FOOL

MARK
TWAIN

A FIRST-CLASS FOOL

MARK TWAIN AND HUMOR

FEATURING THE COLLECTION OF SUSAN JAFFE TANE

Susan Jaffe Tane, Julie Carlsen, Kevin Mac Donnell, and Gabriel Mckee

With essays by John Bird, Julie Carlsen, James E. Caron, Mark Dawidziak, Kerry Driscoll, Joe B. Fulton, Alan Gribben, Benjamin Griffin, Judith Yaross Lee, Kevin Mac Donnell, Gabriel Mckee, Nichole Misako Nomura, R. Kent Rasmussen, David E. E. Sloane, and Barbara E. Snedecor; with an afterword by Declan Kiely

THE GROLIER CLUB
NEW YORK, 2025

"'TURN ONE SUMMERSET, OR MAYBE A COUPLE'"

Contents

Mark Twain

FROM THE BUST BY KARL GERHARDT.

Heliotype Printing Co. Boston and New York.

Preface

SUSAN JAFFE TANE

Fifteen years ago, my budding Mark Twain collection was exhibited at the Cornell University Library. Anne R. Kenney, the Carl A. Kroch University Librarian, was proud to feature the exhibition, *Known to Everyone—Liked by All*, as the highlight of the 2010 academic year. The accompanying book was painstakingly written and edited by Lance J. Heidig. Sadly, my dear friends Anne and Lance have since passed away.

I owe enormous gratitude to Cornell Librarian Katherine Reagan for holding my hand, offering encouragement, and bringing both my Edgar Allan Poe and Mark Twain collections to the University's Library.

Another thank you goes to Stephan Loewentheil of Luxury Catalogs, who introduced me to the pleasures of collecting my favorite nineteenth-century authors, and to Kevin Mac Donnell of Mac Donnell Rare Books. Both served as valued mentors, guiding me through establishing a world-class collection.

Mounting an exhibition requires hard work, expertise, and patience, and I was fortunate to have Gabriel Mckee and Julie Carlsen as my back-up team. As always, they made sure everything was perfectly done while meeting all deadlines. Additional thanks are due to Brent Reidy and my other friends and colleagues at The New York Public Library for partnering on this exhibition.

What started out as a fun hobby turned into a full-blown obsession that shaped much of my avocation and social life. I joined the Grolier Club and met like-minded souls who shared my book collecting passion and unbounded enthusiasm. I no longer had to watch my conversationalists' eyes glaze over with polite disinterest.

I have loved Mark Twain's witticisms, laughing at his humorous remarks—even those that have been falsely attributed to him. Among my favorites:

> "Clothes make the man. Naked people have little or no influence in society."

> "It is better to have old second-hand diamonds than none at all."

> "It is better to keep your mouth closed and let people think you are a fool than to open it and remove all doubt."

And now as I age, I keep this one in mind:

> "If you tell the truth, you don't have to remember anything."

OPPOSITE

Plate from: Mark Twain. *Adventures of Huckleberry Finn (Tom Sawyer's Comrade)*. New York: Charles L. Webster and Company, 1885. (Item no. 24)

Introduction

SUSAN JAFFE TANE
GABRIEL MCKEE
JULIE CARLSEN

ABOUT THE EXHIBITION

A First-Class Fool: Mark Twain and Humor examines Samuel Clemens as a humorist and how he crafted the great "Mark Twain" persona, how he adapted that persona to widen his audience, and how Twain has influenced humorists and continues to influence them today.

The exhibition's title is drawn from Clemens's off-the-cuff speech at an 1899 dinner held in his honor at London's Savage Club. The toastmaster, Sir John MacAlister, had facetiously insulted Clemens, stating: "Mr. Clemens had tried to be funny but had failed, and his true role in life was statistics . . . and it would be the easiest task he ever undertook if he would try to count all the real jokes he had ever made." Clemens opened his joking response by declaring: "Perhaps I am not a humorist, but I am a first-class fool–a simpleton; for up to this moment I have believed Chairman MacAlister to be a decent person whom I could allow to mix up with my friends and relatives."

In context, Twain is speaking specifically to MacAlister's jibe. But his self-identification as a "first-class fool" captures his dual literary role as a simple, folksy author and speaker on the one hand, and an intelligent, cultured, and nuanced literary craftsman on the other. Twain worked carefully to construct his public persona, giving his public voice the appearance of something naturalistic and unrehearsed. Mark Twain was the performance of Samuel L. Clemens's lifetime.

Drawn from the private collection of Susan Jaffe Tane and featuring highlights from the Berg Collection at The New York Public Library, *A First-Class Fool* presents first and rare editions of Twain's published works, including presentation copies, first periodical appearances, and uncommon variants; books from Twain's library and other personal effects; Twain's letters to his friends, publishers, and family; photographs; artwork; and ephemera. Many of these items are displayed for the first time in this exhibition.

ABOUT THE CATALOGUE

Through original essays written by leading scholars in the field, this exhibition catalogue further explores how Twain achieved broad appeal by carefully posturing his humor to suit a wide range of audiences, and how he continues to influence humorists today. Each essay is accompanied by an original illustration by Aril McKee, a young cartoonist and Twain fan who demonstrates the continuing appeal of Clemens's works.

It is important for us to acknowledge that many of Mark Twain's works employ outdated language and

OPPOSITE

[Samuel Clemens, former owner.] Williams No. 6 Typewriter. [New York: 1908.] With accompanying personalized burlap case. (Item no. 126)

imagery that does not meet the standards of diversity, equity, and inclusion to which we and the Grolier Club are committed. Presenting this case study of Clemens's talent as a humorist necessitated that we draw on some of those works; we wanted to show Twain as he was, using his own words.

In the same vein, we have not attempted to regularize the names Samuel Clemens and Mark Twain. He used both, and we opted to follow his pattern.

For items discussed in the text that are not pictured, we refer the reader to item numbers in the "Humorous Highlights" section on pages 230–245.

Introduction to the Essays

KEVIN MAC DONNELL

A. F. Bradley. Portrait photograph of Samuel L. Clemens. [New York, ca. 1907.]

A glance at the biographies of those who have contributed the fifteen essays in this volume will reveal that their combined writings account for a majority of the best scholarship published on Mark Twain in the last few decades. It will also be obvious that most of these contributors are writing on aspects of Twain's life and writings in which they have particular expertise, and that the topics cover Twain's entire career and the broad scope of his writings, exploring their impact on American culture and beyond. Every essay draws inspiration from materials in the Twain collection of Susan Jaffe Tane, exhibited at the Grolier Club in 2025—a tribute to the discernment and generous spirit that has guided Susan in the formation of this fine collection.

In the first essay in this volume, Joe B. Fulton begins at the beginning, showing how Twain's famous jumping frog story initially spread his fame and then hopped along by his side for the rest of his life. John Bird presents Twain as a writer for children who understood child psychology and retained his youthful outlook in his three major books for children of all ages—*The Adventures of Tom Sawyer*, *Adventures of Huckleberry Finn*, and *The Prince and the Pauper*. David E. E. Sloane argues convincingly that all of Twain's humor was adult humor, and identifies how that humor functions in several books and shorter writings that would hook any reader, young or old, who had not read Twain before. Twain's approach to writing can be traced to his early experiences as a hard-working journalist, and Benjamin Griffin traces those origins and shows how Twain learned to exploit his material to the fullest.

Twain wrote about three dozen books, but he penned about 50,000 letters during his lifetime, and Barbara E. Snedecor shows how his epistolatory writings are an essential part of his literary output. When Twain wasn't writing letters or books, he was delivering lectures or readings from his works, and Mark Dawidziak, himself a performer, provides insights into Twain's underappreciated status as a masterful stage performer. When Twain wasn't writing letters, or books, or performing on stage, he was traveling, from the beginning of his career to his very last days—across the country and around the world—and Alan Gribben explores how Twain's extensive travels influenced his writings. Mark Twain, the creation of Samuel L. Clemens, was a brand, and Judith Yaross Lee shows how Clemens deployed his brand—sometimes controlling it, sometimes not.

Mark Twain's literary career began out West, and James E. Caron demonstrates how Twain calibrated his comic style, cutting his teeth on the pages of western periodicals before moving East to pursue his growing fame. Twain's writings are largely autobiographical, and R. Kent Rasmussen explores the character of several of these works. The influences on Twain's writings are numerous and varied, and Twain's remarkably broad influence on both literature and culture is complex and multifaceted; as the editor of these essays, I have attempted in my own essay to summarize and sort them out.

The books Twain read were one influence on Twain's writings, and one of the most important books Twain consulted when writing his aborted sequel to *Huckleberry Finn* was Richard Dodge's *Our Wild Indians*, in which he made extensive preliminary notes. Kerry Driscoll tracks those notes closely and discovers how Twain first intended to write his sequel, how he revised his initial plans as he began writing it, and how he abandoned the whole effort after writing slightly more than 200 pages. *Huckleberry Finn* is not the only major American novel that is frequently banned, but it has been banned, edited, and censored longer than any other, and Nichole Misako Nomura writes thoughtfully about that often-troubled history.

Mark Twain once took a break from writing books and letters, giving lectures, and traveling, and invented (and patented) a game. His game failed in the marketplace, but games by others based on Twain's writings and brand have both succeeded and failed, and Gabriel Mckee surveys them. Scholars have never been able to suppress their angst over the duality—the conflict, or perceived conflict—between Samuel Clemens and his public persona, Mark Twain. Julie Carlsen offers a reading of a selection of Clemens's letters based on how he signed them.

Reading and editing these essays has been a pleasure, and it is hoped that future readers will find them useful, informative, and entertaining. But the best things ever written about Mark Twain cannot be found in essays written about Twain by others, but in the writings of Twain himself. Twain was his own favorite topic, and he returns to that topic in an astonishingly high proportion of his writings. The reader in search of Mark Twain only needs to turn to the pages of any of his books.

Jeremiah Gurney. Carte-de-visite photograph of Mark Twain. New York, [ca. 1871]. (Item no. 113)

“Jim Smiley’s Jumping Frog” and Mark Twain’s Leap to Fame

JOE B. FULTON

“Well—I don’t see no points about that frog that’s any better’n any other frog,” argued the stranger. “Maybe you don’t,” Jim Smiley countered. “Maybe you understand frogs, and maybe you don’t understand ’em” (*Early Tales* 2:286). Fresh from the California mining camps, “Jim Smiley and His Jumping Frog,” Mark Twain’s story of two inveterate gamblers betting on the jumping abilities of two frogs, was published in the *Saturday Press* on November 18, 1865, and “set all New York in a roar” (*Early Tales* 2:271). The story was rapidly reprinted in newspapers around the country and eventually around the world to “India, China, England,—& the reputation it made for me has paid me thousands & thousands of dollars,” Twain told Jim Gillis (UCCL 00416, Twain to Gillis, 26 Jan. 1870) (**page 13**). The narrative of Twain hearing the story and writing the classic frontier yarn is one of those rare literary legends that just happens to be true.

Angel’s Camp in January 1865 was a rough-and-tumble mining outpost located between Carson City, Nevada, and San Francisco, California. After having fled Carson City following his satire of Union fundraising efforts in late May 1864, Sam Clemens departed San Francisco in December of that same year, having been fired from the *Morning Call*. Immured by interminable winter rains, the writer found Angel’s Camp more congenial than either city, weather notwithstanding. Clemens had adopted the pen name Mark Twain in 1863 and with it achieved regional fame and notoriety, but seated near the fireplace at Tryon’s Hotel at Angel’s Camp in January 1865, he heard the story that would make his career. Most of the rainy-day tales have been forgotten, but among them was a story told by former river pilot Ben Coon about a jumping frog.

The essence of Ben Coon’s story about another miner, Coleman, was simple, and Twain captured it in his notebook: “Coleman with his jumping frog—bet stranger $50—stranger had no frog, & C got him one—in the meantime stranger filled C’s frog full of shot & he couldn’t jump—the stranger’s frog won” (*Mark Twain’s Notebooks* 1:80). The outline might not presage literary greatness, but in a letter to Jim Gillis, Twain recalled the story as “the one gleam of jollity that shot across our dismal sojourn in the rain & mud of Angel’s Camp” (UCCL 00416, Twain to Gillis, 26 Jan. 1870).

How Twain captured that gleam of jollity provides an important chapter in his development as a humorist and literary artist. When Twain returned to San Francisco, he found a letter from Artemus Ward (Charles Farrar Browne) inviting him to contribute a sketch to a forthcoming volume. Twain thought of the frog story, but it had a

Autograph letter signed "Samuel L. Clemens" to Jim Gillis. Elmira, N.Y., January 26, 1870. (Item no. 91)

In this letter, Clemens recalls his days of "picket-hunting vagabondage" in California with the recipient, specifically the day they "heard that chap tell about the frog & how they filled him with shot"—the tall tale that would inspire *The Celebrated Jumping Frog of Calaveras County.*

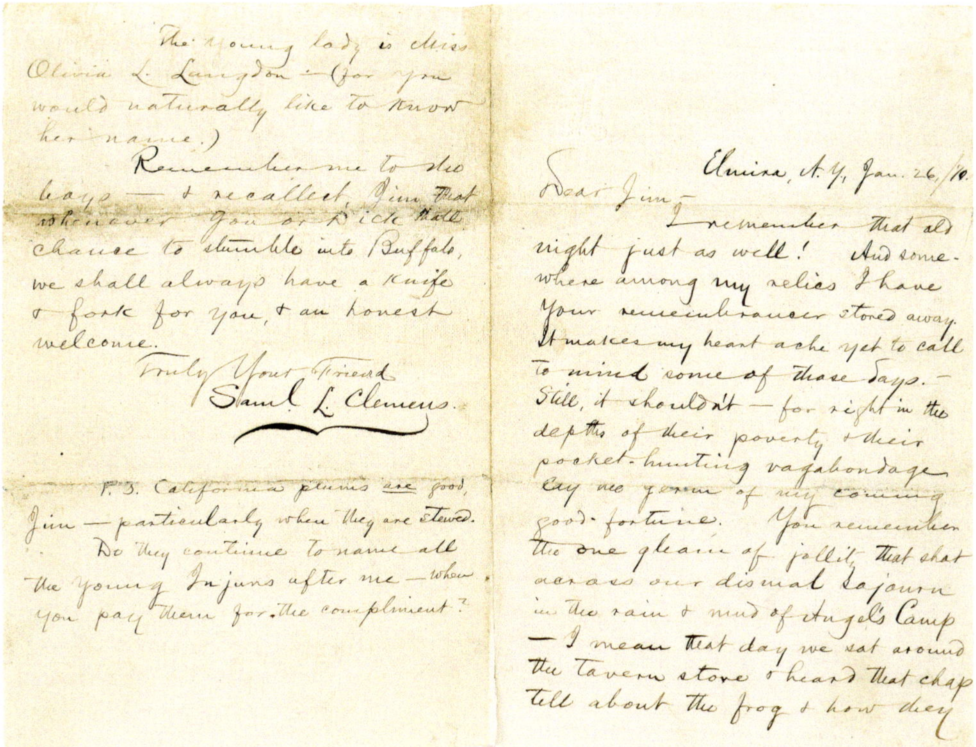

The young lady is Miss Olivia L. Langdon — (for you would naturally like to know her name.)

Remember me to the boys — & recollect, Jim, that whenever you or Dick shall chance to stumble into Buffalo, we shall always have a knife & fork for you, & an honest welcome.

Truly Your Friend
Saml L. Clemens.

P.S. California plums are good, Jim — particularly when they are stewed.

Do they continue to name all the young Injuns after me — when you pay them for the compliment?

Elmira, N.Y. Jan. 26/70.

Dear Jim —

I remember that old night just as well! And somewhere among my relics I have your remembrancer stored away. It makes my heart ache yet to call to mind some of those days. — Still, it shouldn't — for right in the depths of their poverty & their pocket-hunting vagabondage lay the germ of my coming good-fortune. You remember the one gleam of jollity that shot across our dismal sojourn in the rain & mud of Angel's Camp — I mean that day we sat around the tavern stove & heard that chap tell about the frog & how they

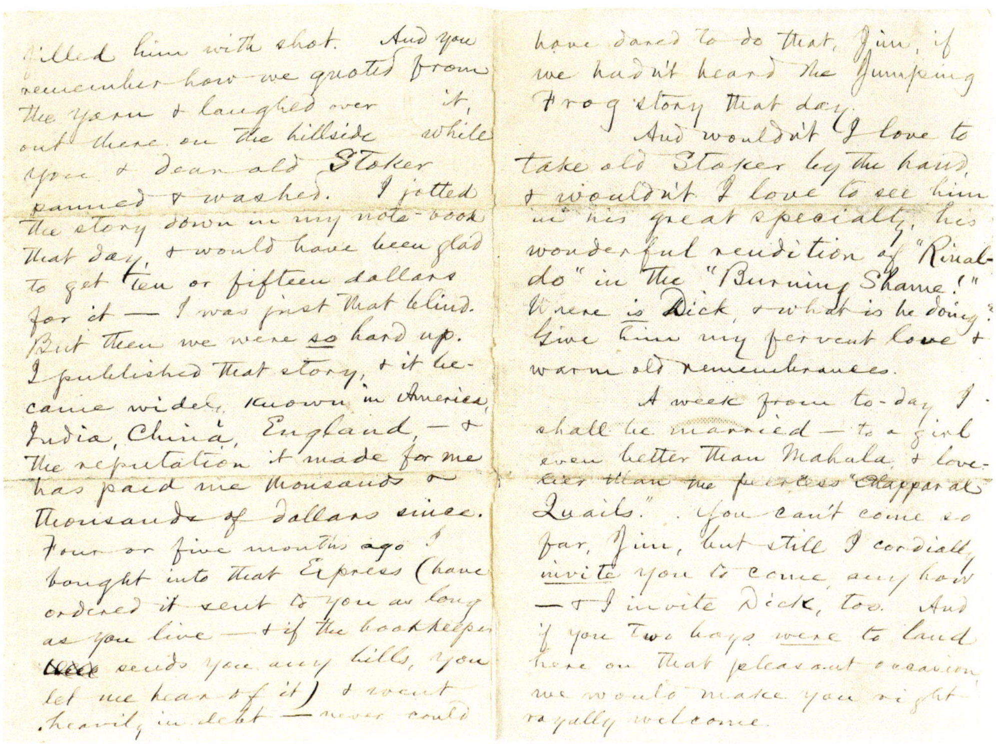

filled him with shot. And you remember how we quoted from the yarn & laughed over it, out there on the hillside while you & dear old Stoker panned & washed. I jotted the story down in my note-book that day, & would have been glad to get ten or fifteen dollars for it — I was just that blind. But then we were so hard up. I published that story, & it became widely known in America, India, China, England, — & the reputation it made for me has paid me thousands & thousands of dollars since. Four or five months ago I bought into that Express (have ordered it sent to you as long as you live — & if the bookkeeper ever sends you any bills, you let me hear of it) & went heavily in debt — never could

have dared to do that, Jim, if we hadn't heard the Jumping Frog story that day.

And wouldn't I love to take old Stoker by the hand, & wouldn't I love to see him in his great specialty, his wonderful rendition of "Rinaldo" in the "Burning Shame!" Where is Dick, & what is he doing? Give him my fervent love & warm old remembrances.

A week from to-day I shall be married — to a girl even better than Mahala, & lovelier than the peerless "Chapparal Quails." You can't come so far, Jim, but still I cordially invite you to come, anyhow — & I invite Dick, too. And if you two boys were to land here on that pleasant occasion we would make you right royally welcome.

"long gestation," as Edgar M. Branch phrased it—too long to meet the deadline (Branch 593). Twain began working with the familiar "frame" structure, in which a more educated narrator introduces a dialect character who tells the story. To write the story, Twain had to find the character and voice to spin the yarn naturally. The story's appeal had little to do with the plot about betting on frogs, the rising action as one frog leaps and the other is so weighted down it finds itself unable to move, the denouement of the trickery revealed, or anything particularly in the *matter* of the story. It was the *way* it was told. Through much of 1865, the frog hopped around Twain's brain, as he drafted versions of the tale, telling and retelling it to friends (part of Twain's creative process for "dialect stuff," as he called it). Through Twain's artistry, the story metamorphosed into a fully developed sketch.

So popular was Mark Twain's story that it leaped to *celebrated* status almost immediately after publication, with Twain changing the title from "Jim Smiley and His Jumping Frog" to "The Celebrated Jumping Frog of Calaveras County" (the county where Angel's Camp is located) when he reprinted it on December 16, 1865, in Bret Harte's *Californian* **(pages 14–15)**. Twain's command of the material increased with other changes, such as removing the introductory address to "A. Ward" when the frog story became the titular sketch of Mark Twain's first book, *The Celebrated Jumping Frog of Calaveras County, and Other Sketches* in 1867 **(pages 16–17)**, edited by Charles Henry Webb. Merle Johnson records that the 1867 volume was copyrighted April 15, 1867, and it seems likely that Artemus Ward's death on March 6 led to his name's removal (Johnson 3). "It was only the frog that was celebrated," Twain recalled. "I was still an obscurity" (*Autobiography* 2:47). That was changing, for reviewers began extolling the author as well as celebrating the frog. Twain recalled the 1867 book fondly: "[Webb] brought it out in blue and gold, and made a very pretty little book of it" (*Autobiography* 2:48). The book was actually bound in a variety of colors, including green (appropriately), as well as lavender, red, and plum (Blanck 3310). Twain's publisher, Charles Henry Webb, declared in the advertisement for the volume that Mark Twain had "scaled the heights of popularity at a single jump" (*The Celebrated Jumping Frog* 4, advertisement).

RIGHT AND OPPOSITE

The Californian, volumes 1–4. San Francisco, May 28, 1864–May 19, 1866. Two bound volumes. (Item no. 60)

Founded by Bret Harte and C. H. Webb, who published *The Jumping Frog* in 1867, *The Californian* contains some of Twain's best humor writing. The October 1, 1864, issue contains his earliest article in the journal signed as Mark Twain: "A Notable Conundrum." The December 16, 1865, issue contains an early West Coast printing of "The Celebrated Jumping Frog of Calaveras County."

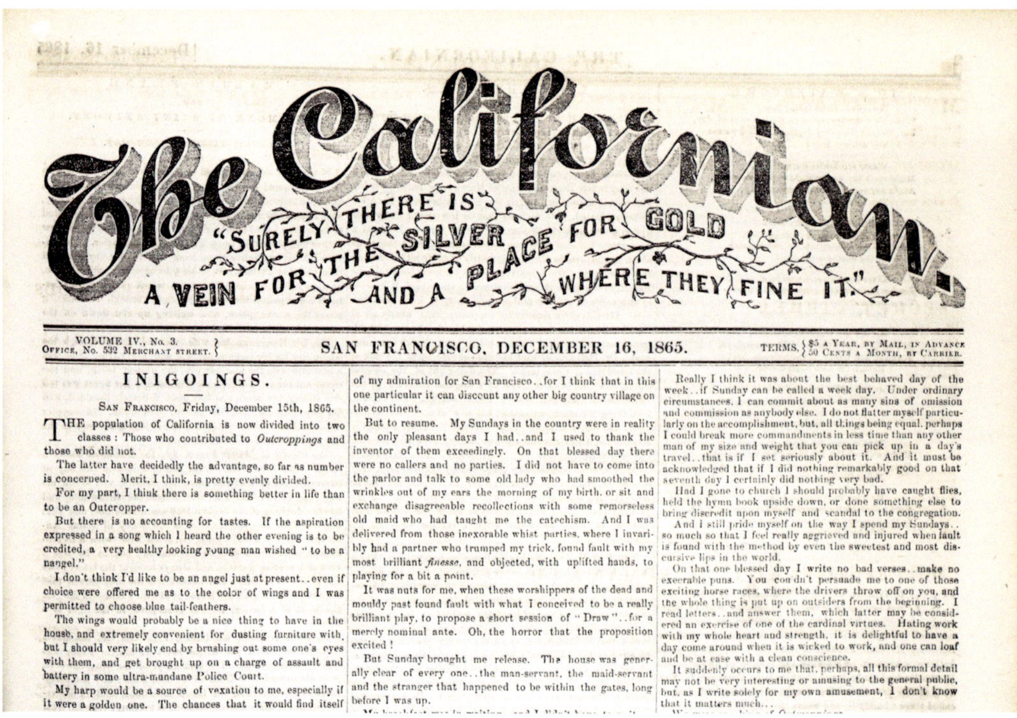

The Californian.

"SURELY THERE IS A VEIN FOR THE SILVER AND A PLACE FOR GOLD WHERE THEY FINE IT."

VOLUME IV., No. 3. Office, No. 532 Merchant Street. | SAN FRANCISCO, DECEMBER 16, 1865. | TERMS, $5 a Year, by Mail, in Advance; 50 Cents a Month, by Carrier.

INIGOINGS.

San Francisco, Friday, December 15th, 1865.

THE population of California is now divided into two classes: Those who contributed to *Outcroppings* and those who did not.

The latter have decidedly the advantage, so far as number is concerned. Merit, I think, is pretty evenly divided.

For my part, I think there is something better in life than to be an Outcropper.

But there is no accounting for tastes. If the aspiration expressed in a song which I heard the other evening is to be credited, a very healthy looking young man wished "to be a nangel."

I don't think I'd like to be an angel just at present..even if choice were offered me as to the color of wings and I was permitted to choose blue tail-feathers.

The wings would probably be a nice thing to have in the house, and extremely convenient for dusting furniture with, but I should very likely end by brushing out some one's eyes with them, and get brought up on a charge of assault and battery in some ultra-mundane Police Court.

My harp would be a source of vexation to me, especially if it were a golden one. The chances that it would find itself

of my admiration for San Francisco..for I think that in this one particular it can discount any other big country village on the continent.

But to resume. My Sundays in the country were in reality the only pleasant days I had..and I used to thank the inventor of them exceedingly. On that blessed day there were no callers and no parties. I did not have to come into the parlor and talk to some old lady who had smoothed the wrinkles out of my ears the morning of my birth, or sit and exchange disagreeable recollections with some remorseless old maid who had taught me the catechism. And I was delivered from those inexorable whist parties, where I invariably had a partner who trumped my trick, found fault with my most brilliant *finesse*, and objected, with uplifted hands, to playing for a bit a point.

It was nuts for me, when these worshippers of the dead and mouldy past found fault with what I conceived to be a really brilliant play, to propose a short session of "Draw"..for a merely nominal ante. Oh, the horror that the proposition excited!

But Sunday brought me release. The house was generally clear of every one..the man-servant, the maid-servant and the stranger that happened to be within the gates, long before I was up.

Really I think it was about the best behaved day of the week..if Sunday can be called a week day. Under ordinary circumstances, I can commit about as many sins of omission and commission as anybody else. I do not flatter myself particularly on the accomplishment, but, all things being equal, perhaps I could break more commandments in less time than any other man of my size and weight that you can pick up in a day's travel..that is if I set seriously about it. And it must be acknowledged that if I did nothing remarkably good on that seventh day I certainly did nothing very bad.

Had I gone to church I should probably have caught flies, held the hymn book upside down, or done something else to bring discredit upon myself and scandal to the congregation.

And I still pride myself on the way I spend my Sundays.. so much so that I feel really aggrieved and injured when fault is found with the method by even the sweetest and most discursive lips in the world.

On that one blessed day I write no bad verses..make no execrable puns. You cou'dn't persuade me to one of those exciting horse races, where the drivers throw off on you, and the whole thing is put up on outsiders from the beginning. I read letters..and answer them, which latter may be considered an exercise of one of the cardinal virtues. Hating work with my whole heart and strength, it is delightful to have a day come around when it is wicked to work, and one can loaf and be at ease with a clean conscience.

It suddenly occurs to me that, perhaps, all this formal detail may not be very interesting or amusing to the general public, but, as I write solely for my own amusement, I don't know that it matters much...

THE CELEBRATED JUMPING FROG OF CALAVERAS COUNTY.

BY MARK TWAIN.

[The *Saturday Press* introduces this sketch in the following complimentary manner: "We give up the principal portion of our editorial space to-day, to an exquisitely humorous sketch—'Jim and his Jumping Frog'—by Mark Twain, who will shortly become a regular contributor to our columns. Mark Twain is the assumed name of a writer in California who has long been a favorite contributor to the San Francisco press, from which his articles have been so extensively copied as to make him nearly as well known as Artemus Ward."]

MR. A. WARD—DEAR SIR: Well, I called on good-natured, garrulous old Simon Wheeler, and I inquired after your friend Leonidas W. Greeley, as you requested me to do, and I hereunto append the result. If you can get any information out of it you are cordially welcome to it. I have a lurking suspicion that your Leonidas W. Greeley is a myth—that you never knew such a personage, and that you only conjectured that if I asked old Wheeler about him it would remind him of his infamous *Jim* Greeley, and he would go to work and bore me nearly to death with some infernal reminiscence of him as long and tedious as it should be useless to me. If that was your design, Mr. Ward, it will gratify you to know that it succeeded.

I found Simon Wheeler dozing comfortably by the bar-room stove of the old dilapidated tavern in the ancient mining camp of Angel's, and I noticed that he was fat and bald-headed, and had an expression of winning gentleness and simplicity upon his tranquil countenance. He roused up and gave me good-day. I told him a friend of mine had commissioned me to make some inquiries about a cherished companion of his boyhood named Leonidas W. Greeley—Rev. Leonidas W. Greeley—a young minister of the Gospel, who he had heard was at one time a resident of Angel's Camp. I added that if Mr. Wheeler could tell me anything about this Rev. Leonidas W. Greeley, I would feel under many obligations to him.

Simon Wheeler backed me into a corner and blockaded me there with his chair—and then sat me down and reeled off the monotonous narrative which follows this paragraph. He never smiled, he never frowned, he never changed his voice from the gentle-flowing key to which he turned the initial sentence, he never betrayed the slightest suspicion of enthusiasm—but all through the interminable narrative there ran a vein of impressive earnestness and sincerity, which showed me plainly that so far from his imagining that there was anything ridiculous or funny about his story, he regarded it as a really important matter, and admired its two heroes as men of transcendent genius in *finesse*. To me, the spectacle of a man drifting serenely along through such a queer yarn without ever smiling was exquisitely absurd. As I said before, I asked him to tell me what he knew of Rev. Leonidas W. Greeley, and he replied as follows. I let him go on in his own way, and never interrupted him once:

There was a feller here once by the name of *Jim* Greeley, in the winter of '49—or maybe it was the spring of '50—I don't recollect exactly, some how, though what makes me think it was one or the other is because I remember the big flume wasn't finished when he first come to the camp; but anyway, he was the curiosest man about always betting on anything that turned up you ever see, if he could get anybody to bet on the other side, and if he couldn't he'd change sides—any way that suited the other man would suit *him*—any way just so's he got a bet, *he* was satisfied. But still, he was lucky—uncommon lucky; he most always come out winner He was always ready and laying for a chance; there couldn't be no solitry thing mentioned but that feller'd offer to bet on it—and take any side you please, as I was just telling you: if there was a horse race, you'd find him flush or you find him busted at the end of it; if there was a dog-fight, he'd bet on it; if there was a cat-fight, he'd bet on it; if there was a chicken-fight, he'd bet on it; why if there was two birds sitting on a fence, he would bet you which one would fly first—or if there was a camp-meeting he would be there reglar to bet on Parson Walker, which he judged to be the best exhorter about here, and so he was, too, and agood man; if he even see a straddle-bug start to go any wheres, he would bet you how long it would take him to get wherever he was going to, and if you took him up he would foller that straddle-bug to Mexico but what he would find out where he was bound for and how long he was on the road. Lots of the boys here has seen that Greeley and can tell you about him. Why, it never made no difference to *him*—he would bet on *anything*—the dangdest feller. Parson Walker's wife laid very sick, once, for a good while, and it seemed as if they warn't going to save her; but one morning he come in and Greeley asked how she was, and he said she was considerable better—thank the Lord for his inf'nit mercy—and coming on so smart that with the blessing of Providence she'd get well yet—and Greeley, before he thought, says: "Well, I'll resk two-and-a-half that she don't, anyway."

Thish-yer Greeley had a mare—the boys called her the fifteen-minute nag, but that was only in fun, you know, because, of course, she was faster than that—and he used to win money on that horse, for all she was so slow and always had the asthma, or the distemper, or the consumption, or something of that kind. They used to give her two or three hundred yard's start, and then pass her under way; but always at the fag-end of the race she'd get excited and desperate like, and come cavorting and spraddling up, and scattering her legs around limber, sometimes in the air, and sometimes out to one side amongst the fences, and kicking up m-o-r-e dust, and raising m-o-r-e racket with her coughing and sneezing and blowing her nose—and always fetch up at the stand just about a neck ahead, as near as you could cipher it down.

And he had a little small bull pup, that to look at him you'd think he warn't worth a cent, but to set around and look onery, and lay for a chance to steal something. But as soon as money was up on him he was a different dog—his underjaw'd begin to stick out like the for'castle of a steamboat, and his teeth would uncover, and shine savage like the furnaces. And a dog might tackle him, and bully-rag him, and bite him, and throw him over his shoulder two or three times, and Andrew Jackson—which was the name of the pup—Andrew Jackson would never let on but what he was satisfied, and hadn't expected nothing else—and the bets being doubled and doubled on the other side all the time, till the money was all up—and then all of a sudden he would grab that other dog just by the joint of his hind leg and freeze to it—not chaw, you understand, but only just grip and hang on till they throwed up the sponge, if it was a year. Greeley always came out winner on that pup till he harnessed a dog once that didn't have no hind legs, because they'd been sawed off in a circular saw, and when the thing had gone along far enough, and the money was all up, and he come to make a snatch for his pet holt, he saw in a minute how he'd been imposed on, and how the other dog had him in the door, so to speak, and he 'peared surprised, and then he looked sorter discouraged like, and didn't try no more to win the fight, and so he got shucked out bad. He give Greeley a look as much as to say his heart was broke, and it was *his* fault, for putting up a dog that hadn't no hind legs for him to take holt of, which was his main dependence in a fight, and then he limped off a piece, and laid down and died. It was a good pup, was that Andrew Jackson, and would have made a name for hisself if he'd lived, for the stuff was in him, and he had genius—I know it, because he hadn't had no opportunities to speak of, and it don't stand to reason that a dog could make such a fight as he could under them circumstances, if he hadn't no talent. It always makes me feel sorry when I think of that last fight of his'n, and the way it turned out.

Well, thish-yer Greeley had rat-tarriers and chicken cocks, and tom-cats, and all them kind of things, till you couldn't rest, and you couldn't fetch nothing for him to bet on but he'd match you. He ketched a frog one day and took him home and said he cal'lated to educate him; and so he never done nothing for three months but set in his back yard and learn that frog to jump. And you bet you he *did* learn him, too. He'd give him a little punch behind, and the next minute you'd see that frog whirling in the air like a doughnut—see him turn one summerset, or maybe a couple, if he got a good start, and come down flat-footed and all right, like a cat. He got him up so in the matter of catching flies, and kept him in practice so constant, that he'd nail a fly every time as far as he could see him. Greeley said all a frog wanted was education, and he could do most anything—and I believe him. Why, I've seen him send Dan'l Webster down here on this floor—Dan'l Webster was the name of the frog—and sing out "Flies! Dan'l, flies," and quicker'n you could wink, he'd spring straight up, and snake a fly off'n the counter there, and flop down on the floor again as solid as a gob of mud, and fall to scratching the side of his head with his hind foot as indifferent as if he hadn't no idea he'd done any more'n any frog might do. You never see a frog so modest and straightfor'ard as he was, for all he was so gifted. And when it come to fair-and square jumping on a dead level, he could get over more ground at one straddle than any animal of his breed you ever see. Jumping on a dead level was his strong suit, you understand, and when it come to that, Greeley would ante up money on him as long as he had a red. Greeley was monstrous proud of his frog, and well he might be, for fellers that had travelled and been everywheres, all said he laid over any frog that ever *they* see.

Well, Greeley kept the beast in a little lattice box, and he used to fetch him down town sometimes and lay for a bet. One day a feller—a stranger in the camp, he was—come across him with his box, and says:

"What might it be that you've got in the box?"

And Greeley says, sorter indifferent like, "It might be a parrot, or it might be a canary, maybe, but it ain't—it's only just a frog."

And the feller took it, and looked at it careful, and turned it round this way and that, and says, "H'm—so 'tis. Well, what's *he* good for?"

"Well," Greeley says, easy and careless, "He's good enough for *one* thing I should judge—he can out-jump ary frog in Calaveras county."

The feller took the box again, and took another long, particlar look, and give it back to Greeley and says, very deliberate, "Well—I don't see no points about that frog that's any better'n any other frog."

"Maybe you don't," Greeley says. "Maybe you understand frogs, and maybe you don't understand 'em; maybe you've had experience, and maybe you ain't only a amature, as it were. Anyways, I've got *my* opinion, and I'll resk forty dollars that he can outjump ary frog in Calaveras county."

And the feller studied a minute, and then says, kinder sad, like, "Well—I'm only a stranger here, and I ain't got no frog—but if I had a frog I'd bet you."

And then Greeley says, "That's all right—that's all right—if you'll hold my box a minute I'll go and get you a frog;" and so the feller took the box, and put up his forty dollars along with Greeley's, and set down to wait.

So he set there a good while thinking and thinking to hisself, and then he got the frog out and prized his mouth open and took a teaspoon and filled him full of quail-shot—filled him pretty near up to his chin—and set him on the floor. Greeley he went to the swamp and slopped around in the mud for a long time, and finally he ketched a frog and fetched him in and give him to this feller and says:

"Now if you're ready, set him alongside of Dan'l, with his fore-paws just even with Dan'l's, and I'll give the word." Then he says, 'one—two—three—jump!" and him and the feller touched up the frogs from behind, and the new frog hopped off, but Dan'l give a heave, and hysted up his shoulders—so—like a Frenchman, but it wa'nt no use—he couldn't budge; he was planted as solid as an anvil, and he couldn't no more stir than if he was anchored out. Greeley was a good deal surprised, and he was disgusted too, but he didn't have no idea what the matter was, of course.

The feller took the money and started away, and when he was going out at the door he sorter jerked his thumb over his shoulders—this way—at Dan'l, and says again, very deliberate: "Well—*I* don't see no points about that frog that's any better'n any other frog."

Greeley he stood scratching his head and looking down at Dan'l a long time, and at last he says, "I do wonder what in the nation that frog throw'd off for—I wonder if there ain't something the matter with him—he 'pears to look mighty baggy, somehow," and he ketched Dan'l by the nap of the neck, and lifted him up and says, "Why blame my cats if he don't weigh five pound," and turned him upside down, and he belched out about a double-handful of shot. And then he see how it was, and he was the maddest man—he set the frog down and took out after that feller, but he never ketched him. And——

[Here Simon Wheeler heard his name called from the front-yard, and got up to see what was wanted.] And turning to me as he moved away, he said: "Just set where you are, stranger, and rest easy—I ain't going to be gone a second."

But by your leave, I did not think that a continuation of the history of the enterprising vagabond Jim Greeley would be likely to afford me much information concerning the Rev. Leonidas W. Greeley, and so I started away.

At the door I met the sociable Wheeler returning, and he buttonholed me and recommenced:

"Well, thish-yer Greeley had a yaller one-eyed cow that didn't have no tail only just a short stump like a bannanner, and——"

"O, curse Greeley and his afflicted cow!" I muttered, good-naturedly, and bidding the old gentleman good-day, I departed.

Your, truly, MARK TWAIN.

THE Annual Christmas Festival of the Trinity Sunday School will take place on Christmas Eve at Platt's Hall. The children of the Protestant Orphan Asylum have been invited, and will be present to participate in the festivities. A Christmas Tree will be prepared for contributions intended for their especial benefit. We trust the tree will be a large one, and that the public will see to it that it be bountifully supplied. Contributions will be received by the Superintendent, Mr. William G. Badger, at Badger & Lindenberg's store. An especially interesting feature will be the presence of the Second U. S. Artillery Band. This Band played the music to which the boys entered Richmond at the time of its capture, and Brigadier-General French has kindly acceeded to the superintendent's request that they be present at the festival.

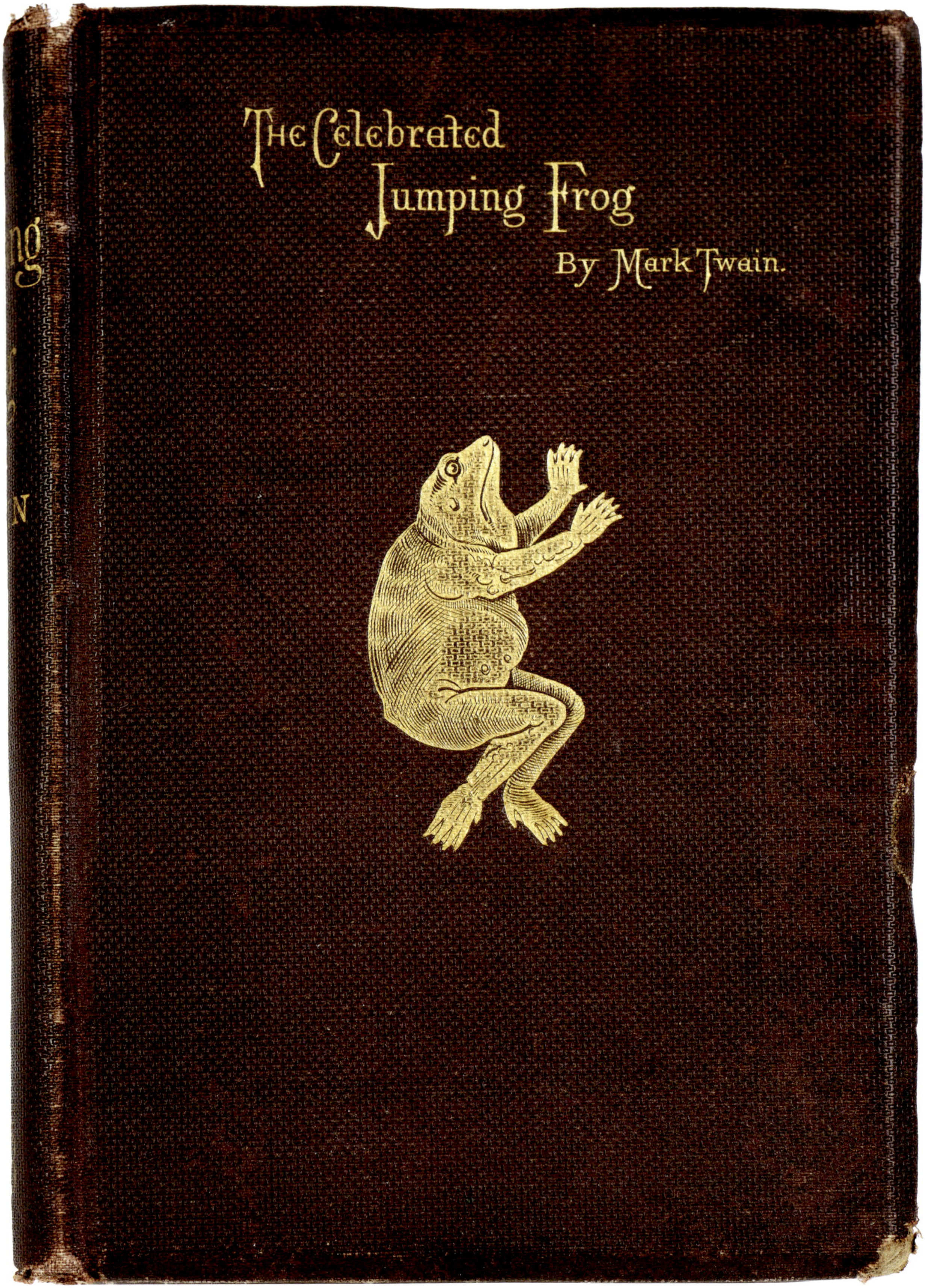
The Celebrated
Jumping Frog
By Mark Twain.

THIS PAGE AND OPPOSITE

Mark Twain. *The Celebrated Jumping Frog of Calaveras County, and Other Sketches*. Edited by John Paul. New York: C. H. Webb, 1867. (Item no. 1)

A year after the story appeared in *The Saturday Press*, Charles Webb published this first book edition of Mark Twain's jumping frog story in 1867 with his own pseudonym John Paul listed as the editor. It quickly sold out, as did early reprints.

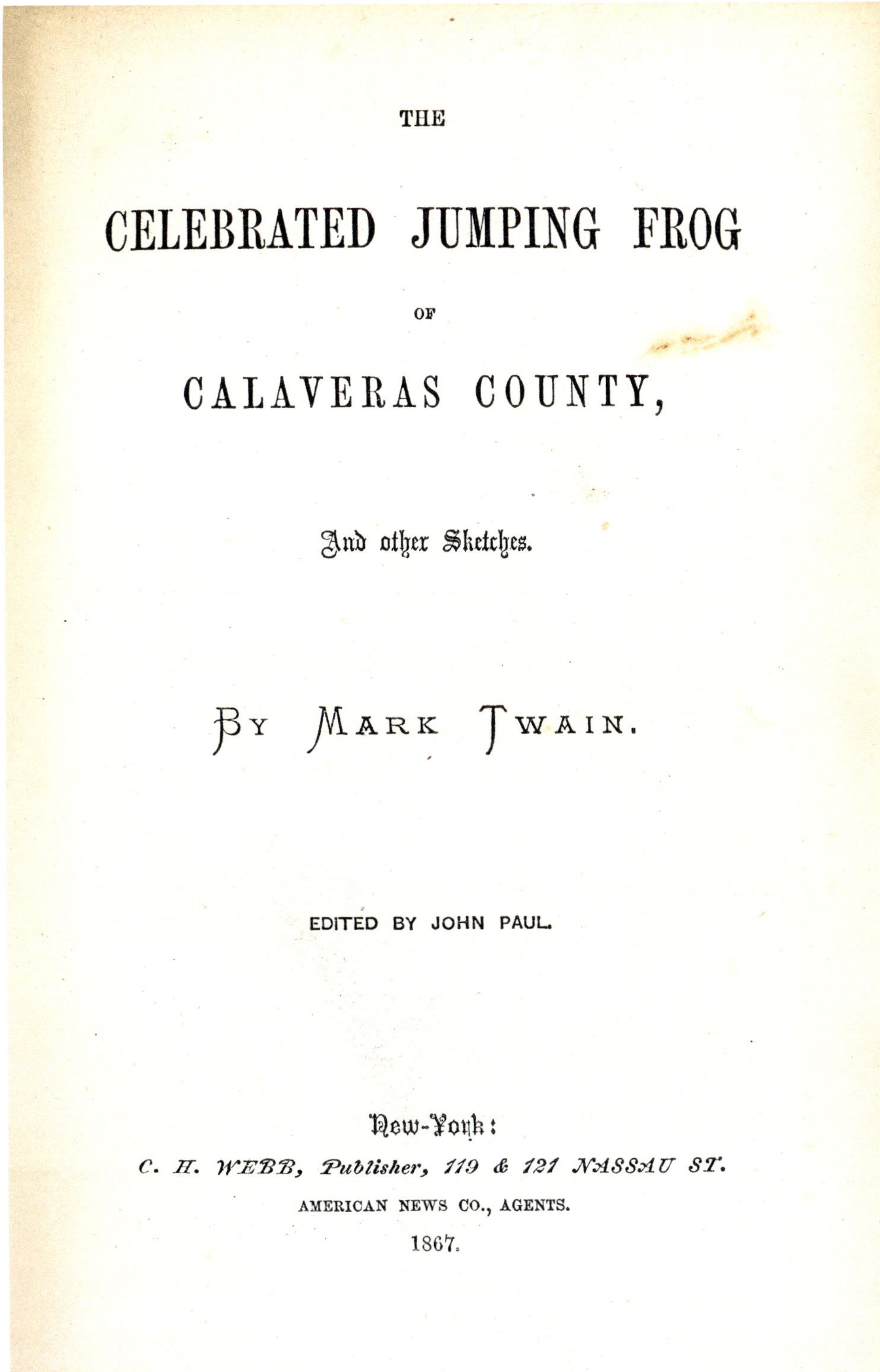

THE

CELEBRATED JUMPING FROG

OF

CALAVERAS COUNTY,

And other Sketches.

BY MARK TWAIN.

EDITED BY JOHN PAUL.

New-York:

C. H. WEBB, Publisher, 119 & 121 NASSAU ST.

AMERICAN NEWS CO., AGENTS.

1867.

Mark Twain. *The Celebrated Jumping Frog of Calaveras County, and Other Sketches.* Edited by John Paul. London: George Routledge & Sons, 1867. (Item no. 2)

This pirated edition of *The Jumping Frog*—the first to be published in the United Kingdom—introduces the unknown Mark Twain to British audiences by quoting *The Saturday Review*: "The CELEBRATED JUMPING FROG may be heartily recommended to any one who is capable of appreciating humor, or enjoying a good laugh."

The Wild West that was nineteenth-century publishing spawned many unauthorized editions of the frog story here and abroad—for indeed, the frog had jumped over the pond and become at least as popular in England as it was in the States. One of these editions was the unauthorized 1867 Routledge edition published in England; that house also published England's first authorized edition in 1870 (Wilson 164) **(page 18)**. Hoping to cash in on the frog's popularity, Twain himself proposed a variety of cheap pamphlets, some of which came to fruition. Clearly, the story of the frog had initial popularity, but it also had legs, enduring appeal.

How to account for that appeal? Mark Twain was an American original, and the jumping frog story—in any of its many forms—has a freshness and vitality to it that characterizes the author's best writing. Twain's language was perfectly attuned to the physical world when he described the frog as landing "down on the floor again as solid as a gob of mud" (*The Celebrated Jumping Frog* 15). Claiming originality for Twain is not to say that the work was *sui generis*. There were earlier versions of the story, and the frog story belonged to a species of literature. Franklin Meine, an avid collector of early humorous writings, began his *Tall Tales of the Southwest* (1930) by asserting that "Mark Twain's early writings marked the climax of a rich development, rather than the beginning of one" (Meine xv). When Twain's book first appeared, writers at the time noted his debt to Sut Lovingood, Johnson Jones Hooper, and others. In Hooper's "The Census Taker," Kit Kuncker names his big yellow dog "Andy, in honor of General Jackson" (165), just as Twain's frog story features Andrew Jackson as a spirited bull pup whose strategy is to seize an opponent "just by the joint of his hind legs and freeze to it—not chaw, you understand, but only jest grip and hang on" (*Early Tales* 2:284–85).

While the frog was Twain's leap to fame, it contributed to a reputation that he was a mere jokester. Twain himself had mixed attitudes toward the story, dismissing it in 1866 as "a villainous backwoods sketch," but continuing to reprint and even tinker with the story (*Early Tales* 2:272). While he chafed under the accusation that his work was inartistic, he did not disown his frog. Indeed, the author updated the story, publishing revised versions and repackaging it for further publications. The frog prodded Twain to pen such manifestos as the 1895 "How to Tell a Story," in which he defended and praised his kind of writing as a "high and delicate art" (201).

Twain's mixed feelings about his frog are apparent in his reaction to Therese Bentzon, pseudonym of

Marie-Thérèse Blanc. Bentzon's "Les Humoristes Américains" appeared in the July 15, 1872, issue of *Revue des deux mondes*, and featured the first French translation of "Jim Smiley and His Jumping Frog." Propelled by a combination of real resentment at her condescending attitude and poor translation and glee at the comic possibilities, Twain responded with "The 'Jumping Frog' in English. Then in French. Then Clawed Back into a Civilized Language Once More by Patient, Unremunerated Toil" (1875) **(pages 20–21)**. In a letter to Olivia Clemens, Twain exulted,

> Got a French version of the Jumping Frog—fun is no name for it. I am going to translate it literarally [*sic*], French construction & all, (apologizing in parenthesis where a word is too many for me) & publish it in the Atlantic as the grave effort of a man who does not know but what he is as good a French scholar as there is—& sign my name to it, without another word. It will be toothsome reading. (UCCL 00909, Twain to Olivia L. Clemens, 26 Apr. 1873)

And so it was, as Twain translated his famous line "Well, I don't see no points about that frog that's any better'n any other frog" into "Eh bien! I no saw not that that frog had nothing of better than each frog" ("The 'Jumping Frog' " 603). Within the essay, he reprinted the famous frog story, retitled as "The Notorious Jumping Frog of Calaveras County," for his frog had metamorphosed from mere jumping frog, to celebrated jumping frog, to notorious jumping frog in just a few leaps. Twain reprinted this version in *Mark Twain's Sketches, New and Old* (1875) **(page 62)**.

The frog appeared in many publications over the years, even having a brief cameo in William Dean Howells's novel *The Rise of Silas Lapham* (1885). In the "Private History of the 'Jumping Frog' Story" (1894), Twain recounted how Professor Henry Van Dyke informed him that the story was of ancient Greek origin, and that he had read "The Athenian and the Frog" in Sidgwick's *Greek Prose Composition*. The resulting "Private History" was Twain's thoughtful rumination on human nature and storytelling; only later did Twain learn that Sidgwick had actually condensed Twain's story and translated it into Greek. Twain included in his essay the original frog story, a translation of Sidgwick's Greek version, and the earlier spoof of Bentzon's French translation. In one form or another, the celebrated, notorious, and companionable frog hopped alongside Twain throughout his career.

With pardonable pride, Twain credited the chance hearing of the yarn at Angel's Camp as "the germ of my coming good-fortune" (UCCL 00416, Twain to James Gillis, 26 Jan. 1870). He wrote these words a week before marrying Olivia Langdon of Elmira, New York. Twain must have felt that the frog had made a prince of him, as in some ways it had. The jumping frog story is a classic of its kind, but other classics and triumphs using the frame structure were to come: "Grandfather's Old Ram" in chapter 53 of *Roughing It* (1872), "The Blue Jay Yarn" in chapter 3 of *A Tramp Abroad* (1880), and *A Connecticut Yankee in King Arthur's Court* (1889).

Even after the masterpieces of *Tom Sawyer* (1876) and *Huckleberry Finn* (1885), the frog was Twain's constant companion. In 1906, origami frogs festooned the tables at the Players Club dinner honoring Twain, and Isabel Lyon recalled how the author returned around midnight "with a Japanese paper frog hanging by a hind leg from his coat lapel" (*Autobiography* 1:547–48). The jumping frog story was not only responsible for Twain's leap to fame, it marked the moment he reached the literary heights to which he aspired. Mary Mason Fairbanks, the mentor Twain had met aboard the *Quaker City*, praised the 1867 volume with the humble amphibian as its title, providing Twain with the occasion for his memorable reply. "*I* don't care anything about being humorous, or poetical, or eloquent, or anything of that kind—the end & aim of my ambition is to be authentic" (UCCL 00196, Twain to Fairbanks, 20 Feb. 1868). With "Jim Smiley's Jumping Frog," Mark Twain grasped the authenticity he craved, and on an international stage at that. There *were* points about that frog, after all.

The Jumping Frog

vous concevez, mais il s'y serait tenu pendu jusqu'à ce qu'on jetât l'éponge en l'air, fallût-il attendre un an. Smiley gagnait toujours avec cette bête-là; malheureusement ils ont fini par dresser un chien qui n'avait pas de pattes de derrière, parce qu'on les avait sciées, et quand les choses furent au point qu'il voulait, et qu'il en vint à se jeter sur son morceau favori, le pauvre chien comprit en un instant qu'on s'était moqué de lui, et que l'autre le tenait. Vous n'avez jamais vu personne avoir l'air plus penaud et plus découragé; il ne fit aucun effort pour gagner le combat et fut rudement secoué, de sorte que, regardant Smiley comme pour lui dire: —Mon cœur est brisé, c'est ta faute; pourquoi m'avoir livré à un chien qui

30

"DAN'L WEBSTER"

THIS PAGE AND OPPOSITE

Mark Twain. *The Jumping Frog; In English, then in French, then Clawed Back into a Civilized Language Once More by Patient, Unremunerated Toil.* New York and London: Harper and Brothers, 1903. (Item no. 3)

Frustrated by the poor quality of unauthorized translations of his works, Twain chose a particularly disagreeable French translation of *The Jumping Frog* and "retranslated" it back into English in order to show how the unskilled adaptation removed the humor from his story. Originally included in *Sketches, New and Old* (1875), it appeared in this separate edition in 1903 with new illustrations by Frederick Strothmann.

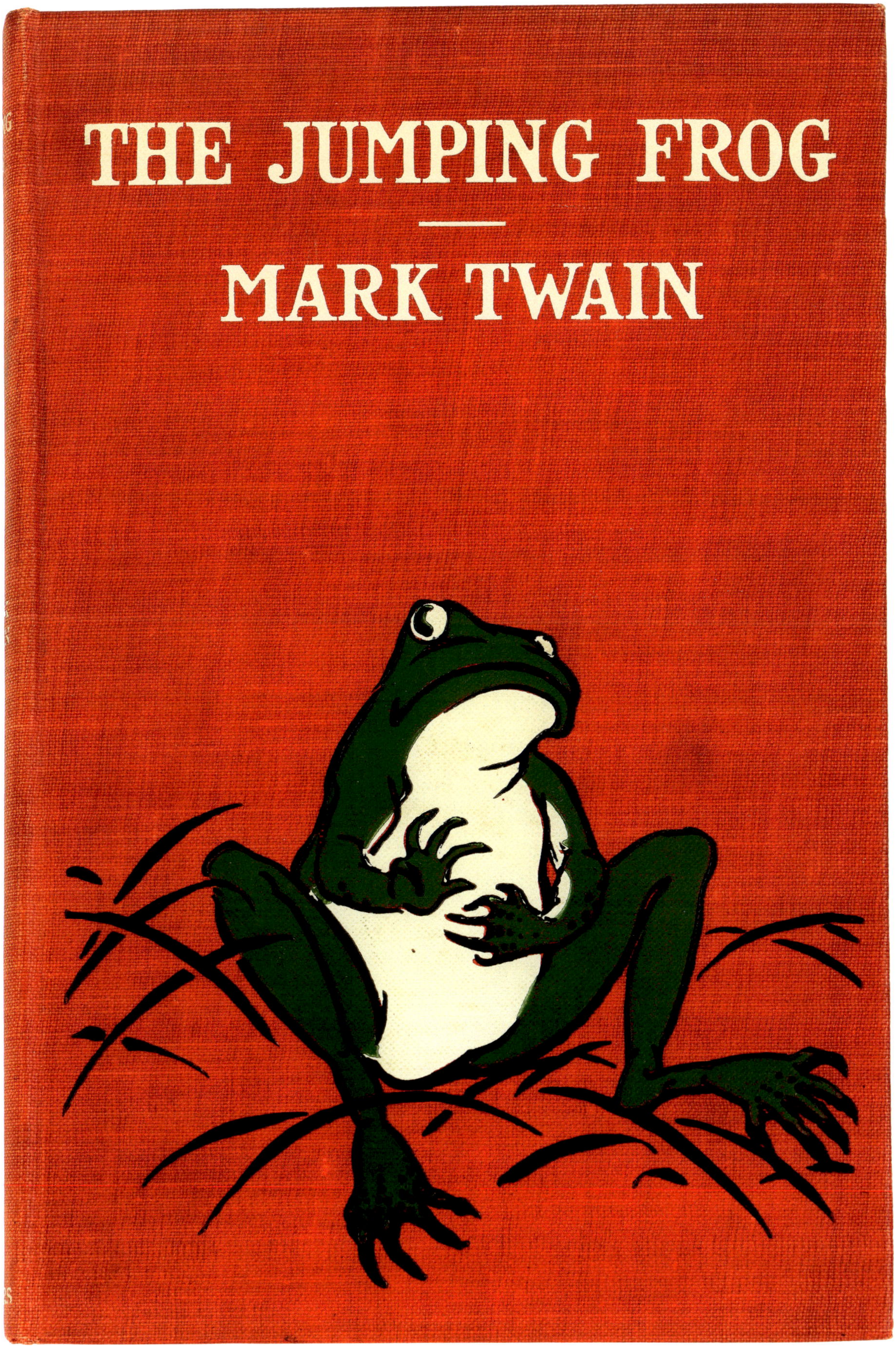
THE JUMPING FROG
MARK TWAIN

THIS PAGE AND OPPOSITE

Samuel L. Clemens. Autograph manuscript table of contents for *Mark Twain's Sketches, New and Old.* [N.p., ca. 1871–1875]. 9 p. (Item no. 84)

Clemens organizes a variety of his magazine and newspaper publications for the collection ultimately published in 1875 by the American Publishing Co. as *Mark Twain's Sketches, New and Old.* The selection and order of texts in this list varies slightly from the published edition.

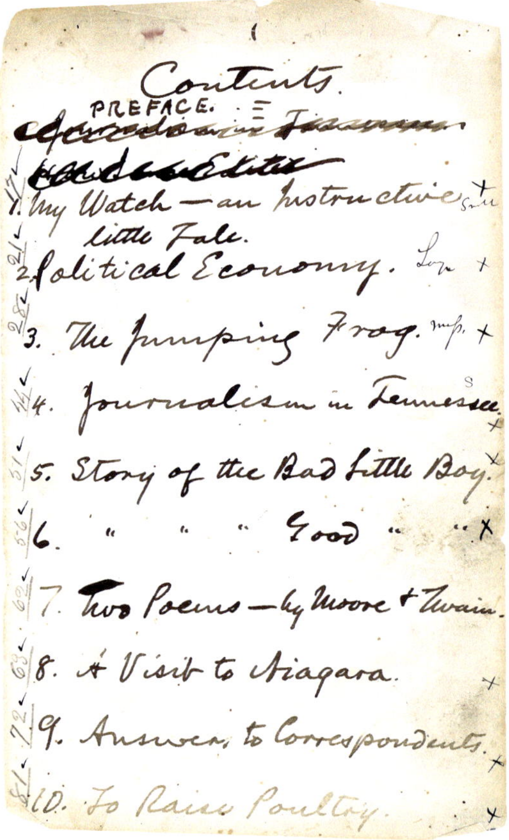

1

Contents.

PREFACE.

~~[illegible]~~

~~[illegible]~~

1. My Watch—an Instructive little Tale.
2. Political Economy.
3. The Jumping Frog.
4. Journalism in Tennessee.
5. Story of the Bad Little Boy.
6. " " " Good " "
7. Two Poems—by Moore & Twain.
8. A Visit to Niagara.
9. Answers to Correspondents.
10. To Raise Poultry.

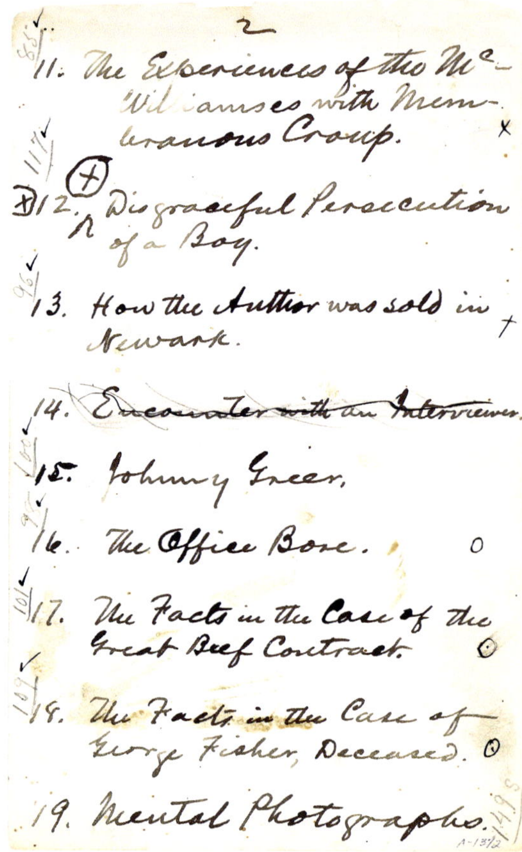

2

11. The Experiences of the McWilliamses with Membranous Croup.
12. Disgraceful Persecution of a Boy.
13. How the Author was sold in Newark.
14. ~~Encounter with an Interviewer.~~
15. Johnny Greer.
16. The Office Bose.
17. The Facts in the Case of the Great Beef Contract.
18. The Facts in the Case of George Fisher, Deceased.
19. Mental Photographs.

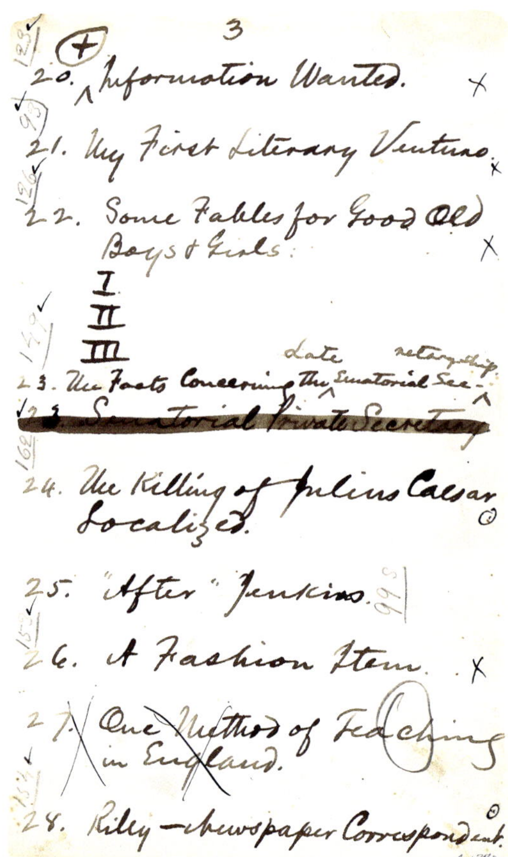

3

20. Information Wanted.
21. My First Literary Venture.
22. Some Fables for Good Old Boys & Girls.
    I.
    II.
    III.
23. The Facts Concerning the late Senatorial Secretaryship.
~~23. Senatorial Private Secretary~~
24. The Killing of Julius Caesar Localized.
25. "After" Jenkins.
26. A Fashion Item.
27. ~~One Method of Teaching in England.~~
28. Riley—Newspaper Correspondent.

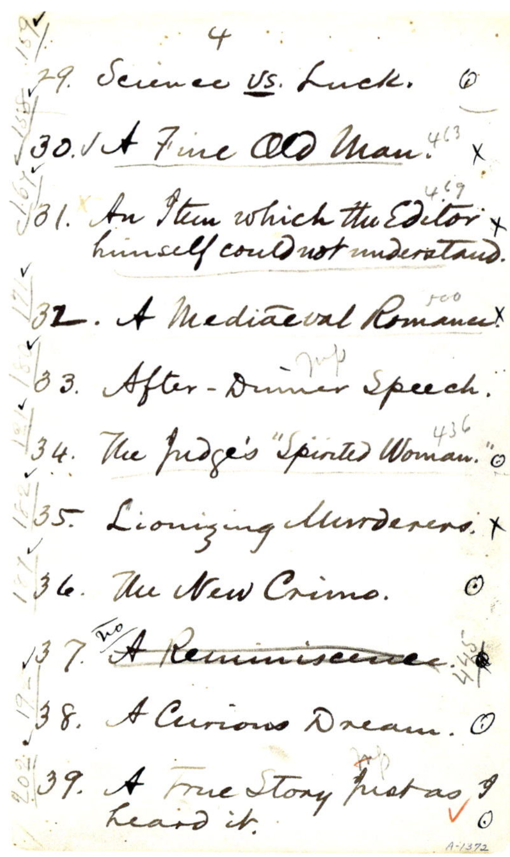

4

29. Science vs. Luck.
30. A Fine Old Man.
31. An Item which the Editor himself could not understand.
32. A Mediaeval Romance.
33. After-Dinner Speech.
34. The Judge's "Spirited Woman."
35. Lionizing Murderers.
36. The New Crime.
37. ~~A Reminiscence.~~
38. A Curious Dream.
39. A True Story Just as I heard it.

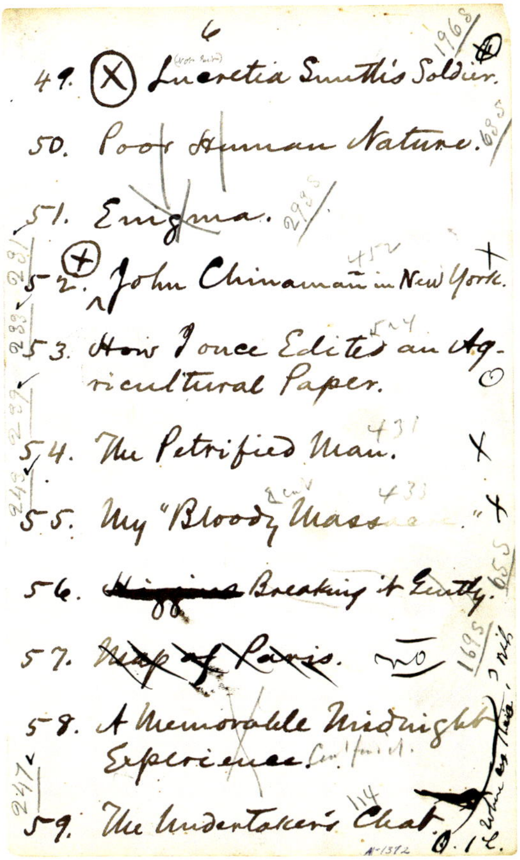
6

49. Lucretia Smith's Soldier.

50. Poor Human Nature.

51. Enigma.

52. John Chinaman in New York.

53. How I once Edited an Agricultural Paper.

54. The Petrified Man.

55. My "Bloody Massacre."

56. ~~Higgins~~ Breaking it Gently.

57. ~~Map of Paris.~~

58. A Memorable Midnight Experience.

59. The Undertaker's Chat.

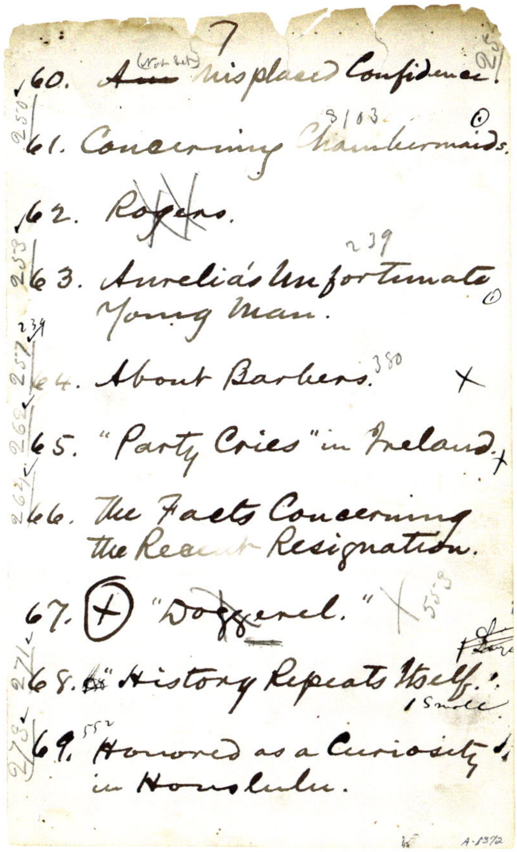
7

60. ~~An~~ Misplaced Confidence.

61. Concerning Chambermaids.

62. Rogers.

63. Aurelia's Unfortunate Young Man.

64. About Barbers.

65. "Party Cries" in Ireland.

66. The Facts Concerning the Recent Resignation.

67. "Doggerel."

68. "History Repeats Itself."

69. Honored as a Curiosity in Honolulu.

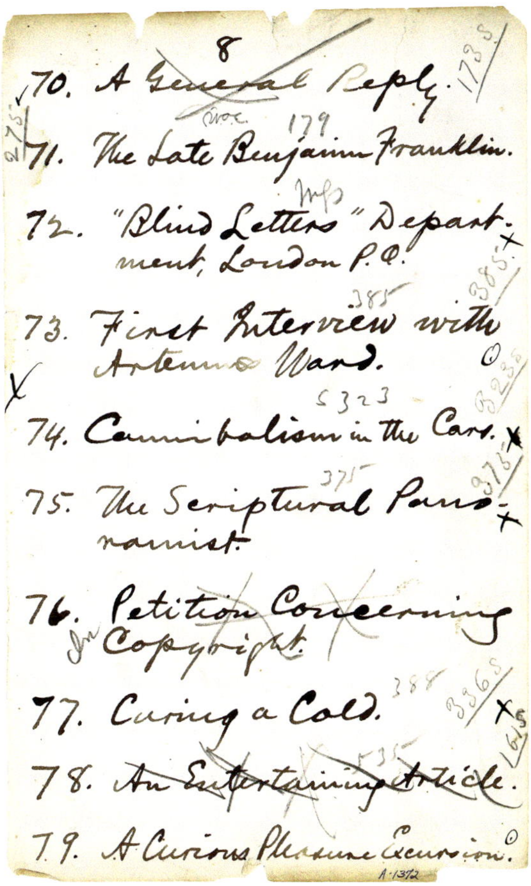
8

70. A ~~General~~ Reply.

71. The Late Benjamin Franklin.

72. "Blind Letters" Department, London P.O.

73. First Interview with Artemus Ward.

74. Cannibalism in the Cars.

75. The Scriptural Panoramist.

76. Petition Concerning Copyright.

77. Curing a Cold.

78. ~~An Entertaining Article.~~

79. A Curious Pleasure Excursion.

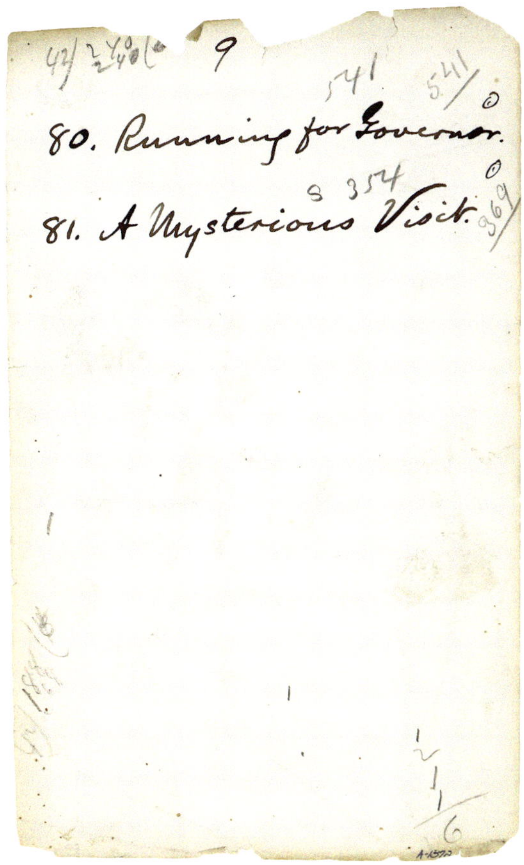
9

80. Running for Governor.

81. A Mysterious Visit.

THIS PAGE AND OPPOSITE

Mark Twain. *The Jumping Frog* [with] *The Private Printing of The "Jumping Frog" Story: An Afterword by Samuel Clemens*. [Easthampton, Mass.]: Cheloniidae Press, 1985. (Item no. 4)

This modern fine press edition of *The Jumping Frog* is one of fifteen unnumbered copies illustrated by Alan James Robinson and bound by Daniel E. Kelm and boxed with a complete suite of wood engravings, a suite of illustrations in proof state, and a copy of the regular edition book.

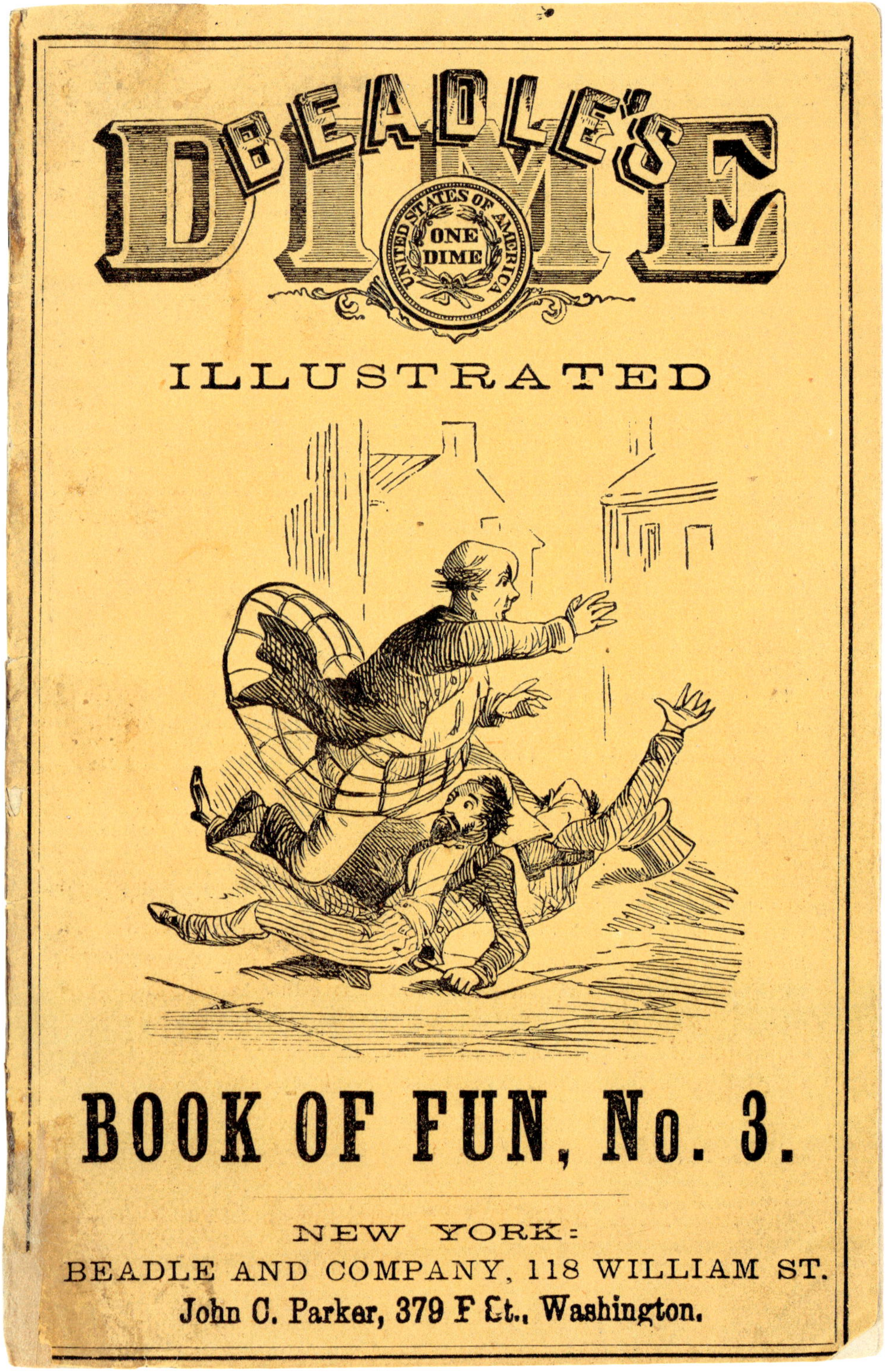

Beadle's Dime Book of Fun, No. 3. New York: Beadle and Company, 1866. In original wrappers. (Item no. 59)

This volume from publisher Erastus Beadle's series of small, inexpensive books—called dime novels for their 10¢ price tags—includes an early printing of "Jim Smiley's Frog," an abbreviated version of the story that would later become *The Celebrated Jumping Frog of Calaveras County*.

Mark Twain. *Mark Twain's Sketches, Number One*. New York: American News Company, 1874. (Item no. 44)

This is the first, failed attempt by Twain to publish his sketches as an inexpensive serial series. He used "The Jumping Frog" as an advertising hook, as seen by the cover illustration of a frog smoking a cigar.

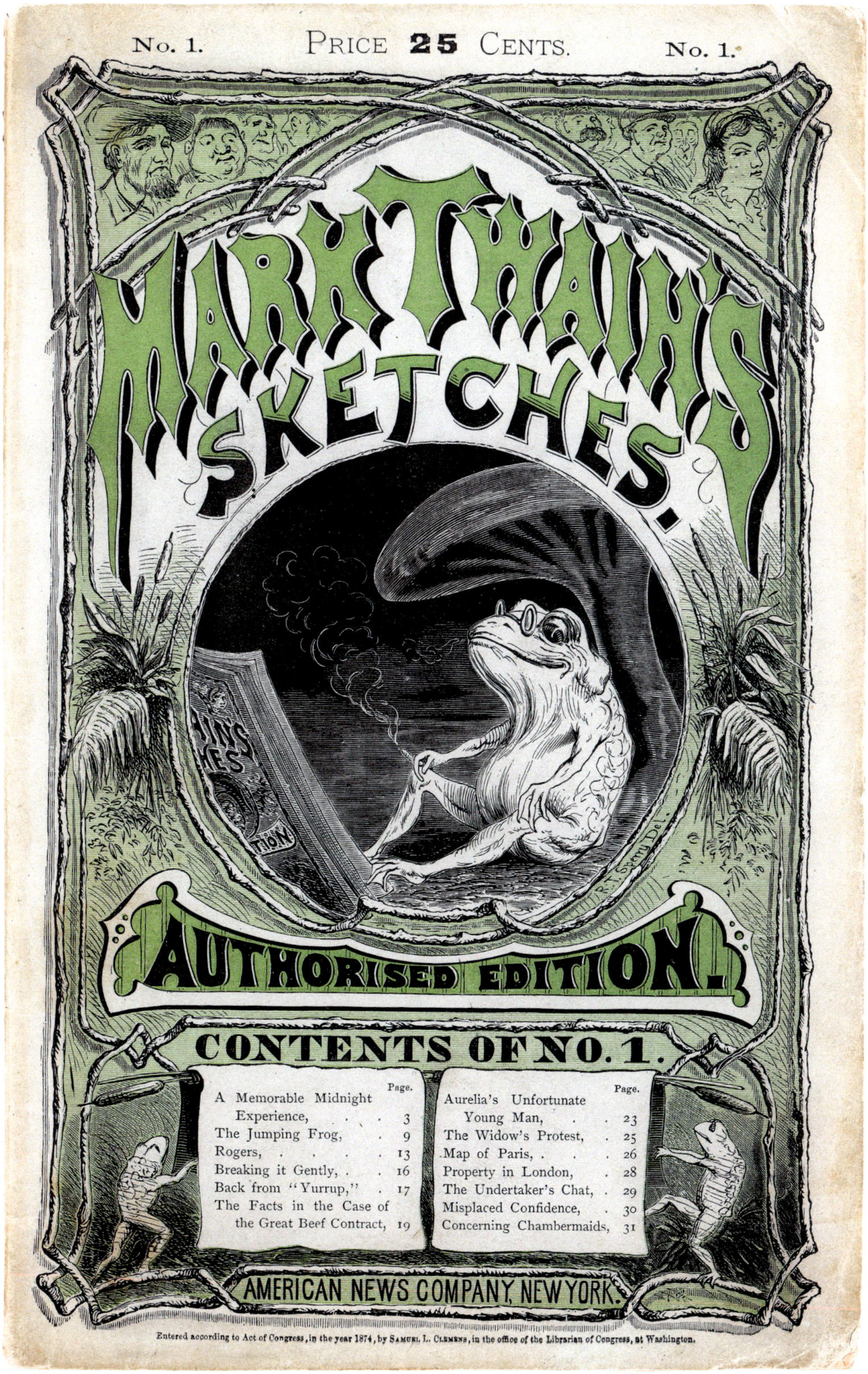

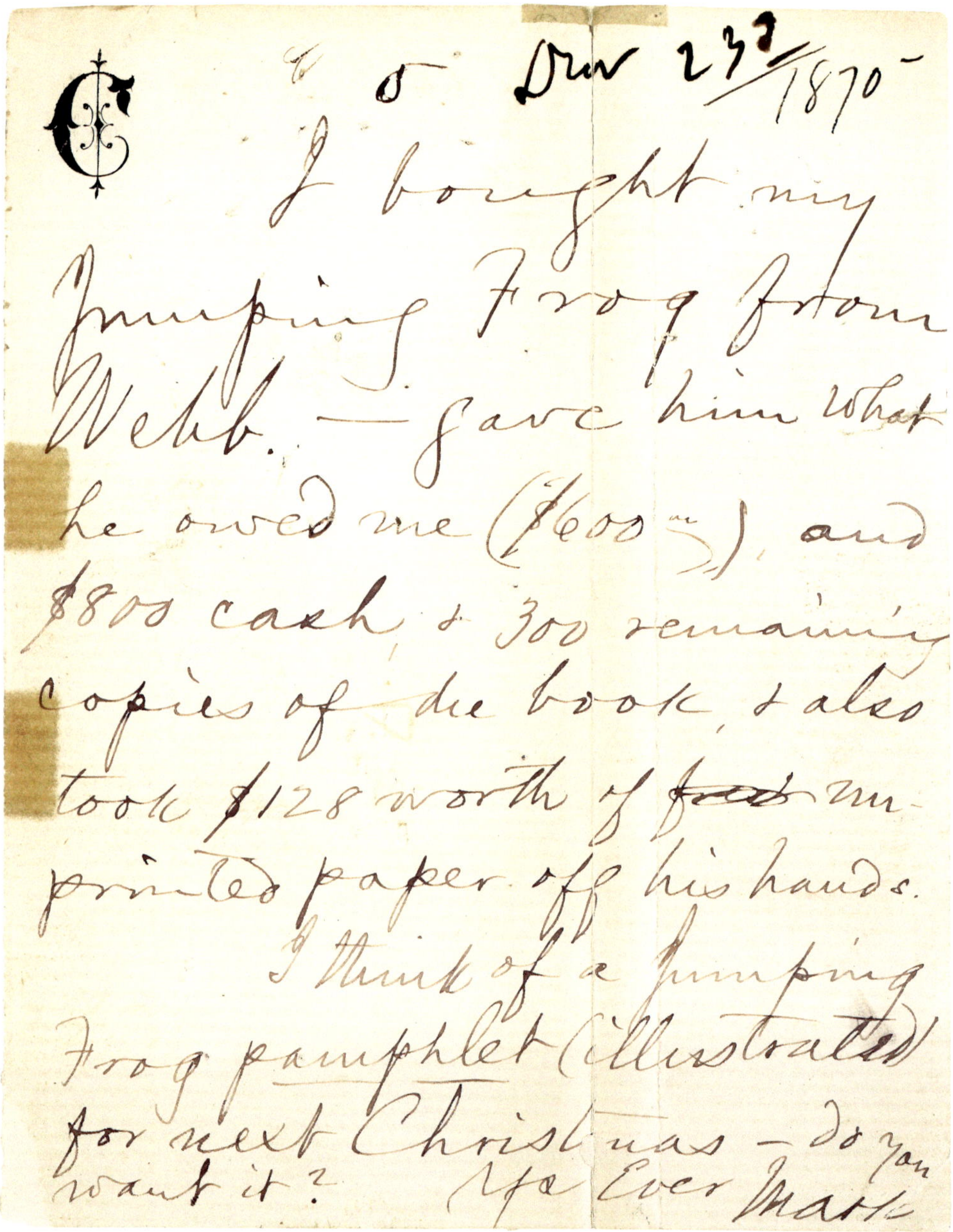

Dec 23d/1870—

I bought my Jumping Frog from Webb.—gave him what he owed me ($600 —), and $800 cash, & 300 remaining copies of the book, & also took $128 worth of ~~[illegible]~~ unprinted paper off his hands.

I think of a Jumping Frog pamphlet (illustrated) for next Christmas—do you want it?

Yrs Ever Mark

LEFT

Mark Twain. Final page from an autograph letter signed "Mark" to publisher Elisha Bliss, Jr. Buffalo, N.Y, December 22, 1870. (Item no. 97)

Charles Webb's 1867 publication of *The Jumping Frog* was an instant popular success, but Webb's publishing operation struggled financially, and Clemens accused him of cheating him out of royalties for the book. In this letter on Clemens's personalized stationery, Twain recounts how he bought the *Jumping Frog* back from Webb, and he offers the publisher Elisha Bliss, Jr., an opportunity to print a new "Jumping Frog *pamphlet*."

OPPOSITE

Plate from: Mark Twain (Samuel L. Clemens). *The Tragedy of Pudd'nhead Wilson and the Comedy Those Extraordinary Twins* [salesman's prospectus]. Hartford: American Publishing Company, 1894. (Item no. 32)

SAMUEL L. CLEMENS (MARK TWAIN).

Mark Twain's Literature for Younger Readers

JOHN BIRD

Mark Twain is a great American writer, but he is also a great children's writer. Throughout his career, he wrote about and for children, using them as protagonists, exhibiting keen insights into the experience of childhood. In his writing, humor was his driving force, and humor is especially important in his fictions that employ children. His two most famous and renowned novels—*The Adventures of Tom Sawyer* and *Adventures of Huckleberry Finn*—have appealed to both children and adult readers since their publication, and the two heroes of these stories have become iconic in the American psyche. At the heart of these two works, as well as another classic, *The Prince and the Pauper*, lies humor, made all the more poignant by its contrast with darkness and seriousness.

THE ADVENTURES OF TOM SAWYER

Published in America's centennial year, 1876, *The Adventures of Tom Sawyer* was the first novel Mark Twain wrote alone (**pages 31–33**). *Tom Sawyer* has become an iconic piece of Americana, a novel that continues to delight both children and adult readers: for children, because it appeals to their own age; for adults, because it appeals to their memories. In both cases, humor is central to the novel's appeal. Twain covered both bases in his preface to the novel:

> Although my book is intended mainly for the entertainment of boys and girls, I hope it will not be shunned by men and women on that account, for part of my plan has been to try to pleasantly remind adults of what they once were themselves, and how they felt and thought and talked, and what queer enterprises they sometimes engaged in.

Twain knew his subject well, since the novel is quite autobiographical: The setting in St. Petersburg, Missouri, is based on his hometown of Hannibal; the time is the 1840s, the years of his childhood; and the characters are based on his family, his friends, and, to a large extent, himself. The novel was a contributor to an emerging genre in the second half of the nineteenth century, the "boy book," with precursors including Thomas Hughes's *Tom Brown's Schooldays* (1857) and Thomas Bailey Aldrich's *The Story of a Bad Boy* (1869) (Gribben, " 'I Did Wish' "; Jacobson).

By the second chapter, Twain captures the reader with a scene that has become famous. Punished by his Aunt Polly for a series of misdeeds, Tom must spend his Saturday whitewashing Aunt Polly's fence. He first tricks his friend Ben Rogers into doing his work for him, convincing Ben that it is not work, but fun; as he tells Ben,

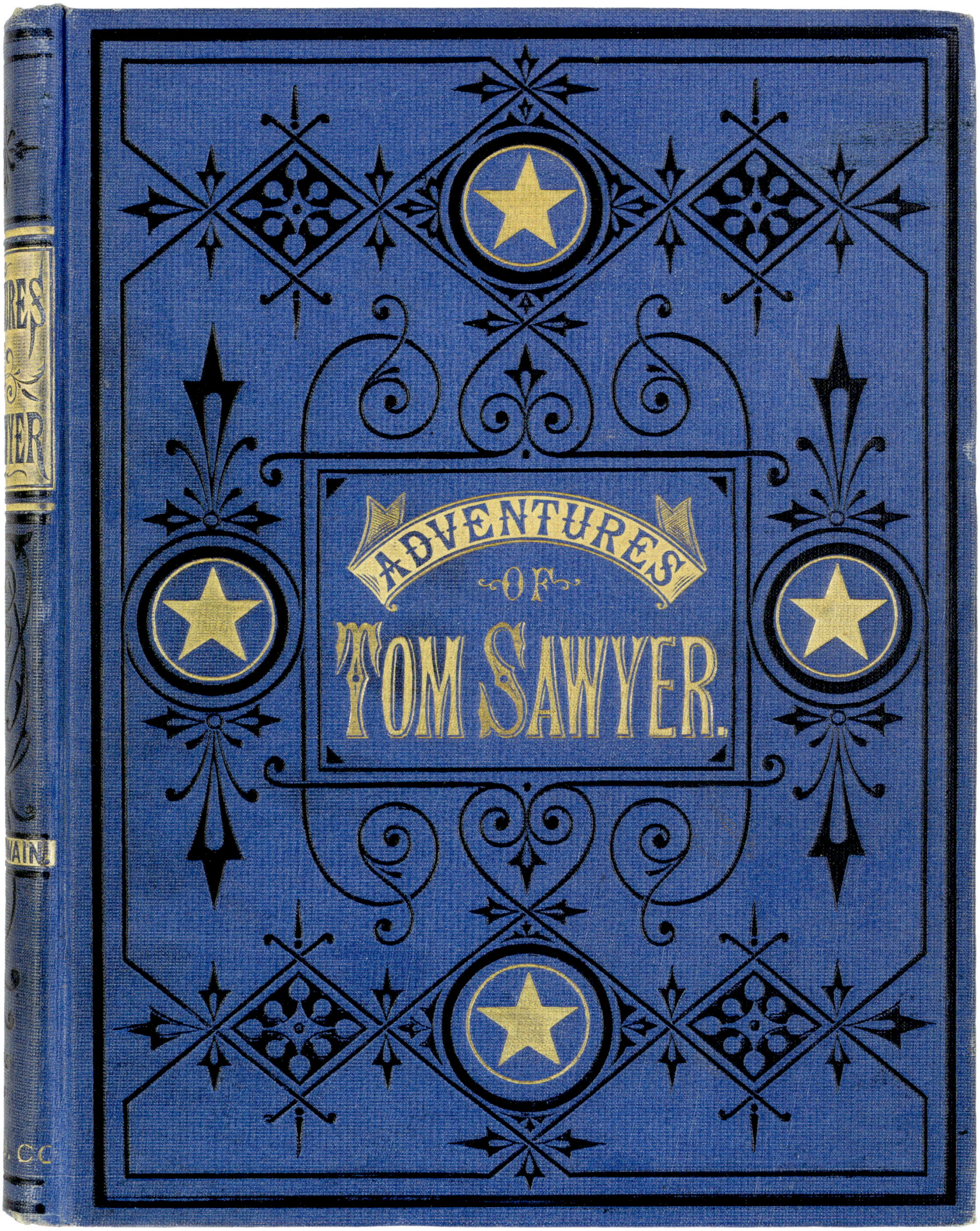

THIS PAGE AND FOLLOWING

Mark Twain. *The Adventures of Tom Sawyer*. Hartford: American Publishing Company, 1876. (Item no. 13)

The first edition of Twain's classic novel about the mischievous, rough-and-tumble Tom Sawyer's amusing adventures along the Mississippi River.

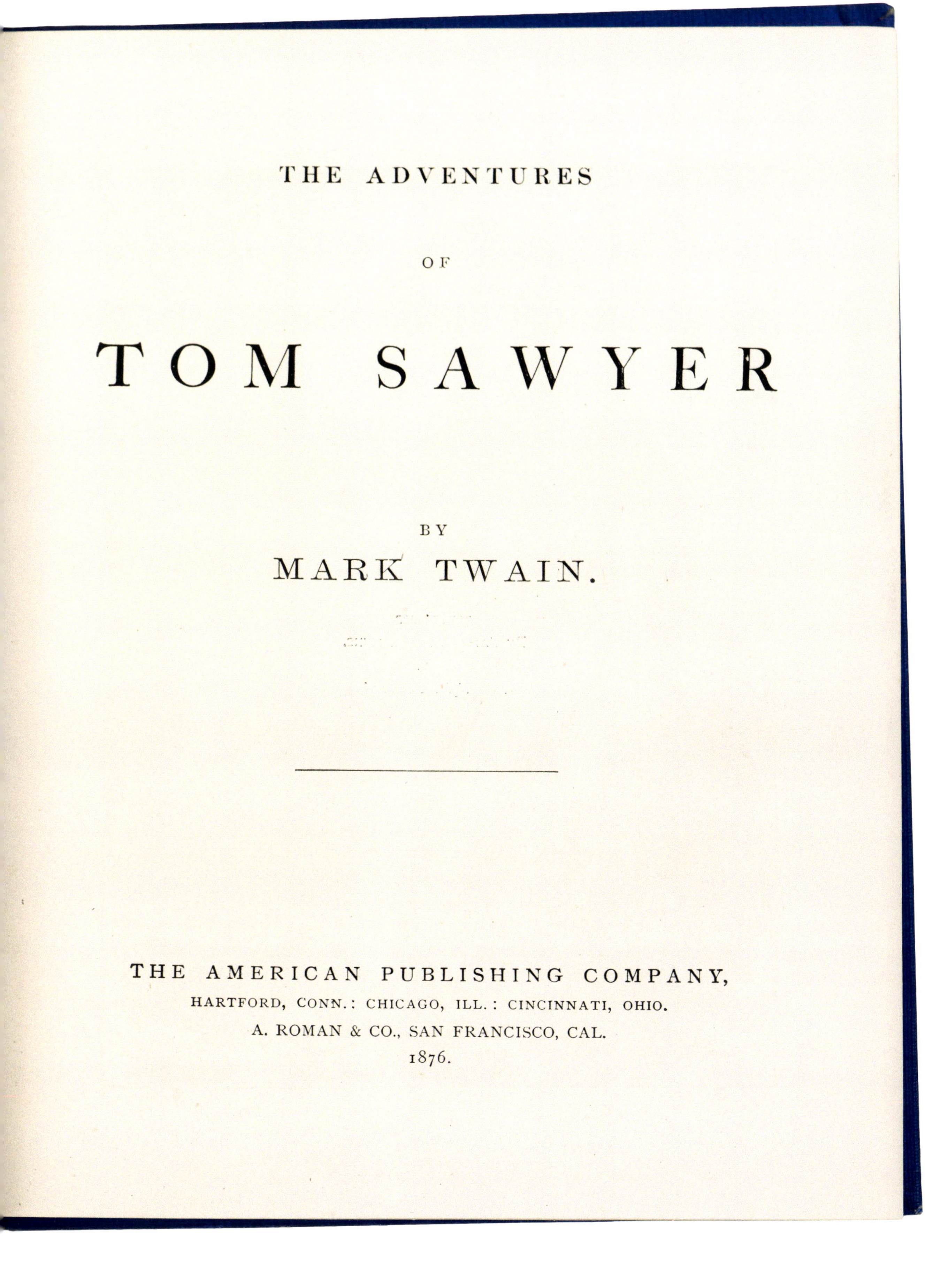
THE ADVENTURES

OF

TOM SAWYER

BY

MARK TWAIN.

THE AMERICAN PUBLISHING COMPANY,

HARTFORD, CONN.: CHICAGO, ILL.: CINCINNATI, OHIO.

A. ROMAN & CO., SAN FRANCISCO, CAL.

1876.

"Like it? Well I don't see why I oughtn't to like it. Does a boy get a chance to whitewash a fence every day?" (*The Adventures of Tom Sawyer* 14). Tom not only gets Ben to do the whitewashing but is also rewarded: Ben gives Tom his apple, then Ben "worked and sweated in the sun," while "the retired artist sat on a barrel in the shade close by, dangled his legs, munched his apple, and planned the slaughter of more innocents" (*The Adventures of Tom Sawyer* 15). One by one Tom tricks his friends into doing the hated work, again receiving rewards for his trickery: a kite from Billy Fisher, a dead rat and a string to swing it with from Johnny Miller, and then a veritable treasure trove—at least, what amounts to treasure for a boy of ten or eleven. The list of treasures is at once comic but also psychologically revealing of the values of childhood:

> twelve marbles, part of a jewsharp, a piece of blue bottle-glass to look through, a spool cannon, a key that wouldn't unlock anything, a fragment of chalk, a glass stopper of a decanter, a tin soldier, a couple of tadpoles, six fire-crackers, a kitten with only one eye, a brass doorknob, a dog collar—but no dog—a handle of a knife, four pieces of orange peel, and a dilapidated old window sash. (*The Adventures of Tom Sawyer* 15)

The whitewashing scene is a tour de force of comic art; if readers remember nothing else about the novel, they remember this scene. It has been endlessly illustrated, notably by Norman Rockwell in a 1936 edition of the novel (Schmidt, "Illustrating *Tom Sawyer*" 214).

Other memorable scenes follow, ably depicting the experience of boyhood: the torture and boredom of school and church and the way Tom relieves that boredom; playing as pirates and Indians with Joe Harper and Huckleberry Finn on Jackson's Island; attending his own "funeral"; and a puppy love romance with Becky Thatcher. Tom Sawyer is a rebel, a "bad boy," but not really bad; as Judith Fetterley termed him in an influential essay, Tom is a "sanctioned rebel," breaking society's norms but rewarded by adult society because he relieves their boredom and constrictions (Fetterley).

Tom even becomes a hero, first at the trial of Muff Potter, when he bravely testifies that Injun Joe was the murderer, then in the cave, when he saves Becky Thatcher and discovers hidden treasure. He is the town's young hero, but Twain abandons his story at these moments of triumph, also abandoning his plan to take Tom to adulthood. For he now had other plans.

ADVENTURES OF HUCKLEBERRY FINN

Adventures of Huckleberry Finn, published in 1885, is that rare sequel that surpasses its predecessor in depth and greatness **(pages 35–36)**. Twain began writing *Huckleberry Finn* immediately after finishing *Tom Sawyer*, the ending of the first novel becoming the opening of the second, but he was to work on his new book in fits and starts for eight years, publishing three other books during the interval.

In a revealing 1875 letter to William Dean Howells, Twain wrote about his decision to end *Tom Sawyer*, but also gave intimations of what would be a pivotal decision about the story that would eventually be its sequel: "I have finished the story & didn't take the chap beyond boyhood. I believe it would be fatal to do it in any shape but autobiographically—like Gil Blas. I perhaps made a mistake in not writing in the first person" (*Mark Twain–Howells Letters* 1:91).

That shift from third-person narration to first-person was to have profound effects on the language, style, and humor of *Huckleberry Finn*. The opening lines of the novel look back to its predecessor but also proclaim a new voice, a liberated voice, one of the great openings of any novel:

> You don't know about me, without you have read a book by the name of "The Adventures of Tom Sawyer," but that ain't no matter. That book was made by Mr. Mark Twain, and he told the truth, mainly. There was things which he stretched, but mainly he told the truth. (*Adventures of Huckleberry Finn* 1)

Because of Huck's naivete and literal-mindedness, almost everything he says has the potential to be humorous, since he only half understands much of what he encounters. Huck's narration is riddled with humor that he doesn't get while the reader laughs heartily, and much humor emerges from the comic dialogues between Tom and Huck in the beginning and ending of the novel, and between Huck and Jim in the middle.

In a holdover from the previous novel, Tom Sawyer dominates the first three chapters, forming "Tom Sawyer's Gang," devoted to committing "robbery and murder" (*Adventures of Huckleberry Finn* 10). Tom, steeped in the sensational dime novels of that era and classic literature he has read but only half understands, embarks on play as if it is real. But literal-minded Huck really expects it to be real, arguing with Tom in comic dialogue when Tom tries to rationalize his fantasies, as when they go after "a whole

And how far a body can hear on the water such nights! I heard people talking at the ferry landing. I heard what they said, too, every word of it. One man said it was getting towards the long days and the short nights, now. 'Tother one said

TAKING A REST.

this warn't one of the short ones, he reckoned—and then they laughed, and he said it over again and they laughed again; then they waked up another fellow and told him, and laughed, but he didn't laugh; he ripped out something brisk and said le

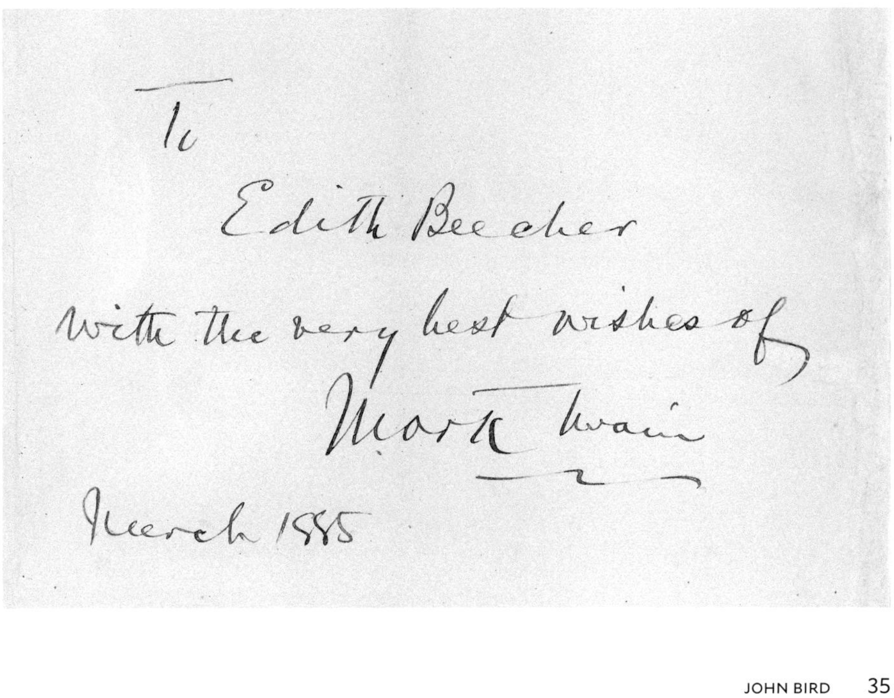

To
Edith Beecher
with the very best wishes of
Mark Twain
March 1885

THIS PAGE AND FOLLOWING

Mark Twain. *Adventures of Huckleberry Finn (Tom Sawyer's Comrade)*. New York: Charles L. Webster and Company, 1885. Publisher's green cloth. (Item no. 24)

First edition of Twain's popular sequel to *Tom Sawyer*. He presented this copy to Edith Beecher, the granddaughter of Henry Ward Beecher and grandniece of his Hartford neighbor Harriet Beecher Stowe, and signed it "Mark Twain."

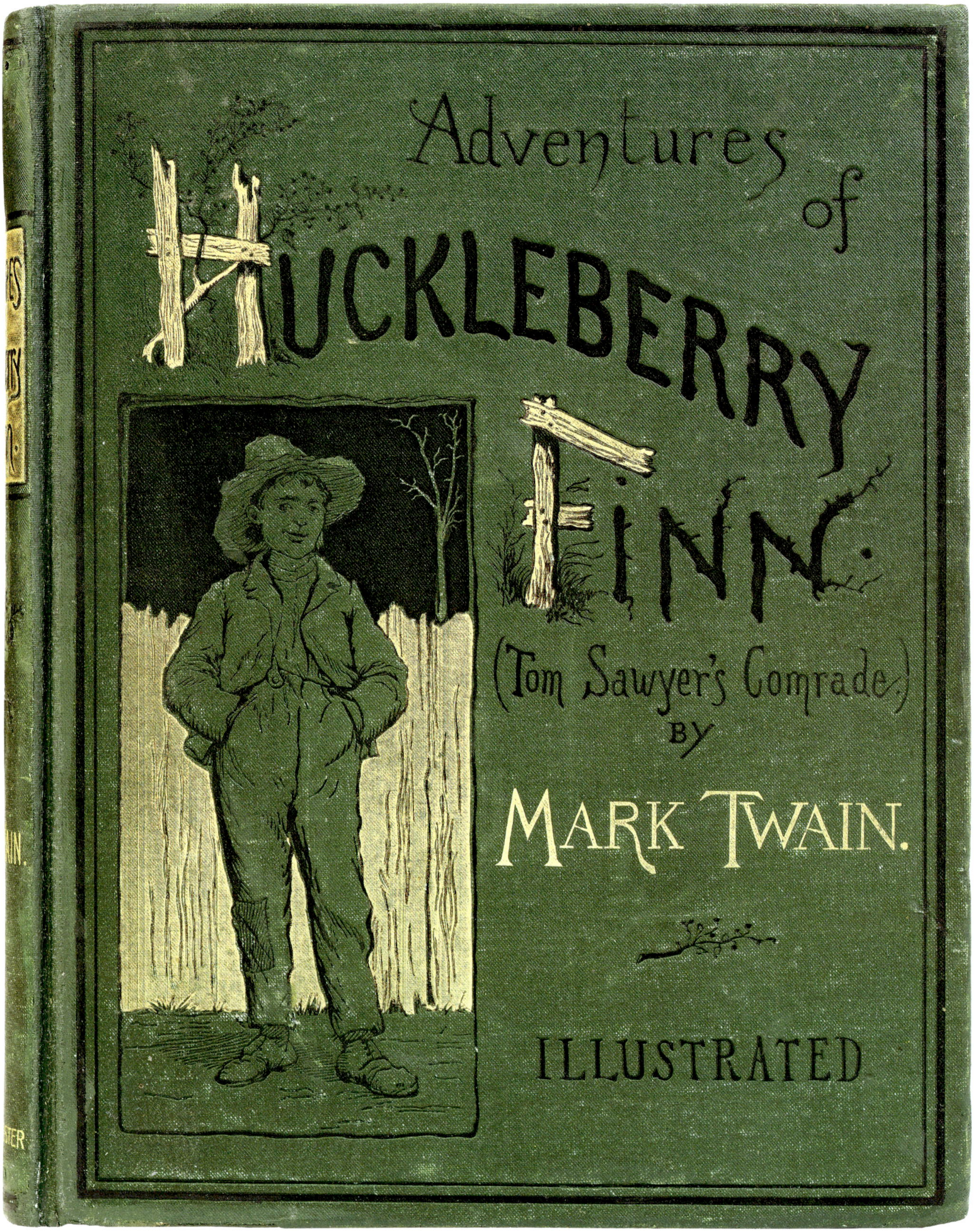
Adventures of
HUCKLEBERRY FINN.
(Tom Sawyer's Comrade.)
BY
MARK TWAIN.
ILLUSTRATED

parcel of Spanish merchants and rich A-rabs . . . with two hundred elephants, and six hundred camels, and over a thousand 'sumter' mules, all loaded down with di'monds" (*Adventures of Huckleberry Finn* 15). Huck says he wants "to see the camels and elephants," so he joins the "ambuscade." "But there warn't no Spaniards and A-rabs," he says. "It warn't nothing but a Sunday School picnic, and a primer class at that" (*Adventures of Huckleberry Finn* 15). But Tom will not let go of his illusions, and the comic argument that follows marks the contrast between romanticism and realism, with the latter winning out. With that, Tom's dominance ends, because Huck becomes a captive of his abusive, alcoholic father, Pap Finn. When Huck escapes, in an inventive scheme that is a delight to both young and old readers, he meets up with the runaway slave Jim on Jackson's Island, and now the real adventures begin.

Huck and Jim running away down the Mississippi on a raft has become an important American symbol. Despite the seriousness of their predicament, humor abounds, both in Huck's comic misunderstandings and in the comic dialogues between Huck and Jim, this time with Huck taking the Tom Sawyer role and Jim the Huck role of common sense and realism. In their arguments about Solomon and the nature of kings, Jim's logic gets the best of Huck's reliance on book reading that he doesn't fully grasp (*Adventures of Huckleberry Finn* 93–98).

Where *Tom Sawyer* has a dark side, *Huckleberry Finn* is drenched in darkness. But despite its serious themes—slavery, racism, abolitionism, alcoholism, child abuse, theft, violence, and murder—humor shines through on almost every page, the contrasts heightening both the light and dark elements. *Huckleberry Finn*, with its blending of humor and seriousness, is truly a masterpiece of American and world literature.

THE PRINCE AND THE PAUPER

Published in 1881, one of the three books Mark Twain published between *Tom Sawyer* and *Huckleberry Finn*, *The Prince and the Pauper* may at first seem to be an anomaly (**page 38**). As historical fiction, it differs greatly from the novels that bookend it, but it has a connection, in that it too is a "boy book" (Gribben, "Tom Sawyer"). The novel was immediately a favorite of the family, as they felt it showed a side of their father that the world did not otherwise see.

The novel is set in England in 1547, the year of King Henry VIII's death. Henry's son Edward, the Prince of Wales, had been born the same day as Tom Canty, son of an abusive father. The plot revolves around switched identities: Tom Canty stands outside the royal palace, only to be admonished by a guard. Edward sees this and invites Tom in, where Tom tells him of his life in Offal Court. He catches the prince's fancy when he tells him of his games and his sports, and the prince, longing for relief from the constriction of the court, proposes that they exchange clothes. Finding that they look exactly alike, they begin what both of them think will be a brief adventure. The ensuing plot follows Edward's travails as a prince in pauper's clothing and Tom's travails as a pauper out of place in the palace. The humor of the piece derives from the change of places. For example, in chapter 7, Tom suffers through dinner, using the wrong utensils, mystified by the expensive napkin he is afraid of soiling, not recognizing lettuce or turnips, and drinking from the finger bowl, about which he pronounces, "Nay, it likes me not, my lord; it hath a pretty flavor, but it wanteth strength" (*The Prince and the Pauper* 100). Edward has his own misadventures in his pauper's world, but his hardships and what he observes of the seamy side of London make him a more compassionate ruler when the switch is finally resolved and he is restored to his rightful place, the throne of England, as King Edward VI.

Despite its anomalous nature in Twain's canon, *The Prince and the Pauper* has always been one of his most read works. It has spawned a number of adaptations: stage plays, film versions, and animation, including Mickey Mouse in the twin roles. Although the setting, language, and style are not what readers usually expect from Mark Twain, he certainly struck an enduring chord with this tale of switched identities and the adventures and humor that come as a result.

CONCLUSION

Mark Twain was a master of fiction about children, especially boys. He had a keen understanding of child psychology and youthful humor, perhaps because he retained a childlike outlook even in adulthood. Indeed, his wife's nickname for her famous husband was "Youth." Despite his fame, his wealth, his voracious reading, and his globe-trotting travels, he always understood and appreciated childhood: its optimism, its innocence, and most of all, its humor.

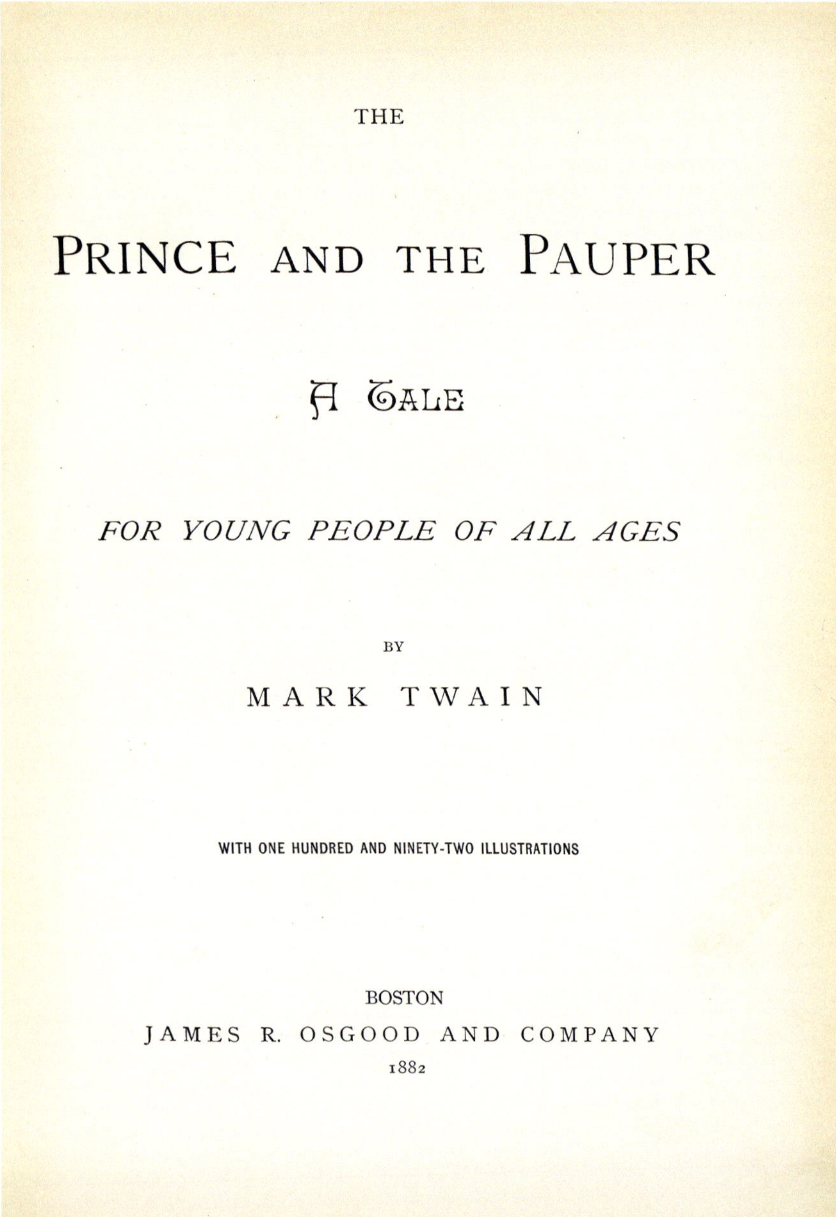

THE

PRINCE AND THE PAUPER

A TALE

FOR YOUNG PEOPLE OF ALL AGES

BY

MARK TWAIN

WITH ONE HUNDRED AND NINETY-TWO ILLUSTRATIONS

BOSTON

JAMES R. OSGOOD AND COMPANY

1882

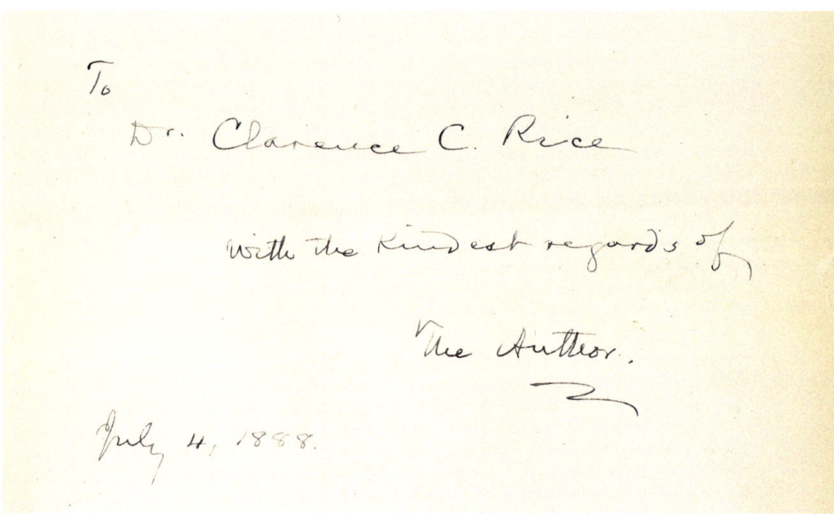

To

Dr. Clarence C. Rice

with the kindest regards of

the Author.

July 4, 1888.

LEFT

Mark Twain. *The Prince and the Pauper: A Tale for Young People of All Ages*. Boston: James R. Osgood and Company, 1882. (Item no. 22)

Twain's first attempt at historical fiction, of which he notes, "It may have happened, it may not have happened: but it could have happened." He presented this copy to Dr. Clarence C. Rice—Clemens's personal physician who introduced the financially troubled author to financial wizard Henry H. Rogers who ultimately led Clemens to solvency—and signed it from "the Author."

OPPOSITE

Mark Twain. *The Adventures of Tom Sawyer*. London: Chatto & Windus, [1877]. (Item no. 14)

A year after its first publication, *Tom Sawyer* appeared in this mass-market "yellowback" edition in Great Britain, featuring a brightly illustrated cover.

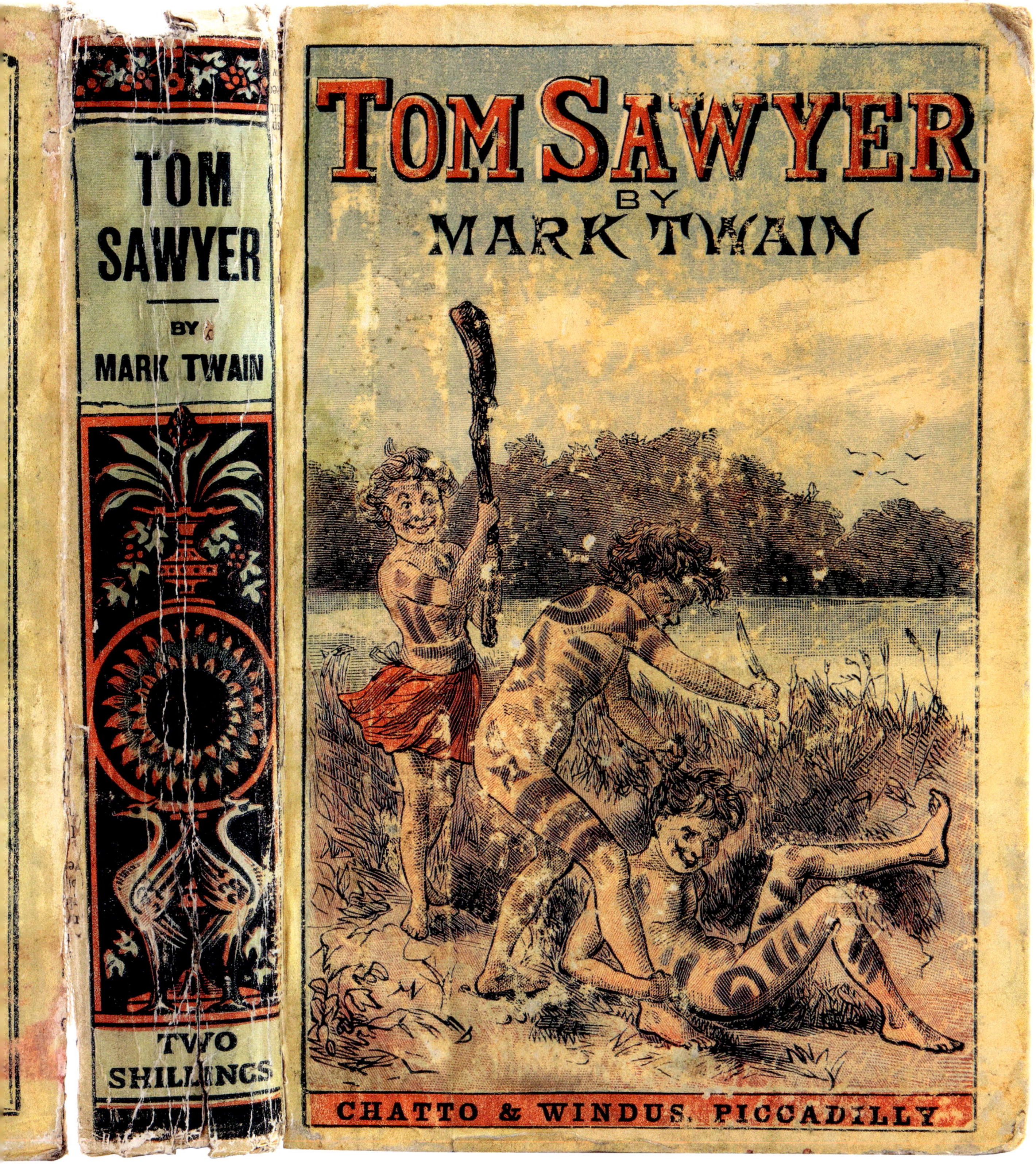
TOM
SAWYER
BY
MARK TWAIN
TWO
SHILLINGS
TOM SAWYER
BY
MARK TWAIN
CHATTO & WINDUS, PICCADILLY

Mark Twain. *Adventures of Huckleberry Finn (Tom Sawyer's Comrade)*. New York: Charles L. Webster and Company, 1885. Sheep binding. (Item no. 25)

The publication of *Huckleberry Finn* was complicated by the discovery in a salesman's prospectus copy of a crude addition to Uncle Silas's trousers. Webster and others suspected a disgruntled engraver. He required the book's salespeople to remove the offending sheet from their samples and return it, and refused to fulfill orders from any who failed to do so; as a result, the "ribald" variant survives in only a single extant prospectus. A few early copies of the book bound in sheep, including this copy, contain the original "curved fly" illustration (preceding the indecent addition). The defaced illustration was corrected in the copies bound in cloth, and the corrected illustration shows a straighter line on the fly of Silas's trousers.

Prospectus for *St. Nicholas for Young Folks*, volume 20, number 12. New York: The Century Company, November 1893. In original wrappers. (Item no. 73)

Mary Mapes Dodge, the founding editor of the children's magazine *St. Nicholas*, advertised Mark Twain's *Tom Sawyer Abroad* in this prospectus for the November 1893 issue. She severely revised the story to the point of bowdlerization, removing references she deemed offensive and elevating Huck Finn's dialect—changes that infuriated Twain.

LEFT

Mark Twain, "editor."
Tom Sawyer Abroad. By Huck Finn. New York: Charles L. Webster and Company, 1894. (Item no. 29)

Twain completed two short sequels to *The Adventures of Tom Sawyer* and left several others unfinished. In *Tom Sawyer Abroad*, Tom and Huck take a hot-air balloon across the Atlantic to Africa.

OPPOSITE

[Unidentified artist.]
A Connecticut Yankee in King Arthur's Court. 1957. Acrylic on board. (Item no. 129)

The comic series *Classics Illustrated* first published its adaptation of Twain's time-travel tale in 1949. For its 1957 reprinting, the story was provided with this new, painted cover depicting a moment of equestrian action.

Mark Twain's Audiences and Voices

DAVID E. E. SLOANE

Readers who were first introduced to Twain, as children, reading *The Adventures of Tom Sawyer* (a book more widely read worldwide than its sequel, *Adventures of Huckleberry Finn*), might wonder whether he wrote adult humor: Twain never wrote any other kind, speaking in terms of ethics, religion, child rearing, and all the rest. The proof is the humor collected in *Sketches, New and Old* (**page 62**), where he tests those subjects in essays he composed as early as his Nevada days in 1863 and into the early '70s for newspaper publication. As he said himself about his thinking: "Information appears to stew out of me naturally, like the precious ottar of roses out of the otter" (*Roughing It*, Prefatory). Information permeated with modern moral standards was his strong suit, and he never wrote otherwise. Twain's social ethics made him a phenom on the West Coast even before he was discovered in the East—his purpose as "the Moralist of the Main" was fixed from the beginning, even though it took many readers, national and international, to catch up with the truth.

His story is even more complicated than that. He had to slip the reputation as a "Phunny Phellow," and then nationally oriented critics gobbled him up as a product of the Native American heartland, just a-slappin' his feet on the Mississippi mud. A more thoughtful evaluation shows something entirely different. "Southwestern humor," the domain to which he was often assigned, was a grotesque misidentification of his real importance to American and world literature. "The South" as our "true frontier" was elevated in our literary history because it represented what some overly influential scholar/pop writers considered to be "true" American (roughhouse/exaggerated) and spoken (vernacular, vulgar) style. That red herring led away from recognizing that American culture and American language had *many* frontiers—including the Far West and California rim, the Old Northeast, the Upper Midwest, and the Urban frontier. If *all* of those had been studied in equal amounts, American culture—and American cultural and literary studies—would not be an isolated academic study. Instead, it would have improved a lot of our lives today—especially the gun culture, treatment of criminals, political activism, the importance of education, and on and on. Twain, by the time of his death, belonged to the world, not just to America. But literary criticism sometimes forgets that fact.

Twain lent his face and name to physical artifacts, not just books on international and national topics but even items like his "self-pasting" scrapbooks (**page 45**), journalistic forays into politics and domestic life, and more. These physical artifacts touch every important facet of

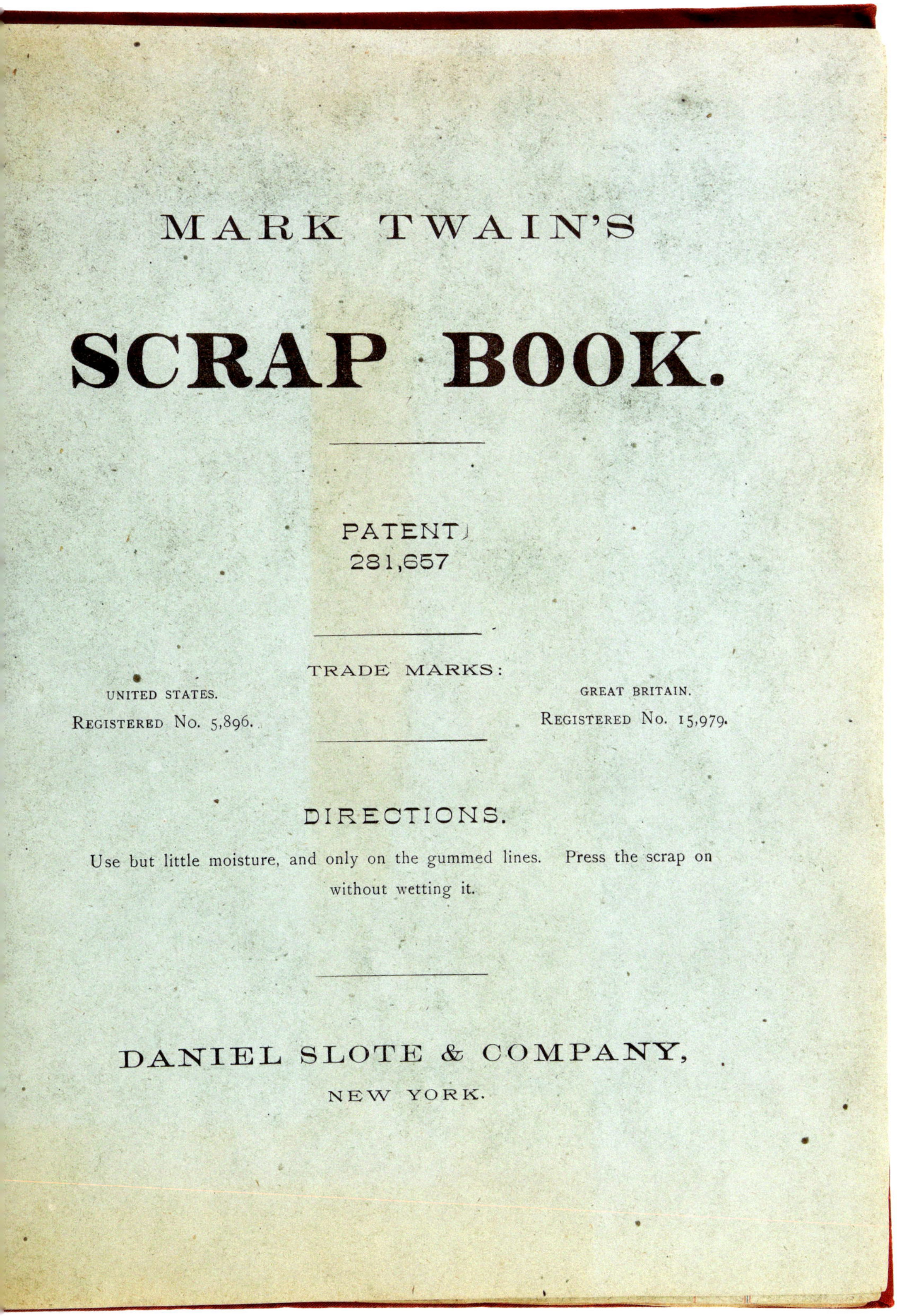

MARK TWAIN'S

SCRAP BOOK.

PATENT
281,657

TRADE MARKS:

UNITED STATES.	GREAT BRITAIN.
REGISTERED No. 5,896.	REGISTERED No. 15,979.

DIRECTIONS.

Use but little moisture, and only on the gummed lines. Press the scrap on without wetting it.

DANIEL SLOTE & COMPANY,
NEW YORK.

Mark Twain's Scrap Book. New York: Daniel Slote & Company, [1892]. (Item no. 168)

Twain patented a self-adhesive scrapbook, which was first issued in 1876. The scrapbook sold well, and was reissued in a variety of sizes and styles for years afterwards.

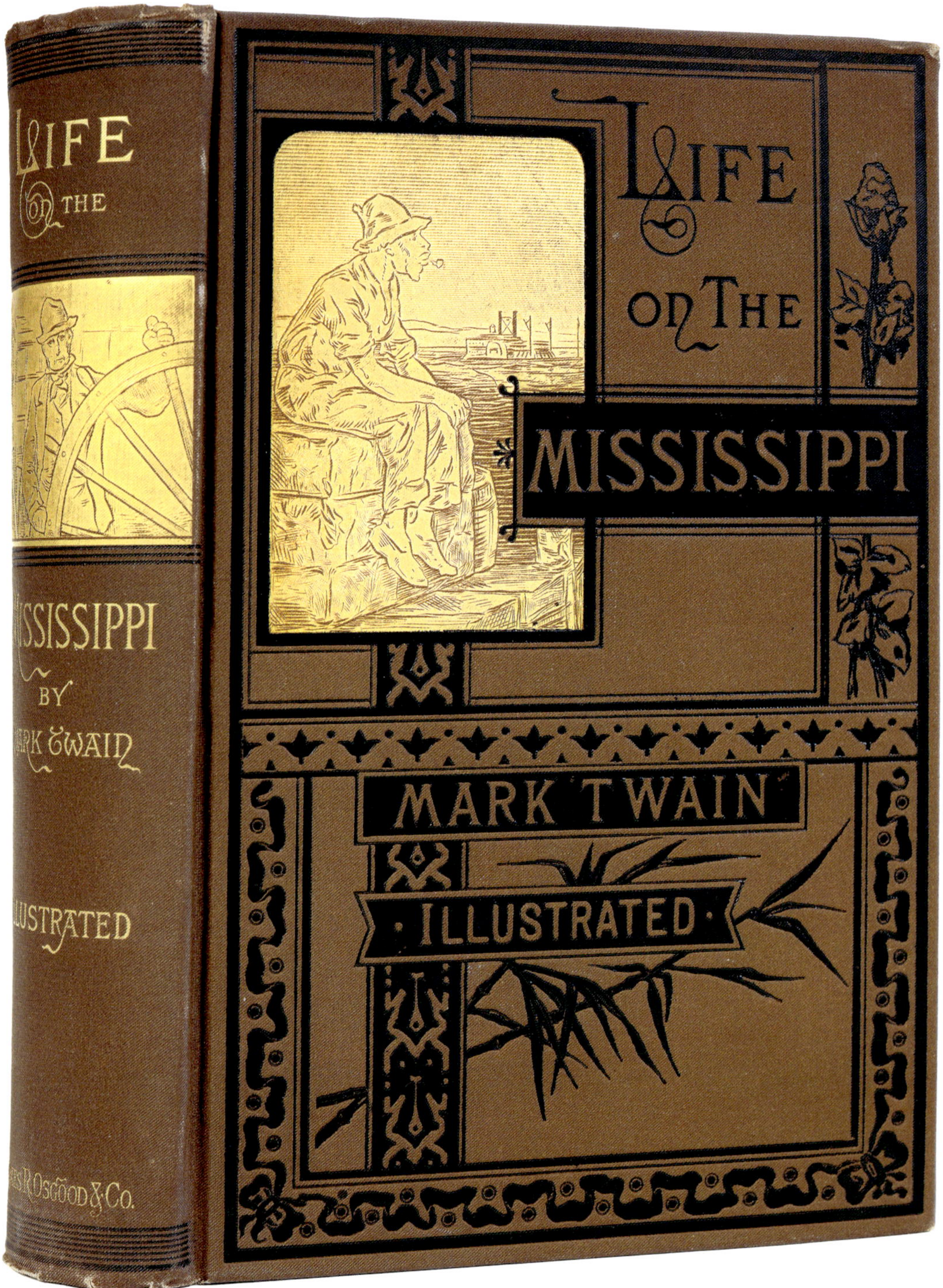

THIS PAGE AND OPPOSITE

Mark Twain. *Life on the Mississippi*. Boston: James R. Osgood and Company, 1883. (Item no. 23)

Here Twain turns his traveler's eye to domestic subjects, recounting his brief career as a riverboat pilot along with the history of the river and numerous tall tales from regions on the river's shore.

Twain and his cultural expectations and personal experience. The artifacts are openly urban, not frontier village and coon-hunting accounts. They are openly literary, elevated and frequently sophisticated in both language and conceptualization, openly social, ethical, and moral in targets for their satire and burlesque, jaundiced in their view of establishments, government, and historical figures. A few critics have always regarded *Sketches, New and Old* as just a pot-boiler, a random collection. Looking at it in the broader context of the span of Twain's career, we recognize it as a powerful kaleidoscope of a whole national culture in Twain's unique voice, covering the period from the 1860s to the early 1870s. That is what drew many readers to Twain in the first place.

Believe it or not, just five Twain pieces can hook a maturing reader on Mark Twain and focus personal and professional goals like few other authors can. The first is "The Lightning Pilot Episode" at the end of chapter 7 of *Life on the Mississippi* (**pages 46–47**). The microcosm of the Pilot house on a riverboat portrays in a single episode the universe defined by a special American skill like that of the professional pilots. What young American reader wouldn't yearn to be worthy of belonging to their guild of high craftmanship and absolute accountability for the welfare of their diverse passengers and their associates? The concerns are as deeply motivated as they are deeply humorous, and fully embedded in the technology of the new industrial world.

The second piece is *The Innocents Abroad* (**pages 52–53 and 108–109**). Any skeptical young reader looking forward to adventuring out into a larger world would be attracted to such a book, although in its early form with

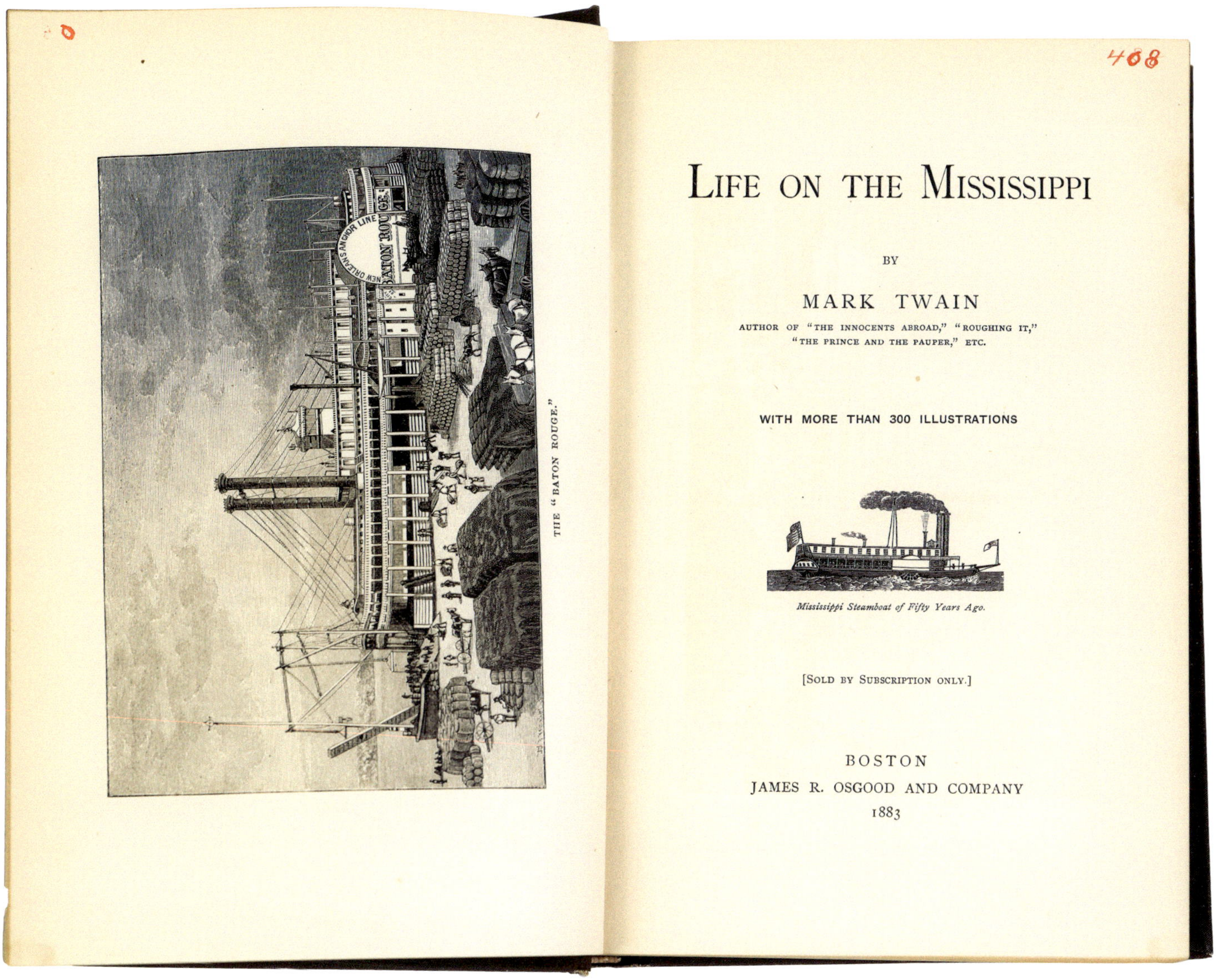

LIFE ON THE MISSISSIPPI

BY

MARK TWAIN

AUTHOR OF "THE INNOCENTS ABROAD," "ROUGHING IT,"
"THE PRINCE AND THE PAUPER," ETC.

WITH MORE THAN 300 ILLUSTRATIONS

Mississippi Steamboat of Fifty Years Ago.

[SOLD BY SUBSCRIPTION ONLY.]

BOSTON
JAMES R. OSGOOD AND COMPANY
1883

illustrations it ran to a whopping 651 pages. Pragmatic post–Civil War readers loved it—Twain among the relics of Europe and the Holy Land at his snarkiest! He wrote like a sarcastic bohemian naif, breathtaking and audacious—and incredibly funny. Twain's neglected forerunners, Artemus Ward, John Phoenix, Q. K. Philander Doesticks, and a few other literary comedians, had paved the way, but their urbane sophisticated allusions and implications were lost on readers who thought America was all buffaloes and Indians. These comedians were embarking on new cultural experiences in a wider world, but their humor was also embedded in history and its meaning, but with sarcastic insights that made the laughs come from a humane as well as a humorous realism. *Mark Twain's Library of Humor* was dominated by them, although Twain noted later that their humor lasted no more than thirty years (**page 49**). Twain outlasted them all. In 1906, he mused that this was because his humor was always sermons, and the humor was let in when it came begging for admission (DeVoto 202f). This was literature almost diametrically opposed to the Old Southwest's worldview.

A third Twain piece was "A True Story" (also included in *Sketches*), better as summer reading with no teacher involved to ram a didactic perspective down a first reader's reading of dewily fresh language and ideas that flowed out of the eastern and national roots of Twain's humor. Many of Twain's works reflect that slant: *Punch, Brothers, Punch*, a brainworm working around the omnibus, an icon of low city life disdained by chauvinistic Southerners (**page 50**), and "A True Story," a story that is actually about a naive northerner—"Misto C"—whose education matures when the former slave "Aunt Rachel" finishes her narrative, "Oh no, Misto C, *I* hain't had no trouble. And no *joy*!" Few teachers can read that sentence the right way in front of a class without tearing up. It is unashamedly sentimental, hardly hard-boiled in southwestern style, despite the richly southern setting and regional characters. The writings of the 1860s had freed Twain from that misconception.

Fourth, there is *Pudd'nhead Wilson*, whose "shoot my half" (of a dog) story got him ostracized by the Southern village loafers (**pages 54–55**). Of course, it would; it was a Yankee story with Yankee irony straight out of P. T. Barnum's *Autobiography*. In an article in *Fetter's Southern Magazine*, Martha McCullouch Williams, a furious former slaveholder, characterized the novel as malicious and misleading, "more than stupid," especially for Twain's use of that joke (Sloane 351–57). African American writers and critics like Ralph Ellison see it differently.

Finally, there is *A Connecticut Yankee in King Arthur's Court* (**pages 56–57**), built around "a Yankee of the Yankees," who cries out on seeing a weeping mother burned at the stake for stealing a small piece of linen to trade for bread for herself and her starving baby:

> A plea was made for her, and her sorrowful story was told in her behalf. She spoke, too, by permission, and said she did steal the cloth, but that her mind was so disordered of late, by trouble, that when she was overborne with hunger all acts, criminal or other, swam meaningless through her brain and she knew nothing rightly, except that that she was *so* hungry! For a moment all were touched, and there was disposition to deal mercifully with her, seeing that she was so young and friendless, and her case so piteous, and the law that robbed her of her support to blame as being the first and only cause of her transgression; but the prosecuting officer replied that whereas these things were all true, and most pitiful as well, still there was much small theft in these days, and mistimed mercy here would be a danger to property—Oh, my God, is there no property in ruined homes, and orphaned babes, and broken hearts that British law holds precious!—and so he must require sentence. (chap. 35)

Other vignettes are more humorous in tone, such as the Yankee's remark that Morgan le Fay had held a man in her dungeon with special hatred, "And yet his crime was committed more in thoughtlessness than deliberate depravity. He had said she had red hair. Well, she had; but that was no way to speak of it. When red-haired people are above a certain social grade, their hair is auburn" (chap. 17). Never forget that Twain was both literary and a comedian. If you can't encompass both, Twain will remain a mystery; all his travel books are semi-fiction. As he was taught in Virginia City by Joe Goodman, "Get your facts first, then you can distort them as much as you want afterwards" (Twain, quoted by Kipling 180).

We also ought to pay a brief tribute in passing to the diaries of Adam and Eve (**pages 58–59**). The stories evoke all the entrepreneurialism, egregiousness, egalitarianism, and empathy of Twain's finest works. Adam and Eve both come to the world as naifs. Both are equivalent in their (mis)understanding of each other and finally in their love. Twain's ironic humor makes a trite theme not only comically engaging but also deeply sensitizing. William Dean

[Mark Twain; William Dean Howells, and Charles Hopkins Clark, eds.] *Mark Twain's Library of Humor*. New York: Charles L. Webster & Company, 1888. (Item no. 55)

Twain nominally edited this compilation of American humor, but Howells and Clark did the lion's share of the editorial work. The book contains short pieces by dozens of authors, and twenty by Twain himself.

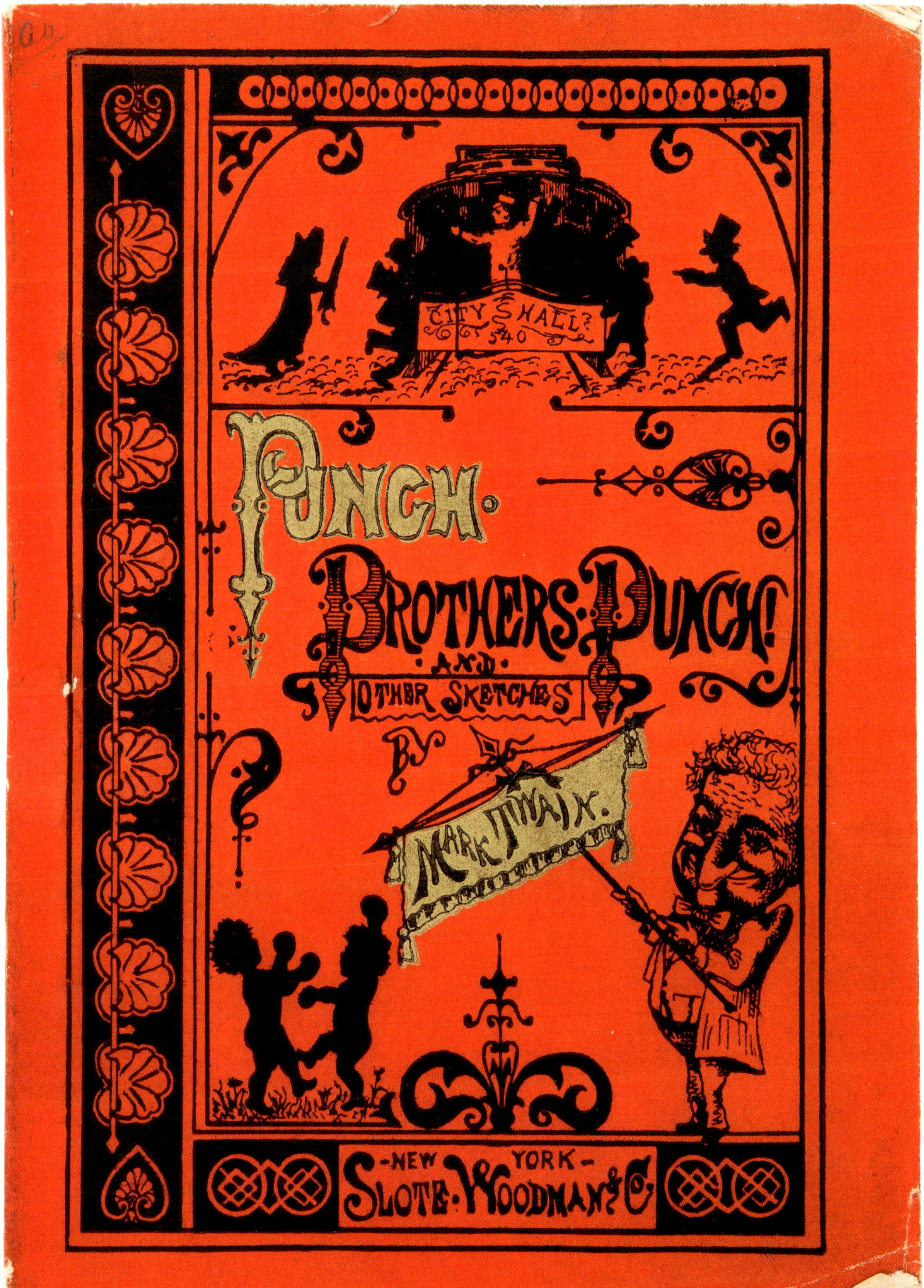
CITY HALL?
540
PUNCH.
BROTHERS: PUNCH!
AND
OTHER SKETCHES
BY
MARK TWAIN.
NEW YORK
SLOTE. WOODMAN & CO.

Howells wanted the Niagara Adam piece for a book promoting the Falls; its origin lay in the publisher's business world. Eve's book changed in visual power through its illustrations to span two centuries, the nineteenth and the twentieth. The illustrations in the first version are cartoonish and comically crude, looking backwards; the second version's illustrations show a fully sexual, beautiful woman in naked outlines—what a contrast! Eve's sacrificial soliloquy on Adam reflects Twain's truest of true loves, not just his wife Olivia's for him, but also his for her. Adam's closing reflection over Eve supersedes outworn religions. His declaration that "wherever she was, there was Eden" places human love at the center of his universe, even above the Bible.

Twain's themes became national after the Civil War. They are good demonstrations of how far Twain had identified with the newspaper culture of the Northeast, the upper Midwest, the intellectual Bohemians of the Pacific Coast, and his enlarged American vision. The collection shows him splitting his life between blue-stocking Elmira and Yankee Hartford, along with his substantial expatriate residences in England, Italy, and Germany. This is why, most broadly of all, the world came to recognize him as the spokesman for all victims of inhumanity and oppression.

Twain's portraits of life along the Mississippi create a world complete in itself, naturally beautiful even in the face of the reality of dead fish on the riverbank in Huck's soliloquy opening chapter 19 of *Huckleberry Finn* **(pages 35–36)**. Likewise, the mature pilot sees as only a professionally trained expert would, in "A Nostalgic View" in chapter 9, often reprinted as "Two Ways of Seeing the River" in *Life on the Mississippi*, one view naive and innocent, the other aware of its dangers and their deadly consequences. The realities Twain captured in the beauty of nature have lasted, not because they are pretty pictures surrounded by amusing Southern anecdotes, but because Twain infused in his word paintings his innocence, idealism, and empathy. These are the themes of *A Connecticut Yankee*, *Pudd'nhead Wilson*, *Huckleberry Finn*, and the kaleidoscope in *Sketches, New and Old*. Together they make up the identity of the single author in our literary history who represents our best and highest hopes for the "American" dream.

The Yankee's demand for a "new deal," and his attempt to make his "man factories" transform medieval England, comprise his deeply American philosophy, but it is also a radical statement akin to Jefferson's claim that the tree of liberty must be watered by the blood of patriots in every generation. Twain's artistry in drawing character and brilliance in capturing comic vignettes and slapstick events makes his novels popular. His underlying vision makes them lasting. When William Dean Howells, Twain's friend and sometimes editor, published "A True Story" in the *Atlantic Monthly*, he told Twain that he would gladly have one hundred more like it. Any literary editor in the Northeast or Midwest would have felt the same. Howells reflected that he knew many writers and they were like each other, but Clemens was sole, incomparable, the Lincoln of our literature . . . and so we see in Mark Twain a profound reflection of ourselves and our hopes.

OPPOSITE

Mark Twain. *Punch, Brothers, Punch! and Other Sketches*. New York: Slote, Woodman & Co., 1878. (Item no. 15)

The eponymous sketch of this collection also appeared under the title "A Literary Nightmare," and concerns Twain's encounter with what would be called in our day an "earworm"— specifically, a catchy jingle written by Isaac Bromley and others about streetcar conductors.

THIS PAGE AND OPPOSITE

Mark Twain. *The Innocents Abroad, or The New Pilgrim's Progress; Being Some Account of the Steamship Quaker City's Pleasure Excursion to Europe and the Holy Land; With Descriptions of Countries, Nations, Incidents and Adventures, as They Appeared to the Author*. Hartford: American Publishing Company, 1869. (Item no. 5)

Mark Twain's first major commercial and popular success, *The Innocents Abroad*—a satirical "anti-travel" book based on his 163-day tour of Europe and the Holy Land—would remain his best-selling book throughout his lifetime.

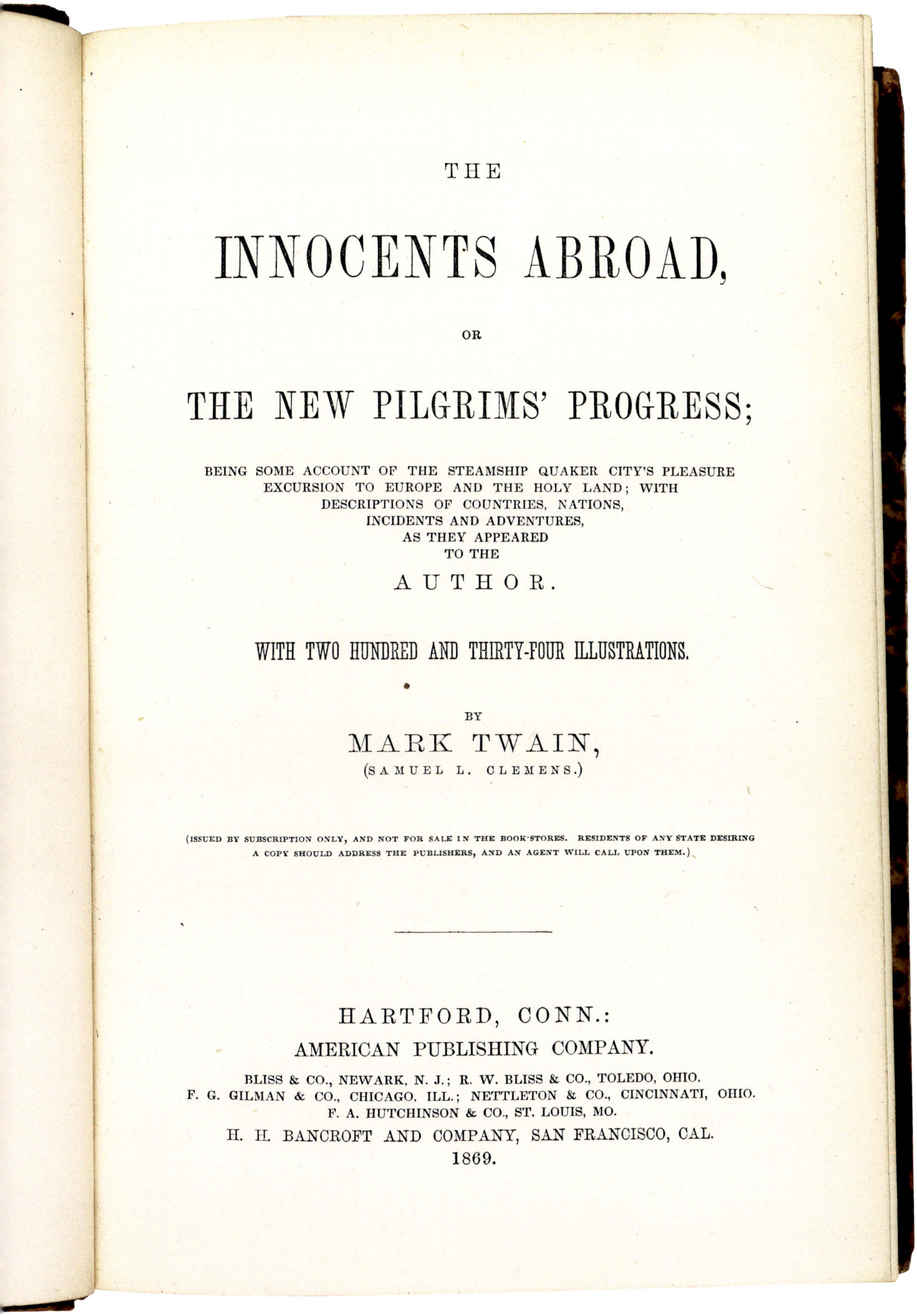

THE

INNOCENTS ABROAD,

OR

THE NEW PILGRIMS' PROGRESS;

BEING SOME ACCOUNT OF THE STEAMSHIP QUAKER CITY'S PLEASURE
EXCURSION TO EUROPE AND THE HOLY LAND; WITH
DESCRIPTIONS OF COUNTRIES, NATIONS,
INCIDENTS AND ADVENTURES,
AS THEY APPEARED
TO THE

AUTHOR.

WITH TWO HUNDRED AND THIRTY-FOUR ILLUSTRATIONS.

BY

MARK TWAIN,

(SAMUEL L. CLEMENS.)

(ISSUED BY SUBSCRIPTION ONLY, AND NOT FOR SALE IN THE BOOK-STORES. RESIDENTS OF ANY STATE DESIRING
A COPY SHOULD ADDRESS THE PUBLISHERS, AND AN AGENT WILL CALL UPON THEM.)

HARTFORD, CONN.:

AMERICAN PUBLISHING COMPANY.

BLISS & CO., NEWARK, N. J.; R. W. BLISS & CO., TOLEDO, OHIO.
F. G. GILMAN & CO., CHICAGO, ILL.; NETTLETON & CO., CINCINNATI, OHIO.
F. A. HUTCHINSON & CO., ST. LOUIS, MO.
H. H. BANCROFT AND COMPANY, SAN FRANCISCO, CAL.
1869.

THIS PAGE AND OPPOSITE

Mark Twain (Samuel L. Clemens). *The Tragedy of Pudd'nhead Wilson, and the Comedy Those Extraordinary Twins*. Hartford: American Publishing Company, 1894. (Item no. 31)

This later Twain novel is steeped in irony: its eponymous character, a lawyer, is dubbed a "Pudd'nhead" not because of his stupidity, but because the unsophisticated inhabitants of his frontier town misunderstand his cleverness. The main plot of the novel updates the basic concept of *The Prince and the Pauper* with biting social criticism, contrasting the lives of a pair of young men—one white, one 1/32 Black (and thus nonwhite under the "one-drop" principle that guided racist legislation of the era)—who are switched in infancy.

PUDD'NHEAD WILSON. 55

"Like it!" and cock his eye to one side to see if Roxy was observing; then, "Awnt it!" and cock his eye again; then, "Hab it!" with another furtive glance; and finally, "Take it!"—and the prize was his. The next moment the heavy implement was raised aloft; the next, there was a crash and a squall, and the cat was off on three legs to meet an engagement; Roxy would arrive just as the lamp or a window went to irremediable smash.

Tom got all the petting, Chambers got none. Tom got all the delicacies, Chambers got mush and milk, and clabber without sugar. In consequence Tom was a sickly child and Chambers was n't. Tom was "fractious," as Roxy called it, and overbearing; Chambers was meek and docile.

With all her splendid common sense and practical every-day ability, Roxy was a doting fool of a mother. She was this toward her child—and she was also more than this: by the fiction created by herself, he was become her master; the necessity of recognizing this relation outwardly and of perfecting

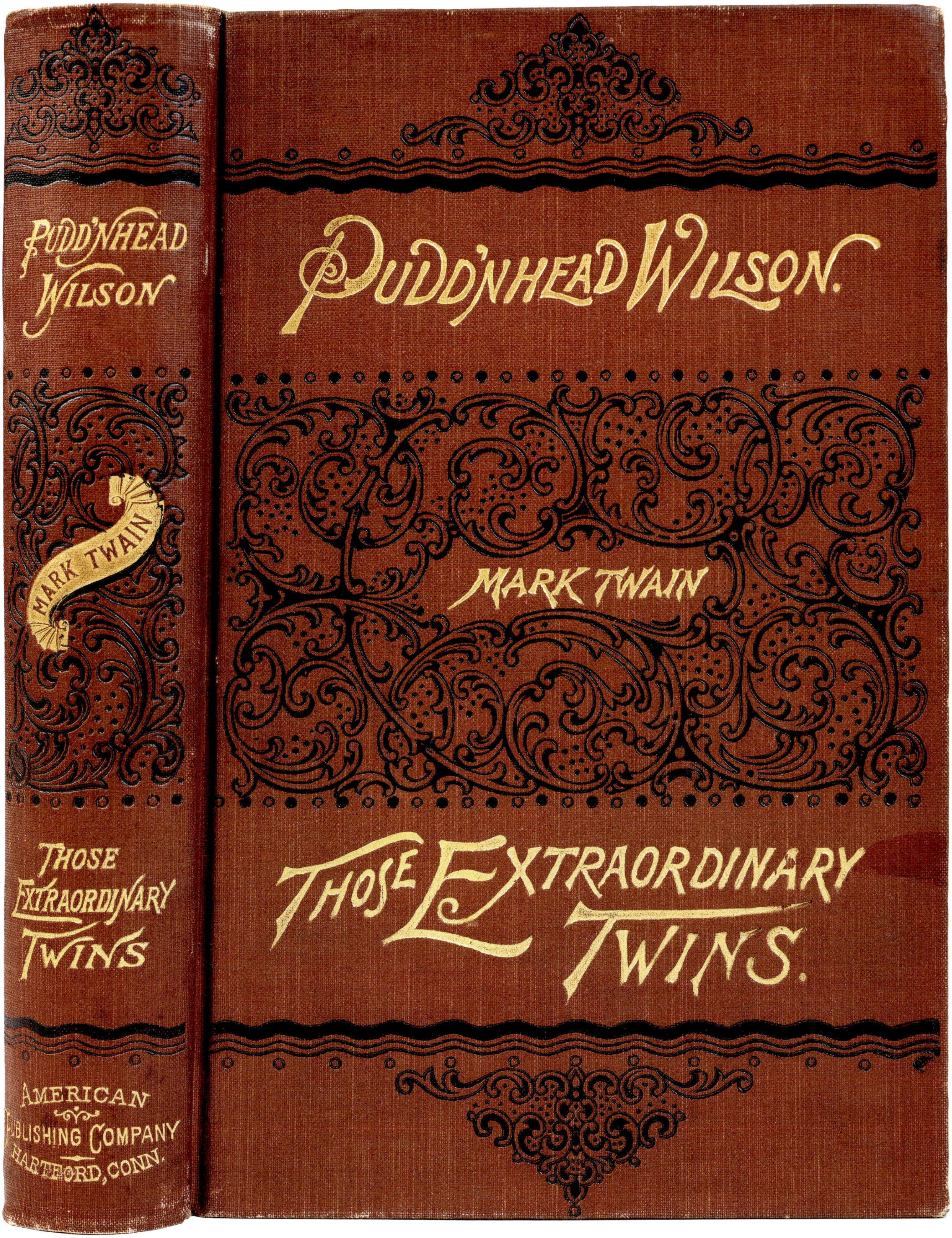
PUDD'NHEAD WILSON
MARK TWAIN
THOSE EXTRAORDINARY TWINS
AMERICAN PUBLISHING COMPANY
HARTFORD, CONN.
PUDD'NHEAD WILSON.
MARK TWAIN
THOSE EXTRAORDINARY TWINS.

THIS PAGE AND OPPOSITE

Mark Twain. *A Connecticut Yankee in King Arthur's Court*. New York: Charles L. Webster & Company, 1889. (Item no. 26)

In Twain's time-travel story, American engineer Hank Morgan finds himself transported to Camelot, bringing progressive values to the age of chivalry. Twain presented this first edition copy to George L. Bell and signed it "the author."

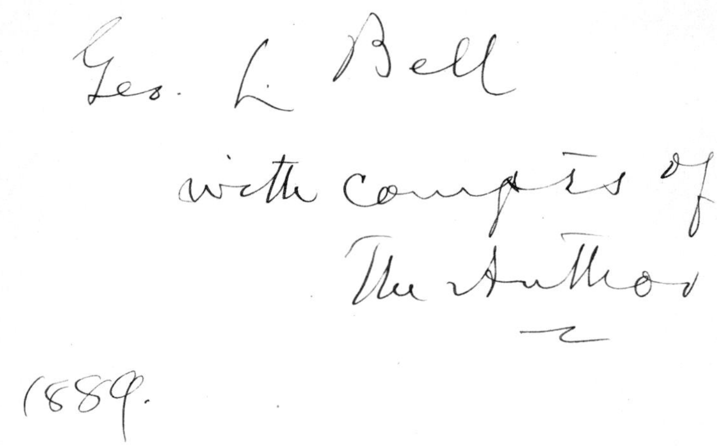
Geo. L. Bell
with compts of
The Author
1889.

"I SAW HE MEANT BUSINESS."

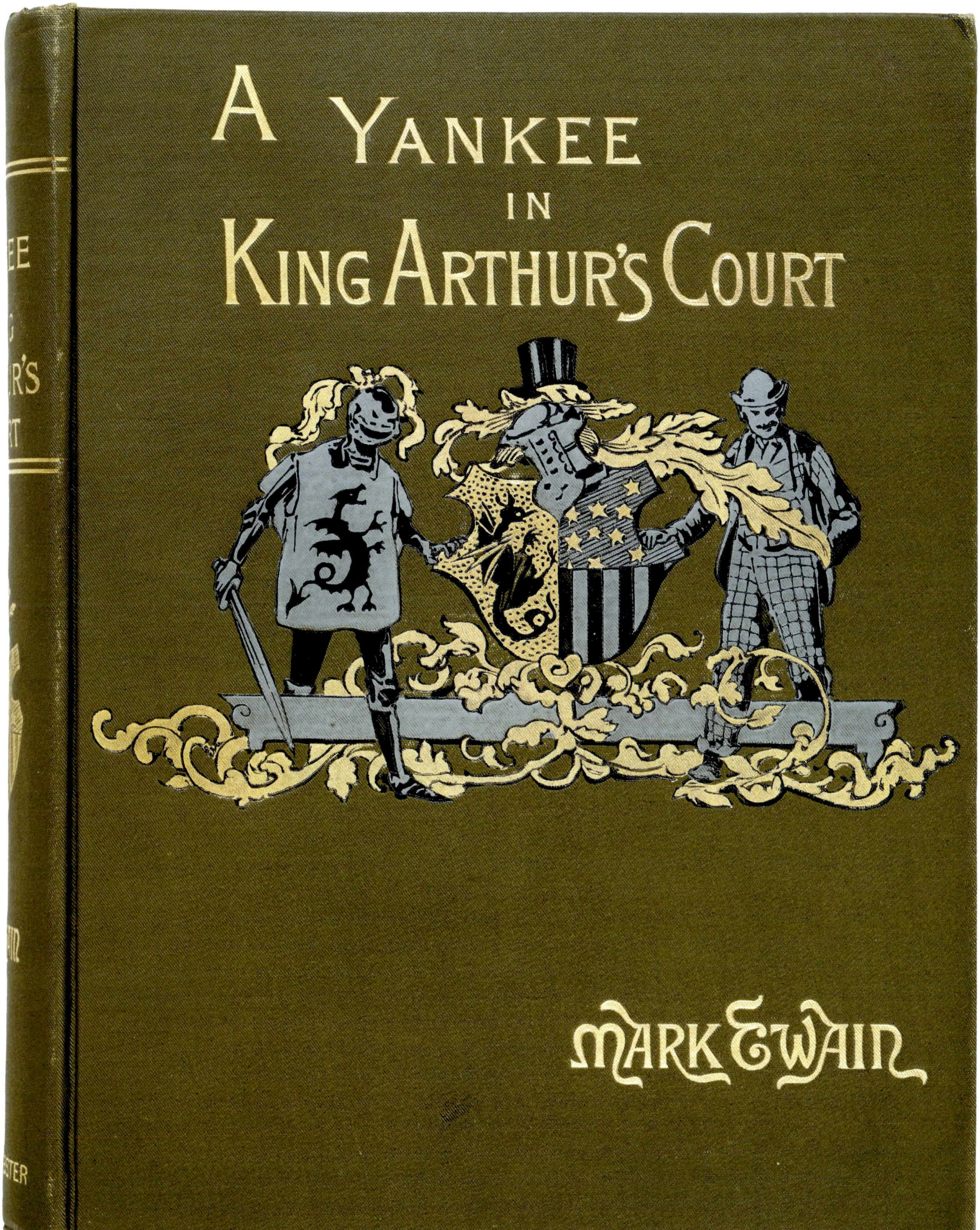
A YANKEE
IN
KING ARTHUR'S COURT
MARK TWAIN

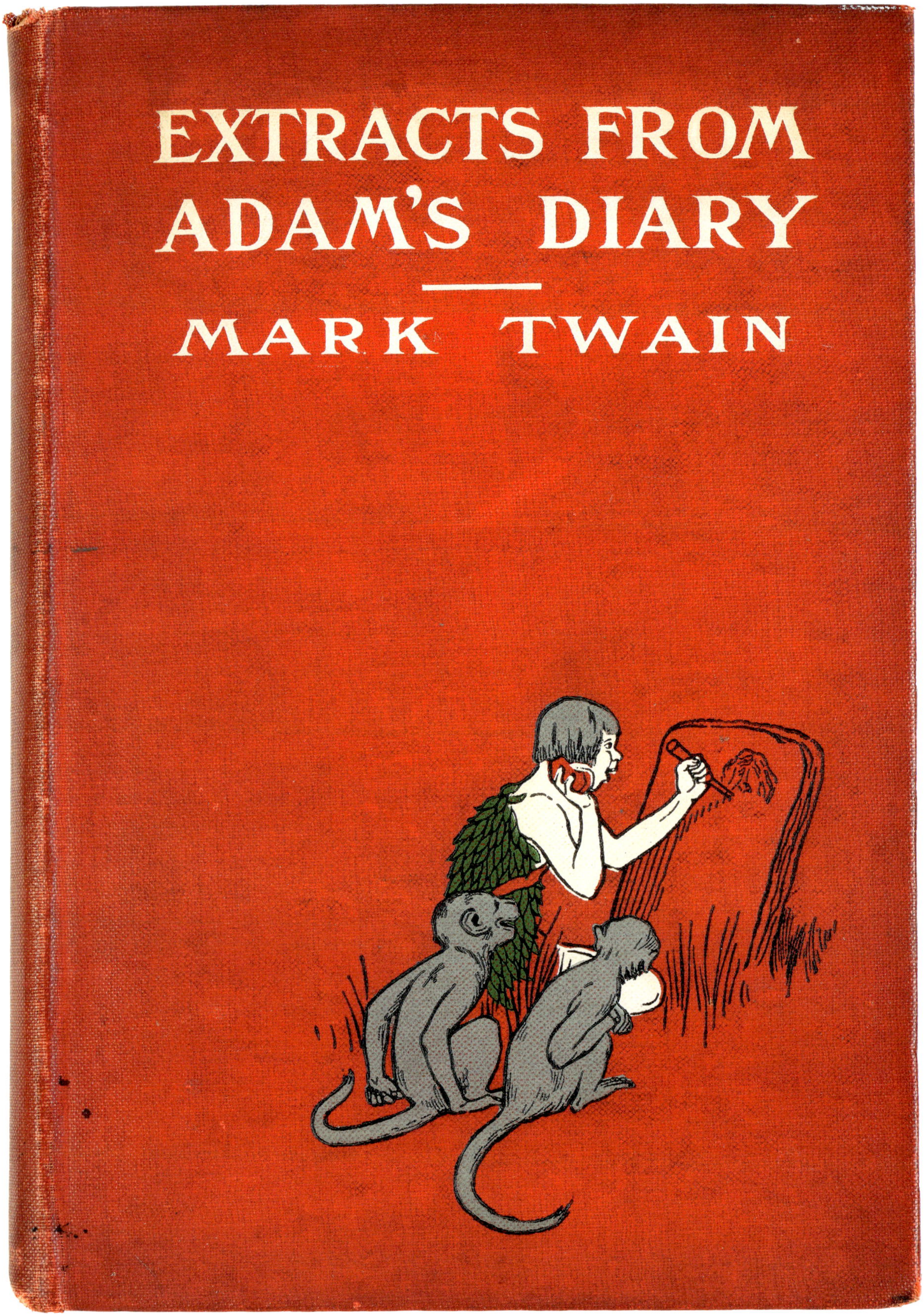
EXTRACTS FROM
ADAM'S DIARY
MARK TWAIN

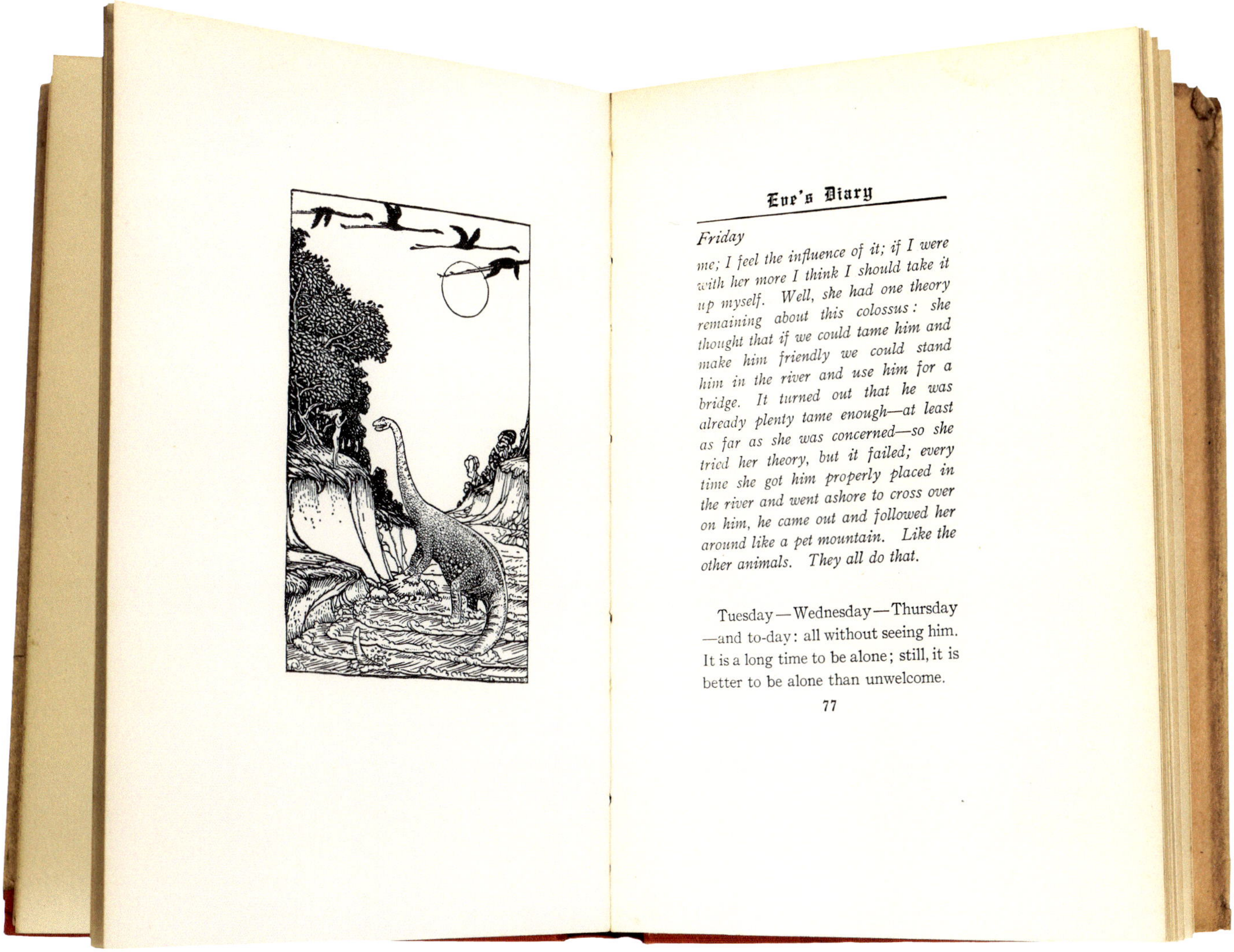

Eve's Diary

Friday

me; I feel the influence of it; if I were with her more I think I should take it up myself. Well, she had one theory remaining about this colossus: she thought that if we could tame him and make him friendly we could stand him in the river and use him for a bridge. It turned out that he was already plenty tame enough—at least as far as she was concerned—so she tried her theory, but it failed; every time she got him properly placed in the river and went ashore to cross over on him, he came out and followed her around like a pet mountain. Like the other animals. They all do that.

Tuesday—Wednesday—Thursday—and to-day: all without seeing him. It is a long time to be alone; still, it is better to be alone than unwelcome.

77

OPPOSITE

Mark Twain. *Extracts from Adam's Diary, Translated from the Original Ms.* London and New York: Harper & Brothers, 1904. (Item no. 35)

ABOVE

Mark Twain. *Eve's Diary, Translated from the Original Ms.* London and New York: Harper & Brothers, 1906. (Item no. 36)

These two novellas purport to tell the biblical story of Adam and Eve from their own perspectives, "translated" here by Mark Twain.

Pedro Carolino. *The New Guide of the Conversation in Portuguese and English. With an Introduction by Mark Twain.* Boston: James R. Osgood & Co., 1883. (Item no. 52)

Carolino published this phrasebook in Portugal in 1855, which because of his unfamiliarity with English syntax contains innumerable unintentionally amusing mistranslations. Clemens discovered the book several years after its original publication and arranged for its verbatim reprinting, declaring in his introduction: "Whatsoever is perfect in its kind, in literature, is imperishable: nobody can imitate it successfully, nobody can hope to produce its fellow; it is perfect, it must and will stand alone: its immortality is secure." Later reissues did add to the original, however, imposing the title *English As She Is Spoke*—a phrase that appears nowhere in Carolino's original.

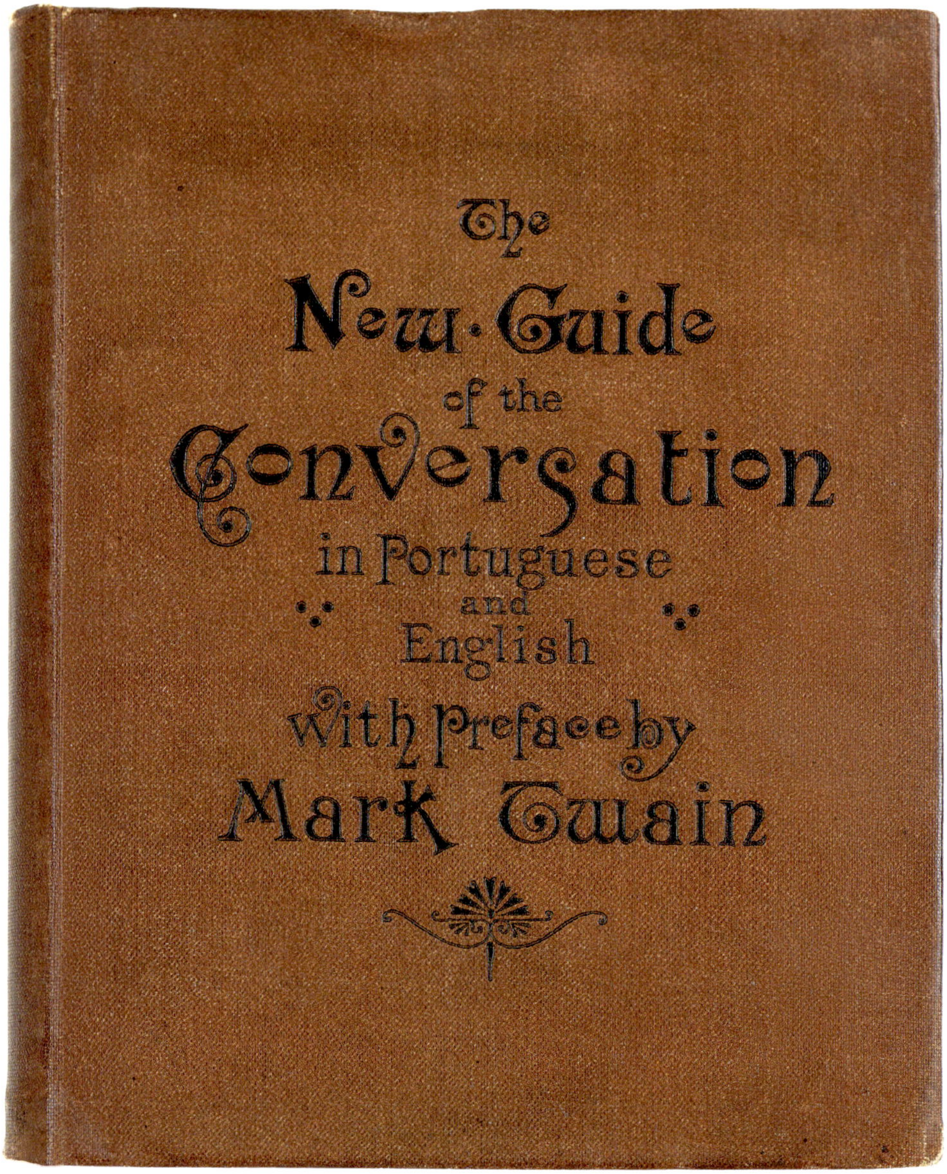

Mark Twain. *A Curious Dream; and Other Sketches.* London: George Routledge & Sons, [1872]. (Item no. 41)

In the title story of this collection, a dreamer experiences a macabre vision of a procession of skeletons who protest that the living have allowed their cemetery to fall into neglect.

BELOW

Mark Twain. *Mark Twain's Sketches, New and Old.* Hartford and Chicago: The American Publishing Company, 1875. (Item no. 46)

Twain edited the amusing sketches in these collections to soften the language from their original American serial publication so that they would be more suitable for British audiences.

OPPOSITE

Mark Twain [edited by Edith Oenone Somerville]. *The Mark Twain Birthday Book.* London: Remington & Co., 1885. (Item no. 53)

Containing over 700 quips, maxims, and quotes from Twain's writings, this British publication is the first compilation of Twain quotations.

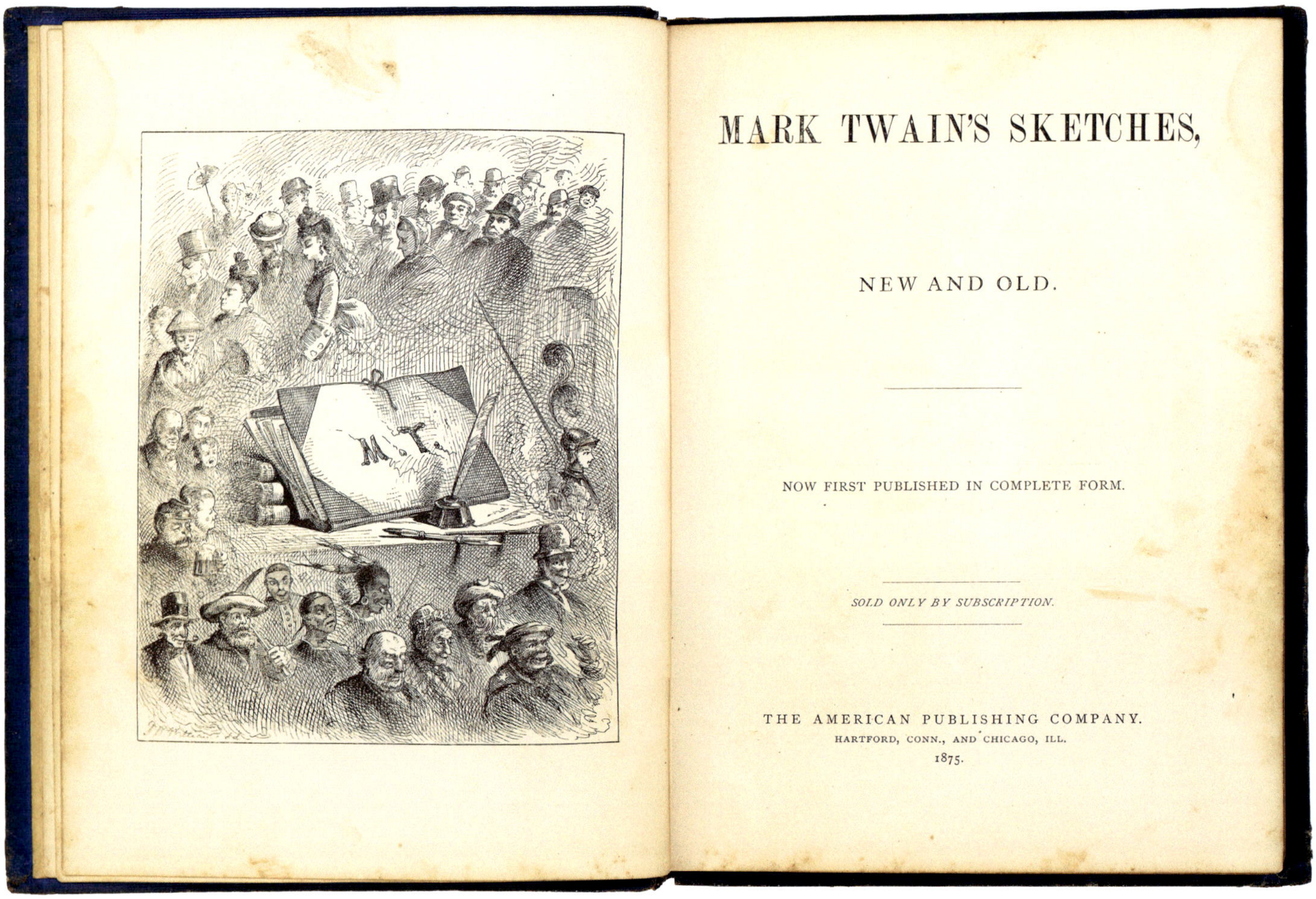

THE
MARK TWAIN
BIRTH-DAY BOOK

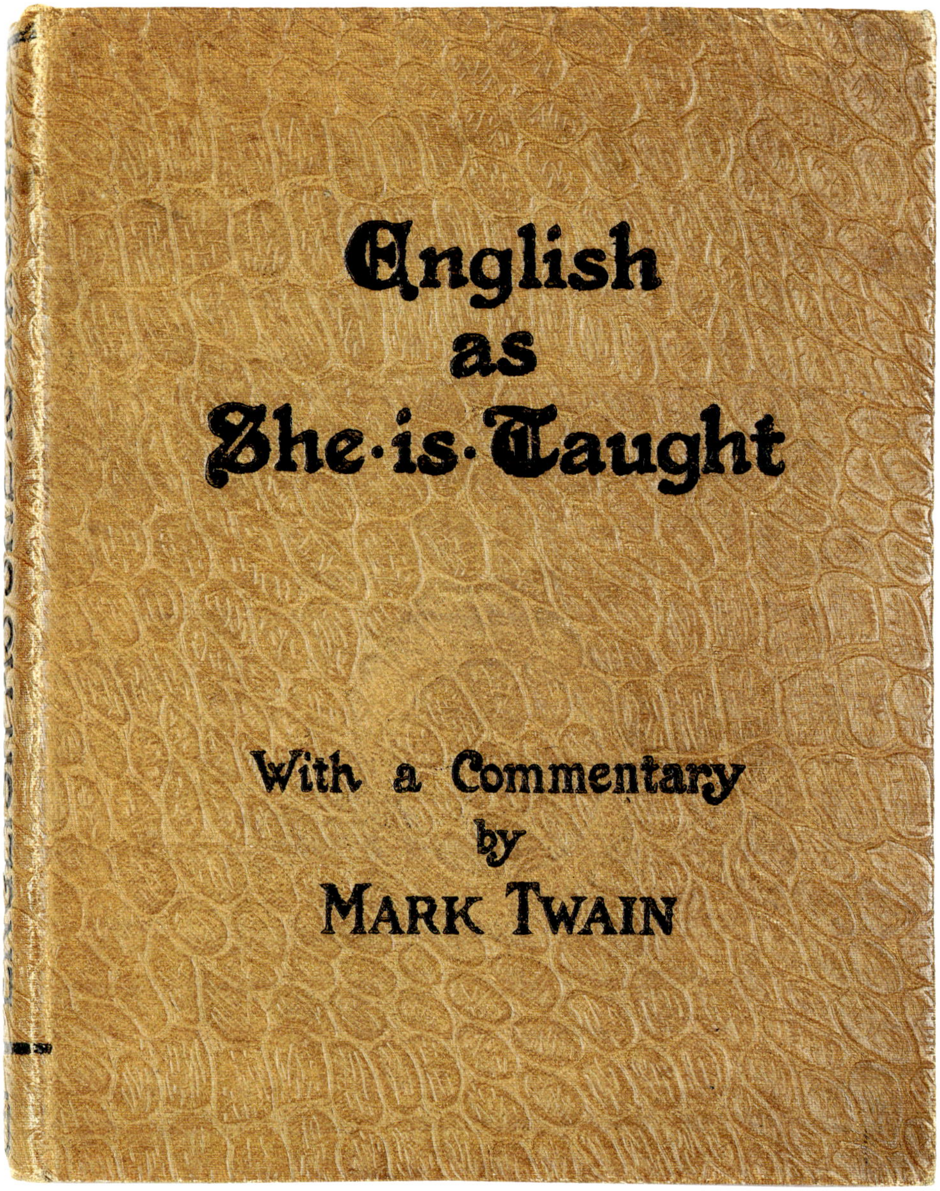

LEFT

English as She is Taught, Being Genuine Answers to Examination Questions in Our Public Schools Collected by Caroline B. Le Row. With a Commentary Thereon by Mark Twain. London: T. Fisher Unwin, 1887. (Item no. 54)

Le Row, a Brooklyn schoolteacher, compiled this booklet of her students' most outrageous answers to test questions. Clemens wrote a glowing review of it for *The Century Magazine*, and read from the book in his lectures. Twain's review was reprinted as an introduction to the book's first English edition.

OPPOSITE

Mark Twain. *The American Claimant*. New York: Charles L. Webster & Co., 1892. (Item no. 27)

Col. Beriah Sellers, a character featured in Twain and Charles Dudley Warner's novel *The Gilded Age*, became a popular character on the stage in an unauthorized dramatic adaptation of the book. Twain acquired the rights to the play and revised it, and it became a successful touring production. Working with William Dean Howells, Twain authored a sequel in which the character, now renamed Col. Mulberry Sellers, gains a hereditary British title. This play was less successful, but Twain adapted the story into his novel *The American Claimant*.

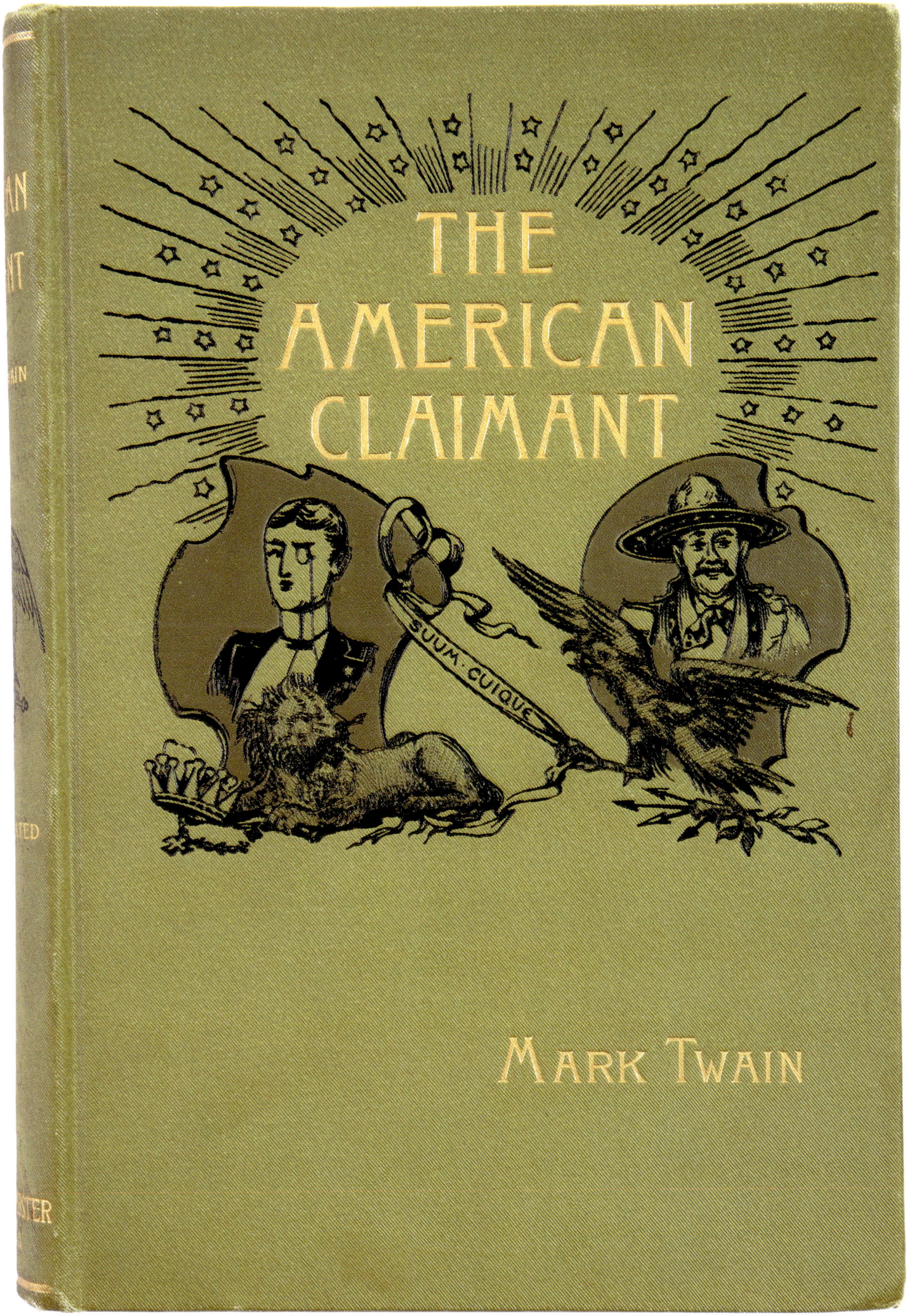
THE AMERICAN CLAIMANT
SUUM·CUIQUE
MARK TWAIN

Mark Twain's Journalism

BENJAMIN GRIFFIN

One of the shortest of the shorter works of Mark Twain is a small card, in the Mark Twain Papers, on which he has written: "CREATING out of NOTHING." At the heart of Clemens's literary-financial economy is Nothing—and the dream of getting something out of it. For him, creation *ex nihilo* is not a theological doctrine but a fact of nature: Some man, somewhere—the Coming Man, the Man of the Hour—will be able to realize something on an investment of nothing. The men who do so are his ideals. They are the investors, who make money breed without working; the miners, who strike a rich vein of gold or silver; the inventors, who bring something new into being and live off the proceeds; the publishers, who turn a book they didn't write into property; the heirs and claimants to fortunes; the hucksters and impostors, too. In his lifetime, Samuel Clemens tried all those roles; but only in language did he find his something-for-nothing. The impulse is worldly enough, it is essentially Gilded Age; yet there is a poetry in it. What is a tall tale but the manufacture, or the glint, of the merest nugget, of an empire, a vast domain, more than the matter gave any promise of supporting?

Why write a story once when you can write it repeatedly? He wrote his reminiscence of "Jim Wolf and the Tom-Cats" in 1867, allowed it to be republished under someone else's name in 1874, considered adding it to *A Tramp Abroad* in 1879, and memorialized the whole affair in an essay published in 1907: "And so that little tale was sold three times. I am selling it again, now," he wrote. "It is one of the best properties I have come across." Another thrice-told (at least!) tale was the shipwreck of the *Hornet*, his first big score as a journalist. Getting himself assigned as a Sandwich Islands correspondent, he produced the first account of that disaster and its lucky survivors. That scoop for the *Sacramento Union* ("Letter from Honolulu"; 7,076 words) was followed by a fuller, more literary treatment for *Harper's New Monthly Magazine* ("Forty-Three Days in an Open Boat," 1866; 10,098 words) (Item no. 65) making use of the survivors' diaries—the still-obscure author's byline being mangled, gallingly, as "Mark Swain." An extract went into the *Jumping Frog* book (1867) **(pages 16–17)**; finally, in 1898, with name recognition no longer a problem, he again adapted "the first magazine article I ever published" as "My Debut as a Literary Person" (11,066 words) and offered it to *Harper's Monthly*, which accepted it—but the *Century Magazine* made a better offer.

Clemens's duties as local reporter for the San Francisco *Morning Call*, a four-page daily he derided as "the washer-woman's paper" (*Autobiography* 2:115), were too routine for his taste, and although he always proclaimed himself a lazy man, slow news days were not congenial to him. But the occasions when he found himself without a subject to write on were, in fact, one of the places where he discovered his special calling. There was simply no keeping him down: With nothing to report, he reports on Nothing. A splendid example is his August 5, 1864, article for the *Call*, indirectly mocking "Almost a Fire" from the previous day's San Francisco *Alta California*. The rival paper's "Almost a Fire" reported on a common enough event in wooden-framed San Francisco, a mishap that, for a short while, promised fairly for a fire. Clemens replied with "Almost an Item," reporting that

> a speck of fire among broken up straw . . . had communicated with the wharf timbers and promised fairly for an item. All this was at the corner of Clay and East streets. We took a position to watch the item growing, but alas! for human hopes; an energetic and public spirited young man who possessed an interest in a ready-made clothing store close by, conceived the wretched idea of squelching the item, which he accomplished with accelerated movements, by anointing the burning materials with a basin of water. ("Almost an Item")

This mocks the *Alta California* and subverts the pages in which Clemens's own article appears, as well. Above all, it foregrounds and advertises his personality: Ostensibly news about San Francisco, it is really news about Samuel L. Clemens. Where the *Alta* had reported on a feeble threat to the city, Clemens chronicles a vicious threat to the reporter's livelihood. The subject of writing has become the effort, the need to write, the death of a young Item killed by tragic mishandling.

Resonances like this are not, of course, always accessible. Few of us are working our way methodically through the San Francisco papers of 1864, and annotated editions of Mark Twain's journalism are not much more numerous. Journalism, even the best and the highest, would not be journalism were it not bound inseparably to its time and place. Its point, its flavor, its very comprehensibility, are dependent on the local milieu, on a mastery of details now only to be recovered by gray, meticulous scholarship. As Clemens went from local journalist to "Literary Person," he did not shed the local color he had mastered as a journalist, but he came to frame it differently, to assume a less thoroughly initiated reader.

In trying to reach a national audience, Clemens could not and, as a rule, did not want to suppress reprintings of his articles. The universal practice of newspaper "exchanges"—the wholesale reprinting of material culled from competitor journals—helped to spread his name and fame. In 1871, *The Day's Doings* **(pages 68–69)** reprinted four of his pieces from *The Buffalo Express*, of which he was then the editor. It would have been unlike Clemens to object to these reprints, though to appear in *The Day's Doings* was to keep questionable company. That journal belonged to the disreputable class of illustrated newspapers; it ran to the "romantic" (the lurid), and it was published by newspaper mogul Frank Leslie under a series of pseudonyms. The London edition ceased operations after prosecution by the Society for the Suppression of Vice. Clemens was in agreement with the Society's aims, arraigning *The Day's Doings* as one of the scandalous journals that "flourish in the land unmolested by the law, because the *virtuous* newspapers long ago nurtured up a public laxity that loves indecency and never cares whether laws are administered or not" (*Mark Twain's Speeches* 48). But it does not appear that he objected to the piracy, as long as it was in a journal. Book publication, however, he saw as the author's prerogative; and the piracy of his shorter works in unauthorized collections started his lifelong pursuit of malefactors and his crusade promoting a system of international copyright.

From Mark Twain's journalism there erupts periodically a fervor, or rancor, that is made all the more powerful by his perfectly judged vernacular. From his dilation on the meager subject there emerges his indirection, his irony. This copious spinning-out is not only another way to augment scanty material and get something for nothing: It is a breakthrough in comic writing, a satirical voice fresher and livelier than any in his time. The early journalism from California already shows his mastery in this kind. The irony in Pap Finn's rant about a free Black man—"Call this a govment!"—is already full fledged in his 1866 mock-defense of police brutality in the San Francisco jail:

> And why shouldn't they shove that half senseless wounded man into a cell without getting a doctor to examine and see how badly he was hurt, and consider that next day would be time enough, if he chanced to live that long? And why shouldn't the jailor let him alone when he found him in a dead stupor two hours after—let him alone because he couldn't wake him—couldn't wake a man who was sleeping and with that calm serenity which is peculiar to men whose heads have been caved in with a

club—couldn't wake such a subject, but never suspected that there was anything unusual in the circumstance? Why shouldn't the jailor do so? Why certainly—why shouldn't he?—the man was an infernal stranger. He had no vote. . . . Therefore, when the stranger died at 7 in the morning, after four hours of refreshing slumber in that cell, with his skull actually split in twain from front to rear, like an apple, as was ascertained by post mortem examination, what the very devil do you want to go and find fault with the prison officers for? You are *always* putting in your shovel. ("What Have the Police" 197)

Mark Twain always claimed to despise the trade of journalism, and to dislike writing. Yet he was unable to stop; and this is obviously from internal, not external, compulsion. We can understand this somewhat better when we read him on creation as a passive experience, a simple transcribing of something that came from outside himself (like Stravinsky on *The Rite of Spring*). We get all our ideas "from the outside," he maintained; if he laid claim to the proceeds, it was as a discoverer, not as a maker. There is a key testimony in the *Autobiography*:

> As long as a book would write itself I was a faithful and interested amanuensis, and my industry did not flag; but the minute that the book tried to shift to my head the labor of contriving its situations, inventing its adventures and conducting its conversations, I put it away and dropped it out of my mind. (2:196)

Books that write themselves, ideas from outside, geese that lay golden eggs; "CREATING out of NOTHING." The figure of the Journalist, by contrast, stood for the poor sucker who has to work at it. But after all, it is possible to take Mark Twain too seriously. The sheer bulk of his journalism, and the brilliance of so much of it—most of all, his frequent disparagement of journalism and journalists—point finally to a deeply felt vocation.

The Days' Doings.
An Illustrated Journal of Romantic Events, Reports, Sporting & Theatrical News, at Home & Abroad.
Vol. I.—No. 15.] PUBLISHED AT No. 300, STRAND, LONDON, W.C.—SATURDAY, NOVEMBER 5, 1870. [PRICE THREEPENCE. Registered at the G.P.O. as a Newspaper.
CAPTURE OF THE NOTORIOUS BRIGAND PILONE, NEAR NAPLES.

THIS PAGE AND OPPOSITE

The Day's Doings: An Illustrated Journal of Romantic Events, Reports, Sporting & Theatrical News, at Home & Abroad, volumes 1–2. London: W. D. Waller, July 30, 1870–July 23, 1871. Bound volume. (Item no. 62)

The sensational and richly illustrated English magazine *The Day's Doings* reprinted Mark Twain's "Map of Paris" first printed in his own magazine *The Buffalo Express* in the November 5, 1870, issue. Twain teasingly laments that the map was printed backwards, and explains that "this is the first time I attempted to draft and engrave a map, or attempt anything in this line of art at all" and "I have never had so much trouble with anything in my life as I did with this map." Still, he notes that it is perfectly readable to left-handed people and that it can also be viewed easily using a mirror, and he even suggests that the reader frame the map for future reference. Although he did not "fix" the illustration, Twain did tweak the piece for British audiences by substituting Europeans for Americans in the "official" praise that follows his text.

NOVEMBER 5, 1870.] THE DAYS' DOINGS. 11

We have received from our esteemed contributor, Mr. Mark Twain, the above map, and we give his explanation of the same which is as follows:—

The idea of this map is not original with me, but is borrowed from the *Times*, and the other great metropolitan journals.

I claim no other merit for this production (if I may so call it) than that it is accurate. The main blemish of the newspaper maps, of which it is an imitation, is that in them more attention seems paid to artistic picturesqueness than geographical reliability.

Inasmuch as this is the first time I ever tried to draft and engrave a map, or attempt anything in this line of art at all, the commendations the work has received and the admiration it has excited among the people have been very grateful to my feelings. And it is touching to reflect that by far the most enthusiastic of these praises have come from people who know nothing at all about art.

By an unimportant oversight I have engraved the map so that it reads wrong end first, except to left-handed people. I forgot that in order to make it right in print it should be drawn and engraved upside down. However, let the student, who desires to contemplate the map stand on his head or hold it before a looking-glass. That will bring it right.

The reader will comprehend at a glance that that piece of river with the "High Bridge" over it got left out to one side by reason of a slip of the graving-tool which rendered it necessary to change the entire course of the River Rhine or else spoil the map. After having spent two days in digging and gouging at the map, I would have changed the course of the Atlantic Ocean before I would have lost so much work.

I never had so much trouble with anything in my life as I did with this map. I had heaps of little fortifications scattered all around Paris, at first; but every now and then my instruments would slip, and fetch away whole miles of batteries, and leave the vicinity as clean as if the Prussians had been there.

The reader will find it well to frame this map for future reference, so that it may aid in extending popular intelligence, and dispelling the widespread ignorance of the day.

MARK TWAIN.

OFFICIAL COMMENDATION.

It is the only map of the kind I ever saw.
W. E. GLADSTONE.

It places the situation in an entirely new light.
BISMARCK.

I cannot look upon it without shedding tears.
BESLEY (Mayor).

My wife was for years afflicted with freckles, and though everything was done for her relief that could be done, all was in vain. But, sir, since her first glance at your map, they have entirely left her. She has nothing but convulsions now.
J. SMITH.

It is very nice, large print.
NAPOLEON.

If I had had this map, I could have got out of Metz without any trouble.
BAZAINE.

I have seen a great many maps in my time, but none that this one reminds me of.
TROCHU.

It is but fair to say that in some respects it is a truly remarkable map.
PROFESSOR HUXLEY.

I said to my son Frederick William, "If you could only make a map like that, I would be perfectly willing to see you die—even anxious."
WILLIAM III.

THERE is a woman's club at Marseilles, at which one of the orators recently proposed that the scaffold should be permanent, and that the first victim should be the Bishop of Marseilles.

CORRESPONDENCE.

[FROM INSIDE PARIS.—LETTER II.]

"Ah! Balloon" Post, *viâ* St. Cloud,
PARIS, *Nov.* 1*st*, 1870.

MADEMOISELLE THÉRÈSE GOBERMOUCHE to MISS SARAH BROWN, à Londres.

CHÈRE SALLY,—Goodness gracious knows if ever this will reach you; what with reducing one's letter by photography to the size of a needle's point, and then its having to be magnified by a forty-horse power back into legibility, *après* to send it *à ballon* by the clouds,—a worse conveyance for news than boat, rail, or 'bus, though one may say its "in nubibus" I cannot help exclaiming with Madame de Quelquechose, and the Duke of Argyle, *la belle chose que la poste*.

A propos of clouds, a savant has a plan for forwarding ours by a very ingenious method; the *modus operandi* is as follows:—An aëronaut ascends to the proper altitude in a balloon, and with a light gauze net catches a small cloud; this being brought to earth, the silver lining is ripped out, coined into five-franc pieces (the profits from this source alone are expected to pay working expenses); the cloud is then thoroughly dessicated, its fleecy body rolled flat, and printed on both sides in close type; afterwards it is subjected to the chemical action of carburetted hydrogen and chloric ether, by a process which is the secret of the inventor. It is supposed the French correspondence will fall flat to the ground when the gas has evaporated. The inventor is M. Chato Desparne, a Gascon.

What with the scarcity of paper, which I need not tell you, dear, is very embarrassing—for one must have lots of papers for papillottes,—and the stringent regulations for writing small and close, they are already talking of forbidding the use of capital letters, because they take up too much room; in fact, *entre nous, ma chère*, I believe we shall *lose the capital* shortly. The daily papers have already dwindled to the size of a square on the chessboard, owing, it is said, to requirements of the Government for bank-notes of one franc, silver having long since disappeared, and, as to *centimes*, one can no longer get them save among *nos intimes*.

Yesterday I enlisted in the—don't laugh, its amazing. I know you'll think me insane—Amazons of the Seine. *Chef de bataillon*, M. Felix Belly. Yes, my dear; I always felt my heart stirred somehow at the sight of *them*, and now I shall really wear *them*. The colour is not yet quite decided, but *they* are to be baggy *à la Zouave*. I am so delighted, you cannot think! Yes, my dear; I shall shortly appear like a Drury-lane pantomime with a pair of pantaloons! The regulations are very strict. No one is admitted to the corps unless introduced by a military man who can state that he has known the lady some time. This is a guarantee of respectability. Nothing can exceed the kindness of the officers, and the interest they take in the corps. They have promised to drill us effectually; and I have no doubt a short time will show a difference in our walk, carriage, and general *bearing*. I can sing nothing but,—

"La donna è *mobile*."

We chose M. Belly for our commanding officer, I suppose, because he is naturally bellicose. There is a fable we learned, you remember, dear, in which the members of the body obeyed the belly, and I believe nothing but confusion came of the arrangement; but the members of our corps have great faith in their leader's skill as a belligerent.

I must break off here: Chère Mignon, the photographer, is waiting for my letter,—seventeen military friends have volunteered to accompany me to drill,—I have my new uniform to try on,—Adolphe is down stairs humming "*Que j'aime cette petite militaire*,"—and I am burning with a martial ardour which can only be equalled by the warmth of my friendship for my dear little Sally.

THÉRÈSE GOBERMOUCHE.

WAR DOINGS.

A CORRESPONDENT narrates the following sad incident of the battle-field:—"The day after the battle of Sedan I was traversing the battle-field, when I chanced on the corpse of a French cavalry officer. His chest had been stove in by the fragment of a shell. He was evidently a man of family; the beautifully clean-cut head and the delicate feet betokened breeding. The vultures had already been about him. An open (and looted) pocket-book lay in the cavity of his wound. I picked it up, and found in it his name—that of one of the first families of France. I tore the leaf out—daintily—for the book was blood-boltered, and had turned to leave, when I noticed that the right hand of the dead man was gloved, and that under the glove on the second finger there was a rising that seemed to betoken the presence of a ring. I had taken the address from the pocket-book, I need not say with the intent to write to the friends of the dead man, and it seemed to me that his ring would be a souvenir for them which they could scarcely overvalue. Stooping, I unbuttoned the glove and gradually worked it off the rigid clenched hand, to find on the finger a beautiful ring with a massive stone set in the gold. I spent many minutes trying to work it off the dead hand, but the joints had already puffed and I could not, so I pulled on the glove again as well as I could, threw something over the face of the dead officer, and went on my way. As I came back I noticed some one stooping over the corpse. He sneaked off as I came up, casting hangdog looks behind. I found that the dead man's finger had been hacked off for the sake of the ring. The finger lay there beside the mutilated hand. I chased the dog and caught him. He was a Belgian with the red cross on his arm, and he swore profusely that he had not done the ghastly deed. Not being a gendarme, I did not like the responsibility of pistolling him as he stood, although I should have accepted in his instance the blood-guiltiness with alacrity. I spoiled a good riding-whip over his back, and then let him run."

PARIS is not yet taken, but the pen with which Count Bismarck is to sign the treaty of peace is already prepared. Herr Bissenger, of Pforzheim, has manufactured out of massive gold an imitation of an ordinary stout goosequill. The quill itself is polished, in order that it may be more conveniently handled; but the feather closely resembles a real quill, every fibre being represented, while the back of the feather is thickly studded with brilliants, and below them a count's coronet and Bismarck's monogram are engraved. Besides the engraver and maker, two goldsmiths were engaged on it for five weeks. The gold employed is of 18 carats, and that part in which the brilliants are set is of 21 carats.

THE Saarbruckians have naturally kindly hearts, but familiarity with the sights of war has blunted their sensibilities. After the 2nd of August a man with a flesh wound was the centre of a knot of sympathizing citizens. After Spicheren, the whole town, even the women and children, wrought unremittingly for two days and two nights in bringing the wounded off the field; the men exclaiming with horror as they passed the mangled corpses, the women weeping as women will, at the sight of so much suffering. The other day a train of sadly-wounded men were borne on stretchers from the railway station down through the principal street of St. Johann to one of the hospitals. Some of them were terrible cases; through the hand-ambulance on which one poor fellow lay the blood was dropping on the paving stones. But the children playing in the gutter never looked up, the women gossiped placidly by the street pump without so much as a casual glance at the sufferers, and the men did not take the pipes from their mouths. Such processions have been so common, that compassion, although not withered up, has grown somewhat tough.

WE have been anticipated by the Germans in some of our postal-card experiences, and we must be very silly if we cannot profit in some manner by the same. Here is one example of German experience:—At Dresden a gentleman received a card, some weeks ago, conveying the following message:—"I have lost my purse yesterday at the Elbe Baths with three napoleons in it. I dropped it close to the water mark, where it must lie still. As you are a good diver, pray go a-bathing with me this evening at six." The gentleman kept the appointment, and was surprised to see two or three postmen go into the bath just before him. Having undressed, he went out to the platform, and there his astonishment increased; for, in spite of the unusual hour, there were numbers of men there, some of whom it needed not the sight of the post-office uniforms in the undressing-room to proclaim post-office clerks, for they were well-known faces from the receiving counters. They all kept near the water mark, a place generally very little frequented, and took uncommonly long dives. The writer of the card was sitting at a little distance, evidently enjoying the sight. As the disappointed clerks returned from their aquatic search, they found an inscription in chalk on the door: "Strict secrecy observed with regard to all postal communications." It was only then that they perceived that they had been made the butt of a joke.

IT seems doubtful which is better and more palatable food—horse-flesh or donkey's-flesh. Both form now almost the staple food of the population of Paris—at least, of the lower classes. Donkey's-flesh is sold at 30 cents. the kilogramme. How scarce other meat is, will be best understood from the fact that, at a dinner-party at the Minister's (J. Favre) three cutlets were served for seven guests. Nobody touched them, from modesty, but a ham was attacked with great vigour instead. The splendid Prussian horses so much admired at the Exhibition of 1867, and made a present of to Napoleon III. by the Emperor Alexander, have been sold for 400 fr. each. Before the siege they were valued at 23,000 fr. each. There are Seine fish still to be had in Paris, and so are vegetables, but both are by this time very scarce.

WHAT strikes one the most forcibly in all this is the utter want of patriotism shown by all classes of the French. After all they have said and written, and sung, they must have led Europe to believe that all the valid men in France would spontaneously fly to arms, and never lay them down whilst a Prussian remains in the country: the contrary has been the rule on the left bank of the Seine. Every man who could escape from taking up arms has done so, and the National Guard, in place of retiring upon the forts around Paris in order to assist in their defence, hastened (their officers showing the example) to divest themselves of their uniforms, and to deliver up their arms, which were ignominiously broken, and the pieces thrown into the Seine.

MARSHAL BAZAINE left Metz on the day of the capitulation, on account of his unpopularity with the soldiers and citizens who were opposed to the surrender, and because of the insecurity of his life.

LEFT

The Galaxy, volume 9, number 5. New York: Sheldon & Co., May 1870 in original wrappers. (Item no. 63)

Clemens was given artistic license to start a humor department for *The Galaxy*; his resulting "Memoranda" was a feature of every issue and advertised on many of the front wrappers: "MARK TWAIN, the Great Humorist, writes for The Galaxy, every month."

OPPOSITE

Kelley's Weekly, A Journal of the Times, volume 1, number 1. New York: A. A. Kelley & Co., November 30, 1867. Disbound. (Item no. 69)

The New York magazine *Kelley's Weekly*—a rare and presumably short-lived publication styled after *Harper's Weekly*—featured an early reprint of Mark Twain's "A Yankee in the Orient" first published in the *New-York Daily Tribune* on October 25 in its debut issue.

KELLEY'S WEEKLY,

A JOURNAL OF THE TIMES.

Vol. I.—No. 1.] NEW-YORK, SATURDAY, NOVEMBER 30, 1867. [SINGLE COPIES TEN CENTS. $4.00 PER YEAR IN ADVANCE.

ENTERED according to Act of Congress, in the Year 1867, by A. A. KELLEY & Co., in the Clerk's Office of the District Court for the Southern District of New-York.

THE RECENT COLLISION IN THE BAY.

As the sloop David Sands was passing Governor's Island, at two o'clock on the morning of the 28th ult., she was run into by the steamship Leo, of the Savannah line. The collision, of course, caused the greatest confusion on board both vessels. There were five men on the sloop. Their consternation at the shock, the crashing of timbers, and the inrushing of waters, cannot be described. Hastily examining the sloop, they found that she was nearly cut in two, and was rapidly sinking. They immediately made every effort to escape. The captain, William Coleman, and his brother saved themselves, and were picked up by the Leo's boat. Almost immediately after, the sloop sank, and James Hazzard, part owner of the sloop, Samuel B. Goodwin, and Thomas Charity (colored), were drowned. Two of these had jumped into the small boat without having cast off the painter, and were carried down with the sloop, while the other had leaped overboard. Captain Dearborn, of the Leo, gives the following version of the accident: "As the steamship Leo was coming into the East River at two o'clock in the morning, she came in collision with the sloop David Sands, of Fishkill. The sloop was sunk, and three of her crew drowned, the captain and his brother being saved by the Leo's boat. Two others leaped into the sloop's boat, but did not cast off the painter, and went down with the sloop. One jumped overboard and was drowned. The cause of the collision was the failure of the sloop to show her side-lights. At the time of the collision the steamer's engines were stopped and reversed. I hailed the sloop, and told her to keep off; if she had done so, the collision could not have occurred."

ACCIDENT ON THE EAST RIVER, OCTOBER 28TH, 1867.

HARPER'S
NEW
MONTHLY
MAGAZINE
HARPER'S
SEPTEMBER
Three Gringos in Central America
RICHARD HARDING DAVIS
Mental Telegraphy Again.
MARK TWAIN
The German Struggle for Liberty
POULTNEY BIGELOW
The Evolution of the Cow-Puncher
OWEN WISTER
Arabia—Islam and the Eastern Question
DR. WILLIAM H. THOMSON
Short Stories by THOMAS A. JANVIER
IAN MACLAREN, and
JULIAN RALPH
&c., &c., &c.

OPPOSITE

Edward Penfield. Poster advertisement for the September 1895 issue of *Harper's*. [New York: Harper & Brothers, 1895.] (Item no. 133)

Mark Twain's "Mental Telegraphy Again" is prominently featured in this striking advertisement for *Harper's* magazine.

RIGHT

Samuel L. Clemens. Autograph letter signed "Clemens" to Elisha Bliss, Jr. Buffalo, N.Y., October 26, 1870. (Item no. 94)

Clemens denies Bliss's request that he stop writing for *The Galaxy* in this letter, contending that "it is good advertising for me—as you show when you desire me to quit."

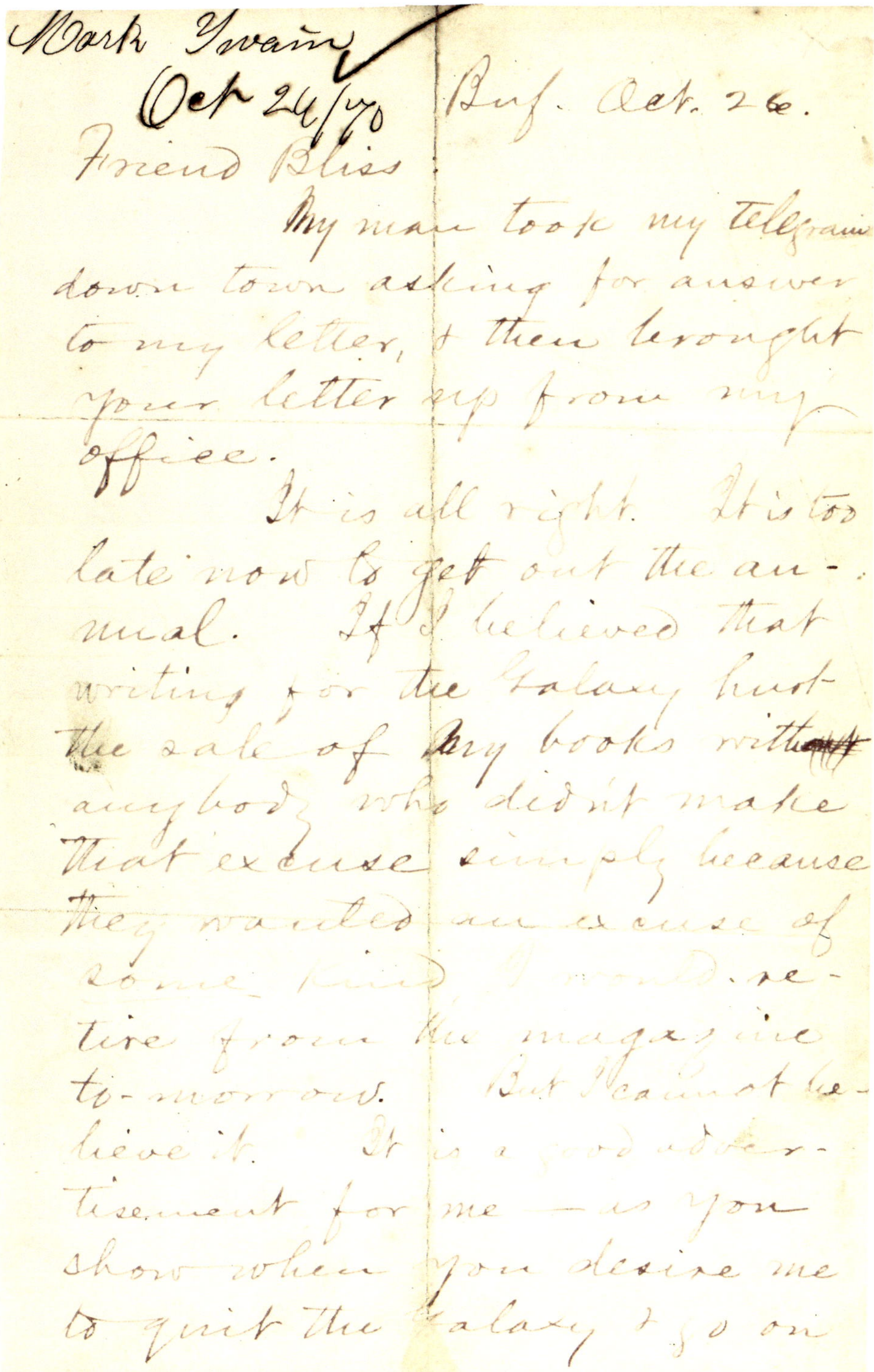

Mark Twain
Oct 24/70

Buf. Oct. 26.

Friend Bliss

My man took my telegram down town asking for answer to my letter, & then brought your letter up from my office.

It is all right. It is too late now to get out the annual. If I believed that writing for the Galaxy hurt the sale of my books with anybody who didn't make that excuse simply because they wanted an excuse of some kind I would retire from the magazine to-morrow. But I cannot believe it. It is a good advertisement for me — as you show when you desire me to quit the Galaxy & go on

"Yrs Truly, SLC": Mark Twain's Letters

BARBARA E. SNEDECOR

Fans of Mark Twain know him best through his novels and stories and perhaps through his interviews and speeches. His literary output was impressive, including, according to biographer Ron Powers, "nearly 30 books, thousands of newspaper and magazine pieces, 50 personal notebooks, and some 600 other literary manuscripts—fragments, chapters, drafts, sketches—that he never published." Then there are his personal letters. Scholars have estimated that he wrote at least 50,000 in his lifetime, making him one of the most prolific letter writers in American history. Add to that the additional estimate that new letters are being discovered at the rate of about three per month, and insights into the life and mind of this beloved author through the treasure trove of his letters seem capable of unlimited expansion.

Samuel Clemens, ever the marketeer and self-promoter, was likely aware that his letters would make good reading even after "the report of his death" was no longer "exaggerated," but fact. Mark Twain scholar Shelley Fisher Fishkin notes that Clemens penned that famous line, by the way, in London on 31 May 1897, to American journalist Frank Marshall White. Clemens explained that a cousin, James Ross Clemens, was ill—*not* Mark Twain (134). That brief note was signed, in capital letters, MARK TWAIN. Samuel Clemens signed his letters and notes in various ways, beginning, in 1863, to use Mark, MARK TWAIN, and Mark Twain. Throughout his life, he interchanged Sam., Sam. L. Clemens, Sam L. Clemens, Sam. Clemens, S.L.C., Saml L. Clemens, Saml. L.C., S.L. Clemens, and sometimes simultaneously Saml. L. Clemens and Mark Twain. Over the years, private and public collectors, and the superb editorial staff at the Mark Twain Papers, have allowed public access to the letters to grow. The result? Illuminating views are available to the everyday reader—not only of Clemens's mind but also of his sometimes elegant—and even sometimes erratic and sometimes illustrated—handwriting. This tangible aspect of an epistolary past is now and then forgotten in the present world of keystroking and swiping. Letters written with ink on paper offer connectivity not only to the thoughts of the writer—and in this case to a brilliant, alert mind—but also to the pure physicality and effort of writing, of crossing out, underlining, and reconsidering word choice.

It is impossible to discuss the whole of Clemens's letters here, but three examples are offered. First, in the early days of his courtship, we are privy to Clemens's ardent appreciation of and sometimes urgent need for letters from his betrothed, Olivia Louise Langdon. Writing from New York City just a week after the couple's "unofficial" engagement, in a letter that would eventually fill twenty-seven pages, Samuel gushes:

> My Dear, Dear Livy: A blessed peace has folded its wings over my spirit, & I am at rest. For your letter is come! It seemed to me that my feet could not carry me fast enough—to my room, to read it. Now that I *have* read it, & re-read it, I am perfectly satisfied and happy—for you are well. And you are not only well, but you are coming to love me better and better. (UCCL 02724, Twain to Langdon, 4 Dec. 1868)

A week later, overly sensitive to Olivia's closing in a letter just received, Samuel fretted,

> Why *Livy!* [. . .] *Don't* scare a body that way again. I *always* look at the end of a letter *first*, to see how it is signed (because the *mood* of the writer crops out there & you know what to expect,)—& behold, there was your *entire* name displayed in frozen & awful solemnity! I expected what I so love to see (& if *must* confess such lack of decorum, *kiss*,) viz., 'Lovingly, Livy'—& found (as I thought,) only 'LIVY L. LANGDON.' I imagined all kinds of horrors at once. (UCCL 00205, Twain to Langdon, 12 Dec. 1868)

In these two telling excerpts, Samuel reveals his early joy and evident anxiety as suitor.

A second view—a glimpse of Samuel Clemens the writer, through correspondence with his close friend William Dean Howells—novelist, critic, and editor of the *Atlantic Monthly*—offers insight into tactics he considered during the composition of *The Adventures of Tom Sawyer*. Following the completion of the manuscript, Clemens reveals:

> My Dear Howells: I have finished the story & didn't take the chap beyond boyhood. I believe it would be fatal to do it in any shape but autobiographically—[. . .] I perhaps made a mistake in not writing it in the first person. If I went on, now, & took him into manhood, he would just be like all the one-horse men in literature & the reader would conceive a hearty contempt for him. It is *not* a boy's book, at all. It will only be read by adults. It is only written for adults. [. . .] I wish you would promise to read the MS of Tom Sawyer some time, & see if you don't really decide that I am right in closing with him as a boy—& point out the most glaring defects for me. It is a tremendous favor to ask [. . .] I don't know any other person whose judgment I could venture to take fully & entirely. (UCCL 01247, Twain to Howells, 5 July 1875)

Clemens appears here as an early, developing novelist, trusting his narrative instincts but also seeking confirmation that his creative impulse is correct.

Finally, a brief glimpse into Clemens's sense of humor appears in the following note to his beloved minister friend, Joseph H. Twichell, pastor of the Asylum Hill Congregational Church in Hartford, Connecticut. With no opening, Clemens writes:

> Religious Conundrum suggested by my present disease.
> *Question*: If a Congress of Presbyterians is a PRESBY*tery*, what is a Congress of dissenters?
> *Answe*r: A DYSentery.
> Joe, you can sell the above to some religious paper or get it off on Dean Sage as original. Yrs Ever, Mark. (UCCL 01291, Twain to Twichell, 29 or 30 Dec. 1875)

Dean Sage was a lawyer friend. Clemens was apparently indisposed enough that the New York *World* dryly reported his sickness in its Personal column: "Mark Twain is recovering from a recent illness" (*Mark Twain's Letters* 606n1). As in so many of his letters, Clemens's playfulness is evident here.

Twain's letters reveal the beloved author in spontaneous brilliance and wit as well as sometimes-acerbic dismay. One letter is written to fellow writer Robert Barr, author of the novel *A Woman Intervenes* (1896). Several are addressed to publishers—among them Elisha Bliss, treasurer and later manager of the American Publishing Company; an unnamed "respectable Boston publisher"; and the editor of *The Galaxy*, either William C. or Francis P. Church. Writing to James M. Tuohy, London correspondent of the New York *World*, Clemens shared thoughts about his short story "Wapping Alice." And Clemens responded to many of his readers who wrote him asking for an autograph. Three letters will here be briefly highlighted.

A letter to Robert Barr was written in September 1897, when Clemens and Olivia, Clara, and Jean, still grieving the death of their daughter and sister Susy a year earlier,

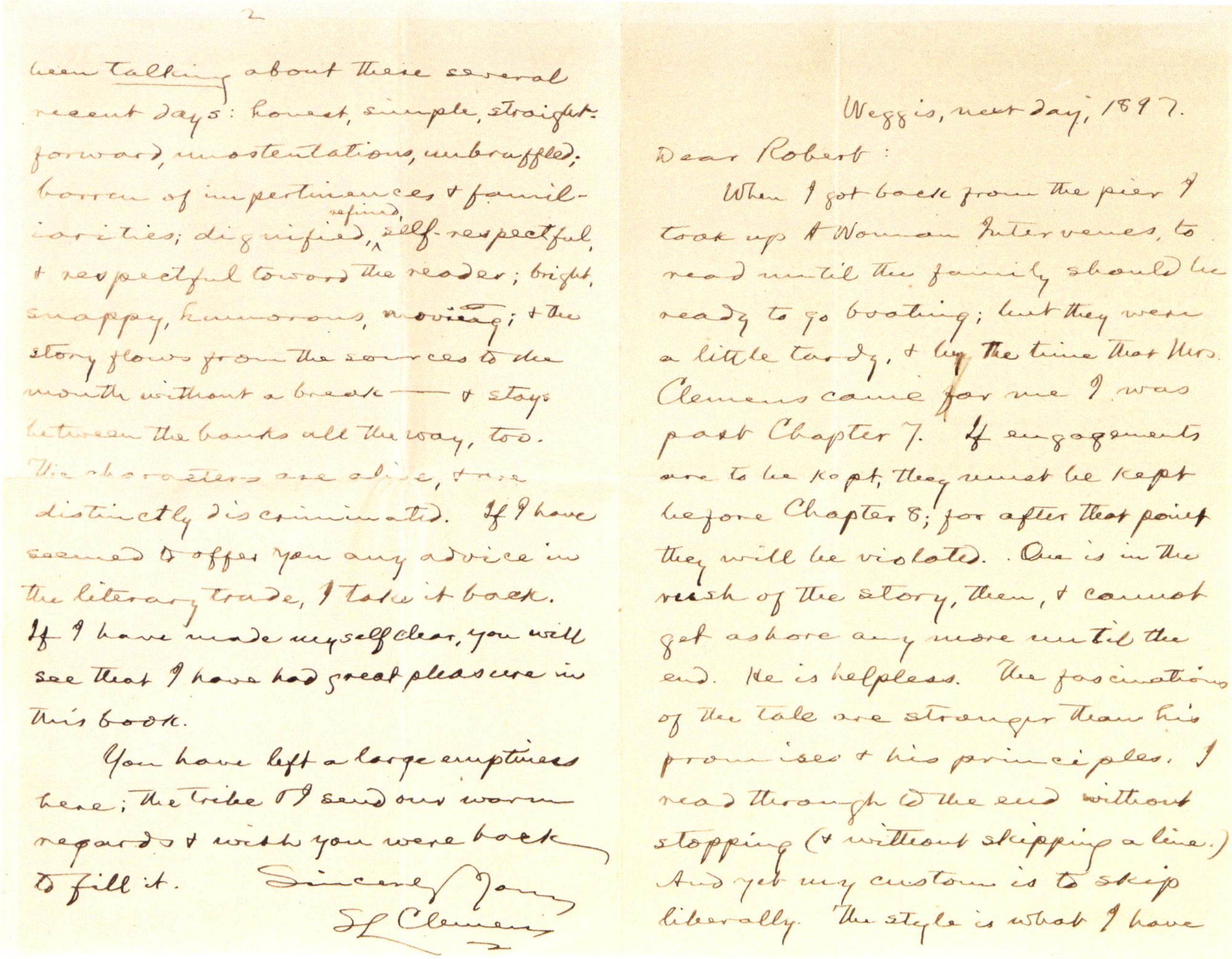

Weggis, next day, 1897.

Dear Robert:

When I got back from the pier I took up A Woman Intervenes, to read until the family should be ready to go boating; but they were a little tardy, & by the time that Mrs. Clemens came for me I was past Chapter 7. If engagements are to be kept, they must be kept before Chapter 8; for after that point they will be violated. One is in the rush of the story, then, & cannot get ashore any more until the end. He is helpless. The fascinations of the tale are stronger than his promises & his principles. I read through to the end without stopping (& without skipping a line.) And yet my custom is to skip liberally. The style is what I have

2

been talking about these several recent days: honest, simple, straight-forward, unostentatious, unbruffled; barren of impertinences & familiarities; dignified, refined, self-respectful, & respectful toward the reader; bright, snappy, humorous, moving; & the story flows from the sources to the mouth without a break — & stays between the banks all the way, too. The characters are alive, & are distinctly discriminated. If I have seemed to offer you any advice in the literary trade, I take it back. If I have made myself clear, you will see that I have had great pleasure in this book.

You have left a large emptiness here; the tribe of us send our warm regards & wish you were back to fill it.

Sincerely Yours

SL Clemens

were living abroad in Switzerland (**page 76**). Clemens had finished *Following the Equator* and was working on a variety of pieces; some he would never finish. Perhaps Barr's *A Woman Intervenes* was just the sort of light reading he needed. In it, a female protagonist is hired by a New York newspaper and sails to London to uncover details of investigations made of Canadian mining properties. A top male reporter had tried and failed to uncover meaningful information, and now a woman would hopefully successfully intervene. Clemens writes to Barr and extolls the virtue of "honest, simple, straight-forward, unostentatious, unbruffled" prose (UCCL 10600, Twain to Barr, 16 Sept. 1897). Clemens additionally likens the movement of a good story to the flow of a river, a comparison possibly stemming from his Mississippi River past.

A letter written to Lillian Gertrude Kimball, English instructor at the State Normal School in Oshkosh, Wisconsin, and author of *The Structure of the English Sentence* (1900) and other books of grammar, was in response to her request for an autograph (**page 77**). In the 1890s and onward, Clemens had begun to pen thoughts about the deplorable status of the human race in letters and notebook entries, most often railing, as to William Dean Howells, against "the usual depravities and basenesses & hypocrisies & cruelties that make up Civilization," and hoping for the eventual damnation of the race (UCCL 05601, Twain to Howells, April 3, 1899). To Miss Kimball, Clemens first riffs on the accidental state of human life, an existence that eludes control, and then adds: "Oh, the delicious Human Race! Always delightful, always funny, never otherwise than funny"; he concludes with disdain for the mistaken belief that humans have any control over their destiny.

A letter to James M. Tuohy (**page 79**), London correspondent for the New York *World*, reveals Clemens's sometimes lengthy composition process. The letter offers insight into a puzzling short story, "Wapping Alice," composed in several iterations over many years and finally

OPPOSITE

Samuel L. Clemens. Autograph letter signed "S. L. Clemens" to Robert Barr. Weggis, Switzerland, [September 16–30], 1897. (Item no. 104)

Clemens writes to his contemporary Robert Barr, praising his novel *A Woman Intervenes* (1896) and reflecting on the qualities of a good novel: "honest, simple, straight-forward, unostentatious, unbruffled; barren of impertinences & familiarities; dignified, refined, self-respectful & respectful toward the reader; bright, snappy, humorous, moving."

BELOW

Mark Twain. Autograph letter signed "Mark Twain" to Lilian G. Kimball. Riverdale, N.Y., March 2, 1902. (Item no. 107)

Twain reflects on life being "only one long Accident, nothing more," noting that "it begins with the Accidents of birth—place, sex, social degree & the formidable & much-determining Accident of Environment."

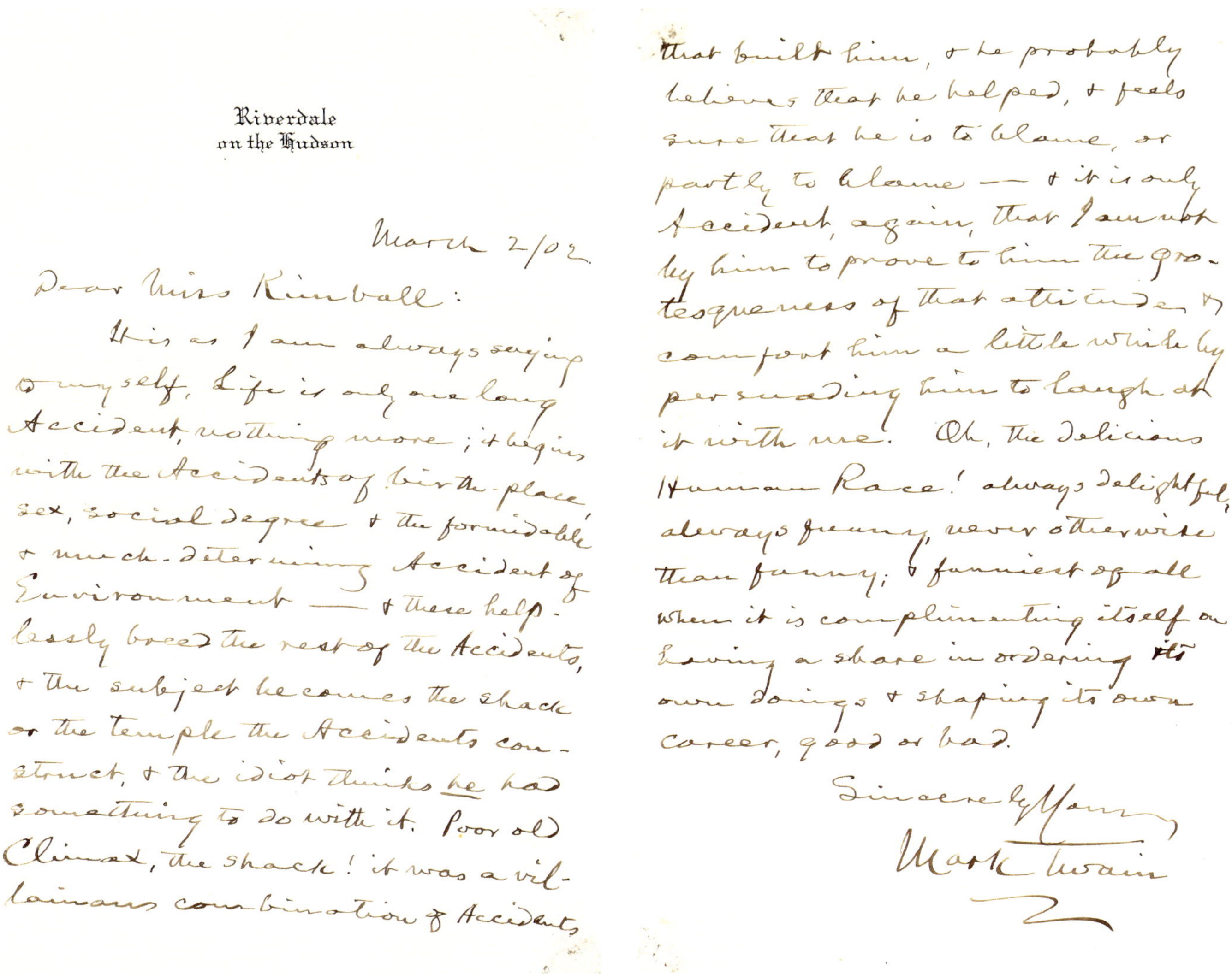

Riverdale
on the Hudson

March 2/02.

Dear Miss Kimball:

It is as I am always saying to myself, Life is only one long Accident, nothing more; it begins with the Accidents of birth-place, sex, social degree & the formidable & much-determining Accident of Environment — & these helplessly breed the rest of the Accidents, & the subject becomes the shack or the temple the Accidents construct, & the idiot thinks *he* had something to do with it. Poor old Climax, the shack! it was a villainous combination of Accidents that built him, & he probably believes that he helped, & feels sure that he is to blame, or partly to blame — & it is only Accident, again, that I am not by him to prove to him the grotesqueness of that attitude, & comfort him a little while by persuading him to laugh at it with me. Oh, the delicious Human Race! always delightful, always funny, never otherwise than funny; & funniest of all when it is complimenting itself on having a share in ordering its own doings & shaping its own career, good or bad.

Sincerely Yours,
Mark Twain

published after Clemens's death. The story originated in an event in the Clemens's Hartford home in 1877, when a family maid set off the burglar alarm to admit her secret lover. Clemens used this plot in his "The McWilliamses and the Burglar Alarm" and then rewrote it in 1897, setting the story this time in the Wapping district of London. This version, however, concludes with a surprising twist of gender. In his letter to Tuohy, Clemens here reveals that the basis of the story is autobiographical in nature. He would again return to discuss the tale years later in an April 10, 1907, autobiographical dictation—indicating the manner in which some of his fictions developed in his mind over time (*Autobiography* 3:39–42).

Further explorations into the engaging and revealing correspondence of Samuel Langhorne Clemens are available thanks to the efforts of the premier Mark Twain Papers and Project, housed at the Bancroft Library, University of California, Berkeley. Interested readers can access six volumes in print (covering 1853–75), and all letters electronically (covering 1853–80), via the website of the Mark Twain Papers. Additional published collections, in print, offer access to Clemens's correspondence with specific individuals, including courtship letters to his fiancé and then wife, Olivia Louise Langdon Clemens; letters to close friends, business associates, and publishers—*Quaker City* traveler and reporter Mary Mason Fairbanks, Boston publisher William Dean Howells, Hartford minister Joseph Hopkins Twichell, oil industry magnate Henry Huttleston Rogers, and Rogers's daughter-in-law, Mary Benjamin Rogers. Letters written by ordinary people *to* Mark Twain are also anthologized. Like the letters discussed above, each of these collections provides delightful and valuable insights.

ABOVE

Autograph postcard signed "S.L.C." [to Frank or Elisha Bliss, Jr.]. [Vienna, Austria, February 11, 1898.] (Item no. 106)

Clemens sends this Austrian production as a sample for a proposed American series of postcards featuring quips and maxims.

OPPOSITE

Samuel L. Clemens. Autograph letter signed "S. L. Clemens" to James Tuohy. Vienna, Austria, November 2, 1898. (Item no. 105)

Clemens offers two new short stories for sale: "The Man That Corrupted Hadleyburg" and "Wapping Alice."

5

Hotel Krantz
Neuermarkt
Vienna, Nov. 10/98.

Dear Mr. Tuohy:

I made a bad miscount. If I am committed to the price I named—$1,600—all right, I stand to it; but if I'm not committed, I'd rather raise it to $2000, if my present count is correct (10,220 words.)

But—committed or not committed—if you find you don't want the tale I shall take it as a great favor if you will mail it to

H. H. Rogers, 26 Broadway, New York.

Sincerely Yours
S. L. Clemens

THIS PAGE AND OPPOSITE

Samuel L. Clemens. Autograph letter signed "S. L. Clemens" to Elisha Bliss, Jr. Buffalo, N.Y., December 2, 1870. (Item no. 96)

Clemens proposes and attempts to negotiate terms for a sequel to *Innocents Abroad*. He urges Bliss to formalize the agreement and cautions him to keep their plans secret: "else we'll have somebody standing ready to launch a book right on our big tidal wave and swim it into a success when it would otherwise fall still-born."

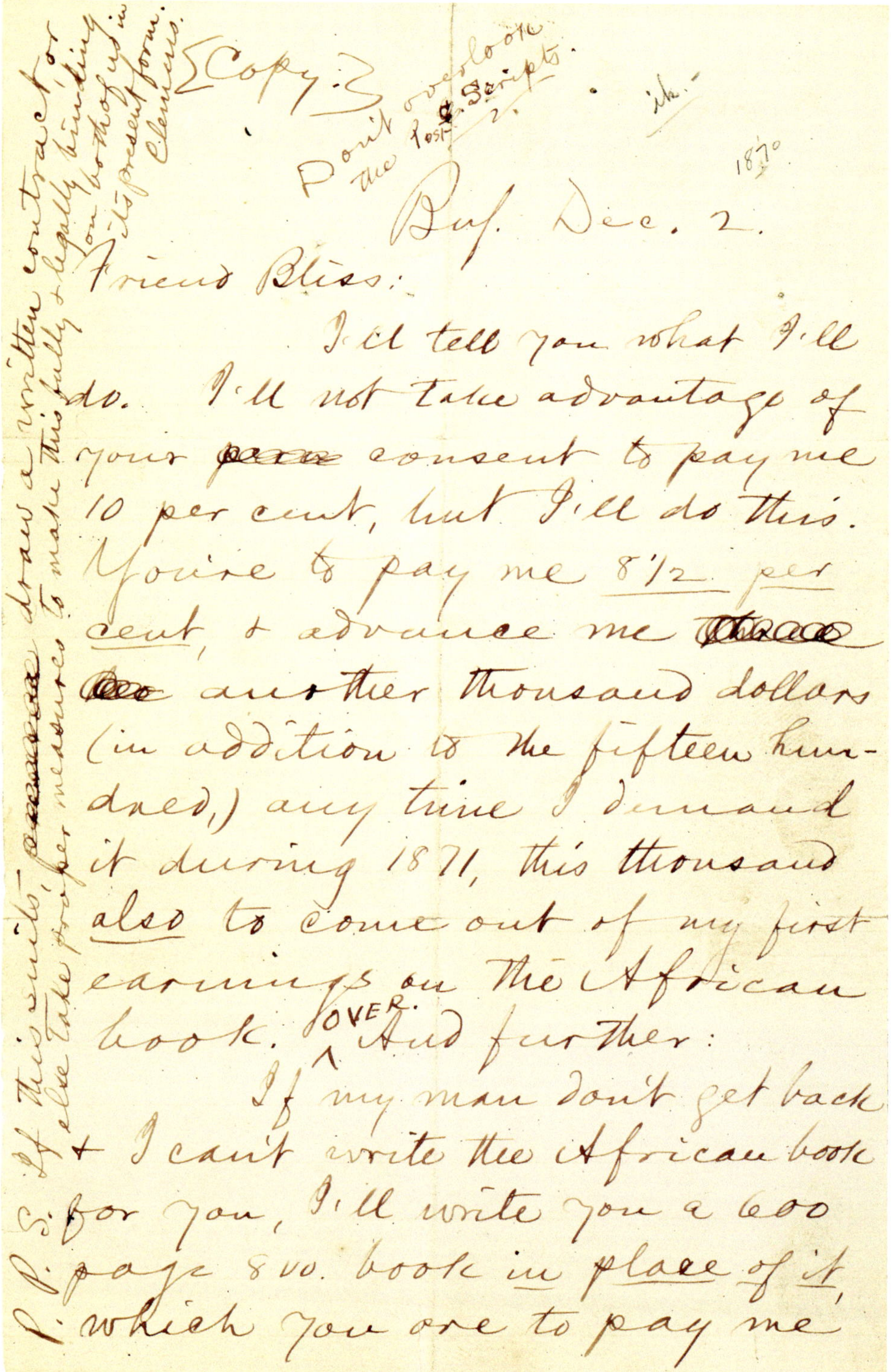

[Copy:]

Don't overlook the Post Script.

1870

Buf. Dec. 2.

Friend Bliss:

I'll tell you what I'll do. I'll not take advantage of your ~~para~~ consent to pay me 10 per cent, but I'll do this. You're to pay me 8½ per cent, & advance me ~~three~~ ~~an~~ another thousand dollars (in addition to the fifteen hundred,) any time I demand it during 1871, this thousand also to come out of my first earnings on the African book. OVER. And further:

If my man don't get back & I can't write the African book for you, I'll write you a 600 page 8vo. book in place of it, which you are to pay me

P.S. If this suits, draw a written contract or else take proper measures to make this fully & legally binding on both of us in its present form. Clemens.

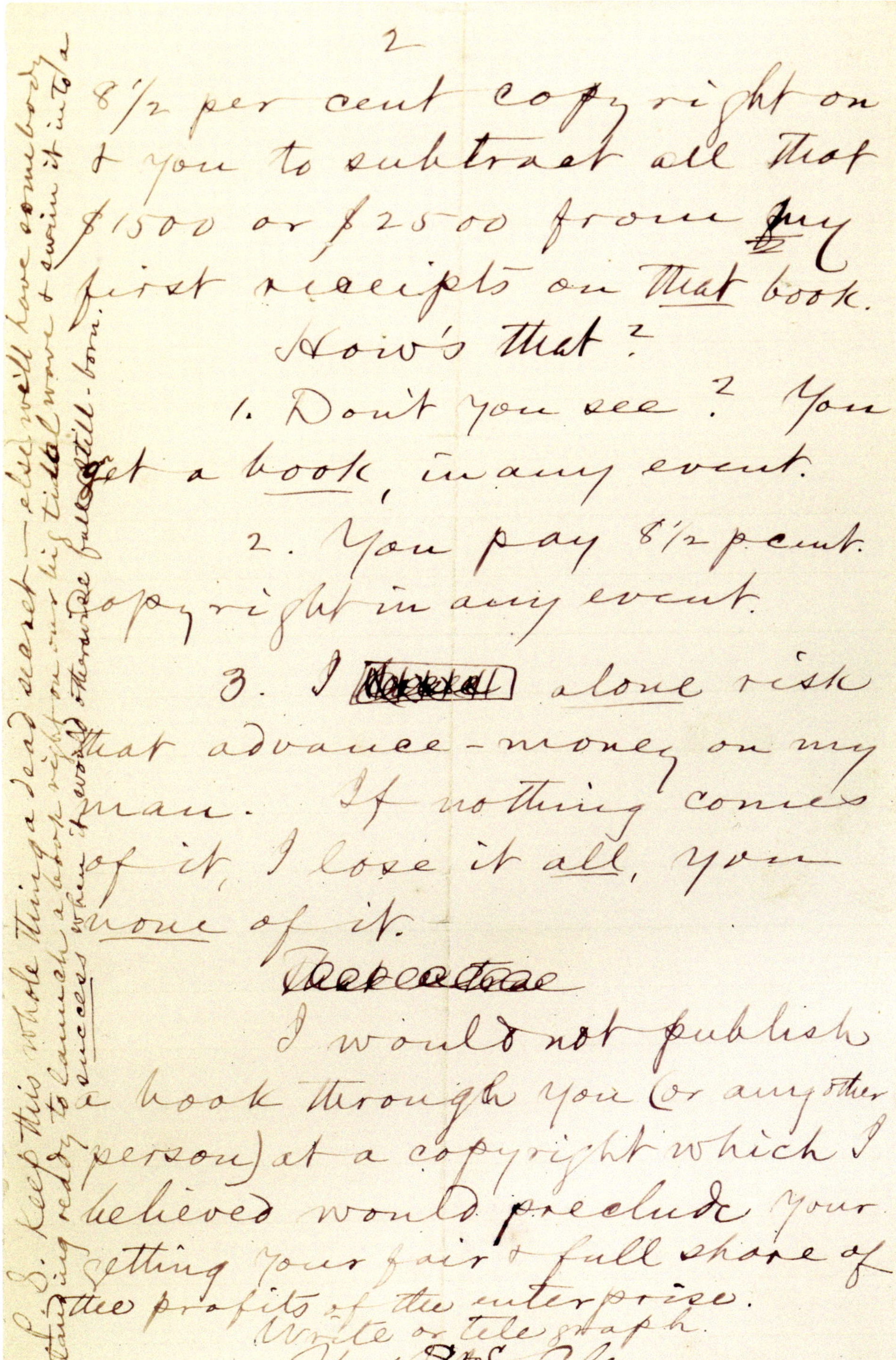

2

8½ per cent copyright on & you to subtract all that $1500 or $2500 from my first receipts on *that* book.

How's that?

1. Don't you see? You get a *book*, in any event.

2. You pay 8½ p. cent. copyright in any event.

3. I alone risk that advance-money on my man. If nothing comes of it, I lose it *all*, you *none* of it.

~~Therefore~~

I would not publish a book through you (or any other person) at a copyright which I believed would preclude your getting your fair & full share of the profits of the enterprise.

Write or telegraph.

Yrs. S. L. Clemens.

P.S. Keep this whole thing a dead secret — else we'll have somebody starting ready to launch a book right on our big tidal wave & swim it into a *success* when it would otherwise be full still-born.

Samuel L. Clemens. Autograph letter signed "S. L. Clemens" to Elisha Bliss, Jr. Hartford, February 19, [1874]. (Item no. 98)

In this letter, Twain offers a humorous reply to Rufus Hatch, managing director of a steamship company, who had requested copies of Twain's publications to stock his fleet's onboard libraries. Twain responds that Bliss should send the books in exchange for disposing of a troublesome relative: "see that my poor old excellent but imperishable aunt Rachel is shipped westward in the slowest & rottenest craft Mr. Hatch can furnish, even if he has to charter one from some other company; & finally, that you personally superintend the embalming of my aunt— for that, you understand, is the main thing." Later in the year Twain reused the name "Aunt Rachel" in the sketch "A True Story, Repeated Word for Word as I Heard It," which recounts a real-life event from the life of Mary Ann Cord, a cook who had been enslaved in Maryland whom Clemens knew at Quarry Farm. There is no connection between Cord and the vexing, imaginary relative of this letter.

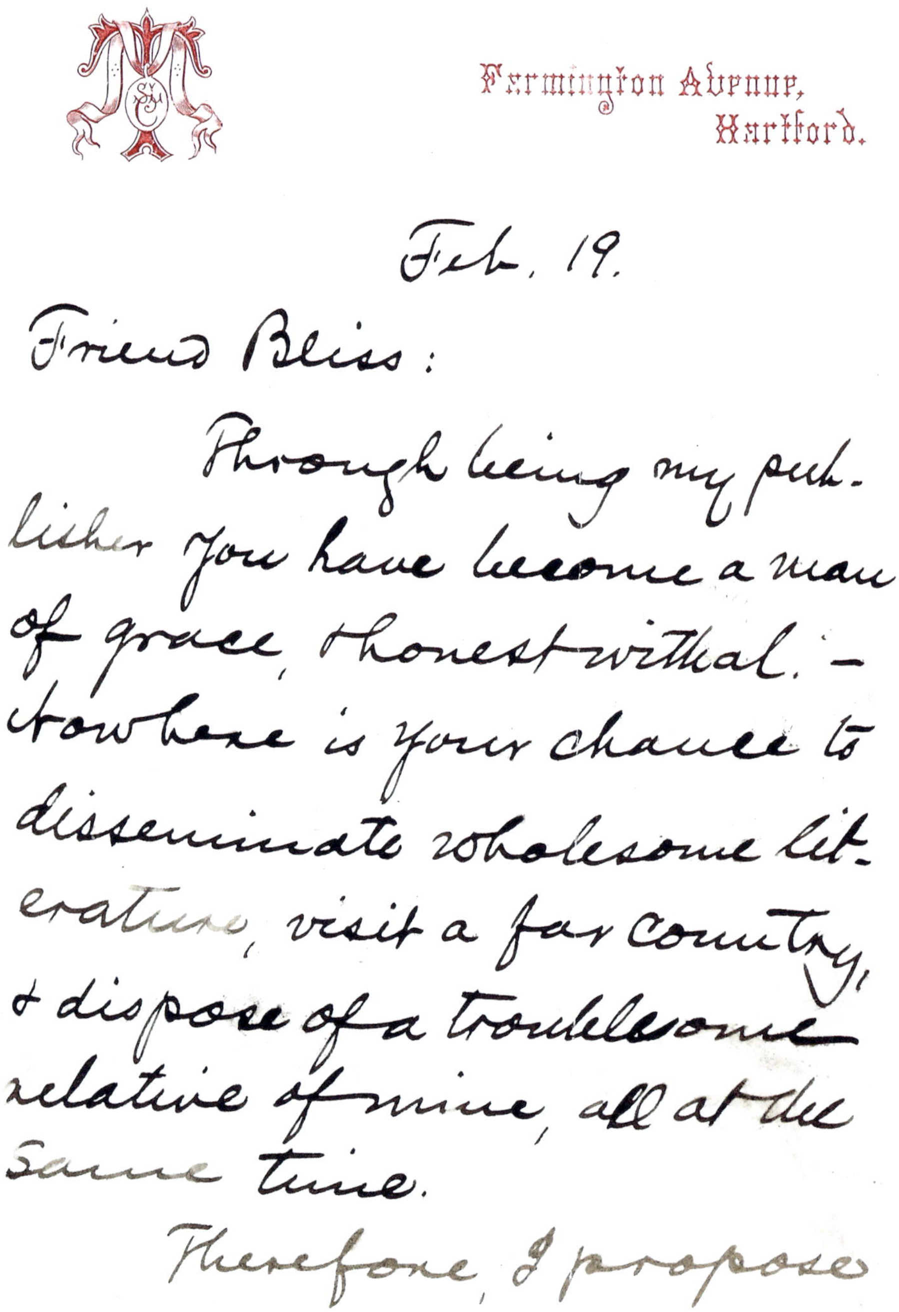

Farmington Avenue,
Hartford.

Feb. 19.

Friend Bliss:

Through being my publisher you have become a man of grace, & honest withal. — Now here is your chance to disseminate wholesome literature, visit a far country, & dispose of a troublesome relative of mine, all at the same time.

Therefore, I propose

Life of "Mark Twain." [Park Place, N.Y.]: Duke Cigarettes; Knapp and Company, Lithographers & Printers, [1888]. (Item no. 145)

Duke Cigarettes' pamphlet series "Histories of Poor Boys Who Have Become Rich, and Other Famous People" offered miniature texts that fit inside a cigarette packet.

Twain on Stage: Lectures and Speeches

MARK DAWIDZIAK

Samuel Clemens is rightly celebrated as a pretty inventive fellow, and one of his greatest inventions was a splendidly amusing alter ego he dubbed Mark Twain. This was much more than just a pen name. This was the public persona Sam assumed to great comic effect and worldwide delight in print, on stage, and in the many interviews he granted reporters as his Mark Twain identity became a wildly popular and lucrative commodity. It was how countless admirers around the globe knew him—or thought they knew him.

Not truly a fictional character, Mark Twain was drawn from slyly chosen aspects of Sam's personality—aspects playfully magnified and whimsically distorted. This extended to his way of speaking. Appearing as Mark Twain during his various successful tours on the lecture platform, he would deliberately exaggerate his Missouri drawl. It had its roots in reality, in what his mother called "Sammy's long talk" (Paine 52). But it wasn't quite the reality. The same could be said of the Mark Twain who appears in the books based on Sam's actual experiences, including *The Innocents Abroad* and *Roughing It*, both rich sources for humorous material used during some of those lecture tours. While that Mark Twain is not quite the reality, either, he is certainly, in cleverly selected ways, reflective of the complex writer lurking behind that nom de plume.

Mark Twain was the face Sam Clemens showed to those attending his lectures and speeches. It was an ongoing and dazzling piece of performance art that began with his professional debut as a humorous lecturer in 1866 and ended with his last public speech in 1909. Publications, ephemera, and artifacts referring to Clemens's professional name also are a reminder that we have always had the pleasure of "knowing" Mark Twain because someone brought him to spectacular life for us by brilliantly portraying him in performance. For sixty-three years, from 1954 to 2017, that someone was Hal Holbrook, who added shadings and dimensions to our perception of Mark Twain by incorporating powerful passages of social criticism that Twain himself never performed or even allowed to be published. Still, materials related to Twain's public performances—including letters (pages 89 and 221), signed menus (pages 90 and 92), a promotional photograph (page 87), and a color cartoon portrait (page 88)—drive home the realization that the first great actor to so triumphantly play Mark Twain on stage was, yes, Samuel Langhorne Clemens.

Those who knew Sam Clemens intimately or socially knew not only that Mark Twain was something of an act, but that it was an act marvelously executed by a great actor. Make no mistake, he was a great actor. Don't breeze past that assertion too quickly. Put that under the glare of the spotlight a moment and give due consideration to its sheer magnitude. By making his "Mark" on stage, Clemens as Twain became one of the most popular humorist-lecturers of his day through deceptively meticulous preparation and rehearsal. Although audiences saw him in lecture and concert halls, opera houses, hotel banquet rooms, school auditoriums, and private clubs, they didn't see the shrewd and assiduous comic master devoting hours to minute matters of memorization, timing, and delivery. He played with pauses, maximizing their effect while establishing himself as the most successful, most accomplished standup comedian of his day. Don't undersell or underestimate that feat, either. The line has been attributed to a few thespians over the decades, but there is that lovely and telling payoff to the oft-told story of the aged actor asked on his deathbed if it is tough to die. His response: "Yes, it is hard to die, but comedy is still harder." Among actors, it is an absolute given that it is far easier to make an audience cry than to elicit their laughter. No less an authority than Britain's reigning Shakespearean player Sir Henry Irving recognized what a high level of art was at play when Mark Twain took the stage. "You made a mistake by not adopting the stage as a profession," Irving told him. "You would have made even a greater actor than a writer" (Paine 571).

Twain actually did adopt the stage as a secondary profession, even if the original goal of that move to the lecture circuit was to support and promote his literary ambitions. By 1866, this was already a well-established route for journalists who, having adopted noms de plume for humorous writing, hoped to see their work collected in book form while building a following on the lecture platform. Charles Farrar Browne, known by his pen name Artemus Ward, helped pioneer this path in the early 1860s. His popularity, deadpan delivery, and droll stage presence were not lost on a friend who recently had adopted a pen name of his own, Mark Twain.

It is believed that Sam Clemens gave his first speech at the age of twenty at a January 1856 printers banquet in Keokuk, Iowa. This was seven years and one month before he began signing articles "Mark Twain" at the *Territorial Enterprise* in the Nevada Territory boomtown of Virginia City. Although he gave a few more speeches between 1856 and his October 2, 1866, appearance at Maguire's Opera House in San Francisco, it was the latter engagement that signaled the beginning of his true baptism-by-limelight. Contemplating a book based on his letters sent to the *Sacramento Union* from the Sandwich Islands, he crafted a talk drawn from this recent stint as a newspaper correspondent. In *Roughing It*, Twain gives an entertaining account of that San Francisco lecture, telling how he showed the manuscript for the talk to several friends. They all shook their heads, certain that he could never be as funny talking as he was writing. "They said nobody would come to hear me, and I would make a humiliating failure of it," Twain recalled, perhaps faithfully (*Roughing It*, chap. 77). The house was full, however, and the lecture was a success. Twain's friends "could not foresee the fact, well recognized by later critics, that . . . the secret of that success lay in his manner and style of speaking rather than the substance of his lecture or in the words themselves," one critic has observed (Lorch 26).

Through the end of November, he delivered his "Sandwich Islands" lecture sixteen more times in California and Nevada. Moving into 1867, he discovered that the "Sandwich Islands" material also worked with Midwest audiences through a five-city tour that took him to Missouri, Iowa, and Illinois. But how would a New York audience receive the wild humorist who had made his name in the West? He scored direct hits that year with May lectures given at the Cooper Institute and Irving Hall in Manhattan and the Athenaeum in Brooklyn. It was a tremendous boost to Twain's growing confidence as a platform performer.

Twain's star status as a public performer was confirmed when he launched his first major lecture tour in November 1868. He gave at least forty-three performances of "The American Vandal Abroad," a lecture drawn from his upcoming book, *The Innocents Abroad*. It was a grueling schedule, taking him to eight states in four months. It paid off handsomely, though, helping to make *The Innocents Abroad* a publishing sensation when it hit print in July 1869. Engaged to Olivia Langdon, Twain believed he would start married life with three reliable sources of income: from books, from lecturing, and from being an editor, columnist, and part-owner of a newspaper. To this end, he purchased a third interest in the *Buffalo Express* in August 1869. Twain ultimately found so much success as an author, he could both give up the newspaper and leave the rigors of the lecture circuit, a level of prosperity very few writers achieved in the nineteenth century.

Halfway through his third major lecture tour, he switched to a talk based on material from his next book, *Roughing It*, paving the way for its publication. By now, Mark Twain was a seasoned performer in full control of his battle-tested stagecraft skills. This was an astonishing accomplishment, Twain fan Kurt Vonnegut wrote in his introduction to *The Unabridged Mark Twain*, because a great writer is almost psychologically incapable of also being a great performer (1:xv). Vonnegut could think of only two other exceptions, Homer and Molière. Although he should have added Dickens to the list, his observation remains sound.

Whether appearing on the lecture circuit or at a banquet, Twain worked diligently to give the impression that he was casually making up the talk as he went along. In truth, every pause and every line was scrupulously prepared. He estimated that it took him three weeks to prepare a seemingly impromptu speech. The master illusionist grew so confident in his abilities, he didn't mind explaining his tricks. "The best and most telling speech is not the actual impromptu one, but the counterfeit of one," Twain said in his 1885 speech "On Speech-Making Reform" (*Mark Twain's Speeches* 2).

Mark Twain as a public performer was far from a static act. Although his primary mission was to entertain, his selections revealed the underlying concern of being perceived merely as a humorist. This can be seen in the variety of choices he made for his 1884–85 tour with author George Washington Cable and his 1895–96 round-the-world tour to help pay off a mountain of debts.

While the public Mark Twain did not turn his severe social criticism into performance pieces, he did modify and alter his voice depending on the circumstances and the audience. A speech in a setting like the Lotos Club (see **pages 90 and 92**) permitted more license and flexibility than a lecture designed for a general audience. Hundreds of encounters with interviewers allowed him in later years to indulge in some of those famously fierce comments on politics, world events, and "the damned human race."

Although Holbrook popularized the image of Twain speaking to audiences dressed in a white suit and puffing on a cigar, a color *Puck* caricature (**page 88**) more accurately shows how he would have appeared on the lecture circuit or at the podium for a speech during most of his life. He was most likely to have worn evening clothes, and the beloved stogie was rarely carried on stage with him.

An American Literary Bureau photo (**page 87**) shows forty-five lecturers, including not only Mark Twain but two other humorists known by comic public personas: Josh Billings (Henry Wheeler Shaw) and Petroleum V. Nasby (David Ross Locke). Each hoped to be seen as the true heir to Artemus Ward, who died of tuberculosis at the age of thirty-two in 1867, but Twain's fame not only eclipsed them all, it endured when, after a generation, their memories faded into obscurity. No one can say if Ward would have matured as a writer. We do know, however, that Twain realized a humorist's long-term survival meant growing and adapting as a literary artist—in print and on stage. "Why have they perished?" Twain said of his fellow humorists in a 1906 autobiographical dictation. "Because they were merely humorists. Humorists of the 'mere' sort cannot survive" (*Autobiography* 2:153).

Despite his great success as Mark Twain, Sam Clemens carried on a bit of a love-hate relationship with his alter ego and the lecture platform. There were times when Sam, always something of a ham, took great delight in acknowledging that Mark Twain had made him "the most conspicuous person on the planet." There were also times when he wearied of being Mark Twain. "I lay awake all last night aggravating myself with this prospect of seeing my hated nom de plume (for I do loathe the very sight of it)," he wrote to his brother Orion (UCCL 00587, Twain to Orion Clemens, 11 and 13 March 1871). If such ambiguity suggests we are wading neck deep into murky psychological waters, that's because we are. Biographers and scholars have routinely delved into ever-intriguing issues of duality, speculating where Mark Twain ended and Sam Clemens began. Public speaking of all kinds put Mark Twain stage center, no doubt, yet the record shows that Mark became an increasingly useful, effective, profitable, and powerful mouthpiece for Sam.

"The Lecture Platform." New York: American Literary Bureau, ca. 1867–1870. (Item no. 111)

Carte-de-visite photograph advertising forty-five available lecturers, including Mark Twain, James T. Fields, Bret Harte, Harriet Beecher Stowe, Ralph Waldo Emerson, Susan B. Anthony, and Elizabeth Cady Stanton.

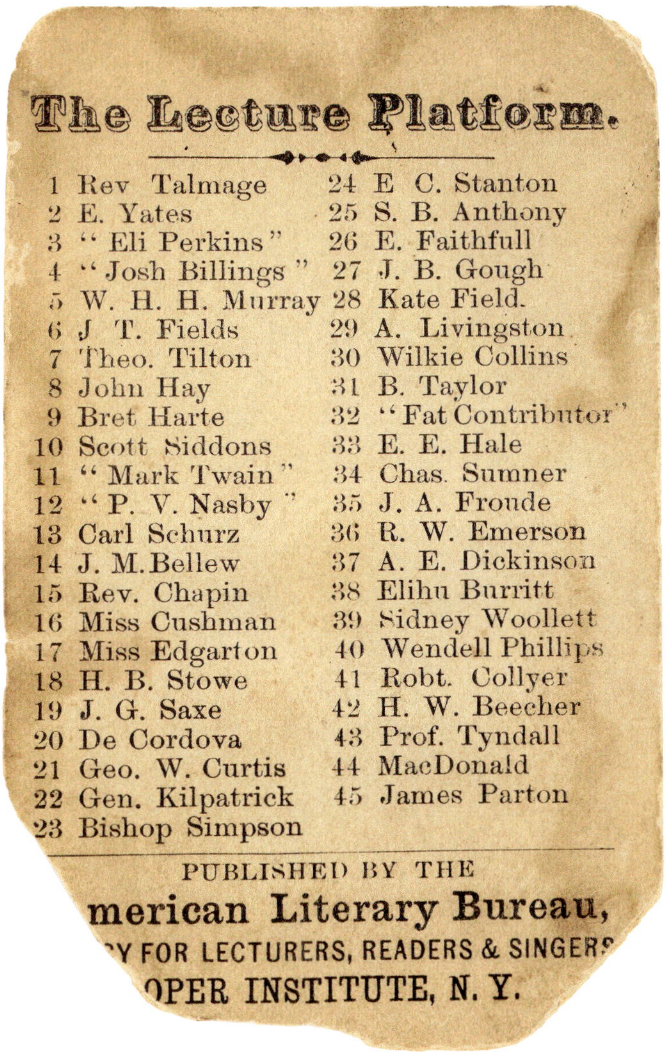

The Lecture Platform.

1	Rev Talmage	24	E C. Stanton
2	E. Yates	25	S. B. Anthony
3	" Eli Perkins "	26	E. Faithfull
4	" Josh Billings "	27	J. B. Gough
5	W. H. H. Murray	28	Kate Field.
6	J T. Fields	29	A. Livingston
7	Theo. Tilton	30	Wilkie Collins
8	John Hay	31	B. Taylor
9	Bret Harte	32	"Fat Contributor"
10	Scott Siddons	33	E. E. Hale
11	" Mark Twain "	34	Chas. Sumner
12	" P. V. Nasby "	35	J. A. Froude
13	Carl Schurz	36	R. W. Emerson
14	J. M. Bellew	37	A. E. Dickinson
15	Rev. Chapin	38	Elihu Burritt
16	Miss Cushman	39	Sidney Woollett
17	Miss Edgarton	40	Wendell Phillips
18	H. B. Stowe	41	Robt. Collyer
19	J. G. Saxe	42	H. W. Beecher
20	De Cordova	43	Prof. Tyndall
21	Geo. W. Curtis	44	MacDonald
22	Gen. Kilpatrick	45	James Parton
23	Bishop Simpson		

PUBLISHED BY THE
merican Literary Bureau,
Y FOR LECTURERS, READERS & SINGERS
OPER INSTITUTE, N. Y.

PUCKOGRAPHS—NEW SERIES, NO. 1.

OFFICE OF "PUCK" 23 WARREN ST. NEW YORK.

MAYER, MERKEL & OTTMANN, LITH. 21-25 WARREN ST. N.Y.

"MARK TWAIN,"
America's Best Humorist.

OPPOSITE

Joseph Keppler. *Mark Twain, America's best humorist*. From *Puck*, new series, number 1. New York: Mayer, Merkel & Ottmann, December 1885. (Item no. 132)

This color plate from the humor magazine *Puck* depicts Twain on stage before an amused audience, surrounded by bird-like representatives of his best-known books.

RIGHT

Samuel L. Clemens. Autograph letter signed "S. L. Clemens" to Daniel or Charles Frohman. New York, February 2, 1890. (Item no. 101)

Clemens denounces a recent stage adaptation of *The Prince and the Pauper* by Abby Sage Richardson as "a mess of idiotic rubbish and vapid twaddle."

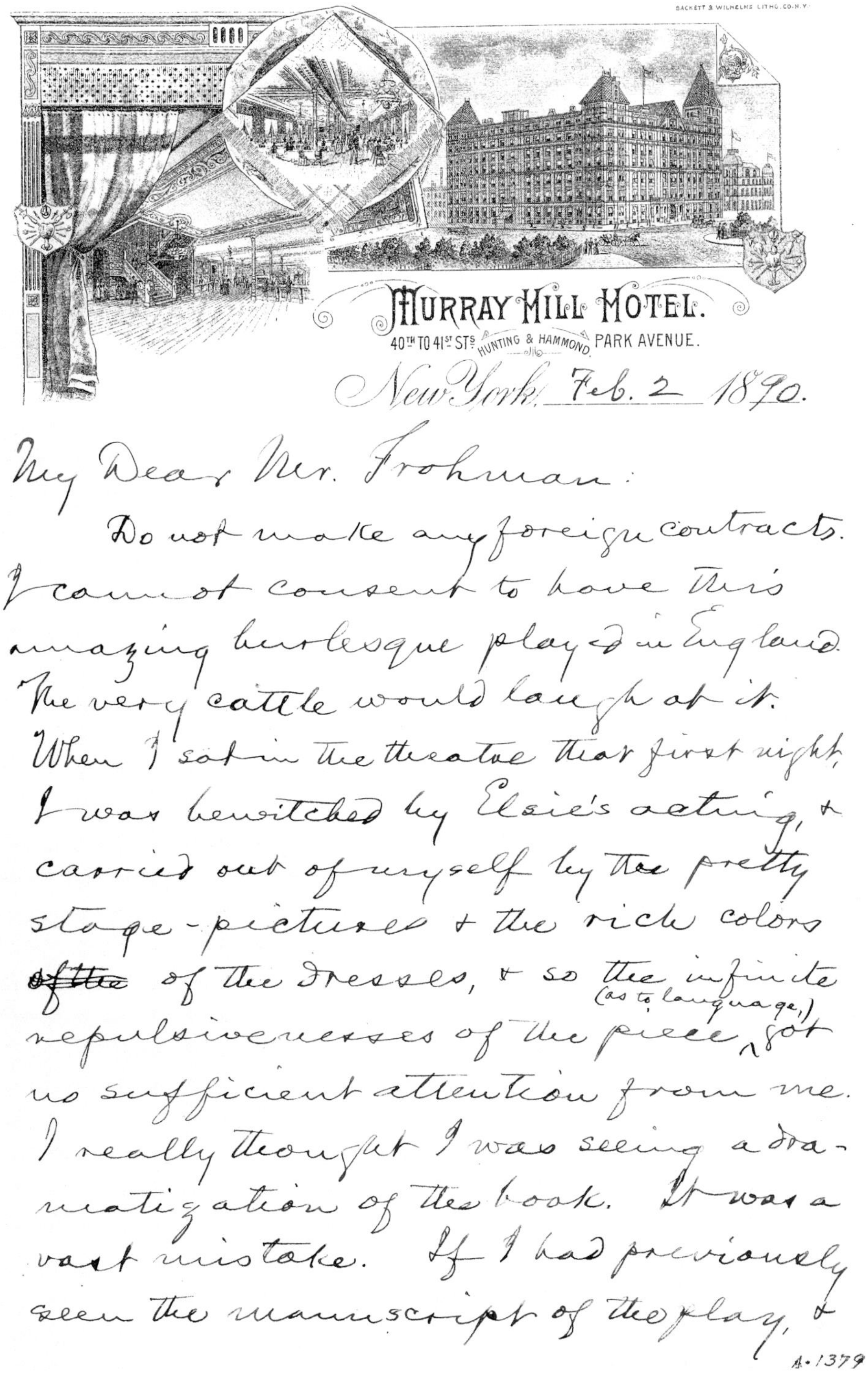

SACKETT & WILHELMS LITHO. CO. N.Y.

MURRAY HILL HOTEL.
40TH TO 41ST STS. HUNTING & HAMMOND. PARK AVENUE.

New York, Feb. 2 1890.

My Dear Mr. Frohman:

Do not make any foreign contracts. I cannot consent to have this amazing burlesque played in England. The very cattle would laugh at it. When I sat in the theatre that first night, I was bewitched by Elsie's acting, & carried out of myself by the pretty stage-pictures & the rich colors ~~of the~~ of the dresses, & so the infinite (as to language,) repulsivenesses of the piece got no sufficient attention from me. I really thought I was seeing a dramatization of the book. It was a vast mistake. If I had previously seen the manuscript of the play, &

A-1379

Lotos Club
Nov. 11th
1893
Lynn Haven Oysters
Chicken Consommé with Quenelles
Olives, Radishes, Celery, Salted Almonds,
Chicken Halibut Cream Sauce
Cucumbers Potatoes Parisienne
Small Patties a la Reine
Larded Tenderloin of Beef with Peas
Potatoes Chateau
Punch Imperial
Stuffed Quail on Toast. Truffle Sauce
Lettuce Salad
Bisquit a la Tortoni
Petits Fours, Fruit
Fromage
Café
Crackers

OPPOSITE

[Lotos Club.] Souvenir menu for dinner at the Lotos Club on November 11, 1893. Signed by Mark Twain and ten of the other attendees. (Item no. 134)

Clemens was an early member of the Lotos Club in New York, one of the oldest literary clubs in the United States. The Club's first formal dinner in its new clubhouse was held in his honor, and the menu was decorated with illustrations of characters from his books.

BELOW

Mark Twain. Autograph letter signed "Mark" to Frank Bliss. Helena, Mont., August 4, 1895. (Item no. 102)

Twain writes to Bliss about the success of his Around the World Tour, boasting, "I always have good houses" despite the Montana heat, and "In a number of instances we have had more people in than were ever in it before, summer or winter."

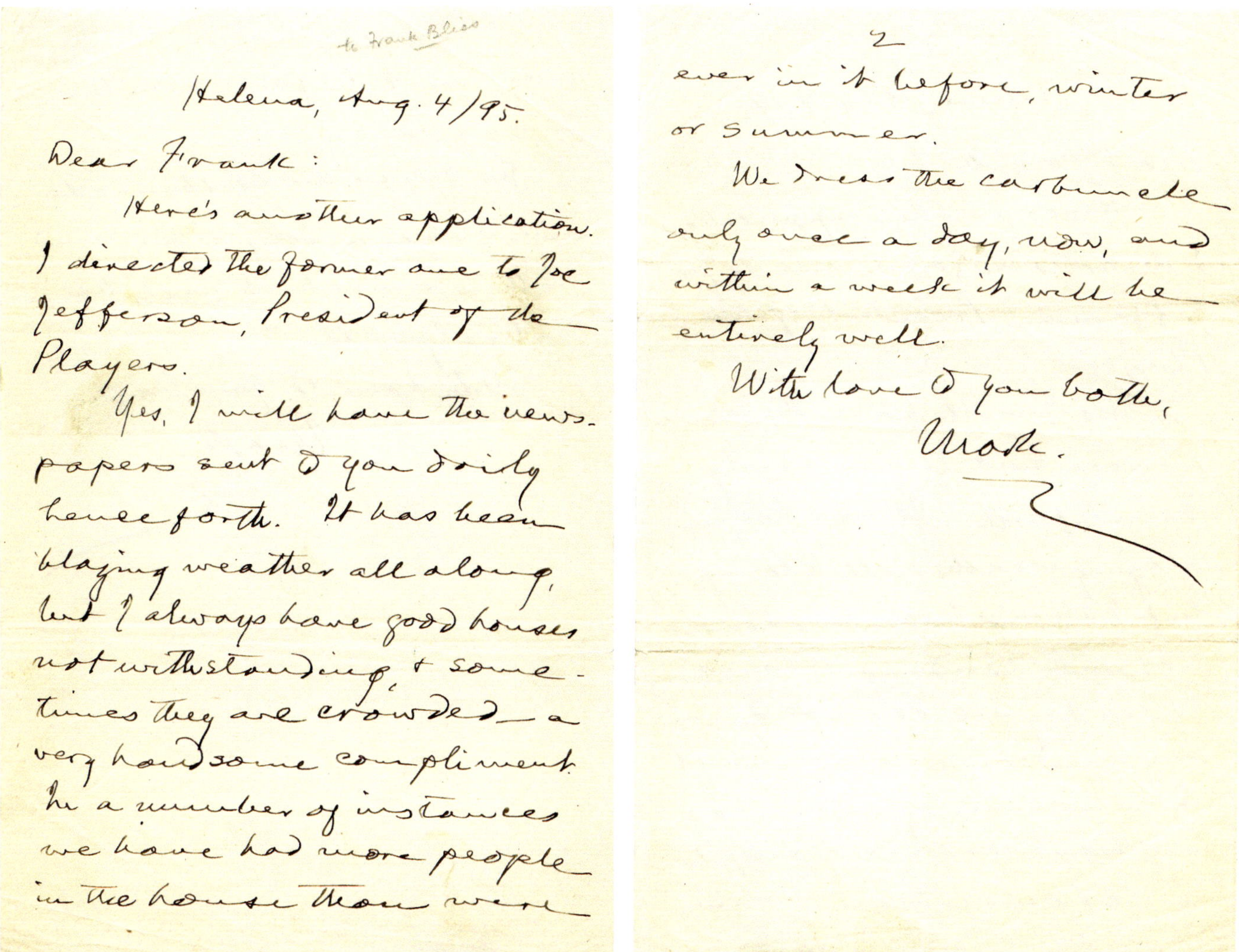
to Frank Bliss

Helena, Aug. 4/95.

Dear Frank:

Here's another application. I directed the former one to Joe Jefferson, President of the Players.

Yes, I will have the newspapers sent to you daily henceforth. It has been blazing weather all along, but I always have good houses notwithstanding, & sometimes they are crowded — a very handsome compliment. In a number of instances we have had more people in the house than were

2

ever in it before, winter or summer.

We dress the carbuncle only once a day, now, and within a week it will be entirely well.

With love to you both,

Mark.

[Lotos Club.] Souvenir menu for dinner at the Lotos Club, June 17, 1902. (Item no. 136)

Clemens spoke at this dinner held in honor of General Horace Porter, a Civil War veteran and US ambassador to France.

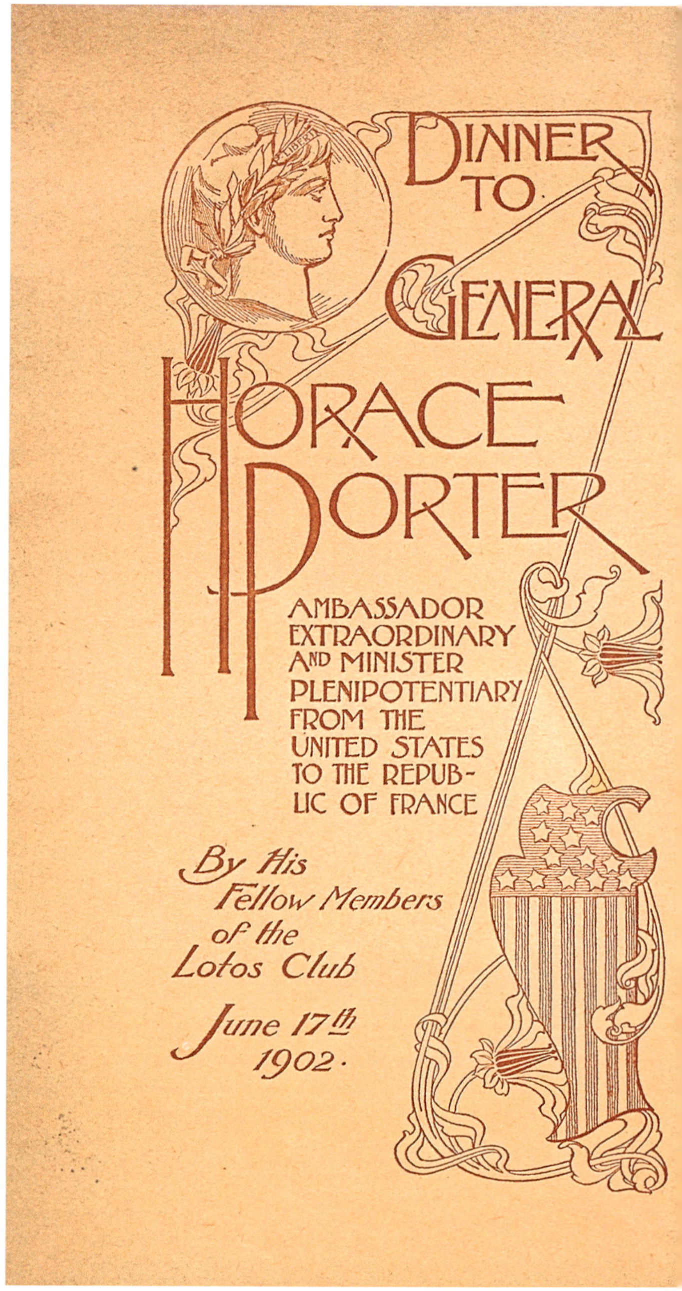

MENU

LITTLE NECK CLAMS — Schloss Vollradser.

STRAINED GUMBO

QUENELLES DE VOLAILLES AU SUPREME

KING FISH SAUTE MEUNIERE, CUCUMBERS.

SWEETBREAD A LA ROCHAMBEAU — Moët & Chandon Brut Imperial

PUNCH LALLA ROOKH

SQUAB SUR CANAPE ASPARAGUS VINAIGRETTE — Chateau d'Arsac.

STRAWBERRY MOUSSE PETITS FOURS

GORGONZOLA AND ROQUFORT CHEESE

CAFE · Apollinaris ·

THIS PAGE AND OPPOSITE

[Engineers Club.] Commemorative volume for the Engineers Club Inaugural Banquet, December 9, 1907. (Item no. 137)

A keepsake for a dinner that featured Andrew Carnegie as guest of honor, this volume, which is bound in Scottish tartan silk and engraved by Tiffany & Co., includes a portrait of Carnegie, illustrations of the Engineers Club clubhouses, the dinner menu and invitation, and other ephemera. It was previously owned by Cleveland engineer Ambrose Swasey, who had the pages signed by Twain, Carnegie, Thomas Edison, and others. Twain entertained the attendees as a speaker, teasing the guest of honor: "just look at Mr. Carnegie's face. It is all scintillating with fictitious innocence. You might think that he had never committed a crime."

Mark Twain
Andrew Carnegie.
John Fritz
Thomas A. Edison
TIFFANY & CO NEW-YORK

Mark Twain Abroad: Travel Writing

ALAN GRIBBEN

Samuel Clemens's first travels away from his hometown, Hannibal, Missouri, were solo journeys in the mid-1850s. He immediately developed three habits that would help earn his livelihood: He recorded his impressions of people and places in notebooks, capitalized on the sights he saw by writing sketches for publication in newspapers, and explored the book collections in every library, hotel, and ship.

When Clemens began piloting on the Mississippi River, of course, he usually had company—other pilots, and sometimes the crew and passengers (see **pages 99–101**). Later he stated that nearly "every well-drawn character in fiction or biography" he read about was someone he already knew—"met him on the river" (*Life on the Mississippi* 217). Following those years (1857–61), perhaps because of the camaraderie he enjoyed on the steamboats and in the ports of St. Louis and New Orleans, he thereafter preferred to bring along someone with whom to share the pleasures and hardships of nineteenth-century travel by stagecoach, railroad, or ocean ships. Often Clemens—or very shortly Mark Twain, the pen name he adopted in 1863—assigned fictional names to these travel companions when he wrote up his experiences for periodicals or gathered his sketches into a travel book. Sometimes he manufactured an irascible personality who would disagree with him on certain points. In a letter published in the April 19, 1866, issue of the Sacramento *Daily Union*, for instance, Mark Twain tries to interest the incorrigible "Mr. Brown" in the gorgeous scenery and exotic food in Honolulu, but Brown will not be placated. He cites minor things that irritate him about Hawaii. Twain objects, "But, Mr. Brown, these are trifles." Finally, Twain gives up, deciding that Brown "is one of those men who always looks at the unpleasant side of everything, and I seldom do" (Blair 29–30).

Mark Twain was hardly the first travel writer to make use of a travel companion. Samuel Johnson traveled to Scotland and the Hebrides with James Boswell, as recounted in *A Journey to the Western Islands of Scotland* (1775). Tobias Smollett went about with his wife and two young women in *Travels Through France and Italy* (1766). Charles Dickens traveled with a party of people in compiling *American Notes* (1842). Still, Mark Twain was arguably the first—or was at least among the most instrumental—in exaggerating and featuring the antics and notions of a barely controlled alter ego seated beside him.

Twain praises and quotes certain passengers on the *Quaker City* and ridicules others in reports he sent during his tour of Europe, Russia, and the Holy Land. The resulting book, *The Innocents Abroad* (1869), launched Twain's national reputation as an impudent, wisecracking traveler, and in his lifetime he would become as well known for this type of travel writing—cheeky, uninhibited observations about remote people and scenes—as for his fiction **(pages 52–53 and 108–109)**.

His later travel books included companion characters as well: *Roughing It* (1872) captures the bone-shaking stagecoach ride that Twain and his older brother Orion took on their way to the Nevada Territory. Miners or journalists typically accompany Twain in the rest of that work. In *A Tramp Abroad* (1880), the Reverend Joseph H. Twichell is with Twain part of the time, though under a pseudonym, "Harris" **(pages 102–103)**. The idyllic raft trip they share on the Neckar River in Germany is one of the book's high points. And Twain took along his publisher James Osgood and a stenographer when he returned to the Mississippi River to collect supplemental material for *Life on the Mississippi* (1883) **(pages 46–47)**.

For Twain's trip around the world in 1895–96, his lecture agent James B. Pond recorded the United States portion of the tour with a camera as well as a journal. Mark Twain's wife Olivia and daughter Clara accompanied him on this grueling but eye-opening venture. Twain's account of that tour, *Following the Equator* (1897), stands out as one of the most conscientious critiques of colonialism in its time **(pages 104–105)**.

In addition to human company, Mark Twain quite early saw the advantages of introducing another type of companion—books written by previous travelers whom he argues with or denounces. Laurence Sterne's *A Sentimental Journey Through France and Italy* (1768) had opened up this line of humor by mocking Tobias Smollett's many complaints about his difficulties in *Travels Through France and Italy*.

The term best fitting Mark Twain's style of introducing others' narratives might be *oppositional* travel writing. Whether he is touring the desert vistas of the Holy Land or gazing at the Taj Mahal, he makes use of disagreements he has with his earlier travelogue competitors, and he won't let them off the hook until he overwhelms their attempts at description and disposes of those who had the audacity to arrive ahead of him.

Beginning with *The Innocents Abroad*, Mark Twain exploits his *oppositional* reading of these literary companions who had visited the sites that Twain intends to describe. He seldom concurs with their impressions. Sometimes he takes pity on the targets of his scorn and renames these hapless victims. When the *Quaker City* passengers tour places prominent in the Christian Bible, Twain reserves his splenetic outbursts for those worshipful pilgrims who preceded him and uncritically gushed in rhapsodic terms over every sight. William C. Prime wrote verbosely and pompously about sights in the Holy Land, and in chapter 50 of Twain's *The Innocents Abroad*, Prime's *Boat Life in Egypt and Nubia* (1866) becomes "Grimes's" *Scow Life in Egypt*. Twain's marginal comments in the pages of a copy of *Boat Life* are caustic: "What a braggart and liar the man is" (35) (Gribben, *MTLR* 2:583).

In chapter 50 of Twain's *The Innocents Abroad*, Prime's other book, *Tent Life in the Holy Land* (1857)—referred to as "Grimes's" *Nomadic Life in Palestine*—serves as a foil for Twain's unflattering descriptions of the desolate landscape at the Sea of Galilee set against the inflated sentimentality of "a *class* of Palestine books." The copy of *Tent Life in the Holy Land* that Twain consulted during his *Quaker City* excursion in 1867 was presented to Elmira College in October 2008 by Irene Langdon, the widow of Samuel Clemens's great-nephew Jervis Langdon Jr. (Gribben, *MTLR* 2:584). Twain's uniformly derogatory marginalia could then be studied: "nauseating drivel" (23), "Always picturesque. Always an ass" (32), "Hogwash" (60), "a terrible man," a "liar" (86), "ignoramus" (88), "thief" (120). Twain was especially offended by Prime's open admission that he borrowed a hammer and chisel to obtain souvenir chips from columns that had stood for millennia in the Valley of Jehoshaphat (120).

For books reporting archeological research, on the other hand, Mark Twain displayed genuine respect. This was one of the objections he raised about Prime. "This *is* cheek," Twain wrote on page 299 of *Tent Life in the Holy Land* where Prime theorized about the Jerusalem gateway: "This fellow, after swelling around ten days, knows more about it than old Robinson, who *studied* those ruins 30 years." Edward Robinson's *Biblical Researches in Palestine, and in the Adjacent Regions. A Journal of Travels in the Years 1838 & 1852* (1856) was one of the books the *Quaker City* passengers were advised to bring on the journey. In *The Innocents Abroad*, Mark Twain seems to rely on Robinson's work more than he acknowledges. Twain also levied on David Austin Randall's *The Handwriting of God in Egypt, Sinai, and the Holy Land: The Records of a Journey from the Great Valley of the West to the Sacred Places of the East* (1862), quoting from it in chapter 52 of *The Innocents Abroad*.

Mark Twain later continued to peruse books about the Holy Land. One that he found especially distasteful was an attempt by the Reverend Edward Payson Hammond to render his impressions in poetic form. Twain mocked these effusions in the margins of a copy of Hammond's *Sketches of Palestine* [1868?] that Twain signed and dated in 1876 (Gribben, *MTLR* 2:307), writing, "And now I've thought out all the rot/That rhymes with vowel E;/Let not this service be forgot—/Ta-ta, Gethsemane" (142). Referring to this author as "putrid" and a "humbug" (148), Twain summed up his opinion on page 153: "We have said our little say,/We have sham'd our little sham,/ We have prayed our little pray—/Yet how few will care a damn." Twain went on to publish a satirical (and anonymous) review of Hammond's volume in the *Atlantic Monthly* in 1877.

After the success of *The Innocents Abroad*, Mark Twain's mode of travel was a confirmed habit: someone he knew and liked in the passenger seat next to him, and a good supply of travel guides and descriptions at his fingertips with which to concur or dispute. Although Twain joked about the occasional unreliability of guidebooks in *A Tramp Abroad* and elsewhere, the fact of the matter is that he was seldom without handbooks such as those published by the firms established by Karl Baedeker (*Southern Germany and Austria*, *Italy*, *London*, *Paris*, *The Rhine*, *Switzerland*) or John Murray (*North Germany*, *Spain*, *Switzerland, Syria and Palestine*) for any nation and city he intended to visit. He was usually complimentary about their assistance.

For the more flowery effusions of independent travelers, he displayed less patience. The description of the Taj Mahal provided by William Wilson Hunter in *The Indian Empire* (1882) Mark Twain cites in chapter 59 of *Following the Equator* as an example of the "fairy structure" too often "built by excitable literary people." Though Twain admired Bayard Taylor, Twain argues in that same chapter of *Following the Equator* that while Taylor's immense praise of the Taj Mahal is merited, the net result nonetheless amounts to "a noble big lie."

To draw contrasts in *Life on the Mississippi* (1883) between the past and the present, Mark Twain ransacked accounts of travel as early as Charles Murray's *Travels in North America During the Years 1834, 1835, & 1836* (1839) (Gribben, *MTLR* 2:523). Chapter 27 relies on Murray for a sense of the river when it was yet untamed to any degree: "The might and majesty of the river," Murray declared, is "fertilizing a boundless valley, bearing along in his course the trophies of his thousand victories over the shattered forest." Twain thoroughly annotated a copy of the Englishwoman Frances Trollope's *Domestic Manners of the Americans* (1832) (Gribben, *MTLR* 2:523), quoting her in chapter 29 about the bad table manners she observed at a hotel in Memphis and calling her "the . . . vigorously hated Mrs. Trollope." In his marginalia in her book and in a section of the manuscript for *Life on the Mississippi* that never got published, Twain paid tribute to Trollope's forthrightness and the accuracy of her criticisms of a new nation. Twain forbore quoting Charles Dickens's unfavorable impressions of cities and people along the Mississippi River, merely alluding to Dickens's displeasure with them, but in an 1895 newspaper interview in Melbourne, Twain granted that Dickens's descriptions of the United States in *American Notes* and *Martin Chuzzlewit* "told us a great many unpleasant truths, but they were truths undoubtedly" (Gribben, *MTLR* 2:199), The portion of *Life on the Mississippi* in which Twain acknowledged the "clear-visioned and accurate" depictions of the raw civilization that Harriet Martineau depicted in her *Society in America* (1837) was discarded before publication. He marked his copy of Martineau's book, and these notes survive. "Horrible," he wrote at the top of page 116 in volume 2 where Martineau unflinchingly discussed the sexual exploitation of enslaved women (Gribben, *MTLR* 2:489).

The titles mentioned here barely suggest the extent of Mark Twain's indebtedness to, and craving for, accounts of journeys in Japan, China, Korea, Russia, and every country and mountain range on the globe. More than 180 books from Twain's library relating to travel survive, and can be documented in auction catalogues from when his library was sold in 1911 and 1951, or can be detected in his writings. Aside from novels and short fiction, travel is the largest category of reading materials that he assembled and annotated. Even earthly destinations did not satisfy Twain's appetite for movement. When advanced age ultimately precluded arduous travel, one of Twain's last sustained works—*Extract from Captain Stormfield's Visit to Heaven*—in 1908 imagines an interstellar voyage by Captain Stormfield, who hurtles through space with Solomon Goldstein and hitches up with Sandy McWilliams and other companions in a Heaven that offers surprises at every turn.

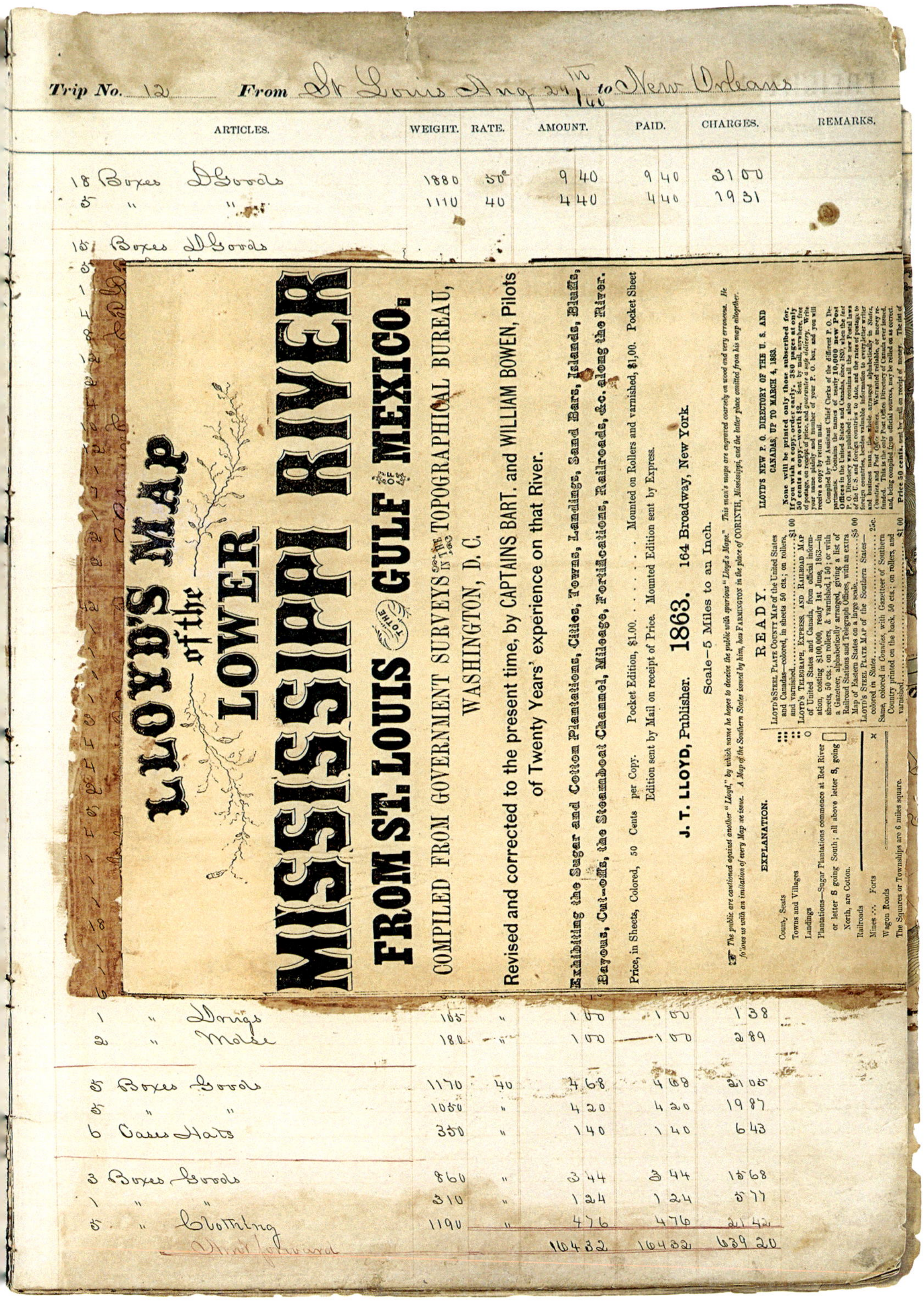

THIS PAGE AND FOLLOWING

Lloyd's Map of the Lower Mississippi River from St. Louis to the Gulf of Mexico. New York: J. T. Lloyd, 1863. (Item no. 122)

Clemens served on a series of steamships beginning in April 1857. He spent most of October of that year on board the *William L. Morrison*, captained by his neighbor, John N. Bofinger. This hand-colored pilot's map of the Lower Mississippi, mounted into a ledger for ease of use, was used on another ship captained by Bofinger, the *Cora Anderson*, and the manuscript notes detail the sorts of cargo that the ship would have transported during Clemens's time as a cub pilot.

FREIGHT LIST, Steamer
SHIPPERS.
EMBARKATION.
CONSIGNEES.
DESTINATION.
MARKS.
Master
ST. LOUIS
ALTON
BELLEVILLE
MISSOURI RIV.
ST. CHARLES
MADISON
ST. CLAIR
MONROE

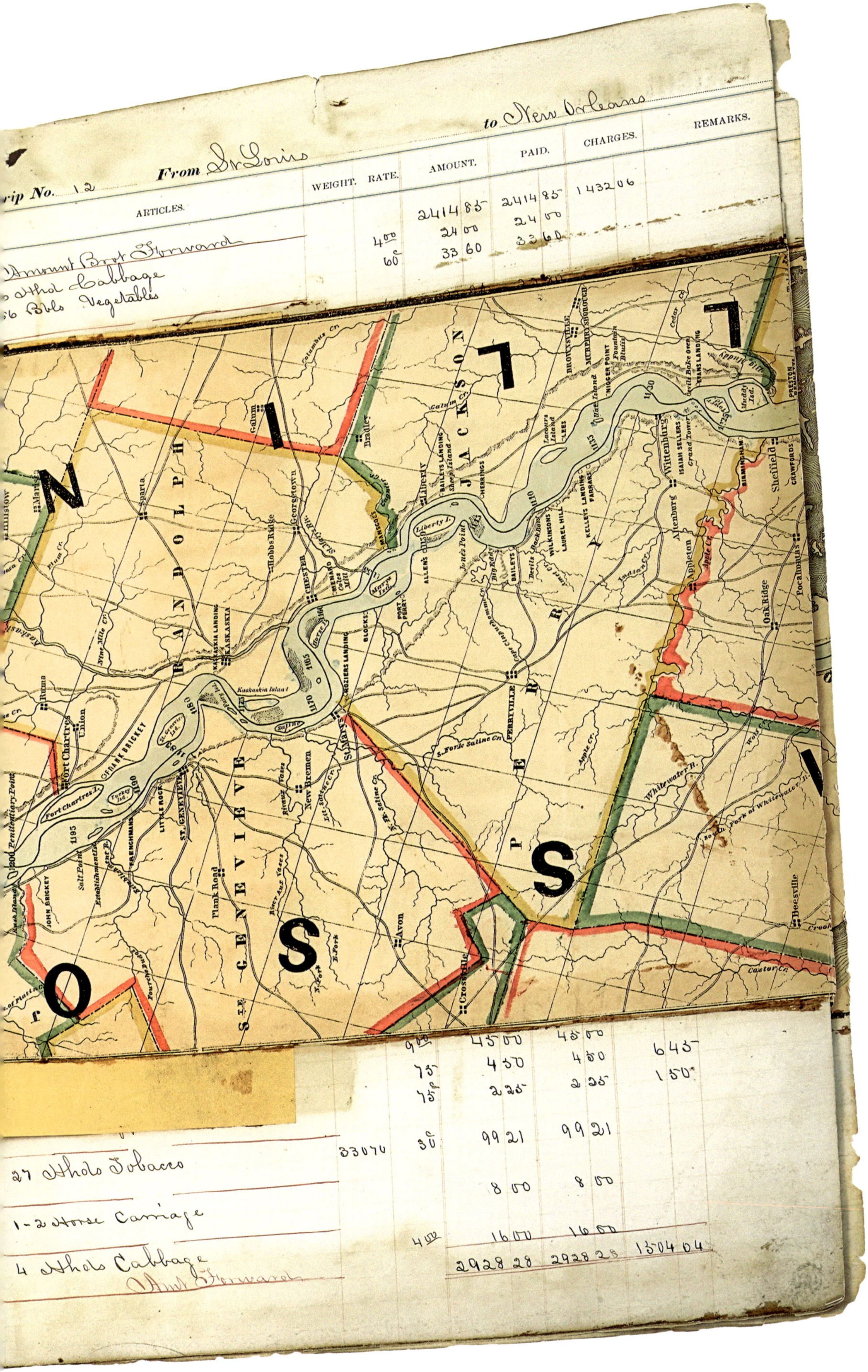

rip No. 12
From St Louis
to New Orleans
ARTICLES.
WEIGHT.
RATE.
AMOUNT.
PAID.
CHARGES.
REMARKS.
Amount Brot Forward
Hhds Cabbage
56 Bbls Vegetables
241485
241485
143206
2400
3360
27 Hhds Tobacco
1-2 Horse Carriage
4 Hhds Cabbage
Amt Forward
292828
130404
RANDOLPH
JACKSON
STE GENEVIEVE
PERRY
Kaskaskia Island
Chester
Kaskaskia
Sparta
Georgetown
Liberty
Perryville
New Bremen
Ste. Genevieve
Wittenburg
Altenburg
Appleton
Oak Ridge
Sheffield
Pocahontas
Avon
Crosstown
Whitewater R.
Fort Chartres I.
Plank Road

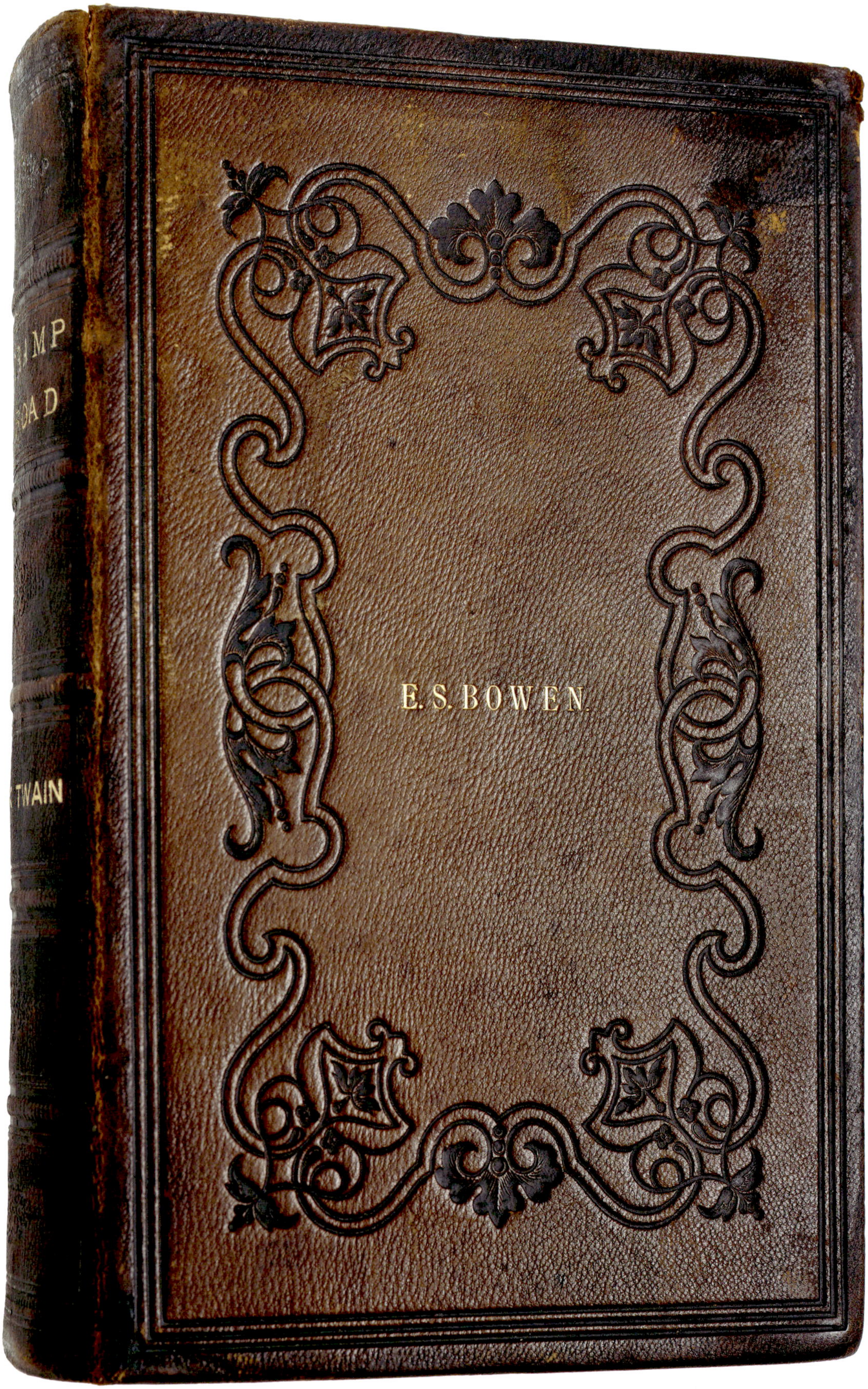
E. S. BOWEN

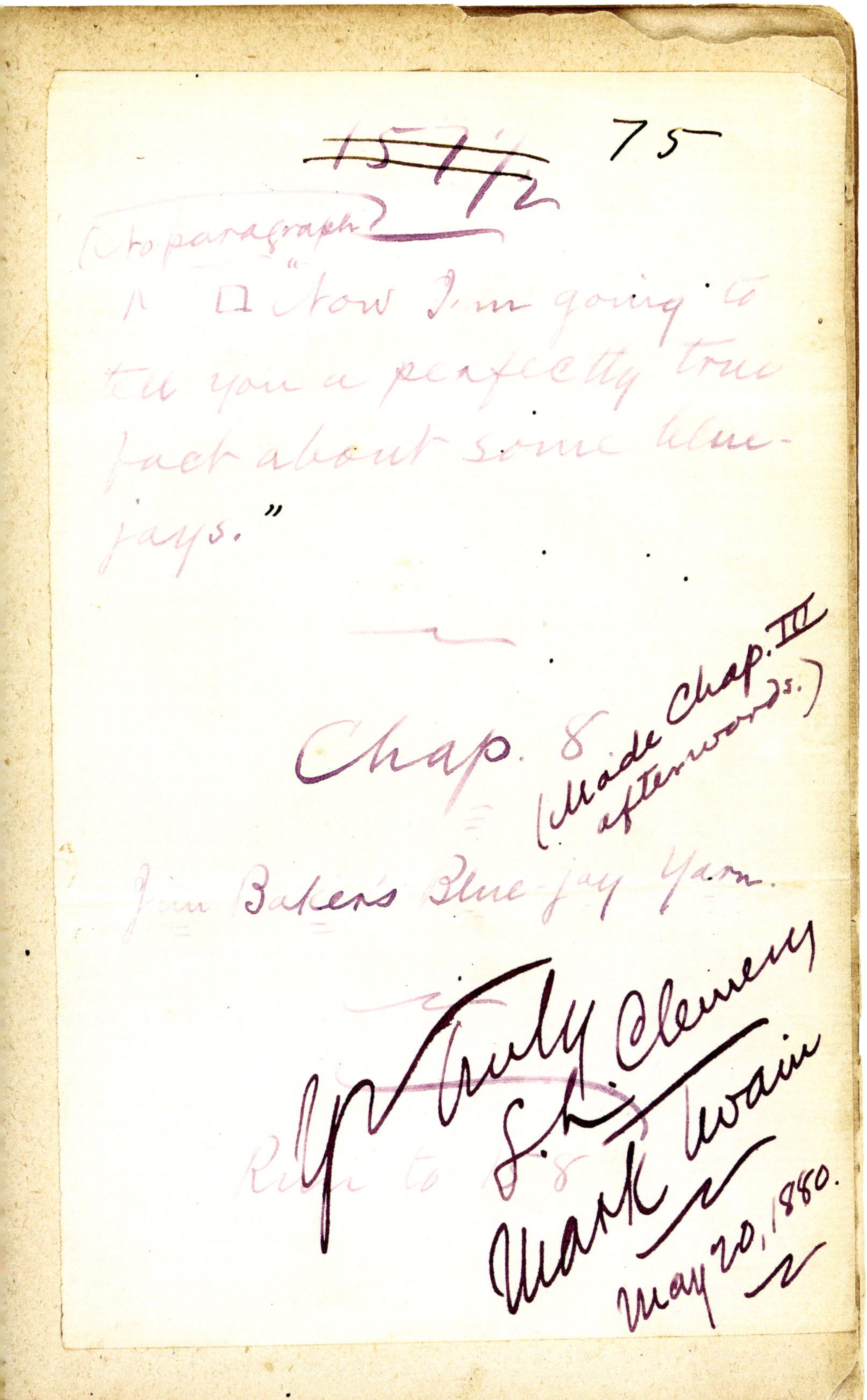

THIS PAGE AND OPPOSITE

Mark Twain (Samuel L. Clemens). *A Tramp Abroad.* Hartford: American Publishing Company, 1880. With a tipped-in page from the book's manuscript and a letter signed "SLC" to "Charley" (Charles Langdon?). (Item no. 16)

Twain's *A Tramp Abroad* details his humorous observations on his travels in central and southern Europe. This copy contains a tipped-in letter in which Twain asks "Charley," presumably his brother-in-law Charley Langdon, to forward the book to supporter E. S. Bowen. He writes: "The correct thing to do on a special occasion is for the notorious author to write his name across a page of MS that helped to make up the book, and send that." This he has done, signing boldly across a page of the book's manuscript: "Yr Truly / S.L. Clemens / Mark Twain."

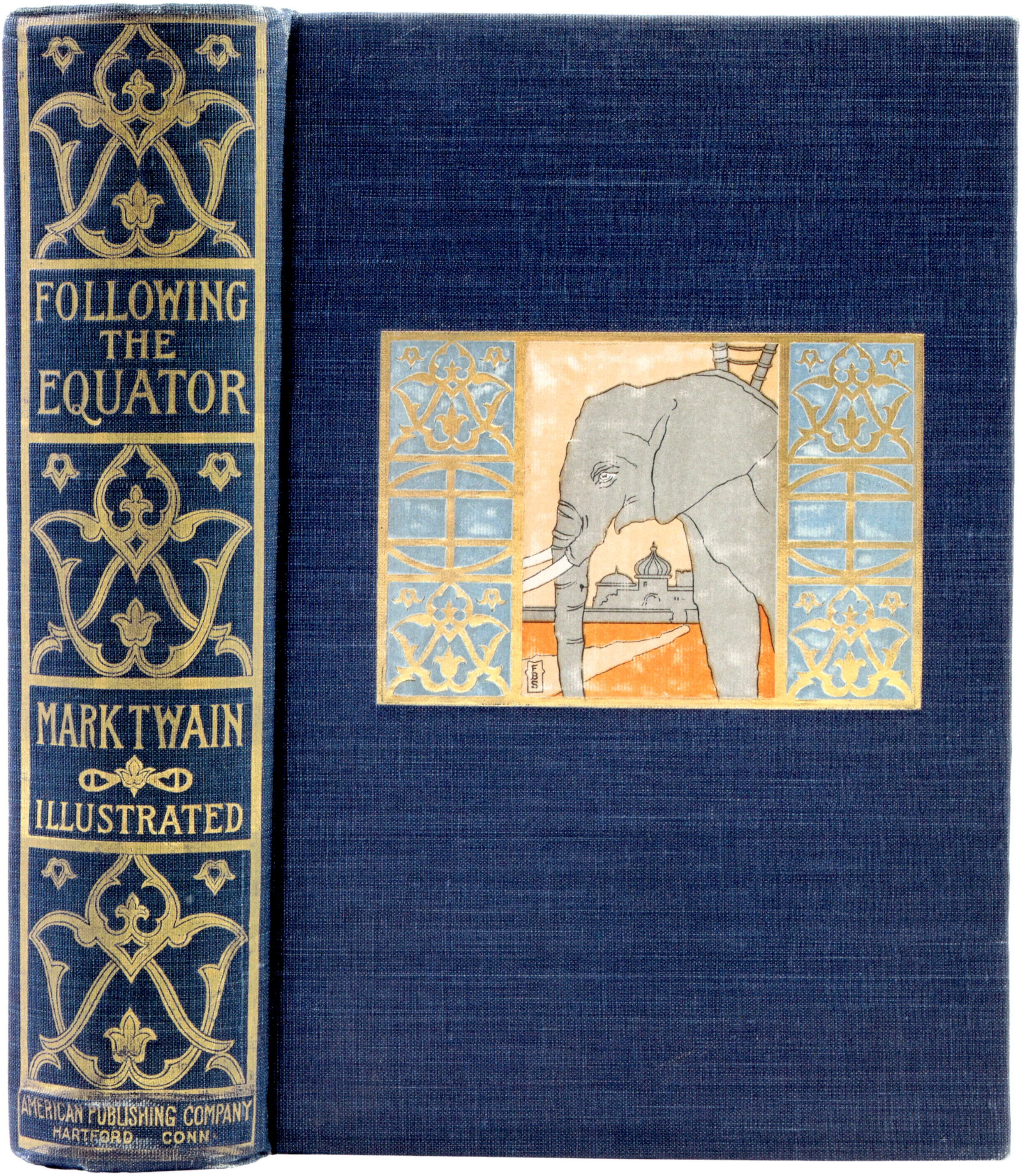
FOLLOWING THE EQUATOR
MARK TWAIN
ILLUSTRATED
AMERICAN PUBLISHING COMPANY
HARTFORD CONN.

THIS PAGE AND OPPOSITE

Mark Twain (Samuel L. Clemens). *Following the Equator: A Journey Around the World.* Hartford, Connecticut: The American Publishing Company, 1897. First edition. (Item no. 33)

Mark Twain invested most of his wealth in a typesetting machine called the Paige Compositor in the early 1890s, and the failure of the firm that designed and manufactured the machine left him on the verge of bankruptcy. To recoup some of his losses, he authored another travel book—*Following the Equator*, published in the UK as *More Tramps Abroad*—which detailed a round-the-world tour of the British Empire's colonies.

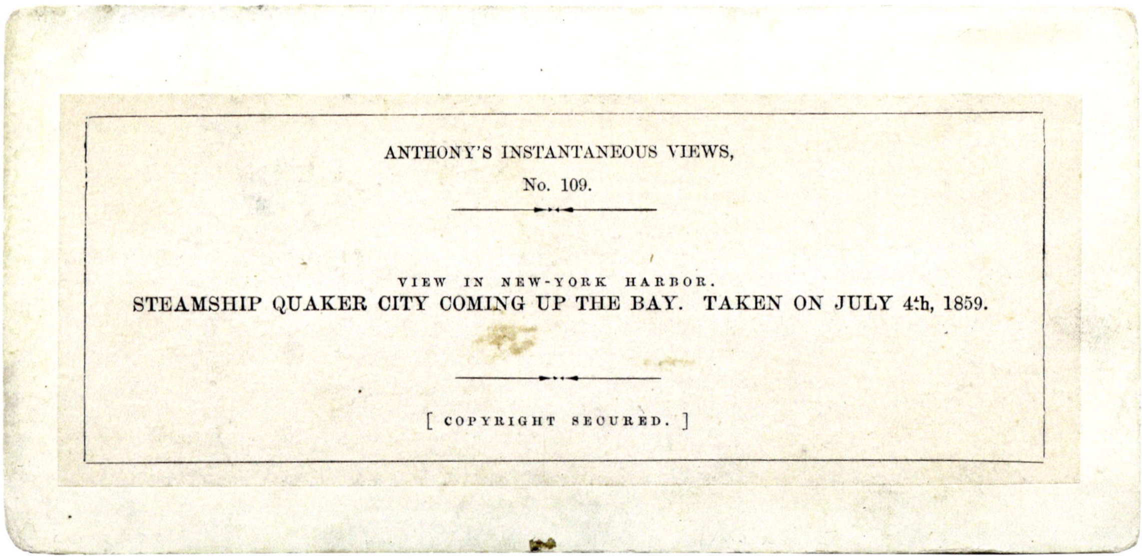

Stereoview of the steamship *Quaker City*. Taken on July 4, 1859. (Item no. 110)

Popular throughout the latter 19th century, stereoview cards present two photographs of the same subject from slightly different angles, which can be viewed as a single three-dimensional image using a special handheld viewer. The title of this card refers to the steamship *Quaker City*, on which Clemens traveled while gathering material for *Innocents Abroad*. But the ship is not the prominent vessel in the foreground of the image; rather it is a smaller vessel visible in the distance.

Mark Twain. *The Innocents Abroad, or The New Pilgrim's Progress; Being Some Account of the Steamship Quaker City's Pleasure Excursion to Europe and the Holy Land; With Descriptions of Countries, Nations, Incidents and Adventures, as They Appeared to the Author*. Hartford: American Publishing Company, 1869. (Item no. 6)

Olivia Clemens's personal copy, bound in a deluxe full morocco binding with her married name stamped on the front cover.

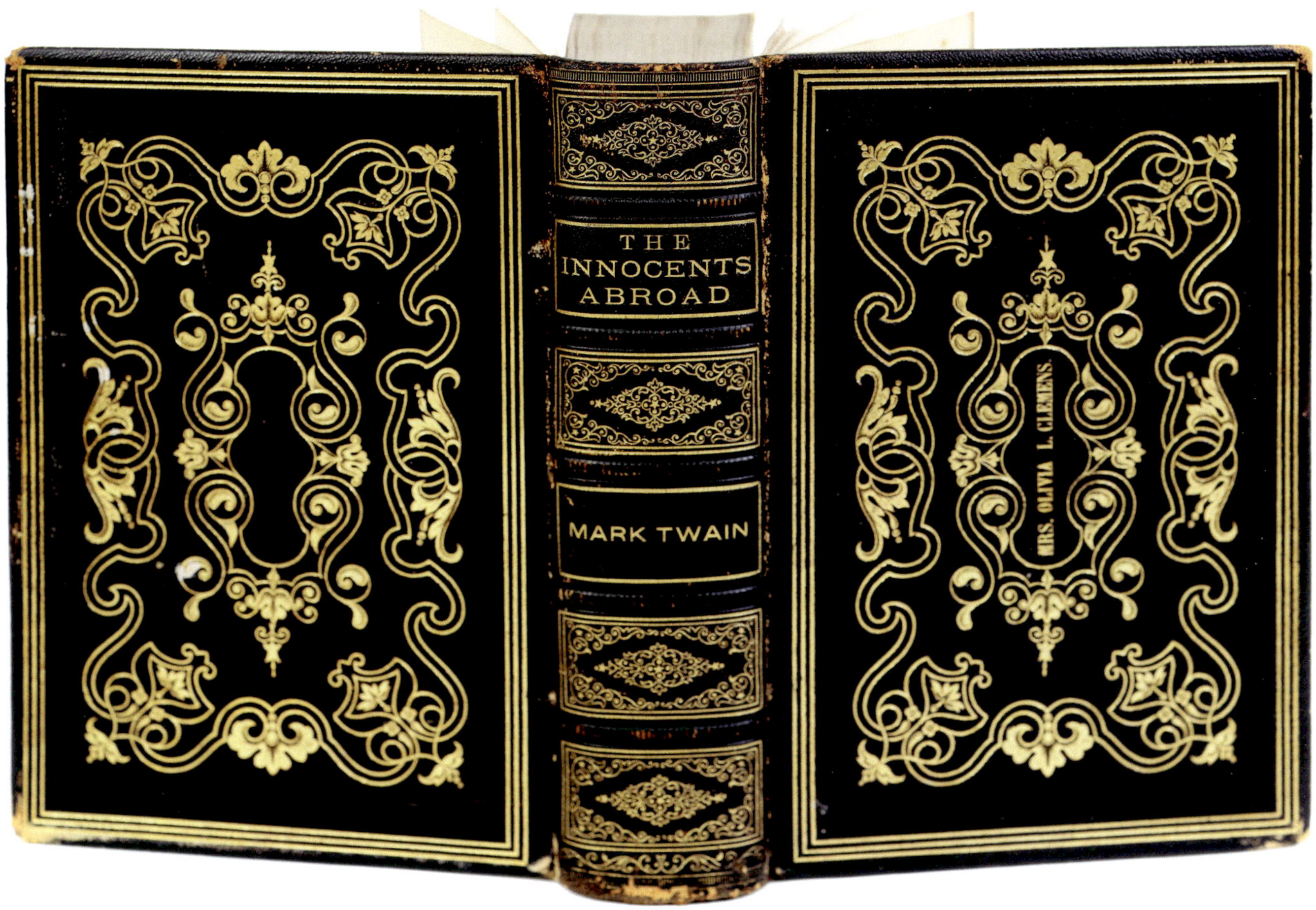

[William Aldrich.] Custom wooden case for salesman's prospectus for *Innocents Abroad*. [Wisconsin, 1869.] (Item no. 7)

Mark, Twain.

Mark Twain. Autograph manuscript, *A Tramp Abroad*, chapter 42: “Switzerland.” [Paris, ca. May 15–May 25, 1879.] 37 p. (Item no. 85)

In the travel book *A Tramp Abroad*, Twain turns his humorist’s eye to Central and Southern Europe, lampooning continental and American attitudes with equally mischievous glee. He opens his chapter on Switzerland by describing the country as “simply a large, humpy, solid rock, with a thin skin of grass stretched over it.”

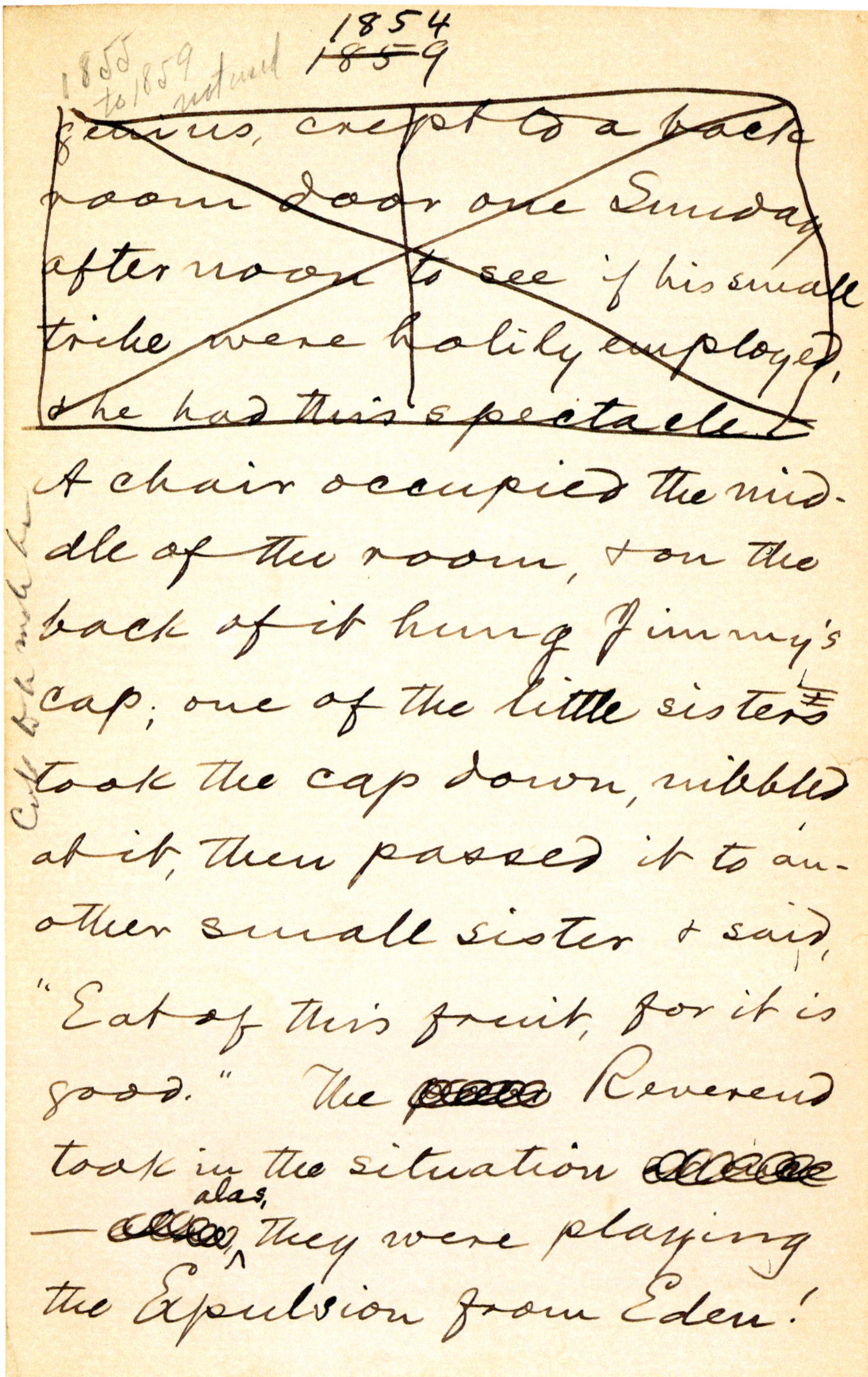

1854
~~1859~~

~~genius, crept to a back room door one Sunday afternoon to see if his small tribe were holily employed, & he had this spectacle:~~

A chair occupied the middle of the room, & on the back of it hung Jimmy's cap; one of the little sisters took the cap down, nibbled at it, then passed it to another small sister & said, "Eat of this fruit, for it is good." The Reverend took in the situation — alas, they were playing the Expulsion from Eden!

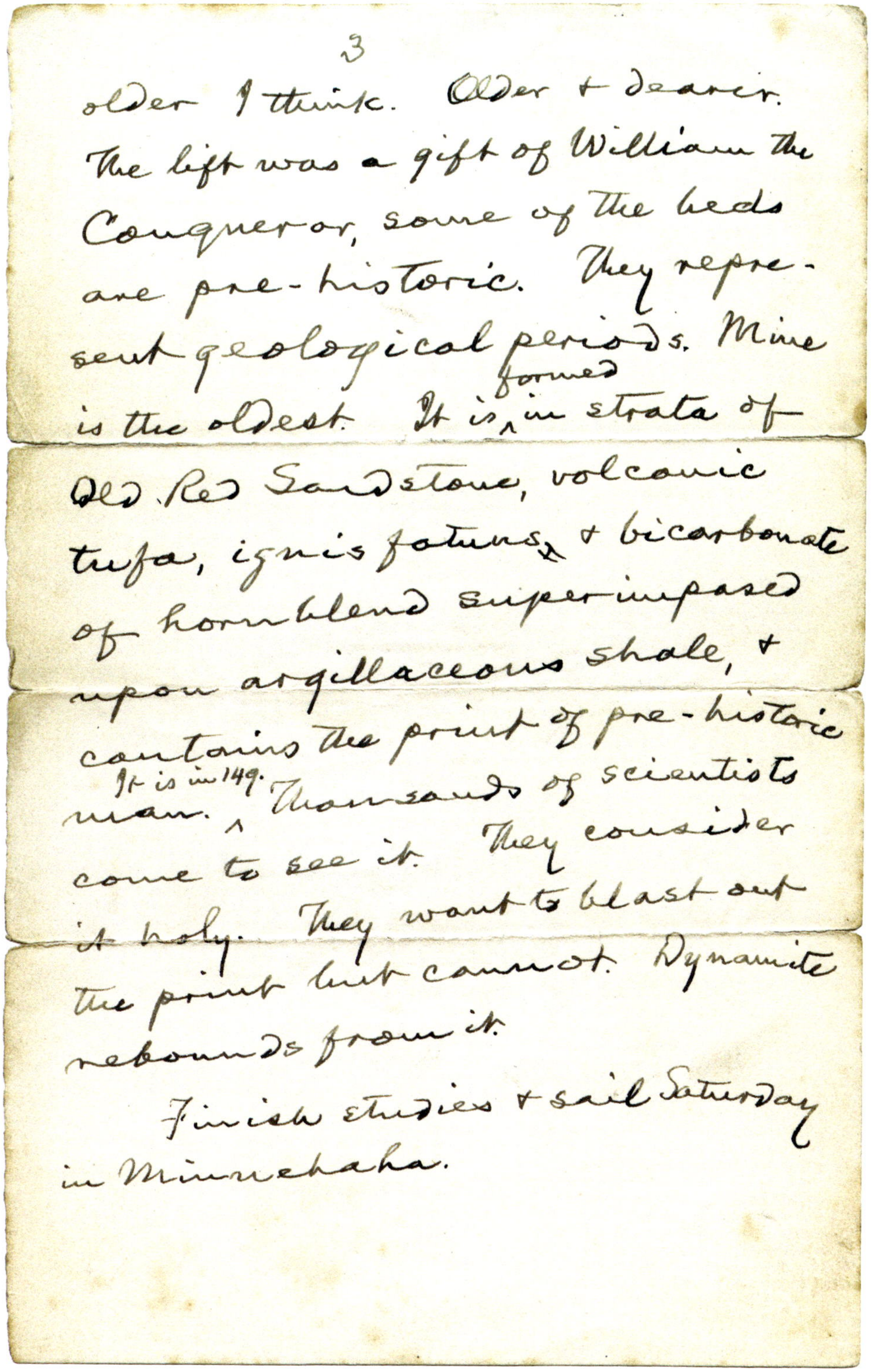

3

older I think. Older & dearer. The lift was a gift of William the Conqueror, some of the beds are pre-historic. They represent geological periods. Mine is the oldest. It is formed in strata of Old Red Sandstone, volcanic tufa, ignis fatuus, & bicarbonate of hornblend superimposed upon argillaceous shale, & contains the print of pre-historic man. It is in 149. Thousands of scientists come to see it. They consider it holy. They want to blast out the print but cannot. Dynamite rebounds from it.

Finish studies & sail Saturday in Minnehaha.

Samuel L. Clemens. Autograph manuscript fragment on "Family Hotels" [draft of letter to John Y. MacAlistair]. [Ca. September 1900.] 3 p. (Item no. 88)

In this manuscript fragment, Clemens gives a humorous description of "all the modern inconveniences" of lodging in London, with particular opprobrium reserved for Brown's Hotel, where he had recently stayed. He writes: "The lift was a gift of William the Conqueror, some of the beds are pre-historic. They represent geological periods. Mine is the oldest."

Mark Twain Commodified

JUDITH YAROSS LEE

Across his career, Samuel Clemens commodified "Mark Twain" by treating it as a brand in the modern sense, a symbol that he could deploy strategically (or withhold) because it attributed his comic persona to commercial products and activities. Previous work that paid by the unit—the em, as a printer; the voyage, as a river pilot; the ounce, as a miner; the column, as a journalist; the performance, as a lecturer—may have shaped his view of authorship as a business enterprise (Gribben, "Autobiography," "Mark Twain, Business Man" 32). But whatever the source, as early as 1872 and as late as 1909, Clemens understood Mark Twain as "a piece of lecturing property"—that is, a commodity—who performed his creativity for profit (UCCL 13454, Twain to Henry Morton Stanley, 1 Sept. 1872; UCCL 08370, Twain to Clara Clemens, 11 and 14 March 1909).

Frederick Waddy captured the essence of the Mark Twain brand in an 1872 caricature of Clemens for London's *Once a Week* illustrated magazine (**page 113**). Captioned only "American Humour," the image of Clemens astride a frog jumping over a hedge merged author, persona, and story into a personification of American comic identity. The caricature not only showed Mark Twain's celebrity three years after *The Innocents Abroad* (1869) brought international fame to the author of "Jim Smiley and His Jumping Frog" (1865), but also proved his brand's power as a marketing tool: The image reappeared a few weeks later on a poster for Twain's February 3, 1873, lecture at the Brooklyn Academy of Music (Frear 189, 173). The caricature points likewise to the commercial context that prompted it: Clemens's first trip to England, where he scouted material for a new book, drew attention to the authorized UK edition of *Roughing It* (Routledge, 1872), and sparked interest in a future British lecture tour. This first international visit after the *Quaker City* voyage joined many domestic efforts across his life, culminating in the trademarks of 1908, to secure the commodity value of the Mark Twain brand even as others sought to profit from it at his expense (see **pages 170–173**).

Clemens's management of the Mark Twain brand took three main forms. Foremost, Clemens jealously guarded the texts of his lectures and writings as economic assets in order to secure their profits for himself. In addition, he selectively extended the brand's comic spirit to other endeavors, including public appearances, interviews, and patented products. On the other hand, he protected the brand's identity by withholding it from activities inconsistent with his comic persona, as when he named his publishing house for his nephew Charles L. Webster and

AMERICAN HUMOUR.

Frederick Waddy, illustrator. *Cartoon Portraits and Biographical Sketches of Men of the Day*. London: Tinsley Brothers, 1873. (Item no. 82)

In this collection of caricatures, Twain is praised as "the best living exponent" of "the peculiar humor invented by our American cousins." A cartoon by Frederick Waddy shows Twain riding a frog as a horse, with the caption "American Humor."

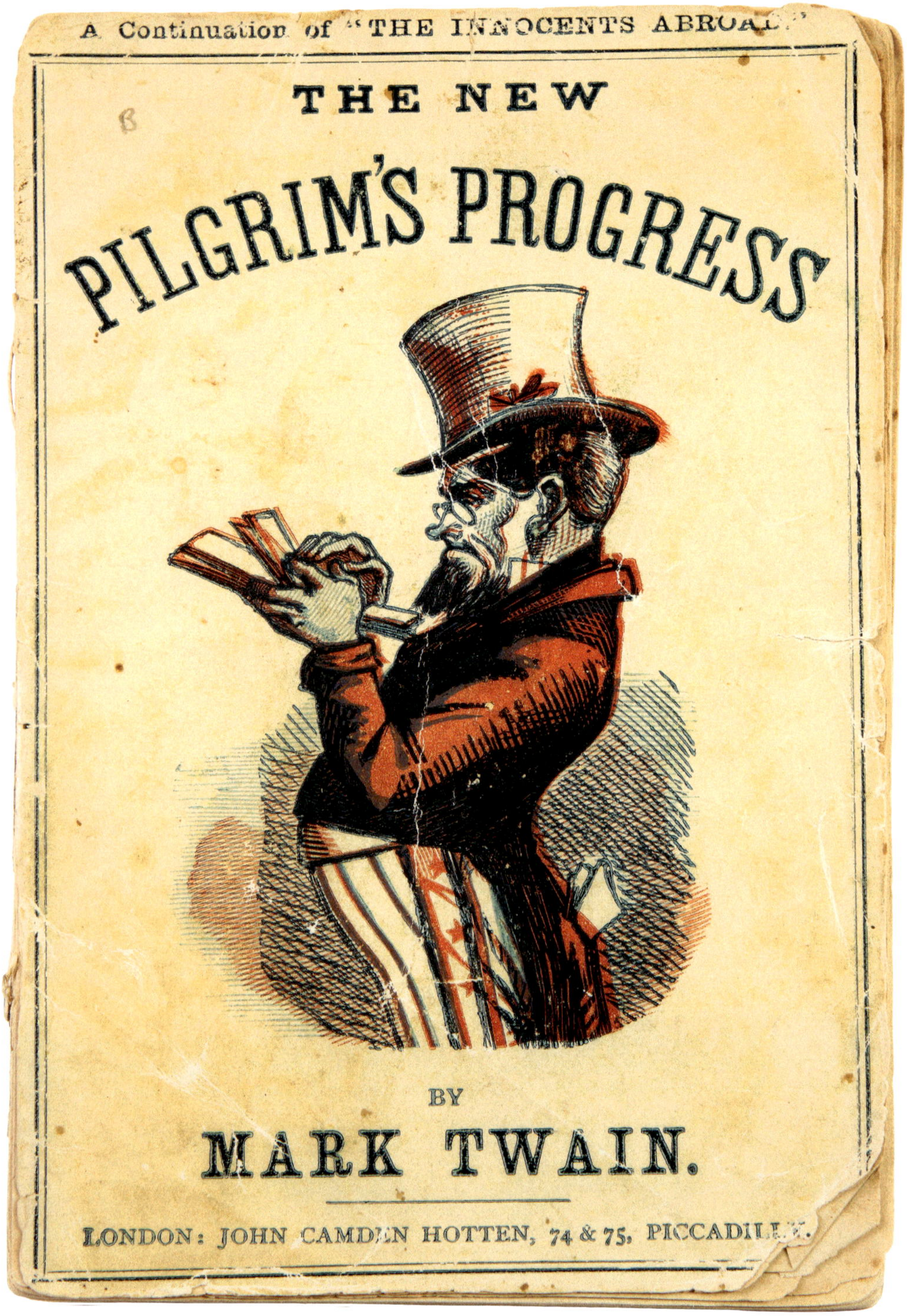

Mark Twain. *The New Pilgrim's Progress. A Book of Travel in Pursuit of Pleasure: The Journey Home*. London: John Camden Hotten, [1870]. (Item no. 8)

London publisher John Camden Hotten exploited the lack of an international copyright treaty to issue pirated editions of many popular American authors. Less than a year after *The Innocents Abroad*'s first publication, Hotten produced his own unauthorized edition, splitting the text into two volumes.

suppressed works from publication during his lifetime. All three approaches showed that Clemens regarded his comic brand as serious business.

Accordingly, he vigorously policed unsanctioned Mark Twain publications through both lawsuits and public complaints. Newspaper reprints of the "Jumping Frog" tale (1865) **(page 14)** unleashed a host of unauthorized volumes that generated great profits for their publishers but produced only fame, not earnings, for Clemens **(page 18)**. John Camden Hotten's wildly successful unauthorized UK editions **(page 114)** drew Clemens's special ire—perhaps intensified by his unhappy experience, the day after docking in England, of seeing a man on his train to London intently reading *The Innocents Abroad* without once cracking a smile (*Autobiography* 2:435). Hotten "embitters his customers against one of the most innocent of men," Clemens complained, citing commercial and moral grounds in a letter to the London *Spectator*, by selling "unrevised, uncorrected, & in some respects, spurious books, with my name to them as author"—that is, by sullying his reputation—and causing "the sorrow that is slowly but surely undermining my health." He drove home the point by imagining a fitting colophon for the unscrupulous publisher: "a picture of a man with his hand in another man's pocket, & the legend 'All Rights Reserved' " ("Mark Twain and His English Editor" 1202).

Here and in copyright suits to follow over the next four decades, Clemens conflated the textual tradition of copyright with the commercial tradition of trademarks, long used to identify craftsmanship of silver and other handiwork and formalized by Congress in 1870 to authenticate products such as patent medicines and spirits. Trademarks therefore went beyond denoting contents and differentiating their origins to connoting quality as early as 1872, when Clemens informally seized on the Mark Twain brand and began defining it (Lee, "Brand" [2014] 43–44, *Twain's Brand* 10–26). His view of the Mark Twain pseudonym as a trademark confused authenticated contents with intellectual property, as the judge ruled in *Clemens v. Such* (New York, 1873) when he insisted, "Trade marks only protect vendible merchandise, and can not be applied to or protect literary property" (Schmidt, "Special Feature"). But Clemens lacked any other equity claim in a time when American copyrights lacked international standing and newspaper publication put works in the public domain. Trademarks for liquor provided his unacknowledged model. His metaphorical claim in *Such*, that "an author cannot bunch a mass of disconnected humorous sketches together & publish the same without sickening the public stomach & damaging his own reputation" (quoted in Feinstein 20–21), became literal eight years later, when he visited Montreal to register the UK copyright on *The Prince and the Pauper* (1882) (Item no. 21). There he offered the hope that "a day will come when . . . literary property will be as sacred as whisky":

> . . . if you steal another man's label to advertise your own brand of whisky with, you will be heavily fined and otherwise punished for violating that trademark; if you steal the whisky without the trademark, you go to jail; but if you could prove that the whisky was literature, you can steal them both, and the law wouldn't say a word. It grieves me to think how far more profound and reverent a respect the law would have for literature if a body could only get drunk on it. ("Mark Twain in Montreal")

Lawsuits and sales involving liquor companies also provided the model for his view of his pseudonym's financial value, its "brand equity" in modern parlance (Lee, "Brand" [2014] 44–45). He pegged its value at more than $1 million in 2024 dollars when, according to a contemporary newspaper report, he told a court in 1891 that "any book by him was worth $30,000 before he had written a line of it" ("Round About Gotham"). But it would be surprising, indeed, had the co-author of the novel that named *The Gilded Age* (1873) failed to commodify his economic activities and their personification in Mark Twain.

Recognizing Mark Twain's commodity value early in his career led Clemens to extend his brand to products and activities beyond writing, a management strategy known today as brand extension. Mark Twain's Patent Scrap Book (U.S. Pat. #140245, 24 June 1873) **(page 45)** had no comic aura itself, but ads highlighted the comic brand by labeling an image of Samuel Clemens with the pseudonym and featuring an illustrated burlesque narrative in which the self-pasting pages avert disaster. He kept his brand in the news through the modern media phenomenon of the pseudo-event, an incident created for the purpose of generating media reports. His pioneering example appeared early in the history of the newspaper interview as a genre, when his publicity stunt of walking with William Dean Howells from Hartford to Boston, reported as "Mark Twain as a Pedestrian" and "Mark Twain: His Recent Walking Feat" (both 14 Nov. 1874) in the *Boston Evening Journal* and *Hartford Times*, gave him the opportunity to plug his play *Colonel Sellers*, then running in New York (Scharnhorst

Mark Twain. *The Prince and the Pauper: A Tale for Young People of All Ages*. Montreal: Dawson Brothers, 1881. (Item no. 21)

Clemens long sought to protect his work from unauthorized use, especially outside of the bounds of US law; he published this edition to establish copyright in Canada and to discourage potential piracy.

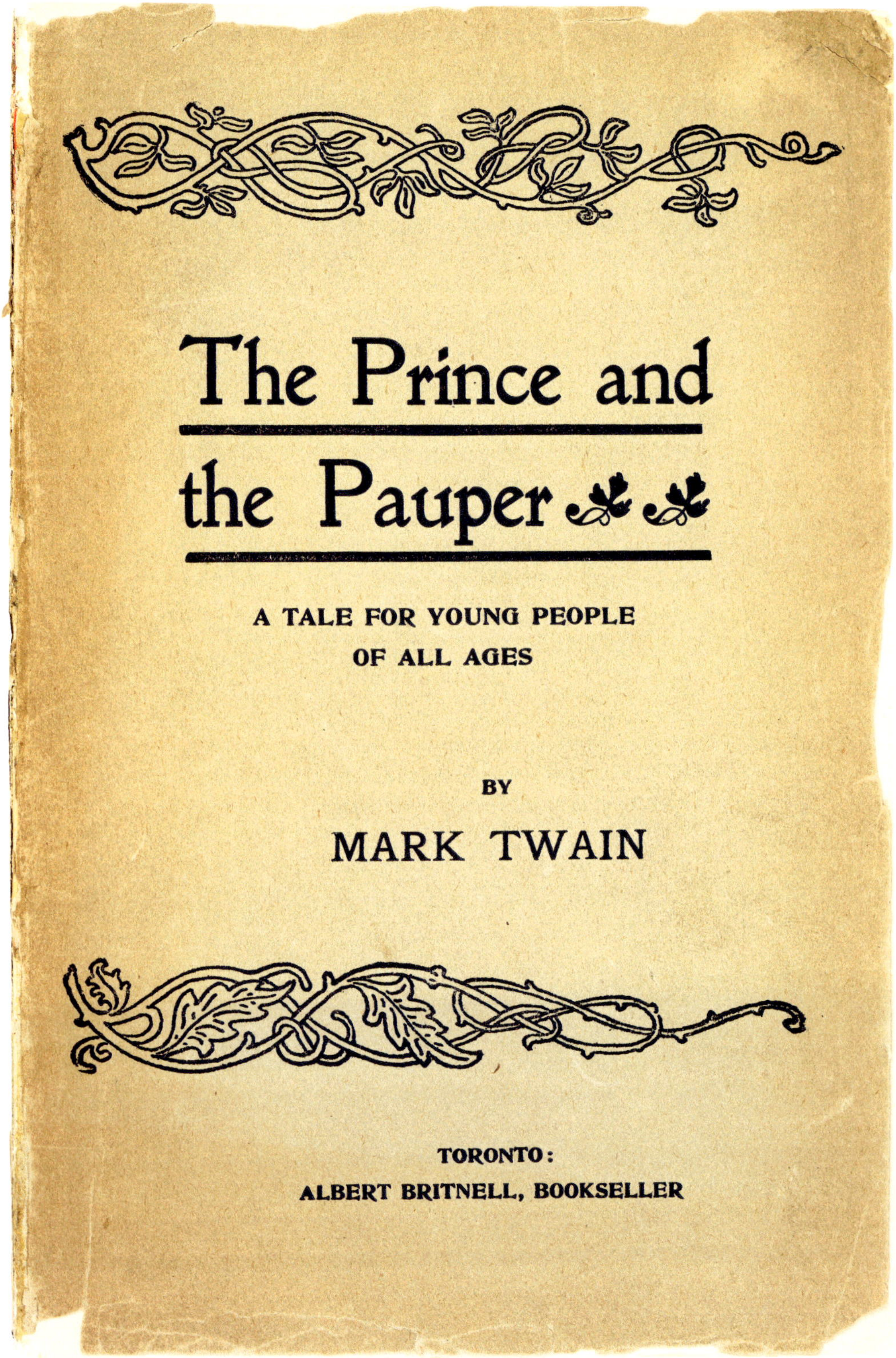

2–4). *Mark Twain's Library of Humor* **(page 49)** reprised the scrapbook marketing strategy in a generic humor anthology edited mainly by Howells and Charles Hopkins Clark, with Clemens's willingness to extend and cash in on the Mark Twain brand manifest in both the title and the facsimile handwritten "Compiler's Apology" boldly signed "Mark Twain" (Lee, "Brand" [2014] 46–47). Other brand extensions included the various uniform editions that began collecting his still-expanding corpus from 1896 onward, recycling his copyrights while marketing old works in a mode that conferred literary stature.

Clemens had his business manager Ralph Ashcroft to thank for the two ultimate extensions of the Mark Twain brand: the Mark Twain Company (incorporated December 22, 1908), to secure Clemens's intellectual property for his surviving daughters, Clara and Jean, by managing his royalties after the copyrights ran out; and four US trademarks for uses of the name "Mark Twain" in a specialized font with an etched image of Samuel Clemens and facsimile "Mark Twain" signature underneath (Lee, "Brand" [2017] 43–50). Both solidified the Mark Twain trademark in myth if not in fact. In this way, the comic branding process that Clemens first noted in the lecture hall eventually moved to less overtly performative venues in order to trade, in the literal commercial sense, on the symbolic value of Mark Twain's brand.

The *Mark Twain's Memory-Builder* game (1891) **(page 205)** had much less success than *Mark Twain's Scrap Book*, likely because it lacked a comic connection, but its comparative failure validated Clemens's third strategy for brand management: withholding the Mark Twain brand from activities inconsistent with or potentially damaging to his reputation as a writer. He named his publishing firm for his nephew Charles L. Webster to protect his own work from appearing self-published and to prevent works like Ulysses Grant's *Personal Memoirs* from having a comic label. He likewise kept the name "Mark Twain" off writings that he considered inconsistent with his reputation as a humorist and public figure. He published the *Personal Recollections of Joan of Arc* serially in *Harper's Magazine* (1895–96) **(page 118)** so that readers would not expect a comic tale. He suppressed "Date: 1601" **(page 119)** for its obscenities, "The War Prayer" (comp. 1905, pub. 1923) (Item no. 48) for its religious politics, and the *Autobiography* for its frank opinions **(pages 153–155)**. And he protected both the social and commodity values of his brand name when he quietly transferred all real and intellectual property to his wife in 1894 before declaring his publishing house bankrupt and promising to pay all its debts with the worldwide tour that became *Following the Equator* and *More Tramps Abroad* (1896) **(pages 104–105 and 233)**.

Clemens's pioneering management of the Mark Twain brand inspired other enterprises to exploit it, too. In concert with its serial publication of *The Tragedy of Pudd'nhead Wilson* from December 1893 to June 1894, the Century Company offered *Pudd'nhead Wilson's Calendar* for 1894 as a premium to newsstand readers and new subscribers **(pages 120–121)**. Harper Brothers followed suit with the *Mark Twain Calendar for 1910* **(page 122)** to advertise the National Edition of the *Works*. Clemens mounted the lecture platform to promote work by other writers, as when he introduced readings by Bill Nye and James Whitcomb Riley, who had recently published *Fun, Wit, and Humor* (1888), at Tremont Church in Boston on February 28, 1889 **(page 123)**. And he attached the Mark Twain brand to political causes, such as advocacy by the Congo Reform Association, which commissioned his anti-imperialist satire *King Leopold's Soliloquy* (1905) **(page 124)**. During Clemens's lifetime, Parker Brothers deftly borrowed the brand's cachet without the label for their first game, the punningly named *Amusing Game of Innocence Abroad* (ca. 1888–90) **(page 125)**, which they later reissued with the nostalgic title *The Good Old Game of Innocence Abroad* **(page 125)**. In the century since his death, Mark Twain's brand has retained, if not increased, its power. His paeans to childhood have inspired two Tom Sawyer games **(pages 210 and 211)** as well as films and comic books. Cigar manufacturers have found him repeatedly useful **(pages 170–173)**. Indeed, the Kennedy Center's annual Mark Twain Prize for American Humor—which honors his memory with a bronze bust while celebrating a wide range of comic luminaries, most of whom perform humor but do not write for publication—proves that Mark Twain's economic and cultural capital remains intact.

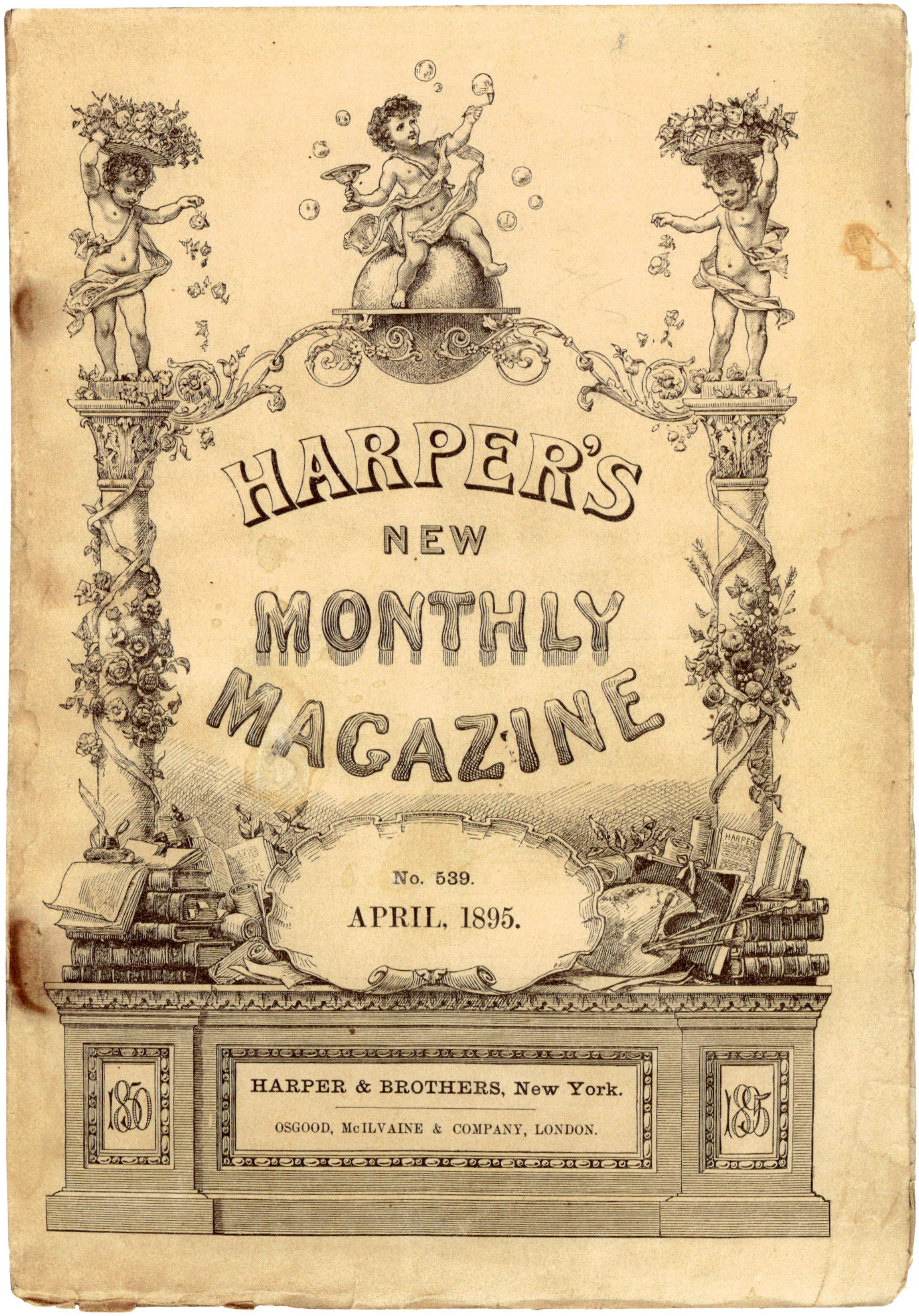

Harper's New Monthly Magazine, volume 90, number 539. New York: Harper & Brothers, April 1895. In original wrappers. (Item no. 66)

Twain's *Personal Recollections of Joan of Arc* was serialized in thirteen issues of the prominent New York magazine *Harper's Monthly*, beginning in April 1895. Because the text was intended as serious, Clemens wanted it to appear anonymously, but *Harper's* advertised the serial as being written by "one of the most successful among American writers of fiction," and the initial installments appeared under the byline of "the Sieur Louis de Conte"—a name that conceals Clemens's initials. Rumors of his authorship spread, and Harper & Bros. published the book as a single volume with the de Conte pseudonym on the title page, but the name "Mark Twain" on the book's cover.

RIGHT

[Mark Twain.] *Conversation as it was by the Social Fireside in the Time of the Tudors. Date—Sixteen Hundred One.* [New York?]: Privately printed, November 20, 1904. (Item no. 19)

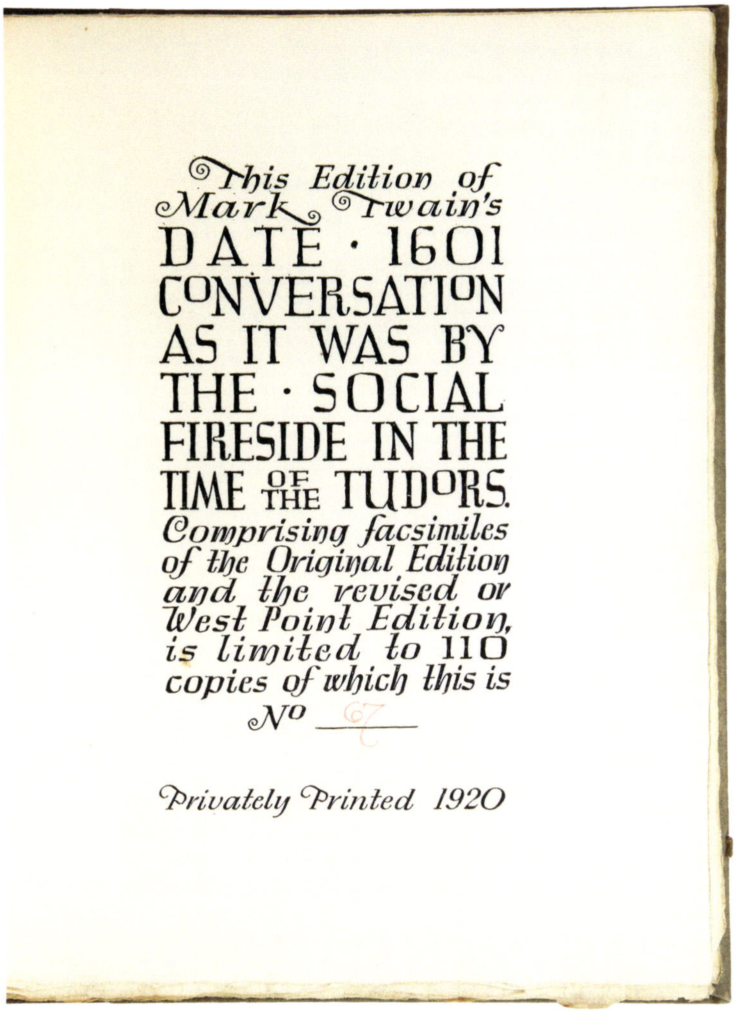

BELOW RIGHT

Mark Twain. *Date, 1601: Conversation as it was by the Social Fireside in the Time of the Tudors.* [New York]: Privately printed [for Merle Johnson and Charles P. Everitt], 1920. (Item no. 20)

Twain first published *1601* in 1880 in an anonymous edition of as few as four copies that he shared with a few close friends. The text is a ribald story in which William Shakespeare, Ben Jonson, and other Elizabethan luminaries discuss flatulence, sex, and other taboo topics. Considered obscene under American law until the early 1960s, it was circulated in a variety of privately printed editions in the decades to come. Twain acknowledged his authorship in 1906, telling librarian Charles Orr: "If there is a decent word findable in it, it is because I overlooked it."

THIS PAGE AND OPPOSITE

Pudd'nhead Wilson's Calendar for 1894. [New York: The Century Co., 1893.] (Item no. 130)

This small pamphlet containing a number of Twain's humorous aphorisms was published as a promotional item for *The Century Magazine*, which serialized *Pudd'nhead Wilson* in 1893–94.

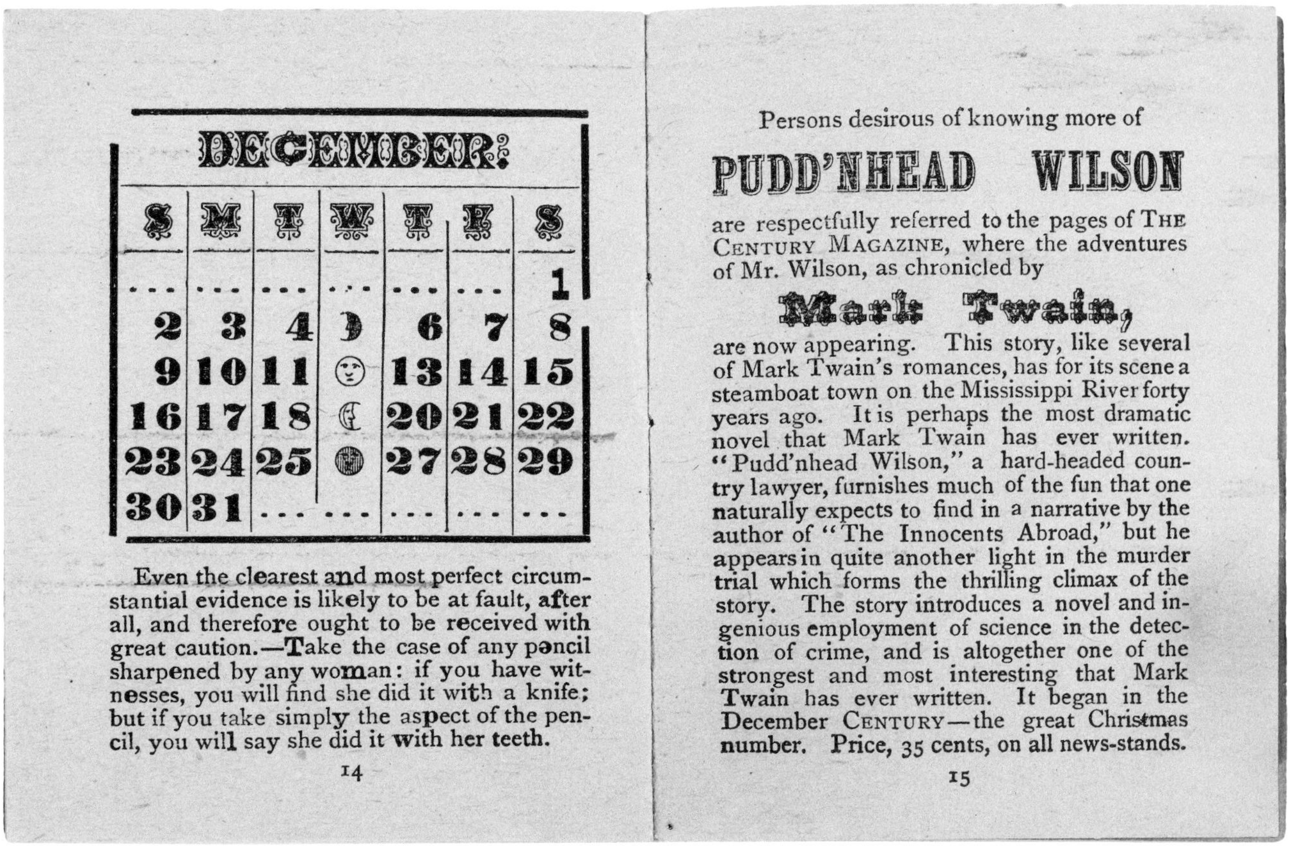

DECEMBER.

S	M	T	W	T	F	S
...	...	...	...	...	...	1
2	3	4	☽	6	7	8
9	10	11	☺	13	14	15
16	17	18	☾	20	21	22
23	24	25	●	27	28	29
30	31	...	...	...	...	...

Even the clearest and most perfect circumstantial evidence is likely to be at fault, after all, and therefore ought to be received with great caution.—Take the case of any pencil sharpened by any woman: if you have witnesses, you will find she did it with a knife; but if you take simply the aspect of the pencil, you will say she did it with her teeth.

14

Persons desirous of knowing more of

PUDD'NHEAD WILSON

are respectfully referred to the pages of THE CENTURY MAGAZINE, where the adventures of Mr. Wilson, as chronicled by

Mark Twain,

are now appearing. This story, like several of Mark Twain's romances, has for its scene a steamboat town on the Mississippi River forty years ago. It is perhaps the most dramatic novel that Mark Twain has ever written. "Pudd'nhead Wilson," a hard-headed country lawyer, furnishes much of the fun that one naturally expects to find in a narrative by the author of "The Innocents Abroad," but he appears in quite another light in the murder trial which forms the thrilling climax of the story. The story introduces a novel and ingenious employment of science in the detection of crime, and is altogether one of the strongest and most interesting that Mark Twain has ever written. It began in the December CENTURY—the great Christmas number. Price, 35 cents, on all news-stands.

15

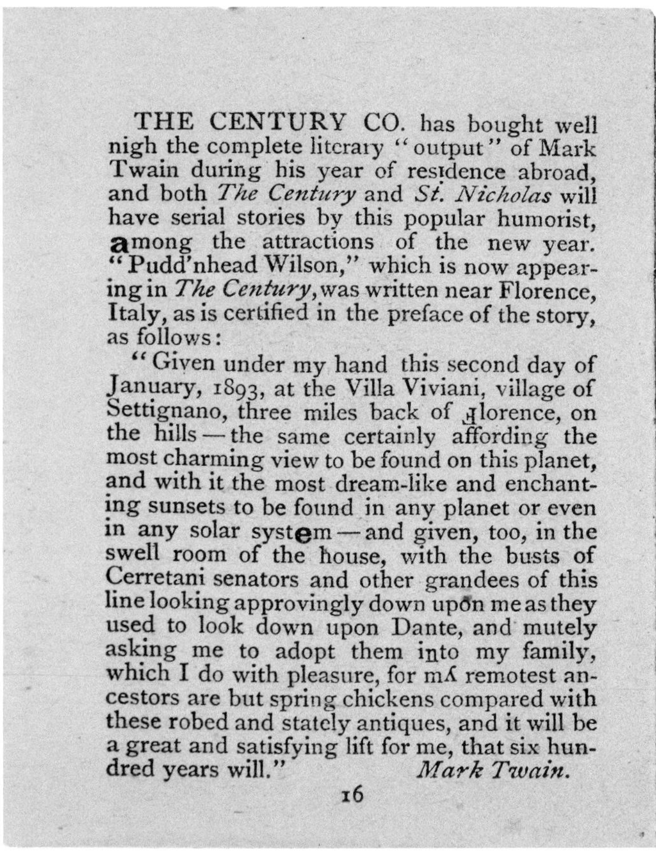

THE CENTURY CO. has bought well nigh the complete literary "output" of Mark Twain during his year of residence abroad, and both *The Century* and *St. Nicholas* will have serial stories by this popular humorist, among the attractions of the new year. "Pudd'nhead Wilson," which is now appearing in *The Century*, was written near Florence, Italy, as is certified in the preface of the story, as follows:

"Given under my hand this second day of January, 1893, at the Villa Viviani, village of Settignano, three miles back of Florence, on the hills—the same certainly affording the most charming view to be found on this planet, and with it the most dream-like and enchanting sunsets to be found in any planet or even in any solar system—and given, too, in the swell room of the house, with the busts of Cerretani senators and other grandees of this line looking approvingly down upon me as they used to look down upon Dante, and mutely asking me to adopt them into my family, which I do with pleasure, for my remotest ancestors are but spring chickens compared with these robed and stately antiques, and it will be a great and satisfying lift for me, that six hundred years will." *Mark Twain.*

16

Portrait of MARK TWAIN,
From an amateur photograph by his friend "Pudd'nhead Wilson."

Mark Twain Calendar for 1910. New York: Harper & Brothers, 1909. (Item no. 162)

An illustrated calendar issued to promote Harper's National Edition of Twain's *Works.*

1910

Mark Twain

JANUARY						
S	M	T	W	T	F	S
..	..	..	..	..	..	1
2	3	4	5	6	7	8
9	10	11	12	13	14	15
16	17	18	19	20	21	22
23	24	25	26	27	28	29
30	31	..	..	..	..	..

When in doubt, tell the truth.
—*Pudd'nhead Wilson's New Calendar*

FEBRUARY						
S	M	T	W	T	F	S
..	..	1	2	3	4	5
6	7	8	9	10	11	12
13	14	15	16	17	18	19
20	21	22	23	24	25	26
27	28	..	..	..	..	..
..	..	..	..	..	..	..

work of such artists as
J. G. Brown, A. B. Frost, Peter Newell, Dan Beard, Frederick Dielman, Etc.
W. T. Smedley, T. de Thulstrup, B. W. Clinedinst, F. Luis Mora, C. D. Weldon, Etc.
E. W. Kemble, C. Allan Gilbert, F. V. Du Mond, Frank J. Merrill, F. B. Opper, Etc.

BINDING AND OTHER DETAILS

The binding is a beautiful dark-red vellum book cloth, with blue title labels stamped in gold. The books are printed on white antique wove paper, especially made for this edition. The size of each volume is 5 x 7 ½ inches.

HARPER & BROTHERS, FRANKLIN SQUARE, NEW YORK

Copyright, 1909, by Harper & Brothers

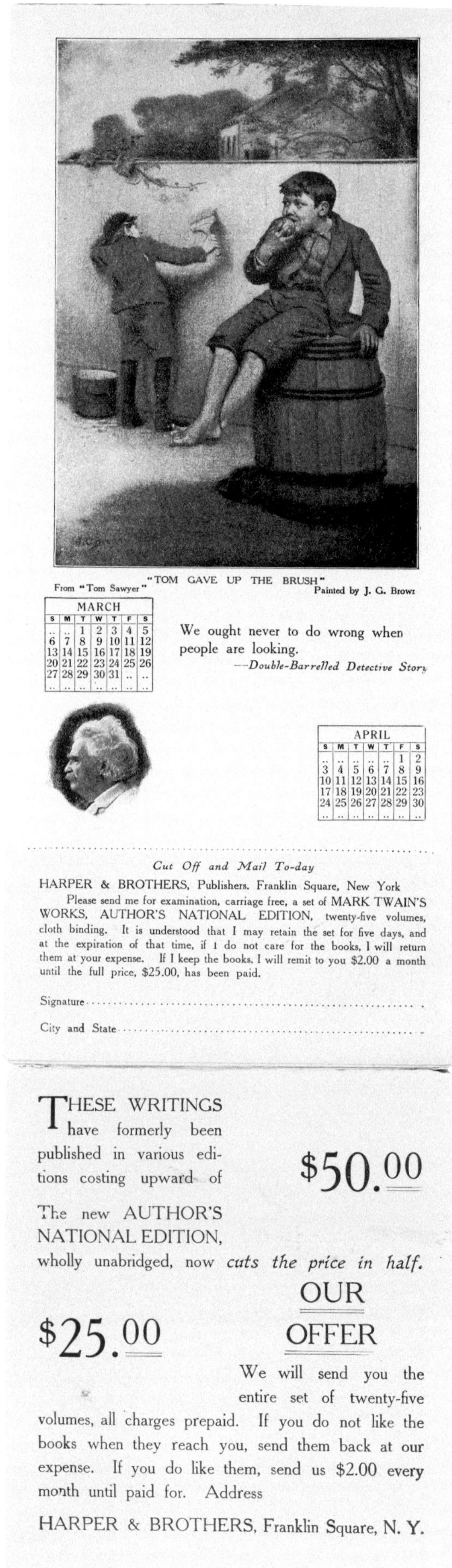

From "Tom Sawyer" "TOM GAVE UP THE BRUSH" Painted by J. G. Browr

MARCH						
S	M	T	W	T	F	S
..	..	1	2	3	4	5
6	7	8	9	10	11	12
13	14	15	16	17	18	19
20	21	22	23	24	25	26
27	28	29	30	31	..	..
..	..	..	..	..	..	..

We ought never to do wrong when people are looking.
—*Double-Barrelled Detective Story*

APRIL						
S	M	T	W	T	F	S
..	..	..	..	..	1	2
3	4	5	6	7	8	9
10	11	12	13	14	15	16
17	18	19	20	21	22	23
24	25	26	27	28	29	30
..	..	..	..	..	..	..

Cut Off and Mail To-day

HARPER & BROTHERS, Publishers, Franklin Square, New York

Please send me for examination, carriage free, a set of MARK TWAIN'S WORKS, AUTHOR'S NATIONAL EDITION, twenty-five volumes, cloth binding. It is understood that I may retain the set for five days, and at the expiration of that time, if I do not care for the books, I will return them at your expense. If I keep the books, I will remit to you $2.00 a month until the full price, $25.00, has been paid.

Signature..

City and State..

THESE WRITINGS have formerly been published in various editions costing upward of $50.00

The new AUTHOR'S NATIONAL EDITION, wholly unabridged, now *cuts the price in half.*

$25.00 OUR OFFER

We will send you the entire set of twenty-five volumes, all charges prepaid. If you do not like the books when they reach you, send them back at our expense. If you do like them, send us $2.00 every month until paid for. Address

HARPER & BROTHERS, Franklin Square, N. Y.

“Smiles and Tears. Programme of readings to be given by James Whitcomb Riley the distinguished poet, and Bill Nye, the famous humorist . . . Mr. S.L. Clemens, ‘Mark Twain,’ will preside.” Boston: F. A. Searle, Printer, [1889]. (Item no. 164)

James Whitcomb Riley and Edgar Wilson “Bill” Nye toured together on the lecture circuit for several years in the 1880s, and for this Boston appearance they were introduced by Twain. In his brief speech, Twain offered an extended, joking presentation of the duo as Chang and Eng Bunker, conjoined twins who had appeared at P. T. Barnum’s American Museum in 1860 and toured for several years thereafter.

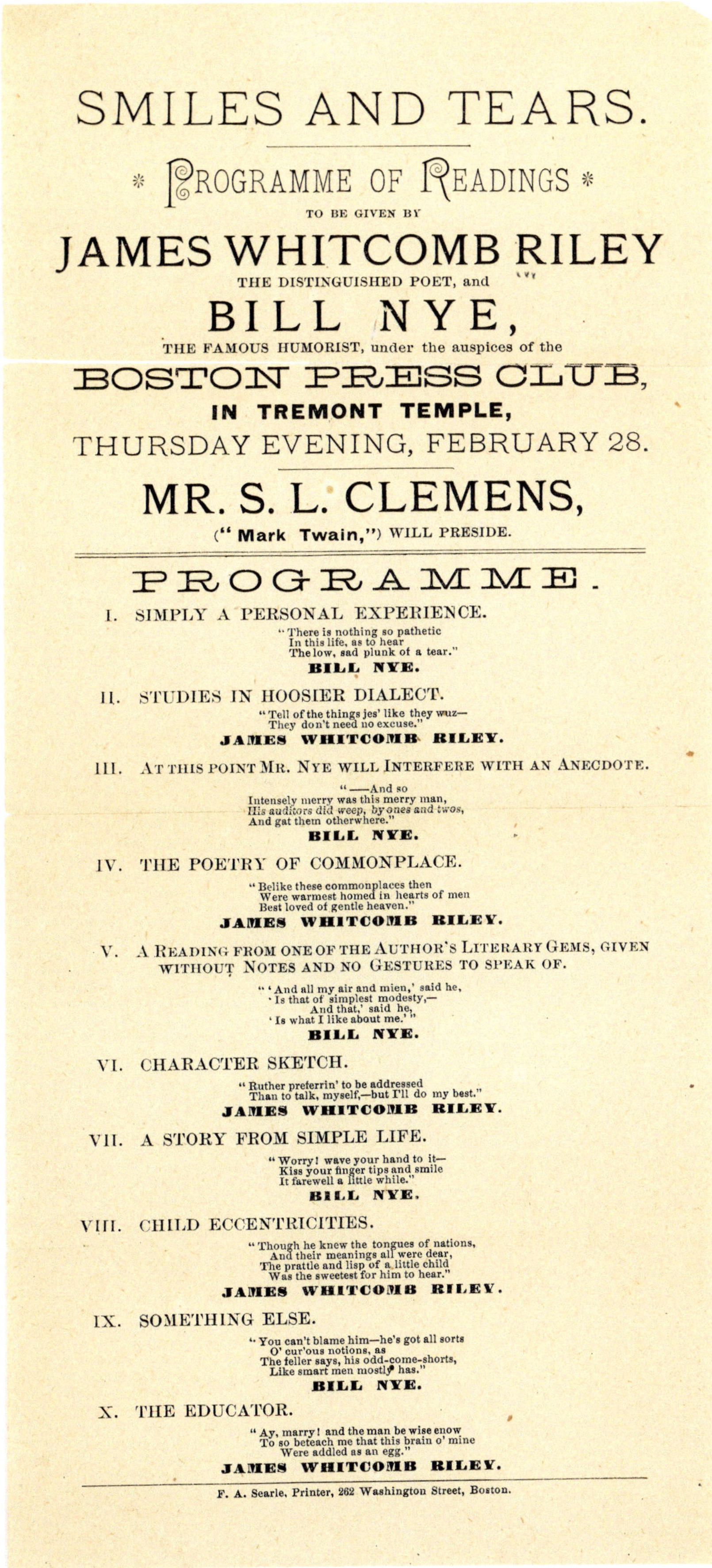

SMILES AND TEARS.

PROGRAMME OF READINGS

TO BE GIVEN BY

JAMES WHITCOMB RILEY

THE DISTINGUISHED POET, and

BILL NYE,

THE FAMOUS HUMORIST, under the auspices of the

BOSTON PRESS CLUB,

IN TREMONT TEMPLE,

THURSDAY EVENING, FEBRUARY 28.

MR. S. L. CLEMENS,

(“ Mark Twain,”) WILL PRESIDE.

PROGRAMME.

I. SIMPLY A PERSONAL EXPERIENCE.

“There is nothing so pathetic
In this life, as to hear
The low, sad plunk of a tear.”

BILL NYE.

II. STUDIES IN HOOSIER DIALECT.

“Tell of the things jes' like they wuz—
They don't need no excuse.”

JAMES WHITCOMB RILEY.

III. AT THIS POINT MR. NYE WILL INTERFERE WITH AN ANECDOTE.

“——And so
Intensely merry was this merry man,
His auditors did weep, by ones and twos,
And gat them otherwhere.”

BILL NYE.

IV. THE POETRY OF COMMONPLACE.

“Belike these commonplaces then
Were warmest homed in hearts of men
Best loved of gentle heaven.”

JAMES WHITCOMB RILEY.

V. A READING FROM ONE OF THE AUTHOR'S LITERARY GEMS, GIVEN WITHOUT NOTES AND NO GESTURES TO SPEAK OF.

“ ‘And all my air and mien,’ said he,
‘Is that of simplest modesty,—
And that,’ said he,
‘Is what I like about me.’ ”

BILL NYE.

VI. CHARACTER SKETCH.

“Ruther preferrin' to be addressed
Than to talk, myself,—but I'll do my best.”

JAMES WHITCOMB RILEY.

VII. A STORY FROM SIMPLE LIFE.

“Worry! wave your hand to it—
Kiss your finger tips and smile
It farewell a little while.”

BILL NYE.

VIII. CHILD ECCENTRICITIES.

“Though he knew the tongues of nations,
And their meanings all were dear,
The prattle and lisp of a little child
Was the sweetest for him to hear.”

JAMES WHITCOMB RILEY.

IX. SOMETHING ELSE.

“You can't blame him—he's got all sorts
O' cur'ous notions, as
The feller says, his odd-come-shorts,
Like smart men mostly has.”

BILL NYE.

X. THE EDUCATOR.

“Ay, marry! and the man be wise enow
To so beteach me that this brain o' mine
Were addled as an egg.”

JAMES WHITCOMB RILEY.

F. A. Searle, Printer, 262 Washington Street, Boston.

Mark Twain. *King Leopold's Soliloquy: A Defense of his Congo Rule.* Boston: The P. R. Warren Co., 1905. Second edition, with the publisher's statement on pink paper tipped in. (Item no. 37)

King Leopold II of Belgium is notorious for the extent of the atrocities he visited on the Congo Free State between 1885 and 1908. In this bleakly satirical pamphlet, Twain presents the king as offering a self-damning "defense" of his actions. The publisher donated the proceeds from the pamphlet's sale to humanitarian aid in the region.

ABOVE

[Mrs. Shepherd.] *The Amusing Game of Innocence Abroad*. Salem, Mass.: Parker Brothers, [ca. 1888–1890]. (Item no. 154)

RIGHT

[Mrs. Shepherd.] *The Good Old Game of Innocence Abroad*. Salem, Mass.: Parker Brothers, [ca. 1901]. (Item no. 155)

George S. Parker copyrighted this map board game in 1888, licensed to his fledgling game publisher by its designer, a Mrs. Shepherd. The subtle change to the title for Twain's *Innocents Abroad* signals the paucity of the game's connection to the book. Still, it proved popular, and was reissued a decade after its original release.

THIS PAGE AND OPPOSITE

Mark Twain. Autograph letter signed "Mark" to Elisha Bliss, Jr. Elmira, N.Y., July 4, 1870. (Item no. 92)

Clemens negotiates a higher royalty fee from Elisha Bliss, Jr., of the American Publishing Company by detailing the generous offer he received from another publisher.

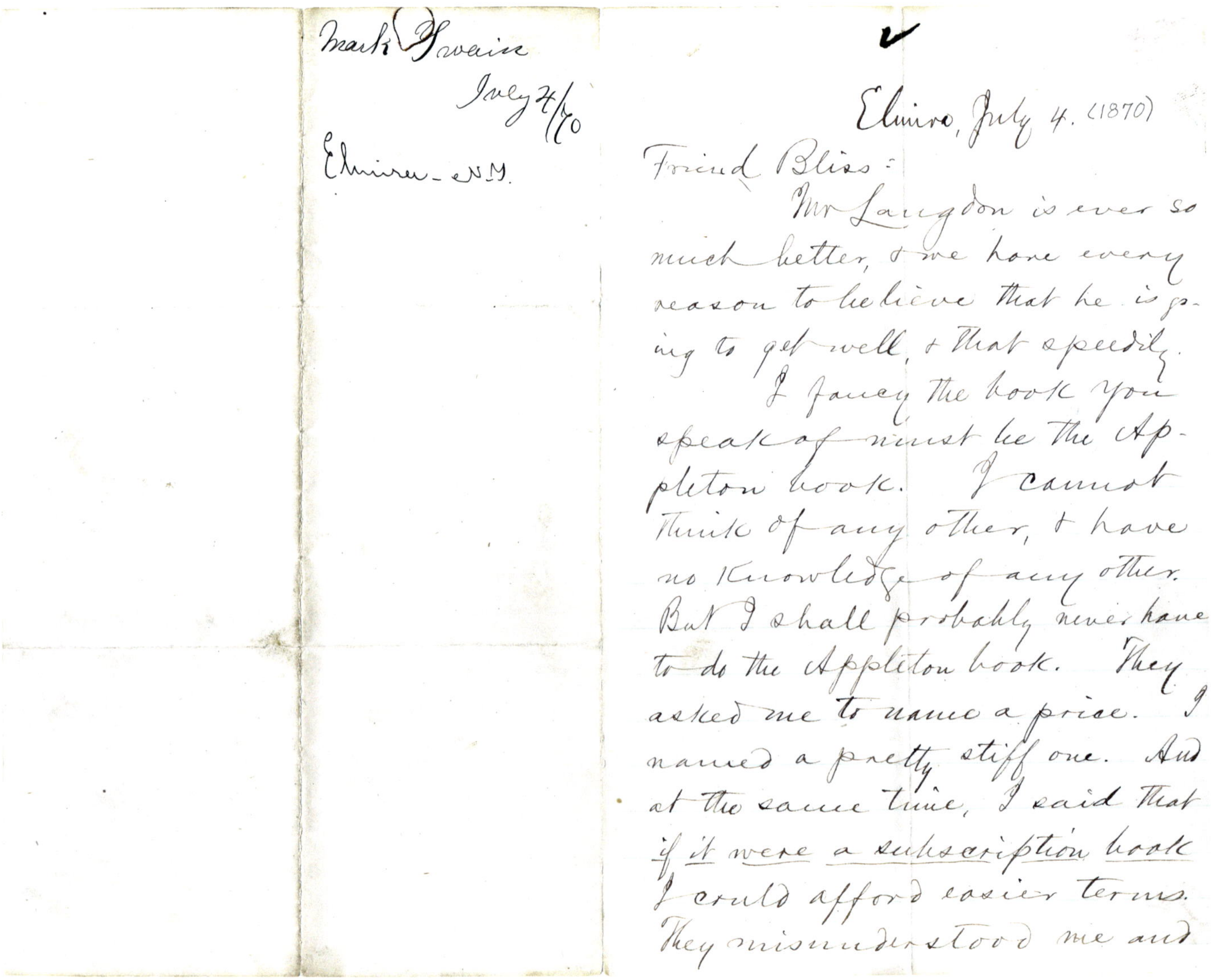

Mark Twain
July 4/70
Elmira – N.Y.

Elmira, July 4. (1870)

Friend Bliss:

Mr Langdon is ever so much better, & we have every reason to believe that he is going to get well, & that speedily.

I fancy the book you speak of must be the Appleton book. I cannot think of any other, & have no knowledge of any other. But I shall probably never have to do the Appleton book. They asked me to name a price. I named a pretty stiff one. And at the same time, I said that *if it were a subscription book* I could afford easier terms. They misunderstood me and thought that I was <u>suggesting</u> that it be made a subscription work — & so they <u>accepted</u> ~~declined~~ my suggestion and offered <u>higher</u> pay than I spoke of. But I wrote them immediately that they had misconstrued me, & that I could not do a <u>subscription</u> book for them <u>at any price whatever</u>. And moreover, that I could do <u>nothing</u> more than the original proposition called for. And that I could not even do that unless I could do it either before or immediately after my Adirondack trip. They have had ~~[illegible]~~ ample time to have written me half a dozen times since, & haven't done it. Therefore it is <u>far</u> from likely that any "humorous book" ~~#~~ will issue from my pen shortly.

If Mr L. gets thoroughly well, in time, my wife & I will go straight from Buffalo to Vergennes, Vt., ~~to~~ at the end of July, & be joined there by the Twichells. It is our shortest & straightest route to the woods.

We shall be here 10 days or 2 weeks yet. Come — come either here or to Buf.

Yrs

Mark.

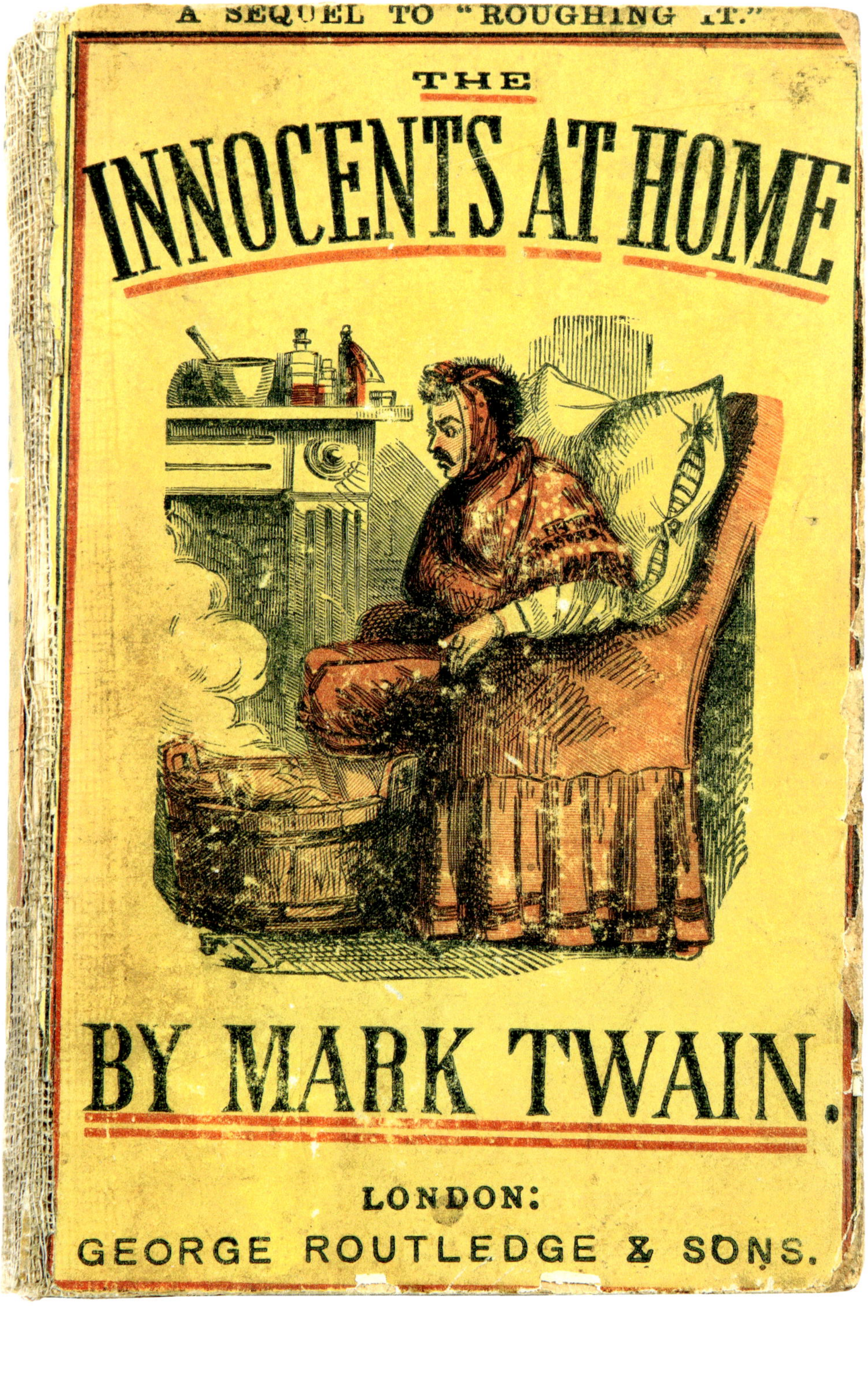

Mark Twain. *The Innocents at Home*. London: George Routledge and Sons, 1872. (Item no. 10)

Because of their length, Twain's books were often split into two volumes for their British mass-market "yellowback" editions. Routledge sought to trade on the success of Twain's most successful book by recalling *Innocents Abroad* with its title for the second half—and kept the second title for its single-volume hard-cover edition.

Autograph letter signed "S.L. Clemens" to Frank or Elisha Bliss, Jr. Vienna, Austria, February 11, 1898. (Item no. 106)

Both during his lifetime and today, Mark Twain was well known for his maxims: quotations that are simultaneously brief, humorous, and wise. In this letter, Clemens informs his publisher that he has assembled a collection of sixty such quotations—not enough for a daily calendar, but ample to produce a series of postcards that he hopes will sell better than his recent *Following the Equator*.

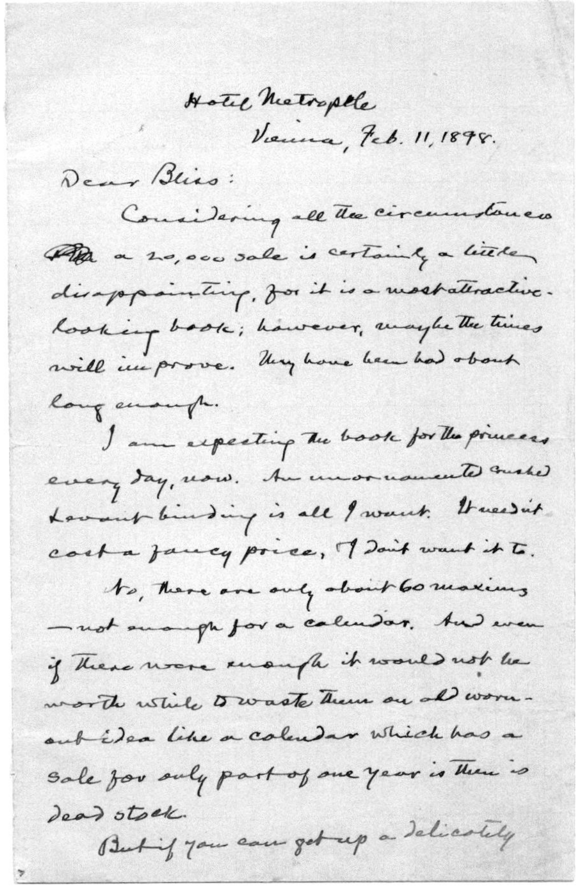

Hotel Metropole
Vienna, Feb. 11, 1898.

Dear Bliss:

Considering all the circumstances a 20,000 sale is certainly a little disappointing, for it is a most attractive-looking book; however, maybe the times will improve. They have been bad about long enough.

I am expecting the book for the princess every day, now. An unornamented crushed Levant binding is all I want. It needn't cost a fancy price, I don't want it to.

No, there are only about 60 maxims—not enough for a calendar. And even if there were enough it would not be worth while to waste them on an old worn-out idea like a calendar which has a sale for only part of one year & then is dead stock.

But if you can get up a delicately

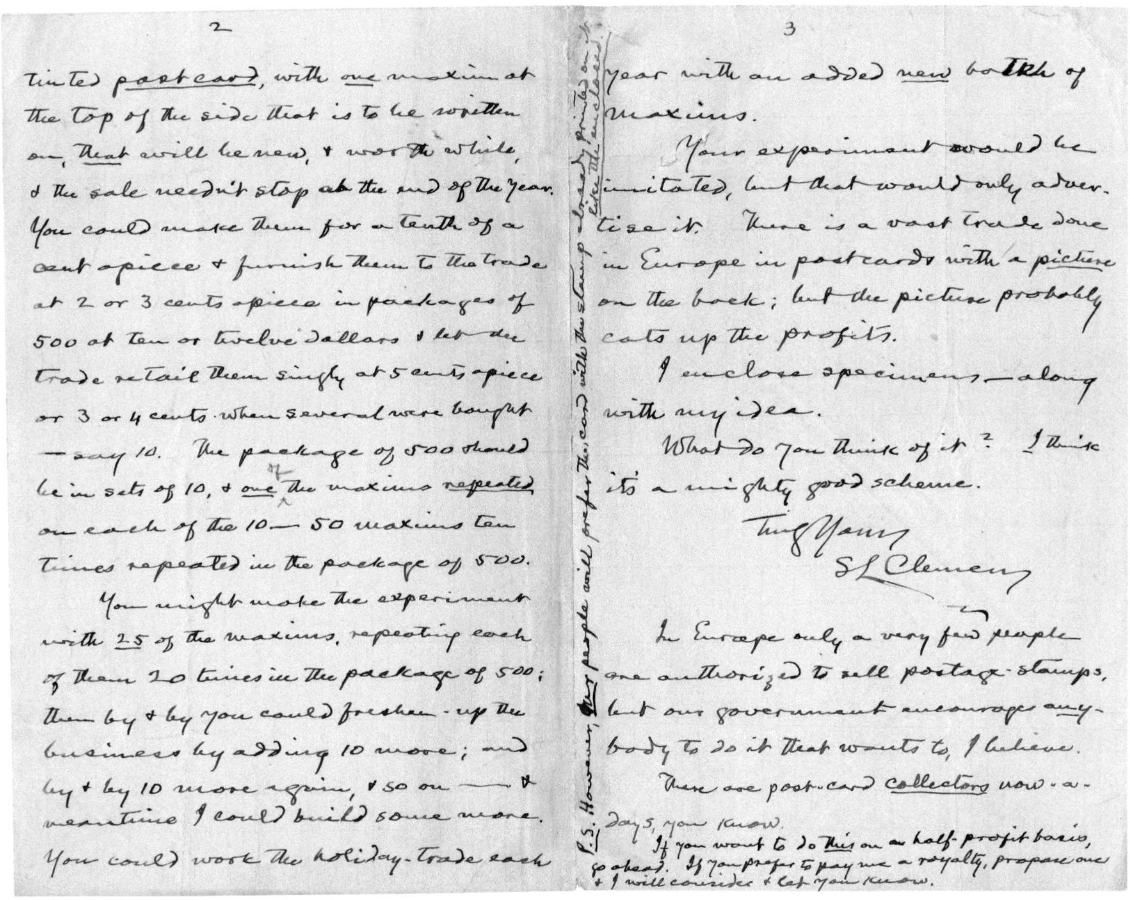

2

tinted postcard, with one maxim at the top of the side that is to be written on, that will be new, & worth while, & the sale needn't stop at the end of the year. You could make them for a tenth of a cent apiece & furnish them to the trade at 2 or 3 cents apiece in packages of 500 at ten or twelve dollars & let the trade retail them singly at 5 cents apiece or 3 or 4 cents when several were bought—say 10. The package of 500 should be in sets of 10, & one of the maxims repeated on each of the 10—50 maxims ten times repeated in the package of 500.

You might make the experiment with 25 of the maxims, repeating each of them 20 times in the package of 500; then by & by you could freshen-up the business by adding 10 more; and by & by 10 more again, & so on—& meantime I could build some more. You could work the holiday-trade each

3

year with an added new batch of maxims.

Your experiment would be imitated, but that would only advertise it. There is a vast trade done in Europe in postcards with a picture on the back; but the picture probably eats up the profits.

I enclose specimens—along with my idea.

What do you think of it? I think it's a mighty good scheme.

Truly Yours
SL Clemens

In Europe only a very few people are authorized to sell postage-stamps, but our government encourage anybody to do it that wants to, I believe.

There are post-card collectors now-a-days, you know.

If you want to do this on a half-profit basis, go ahead. If you prefer to pay me a royalty, propose one & I will consider & let you know.

P.S. However, my people will prefer the card with the stamp printed on it, like the enclosed.

THIS PAGE AND OPPOSITE

Woolson Spice Co. "Shadow Picture [Mark Twain]." Toledo, Ohio: Woolson Spice Co., [1895]. (Item no. 166)

Carefully cutting around the lines on the back of this card will turn the floral illustration on the front into a silhouette portrait of Mark Twain.

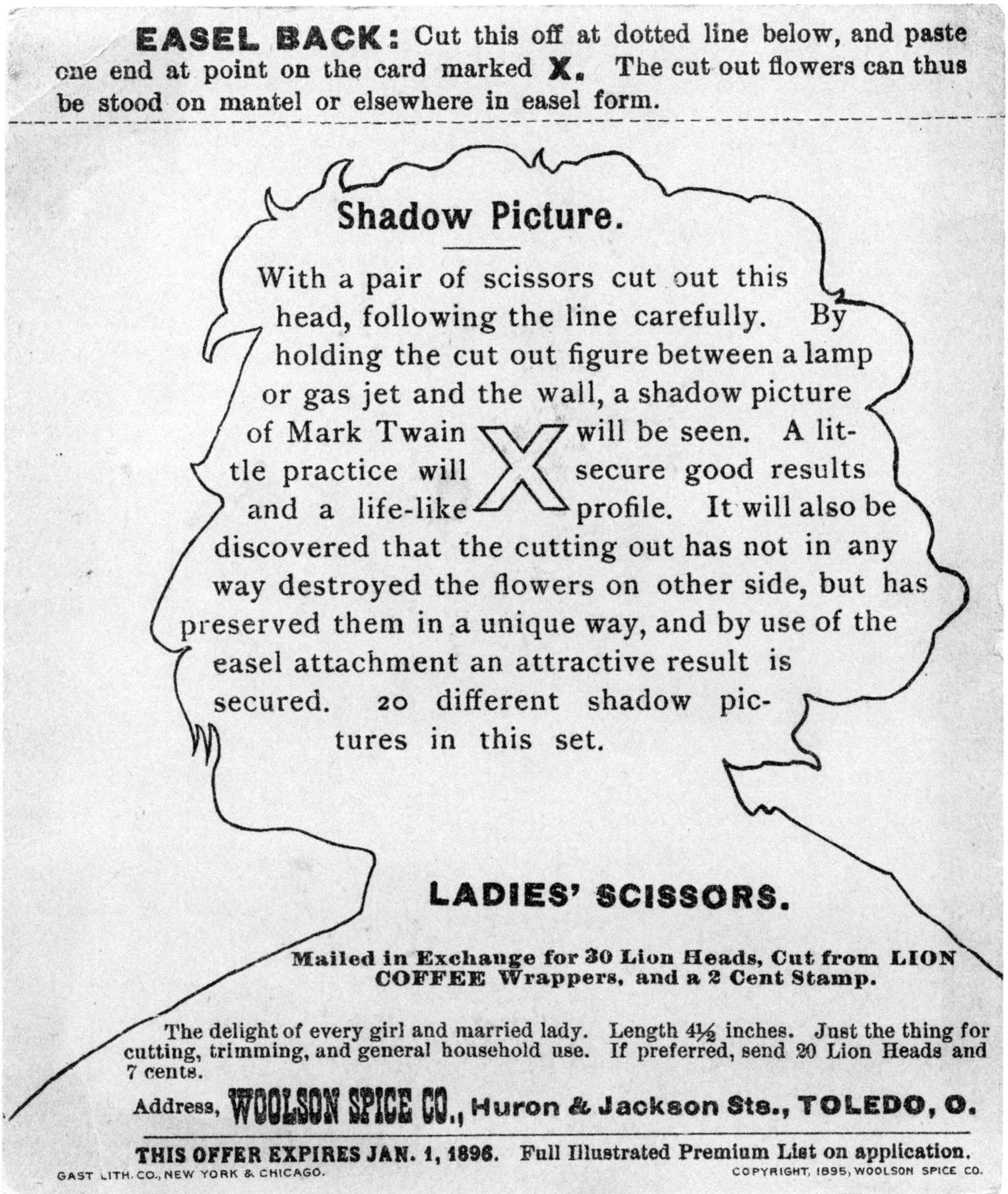

EASEL BACK: Cut this off at dotted line below, and paste one end at point on the card marked **X.** The cut out flowers can thus be stood on mantel or elsewhere in easel form.

Shadow Picture.

With a pair of scissors cut out this head, following the line carefully. By holding the cut out figure between a lamp or gas jet and the wall, a shadow picture of Mark Twain X will be seen. A little practice will secure good results and a life-like profile. It will also be discovered that the cutting out has not in any way destroyed the flowers on other side, but has preserved them in a unique way, and by use of the easel attachment an attractive result is secured. 20 different shadow pictures in this set.

LADIES' SCISSORS.

Mailed in Exchange for 30 Lion Heads, Cut from LION COFFEE Wrappers, and a 2 Cent Stamp.

The delight of every girl and married lady. Length 4½ inches. Just the thing for cutting, trimming, and general household use. If preferred, send 20 Lion Heads and 7 cents.

Address, **WOOLSON SPICE CO., Huron & Jackson Sts., TOLEDO, O.**

THIS OFFER EXPIRES JAN. 1, 1896. Full Illustrated Premium List on application.

GAST LITH. CO., NEW YORK & CHICAGO.

COPYRIGHT, 1895, WOOLSON SPICE CO.

THIS PAGE AND OPPOSITE

Morrell's Mark Twain Calendar [*1946*]. Ottumwa, Iowa: John Morrell & Co., 1945. (Item no. 163)

In this tearaway calendar missing only January, each month is accompanied by a painted illustration by Norman Rockwell and quotation from *The Adventures of Tom Sawyer*.

Tom came upon the juvenile vagabond of the village, Huckleberry Finn, who was carrying a dead cat. "My, he's pretty stiff," said Tom. "Say, what is dead cats good for, Huck?" "Good for? Cure warts with," Huck replied. Then followed a long, detailed discussion of various and sundry methods of removing warts. But the appeal of the dead cat theory prevailed. The two boys agreed to test it that night and thereby stumbled upon the tragedy at the graveyard.
MARCH 1946
Morrell PRIDE Beef
PROVISIONERS SINCE 1827
Compliments of
COMMUNITY MARKET
Government Inspected Meats — Quality - Service - Economy
Telephone 262
LALICH & ORLER, Proprietors
1348 Main Street, Weirton, W. Va.

Huck made corncob pipes and soon the novices, Tom and Joe, were puffing luxuriously. Presently their silences widened, their expectoration marvelously increased. Every pore within their cheeks became a spouting fountain. Both boys were pale and miserable. Joe said feebly, "I've lost my knife. I reckon I better go and find it." Tom said, "I'll help you." When Huck found them later, something informed him that if they had had any trouble they had got rid of it.
One of the paintings made by Norman Rockwell to illustrate the Heritage edition of TOM SAWYER.
JULY 1946
Morrell PRIDE Bacon
PROVISIONERS SINCE 1827
Compliments of
COMMUNITY MARKET
Government Inspected Meats — Quality - Service - Economy
Telephone 262
LALICH & ORLER, Proprietors
1348 Main Street, Weirton, W. Va.

LEFT

Mark Twain bookends. [Bridgeport, Conn.]: Weidlich Brothers, [1947?]. (Item no. 148)

These bookends show a scholarly Twain reading a book that he holds in his lap.

BELOW

United States Postal Service. Tom Sawyer first day of issue cover. Hannibal, Mo., November 30, 1972. (Item no. 165)

Illustrated envelope postmarked in Clemens's hometown on the date of issue of an eight-cent stamp commemorating *The Adventures of Tom Sawyer*.

Royal Bobbles. *American Writers: Mark Twain*. Alpharetta, Ga.: Royal Bobbles, 2015. (Item no. 167)

A limited edition "bobblehead" figurine featuring Twain in his signature white suit.

The Western Experience

JAMES E. CARON

To understand early Mark Twain, one must remember that Clemens created his literary alter ego within the context of mid-nineteenth-century American periodical publication. Moreover, one must recall that the most important genre for the initial success of Mark Twain was the travel letter, written for various periodicals. Though the pen name "Mark Twain" today signifies comic writing for the average American reader, the first bestseller for Sam Clemens was the collection of travel letters that became *The Innocents Abroad* (1869) **(pages 52–53 and 108–109)**

He followed that success with *Roughing It* (1872) **(page 231)**, his account of traveling to the Nevada Territory in 1862, living there and trying his hand at mining before becoming a newspaper reporter and inventing his print alter ego Mark Twain. *Roughing It* also contains a revision of Clemens's first extended effort at travel letters, letters from the Kingdom of Hawai'i, originally published in the *Sacramento Union* (1866). Clemens returned to these successes with *Life on the Mississippi* (1883) **(pages 46–47)**, a travelogue that he first planned just after his return from Hawai'i. There were also two other notable efforts: *A Tramp Abroad* (1880) and *Following the Equator* (1897) **(pages 102–103 and 104–105)**.

Clemens reinvents the travel letter by merging the antebellum comic tradition of mock travel letters, exemplified by Seba Smith's Major Jack Downing, with the highbrow style of travel writing represented by Bayard Taylor. This new kind of travel letter accommodated a mixture of the necessary reportage and expected literary description with comic misadventures as likely to be fictional as not.

Clemens's travel volumes, then, represent an important achievement: adopting the persona of Mark Twain to write comic travel letters. The background for what becomes *Roughing It* is suggested by items from the American West—photographs of important men in the territory of California, some of whom Mark Twain had mocked **(page 137)**; business directories of San Francisco **(pages 138–139)**; and the laws of the Territory of Nevada **(pages 140–141)**, to which Clemens contributed.

Sam Clemens inventing Mark Twain in Nevada and California tells a literary story not just of creating a comic persona (in)famous for its breezy style, which included a fast-and-loose attitude toward journalism and a habit of mocking well-known individuals in the territory. His extended sojourn in the West also gave Clemens the opportunity to evolve Mark Twain from a habitual dispenser of lampoons into a sharp-eyed satirist of the civic scene, both in Virginia City and San Francisco.

[KEY TO BRADLEY & RULOFSON'S "MEN OF MARK."]

A galaxy of persons of distinction on the Pacific Coast, also, embracing many persons of note who have visited California since 1849,—statesmen noblemen, artists, authors and others, whose talent, culture, wealth or birth give them right among the celebrated of the world, published by Bradley & Rulofson as a record of passing events.

OPINIONS:
"Most beautiful work of Art," U. S. GRANT. "Art in your hands surpasses itself," H. H. BANCROFT. "The Finest Photographs I ever had," DOM PEDRO.
"Thanks for kind attention and superb Photographs," SIR HARRY PARKS. "I commend these gentlemen to my friends in the Colonies," SIR REDMOND BARRY.
"The best in the World," KING KALAKAUA. "Your pictures admired by everybody at Melbourne," SIR GEO. FERGUSON BOWEN.
"A better picture than I ever was able to get in Paris, London, or elsewhere, has been taken of me by the firm of Bradley & Rulofson," P. T. BARNUM.
"Many thanks for "Men of Mark," recognize almost every one—grouped so skillfully," WM, T. SHERMAN, General U. S. A.
"All these pictures are splendid specimens of the Art which you have done so much to improve, perfect and illustrate." GOV. WM. IRWIN.

1 Sir Harry Parks
2 Iwakura, Japanese Minister
3 Hon. P. A. Jennings, Australia
4 Mark Twain, Humorist
5 Hon. R. C. McCormick, M. C., Arizona
6 Right Reverend Bishop Kipp
7 Hon. Leland Stanford, ex-Governor, Cal
8 General Coltou, C. P. R. R.
9 Duke de Penthievre, French Navy
10 F. L. Pioche, Capatalist
11 Sir Daniel Cooper " Baronet"
12 Wm. C. Ralston, Banker
13 Mrs. Partington—Mr. B. P. Shillaber
14 Wm. Laird McGregor, Gentleman, London
15 Howard Coit, Board of Brokers
16 Baron von Reibnitz, German Navy
17 Admiral Winslow, U. S. N.
18 Hon. H. H. Haight, ex-Governor, Cal
19 Anson Burlingame, ex-U. S. Minister, China
20 Hon. Frank McCoppin, ex-Mayor, S. F
21 Judge Miller
22 Henry Rochefort, Comunist
23 Loyd Tevis, Wells, Fargo & Co
24 Baron von Holleben, German Minister
25 Col. W. H. L. Barnes, Lawyer
26 Duke of Manchester
27 Brigadier-Gen'l George Crook, U. S. A
28 Prof. L. Agassiz, Naturalist
29 Admiral Farquhaar, R. N
30 Admiral Farragut, U. S. N
31 Pedro Mezarra, Sculptor
32 Postmaster Coey, S. F
33 Hon. Romaldo Pacheco, ex-Governor, Cal
34 Admiral Almy, U. S. N
35 Octavio Pavy, Artic Explorer
36 Hon. Newton Booth. Senator, Cal
37 Prof. D. C. Gilman, University, Baltimore
38 General McLellan, U. S. A.
39 Bret Hart, Poet
40 Joaquin Miller, Poet
41 Charles DeLong, ex-U. S. Minister, Japan
42 Wm. S. O'Brien, Capitalist
43 Jas. C. Flood, Capitalist
44 Count von Moltke, German Navy
45 Hon. A. J. Bryant, Mayor, S. F
46 Judge Dwinnell, District Court
47 Charles Crocker, C. P. R R
48 Brigadier-General John McComb, N. G. C
49 Reverend L. P. Hammond, " Revivalist"
50 Hon. Nathan Clifford, U. S. Supreme Court
51 Hon. H. Peirce, U. S. Minister, Honolulu
52 Viscount of Bom-Ratero, Brazil
53 Arthur T. de Macedo, Brazil
54 Hon. Thos. H. Selby, ex-Mayor, S. F.
55 Peter Donahue, Capitalist
56 Sir George Ferguson Bowen, Australia
57 Hon. Wm. M. Stewart, Senator, Nev
58 James Fair, Capitalist
59 Wm. Bradford, Artic Painter
60 General LaGrange, Sup't Mint
61 Harry Meiggs
62 H. I. M Dom Pedro, Emperor of Brazil
63 General Sherman, U. S. A
64 Hon. Simon Cameron, Statesman, Penn
65 Milton S. Latham, Banker
66 Hon. John P. Jones, Senator, Nev
67 Hon. A. A Sargent, Senator, Cal
68 Judge Delos Lake
69 Hon. Wm. Irwin, Governor Cal
70 James J. O'Kelly, N. Y. Herald
71 Lord D'Arcy Osborne.
72 Fred MacCrellish, S. F. Alta
73 Phil. Roach, S. F. Examiner
74 H. R. M. King Kalakaua, H. I
75 Judge Stephen J. Field, U. S. Court
76 Fred Marriott, S. F. News Letter
77 Hon. Cornelius Cole, ex-Senator, Cal
78 Cyrus W. Field, first ocean cable
79 Loring Pickering, S. F. Bulletin
80 Hon. Wm. Alvord, ex-Mayor, S. F
81 Hon. P. T. Barnum, ex-Mayor, Brid'pt Conn
82 Hon. P. C. Cheney, Governor. New Ham
83 Wm. Lane Rooker, British Consul, S. F.
84 Rev. C. T. Mills, Mills' Seminary
85 Baron von Oestreicher, Austrian Navy
86 Hon. J. S. Hager, Senator, Cal
87 General Schofield, U. S. A
88 I. Friedlander, the Grain King
89 James Donahue, Capitalist
90 Sir Redmond Barry, Australia
91 James Lick, Philantophist
92 Hon. Sharon, Senator, Nev
93 D. O. Mills, President Bank of California
94 Hon. Geo. C. Gorham, Secretary U. S. Senate
95 Col. Tom Scott, Railroad King
96 Duke of Genoa, Italian Navy
97 Hon. H. D. Blaisdell, ex-Governor, Nev
98 Hon. James Otis, ex-Mayor, S F
99 Hon. James A. Johnson, Lt. Governor, Cal
100 H. H. Bancroft, Historian
101 Hon. Wm. Schley, North Weston Railroad
102 Hon. B. Washburn, ex-Governor Mass
103 Hon. John W. Garrett, Prest. B. & O. R. R
104 Hon. H. B. Montefiore, Australia
105 Hon. Henry Failing, ex-Mayor Portland, Or
106 Baron de Roussin, French Admiral
107 Count Destoure, Austria
108 Bishop Kavanaugh, Louisville, Ky.
109 Hon John Parrott, Capitalist
110 Wm. H. Rulofson' " The " Photographer

Entered according to Act of Congress by Bradley & Rulofson, in the office of the Librarian of Congress, at Washington, D. C., 1876.

Henry William Bradley & William Herman Rulofson, photographers. "Men of Mark." San Francisco: Bradley & Rulofson, 1876. (Item no. 116)

A collage made up of 110 separate photographs of famous visitors to Bradley & Rulofson's San Francisco photography studio. Clemens was photographed there in April 1868.

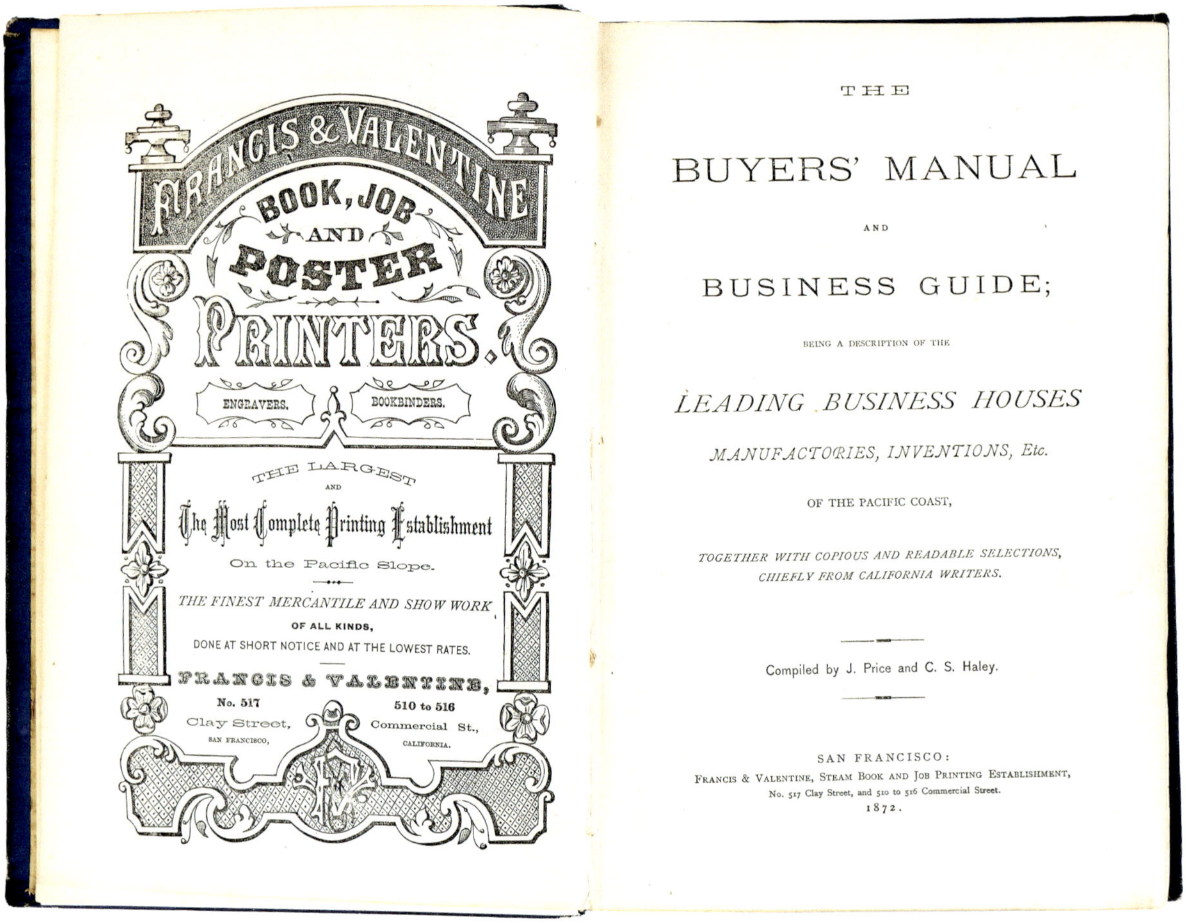

THIS PAGE AND OPPOSITE

J. Price and C. S. Haley (editors). *The Buyers' Manual and Business Guide; being a description of the Leading Business Houses, Manufactories, Inventions, Etc. of the Pacific Coast, together with copious and readable selections, chiefly from California writers.* San Francisco: Francis & Valentine, Steam Book and Job Printing Establishment, 1872. (Item no. 51)

This directory of San Francisco businesses also includes a selection of Californian literature, including Twain's "Jumping Frog," the sketch "The Public to Mark Twain," and the text of a speech he delivered at New York's Aldine Club.

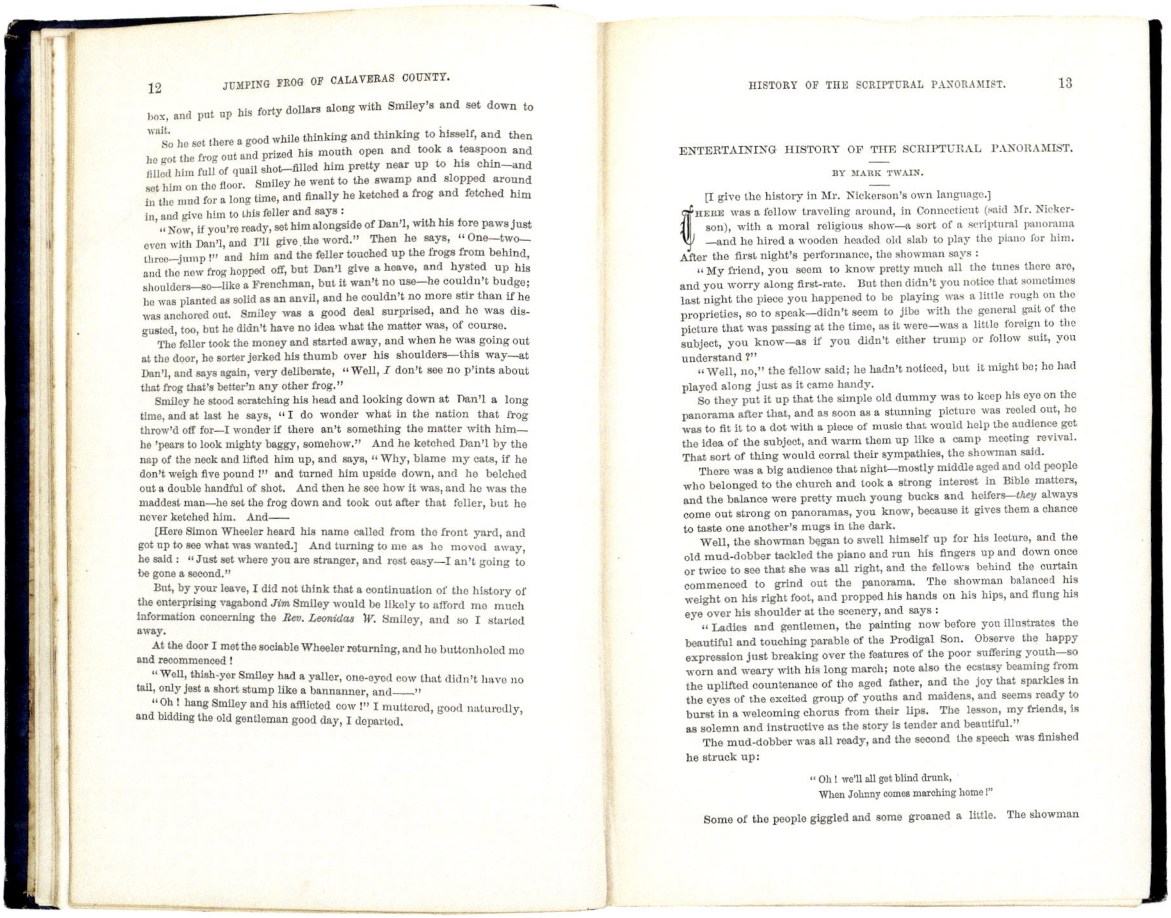

12 JUMPING FROG OF CALAVERAS COUNTY.

box, and put up his forty dollars along with Smiley's and set down to wait.

So he set there a good while thinking and thinking to hisself, and then he got the frog out and prized his mouth open and took a teaspoon and filled him full of quail shot—filled him pretty near up to his chin—and set him on the floor. Smiley he went to the swamp and slopped around in the mud for a long time, and finally he ketched a frog and fetched him in, and give him to this feller and says :

"Now, if you're ready, set him alongside of Dan'l, with his fore paws just even with Dan'l, and I'll give the word." Then he says, "One—two—three—jump !" and him and the feller touched up the frogs from behind, and the new frog hopped off, but Dan'l give a heave, and hysted up his shoulders—so—like a Frenchman, but it wan't no use—he couldn't budge; he was planted as solid as an anvil, and he couldn't no more stir than if he was anchored out. Smiley was a good deal surprised, and he was disgusted, too, but he didn't have no idea what the matter was, of course.

The feller took the money and started away, and when he was going out at the door, he sorter jerked his thumb over his shoulders—this way—at Dan'l, and says again, very deliberate, "Well, *I* don't see no p'ints about that frog that's better'n any other frog."

Smiley he stood scratching his head and looking down at Dan'l a long time, and at last he says, "I do wonder what in the nation that frog throw'd off for—I wonder if there an't something the matter with him—he 'pears to look mighty baggy, somehow." And he ketched Dan'l by the nap of the neck and lifted him up, and says, "Why, blame my cats, if he don't weigh five pound !" and turned him upside down, and he belched out a double handful of shot. And then he see how it was, and he was the maddest man—he set the frog down and took out after that feller, but he never ketched him. And——

[Here Simon Wheeler heard his name called from the front yard, and got up to see what was wanted.] And turning to me as he moved away, he said : "Just set where you are stranger, and rest easy—I an't going to be gone a second."

But, by your leave, I did not think that a continuation of the history of the enterprising vagabond *Jim* Smiley would be likely to afford me much information concerning the *Rev. Leonidas W.* Smiley, and so I started away.

At the door I met the sociable Wheeler returning, and he buttonholed me and recommenced !

"Well, thish-yer Smiley had a yaller, one-eyed cow that didn't have no tail, only jest a short stump like a bannanner, and——"

"Oh ! hang Smiley and his afflicted cow !" I muttered, good naturedly, and bidding the old gentleman good day, I departed.

HISTORY OF THE SCRIPTURAL PANORAMIST. 13

ENTERTAINING HISTORY OF THE SCRIPTURAL PANORAMIST.

BY MARK TWAIN.

[I give the history in Mr. Nickerson's own language.]

THERE was a fellow traveling around, in Connecticut (said Mr. Nickerson), with a moral religious show—a sort of a scriptural panorama—and he hired a wooden headed old slab to play the piano for him. After the first night's performance, the showman says :

"My friend, you seem to know pretty much all the tunes there are, and you worry along first-rate. But then didn't you notice that sometimes last night the piece you happened to be playing was a little rough on the proprieties, so to speak—didn't seem to jibe with the general gait of the picture that was passing at the time, as it were—was a little foreign to the subject, you know—as if you didn't either trump or follow suit, you understand ?"

"Well, no," the fellow said; he hadn't noticed, but it might be; he had played along just as it came handy.

So they put it up that the simple old dummy was to keep his eye on the panorama after that, and as soon as a stunning picture was reeled out, he was to fit it to a dot with a piece of music that would help the audience get the idea of the subject, and warm them up like a camp meeting revival. That sort of thing would corral their sympathies, the showman said.

There was a big audience that night—mostly middle aged and old people who belonged to the church and took a strong interest in Bible matters, and the balance were pretty much young bucks and heifers—*they* always come out strong on panoramas, you know, because it gives them a chance to taste one another's mugs in the dark.

Well, the showman began to swell himself up for his lecture, and the old mud-dobber tackled the piano and run his fingers up and down once or twice to see that she was all right, and the fellows behind the curtain commenced to grind out the panorama. The showman balanced his weight on his right foot, and propped his hands on his hips, and flung his eye over his shoulder at the scenery, and says :

"Ladies and gentlemen, the painting now before you illustrates the beautiful and touching parable of the Prodigal Son. Observe the happy expression just breaking over the features of the poor suffering youth—so worn and weary with his long march; note also the ecstasy beaming from the uplifted countenance of the aged father, and the joy that sparkles in the eyes of the excited group of youths and maidens, and seems ready to burst in a welcoming chorus from their lips. The lesson, my friends, is as solemn and instructive as the story is tender and beautiful."

The mud-dobber was all ready, and the second the speech was finished he struck up:

"Oh ! we'll all get blind drunk,
When Johnny comes marching home !"

Some of the people giggled and some groaned a little. The showman

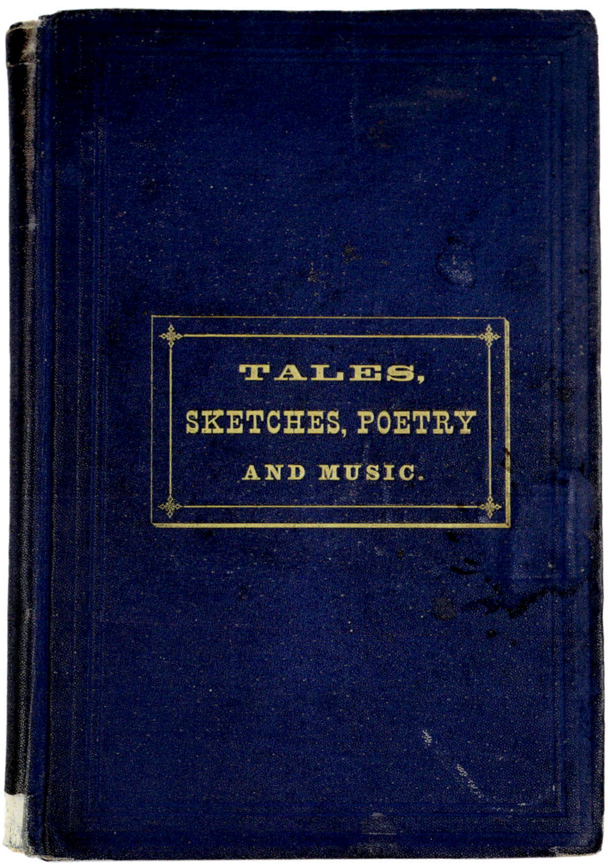

THIS PAGE AND OPPOSITE

Laws of the territory of Nevada passed at the second regular session of the legislative assembly... Virginia [City, Nev.]: J.T. Goodman & Co., Territorial Enterprise, 1863. (Item no. 49)

In November and December of 1862, Clemens worked for Joseph T. Goodman's *Territorial Enterprise*, published in Carson City. During this time, his brother Orion Clemens was Secretary of Nevada Territory, and the two helped draft the language of some of the laws recorded in this volume—though it is impossible to know what texts specifically originated with Clemens's pen. Orion also designed the territory's seal, which appears at the beginning of the volume.

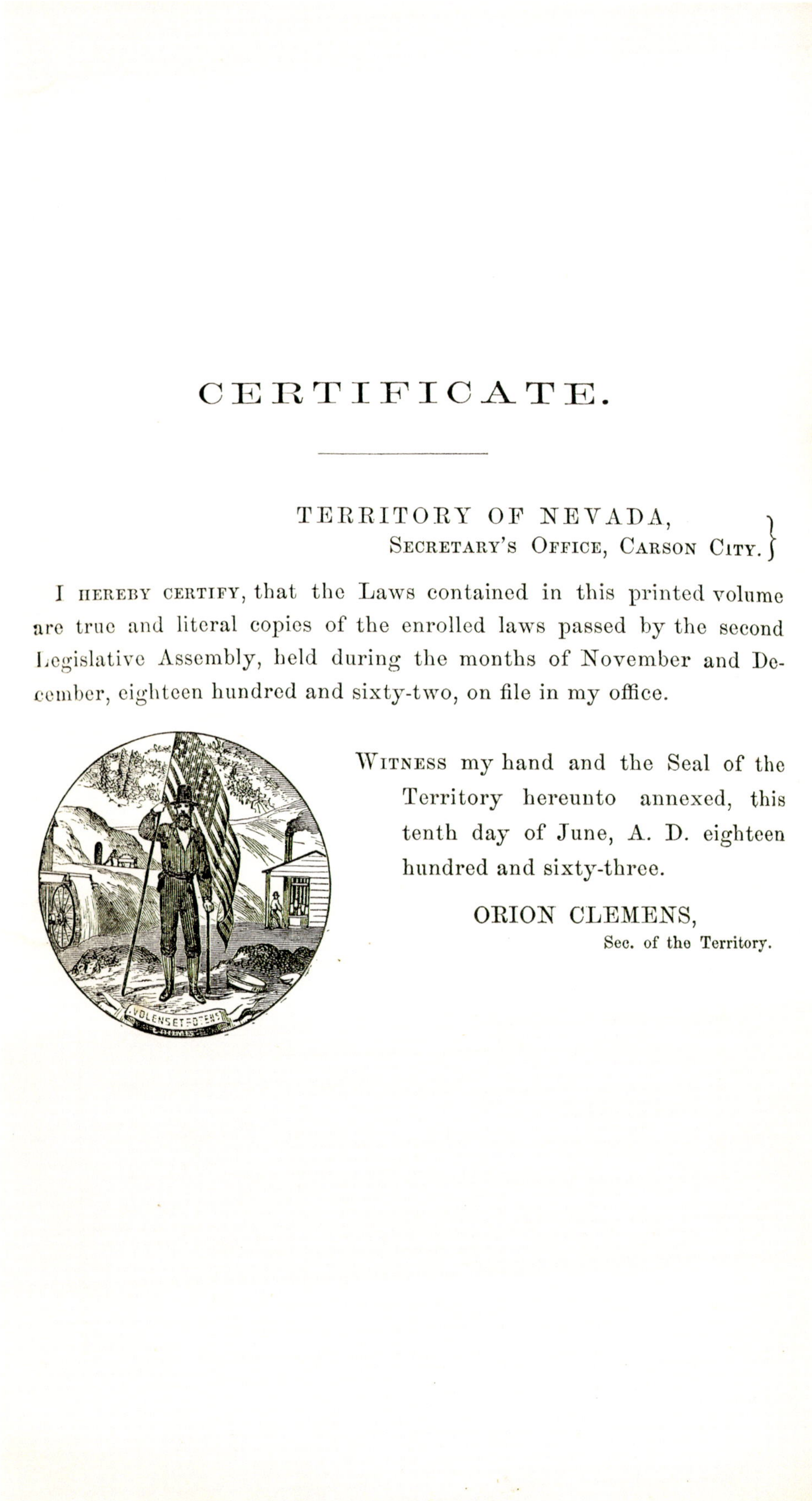

CERTIFICATE.

TERRITORY OF NEVADA,
SECRETARY'S OFFICE, CARSON CITY.

I HEREBY CERTIFY, that the Laws contained in this printed volume are true and literal copies of the enrolled laws passed by the second Legislative Assembly, held during the months of November and December, eighteen hundred and sixty-two, on file in my office.

WITNESS my hand and the Seal of the Territory hereunto annexed, this tenth day of June, A. D. eighteen hundred and sixty-three.

ORION CLEMENS,
Sec. of the Territory.

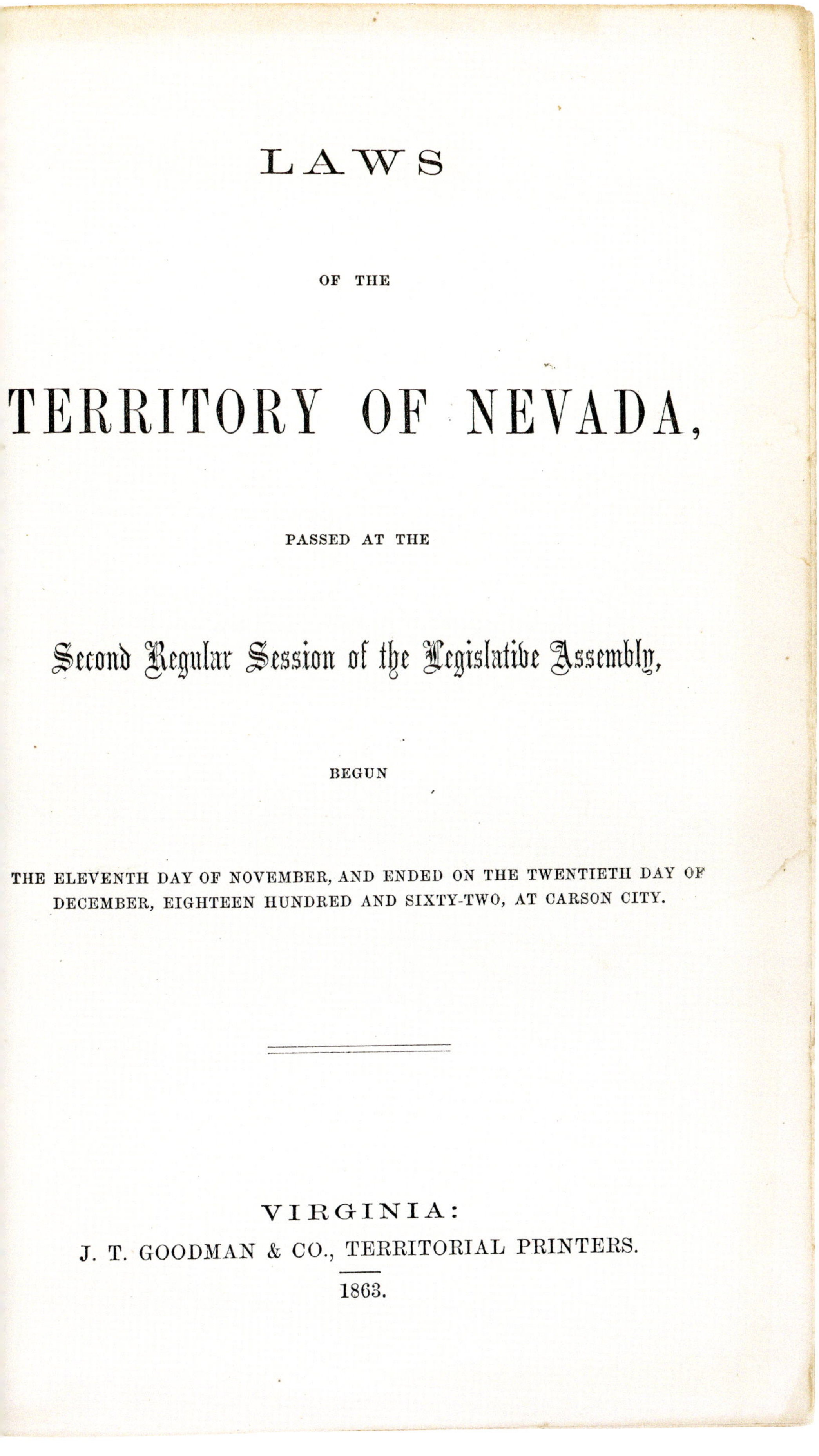

LAWS

OF THE

TERRITORY OF NEVADA,

PASSED AT THE

Second Regular Session of the Legislative Assembly,

BEGUN

THE ELEVENTH DAY OF NOVEMBER, AND ENDED ON THE TWENTIETH DAY OF DECEMBER, EIGHTEEN HUNDRED AND SIXTY-TWO, AT CARSON CITY.

VIRGINIA:
J. T. GOODMAN & CO., TERRITORIAL PRINTERS.
1863.

In the approximately fifteen months of Mark Twain's print existence in the Nevada Territory before he moved to San Francisco, so much of his comic personality had consisted of teasing people that an eighteenth-century English writer like Joseph Addison would have said he had "a humor for raillery." By May of 1864, Clemens, in the guise of his comic alter ego, had made fun of nearly all of the important men in Nevada and California. Clemens had also used his Mark Twain pseudonym to give a fellow newspaper reporter a derisive nickname, "The Unreliable," and then proceeded to fabricate comic stories about his uncouth behavior. These tales were immensely popular and did much to propel Mark Twain's career on the West Coast.

A well-known instance of his early comic pieces, "The Petrified Man," had as a principal target for laughter a coroner, G. T. Sewall. Also, the most well-known of his initial writings after inventing Mark Twain, "A Bloody Massacre Near Carson," worked in some teasing jabs at individuals along with its main satiric attack on the crooked business practices of mining. The habit of comic raillery, however, backfired when Clemens baited the staff of a rival newspaper, the *Virginia City Union*, about their pledges to a Civil War charity, the Sanitary Fund (forerunner of the Red Cross), and when he questioned the motives of prominent Carson City ladies about the disposition of their money raised for the fund. These supposed jokes earned Clemens not one but probably three aborted duels before he quit Virginia City, never again to make his home there. Moving to San Francisco, however, would not deter his humor for raillery.

The Sanitary Fund imbroglio, in truth, was the climax to a litany of perceived sins, at least as far as the self-proclaimed respectable folks in Nevada were concerned. The chief fault was Clemens the reporter too often morphing into Mark Twain the raconteur. Clemens's habit of embroidering the facts or just plain making stuff up particularly incensed a significant portion of his newspaper brethren.

The Mark Twain pen name, when it appeared in February of 1863, signified not only a comic attitude and a play frame; "Mark Twain" also signified to contemporary readers a license alerting everyone that Sam Clemens was just kidding when he said things that were not true about his friends and newspaper colleagues William Wright or Joe Goodman or Clement Rice—or even about fashionable women, as he had done with mock reviews of high society balls. "Mark Twain" meant fun first, not accurate reporting. These meanings, however, were not clear to all readers.

Clemens stood on firmer ground with newspaper colleagues, at least among the other local reporters on rival papers—Clement Rice and Adair Wilson of the *Virginia City Union*, Charles Parker of the *Virginia City Evening Bulletin*, Charles Sumner of the *Gold Hill Daily News*, and of course William Wright of the *Enterprise*—because of the reporters' long-standing custom of ribbing each other.

The initial success of Mark Twain originates with a clever manipulation of the custom. First, Sam Clemens had conformed to the rules of the game, kidding Clement Rice about being an unreliable reporter; he then elaborated on the custom, making up outrageous peccadillos committed by Rice rather than merely ribbing him about actual mistakes in his column. By telling stretchers about the behavior of Rice the Unreliable, Mark Twain in Nevada raised the stakes for which the mock feuds of reporters were usually played. Clemens does not invent the comic game of mock combats in print, but he beat everyone else at it with his extravagant manner of playing.

Many Mark Twain comic squibs and sketches in the Nevada Territory reach toward the outrageous in their imaginative impulse. That impulse carries Clemens beyond merely reporting for a daily newspaper, and it fuels his meteoric success with Mark Twain, ensuring initial publications in literary weeklies. Though Clemens achieved his first big success in newspapers, by 1864 he was also aiming for the more sophisticated readership of the weeklies. The story of Sam Clemens in San Francisco, therefore, becomes the story of how he reworked what could be called "Washoe Mark Twain," in deference to indigenous people in the territory (Caron 85–125). This more literary ambition aimed consistently for the middle to upper class and largely feminine audience that those literary weeklies represented, rather than "the boys" for whom the *Enterprise* staff wrote.

The more literary ambition of Sam Clemens in San Francisco was almost snuffed out at the very beginning when he was hired to be the local reporter for the *San Francisco Call*, which proved to be a mixed blessing. The editors had clearly hired Sam Clemens the reporter rather than Mark Twain the comic character; confidence in his reporting abilities did not include a license to joke. Clemens had to cramp down hard on his Mark Twain style of writing. His job, plain and simple, was reporting local events, a job he called "fearful drudgery—soulless drudgery" (*Autobiography* 2:115). In short order, he was fired. He decided to freelance, and he knew where he would be most welcomed: the highbrow literary journal the *Californian*, edited by Bret Harte and Charles Webb.

Writing for the *Californian*, Clemens reinvented Mark Twain, dispensing comic raillery as a literary critic and a social satirist **(pages 14–15)**. He burlesqued bad writing and chastised the San Francisco police force for its incompetence and corruption. Developing into a freelance writer for literary periodicals implied that the satiric possibilities he found as a *Call* reporter would be given Mark Twain's peculiar comic treatment. Moreover, freelancing not only meant the freedom to be satiric. Mark Twain could also operate as a comic *flâneur* when the character reports on the city scene.

The success of Mark Twain in the world of 1860s periodicals stemmed from extensive experiment and careful calibration of a comic style, one that staked out a large zone of middling taste between belles lettres as one boundary and mass popular literature as another. Clemens writing successfully for varied publications like the *New York Sunday Mercury*, the *San Francisco Golden Era*, and the *Californian* underscores the hierarchical nature of the periodical market when he shifted his focus from newspapers to literary weeklies.

Early on, Mark Twain's most consistent readership straddled lower and upper-middle taste cultures but had some appreciation of high-culture writers, too. Mark Twain spanned literary tastes. That commercial reach rested on a stylistic paradox. Writings signed "Mark Twain" fit comfortably into a standard highbrow view of comic material yet retained a daringly fresh and original quality that nevertheless acceptably packaged the potential subversiveness of comic exuberance, for instance, a comic anger that gives Mark Twain as persona a sharp edge to be used darkly or irreverently. Once Sam Clemens had conquered the literary world of San Francisco, once he transmuted his western experience into literary gold, Mark Twain was well on his way to national fame.

Jeremiah Gurney. Stereoview card of Mark Twain. New York: J. Gurney & Son, [1871]. (Item no. 112)

LEFT

The Overland Monthly, volume 1. San Francisco: A. Roman & Company, 1868. Bound volume. (Item no. 72)

The first four issues of this early Californian periodical contained sketches by Twain, all of which were later incorporated into *The Innocents Abroad*.

OPPOSITE

Oscar T. Shuck (editor). *The California Scrap-Book: A Repository of Useful Information and Select Reading*. San Francisco: H. H. Bancroft and Company, 1869. (Item no. 50)

An early anthology of writing from California, including some of Mark Twain's letters to *The Alta California* that were later incorporated into *Innocents Abroad*.

CALIFORNIA
SCRAP BOOK

Twain's *Autobiography* and Other Nonfiction

R. KENT RASMUSSEN

Although Samuel L. Clemens, aka Mark Twain, is best known as a novelist, most of his published writings are generally classified as nonfiction. From an early age, almost everything he observed fascinated him—from trivial details of ordinary domestic life and personal interrelationships to great scientific discoveries and world affairs. He began his writing career as a journalist, a vocation that trained him to pay attention to both local and world events, while fostering in him lifelong habits of reading and learning. From his late teens until he entered his seventies, he traveled widely and had a diversity of careers and experiences. Along the way, he wrote articles, editorials, and essays on numerous subjects and often worked his knowledge of the world into his fiction and lighter writings—almost always with brilliant humor. Although his writing interests naturally shifted over time, there was one subject in which he *never* lost interest—*himself*. It should thus not be surprising that he is one of the most autobiographical of major American writers.

One clear evidence of Clemens's interest in writing about himself is his heavy use of the first-person voice. His five stout travel books—which constitute the bulk of his nonfiction writings—are almost as much about *him* as they are about the places they describe. *A Tramp Abroad* (1880) **(pages 102–103)**, for example, about his recent tour of Europe, uses the pronouns *I*, *me*, *my*, and *myself* more than 3,000 times—an average of more than once for every two sentences. Many of his editorials and essays are as much about how *he* personally views his subjects as they are about their subjects themselves, and they typically include anecdotes about his own experiences. Indeed, some of his essays may justly be regarded as autobiographical sketches. Two prime examples are "My Boyhood Dreams" and "The Turning Point of My Life."

Clemens's personal presence is also felt in much of his fiction. What may be his most famous novel, *The Adventures of Tom Sawyer* (1876) **(pages 31–33)**, is an embellished fictional re-creation of his experiences and those of people he knew during his boyhood in Hannibal, Missouri. *The Gilded Age* (1874), a novel he co-authored with Charles Dudley Warner, begins with a fictionalized history of his family's migration to Missouri and models one of its characters on Clemens himself. Clemens even appears briefly in *A Connecticut Yankee in King Arthur's Court* (1889) **(pages 56–57)**, in which he serves as the frame narrator of an epic fantasy about a nineteenth-century American who travels back to sixth-century England.

Although it is clear that a strong autobiographical current flows throughout Clemens's writings, it can be argued that he never wrote a book everyone would regard as a true "autobiography." That may seem shocking, especially in view of the fact that at least ten different versions of Clemens's autobiography have been published. To account for this apparent discrepancy, we must consider what we mean by "autobiography." A generally understood definition is a chronologically arranged narrative of a person's own life that accounts for significant events and reflects on their significance in the author's personal development. Clemens wrote a great deal—a truly great deal—about the *events* of his own life, but he paid little attention to chronology and was rarely deeply introspective.

One of Clemens's earliest books is a slim volume titled *Mark Twain's Autobiography and First Romance* (1871). That, anyway, is the title on the American edition's cover. Inside, the title page reads: *Mark Twain's (Burlesque) Autobiography and First Romance*, with the parenthesized "Burlesque" printed in such tiny type it might easily be overlooked. Labeling the book a "burlesque," of course, signals that it is probably humorous and not a true autobiography. In fact, that book is not even a mock autobiography! Its primary text is actually a burlesque history of Clemens's mostly fictitious ancestors with nothing about his own life. The pirated Canadian edition (**page 147**) bears yet another title on its cover, as well as additional contents that make it larger than the first American edition. Among that edition's added texts is an 1,800-word sketch with some autobiographical relevance: "My Late Senatorial Secretaryship" (1868). Clemens actually served as a US senator's private secretary for a few months, but the sketch is mostly facetious. Clemens published the book to capitalize on the fame his first major book, *The Innocents Abroad* (1869), was then bringing him. Typically ignored in the Mark Twain canon, *Mark Twain's (Burlesque) Autobiography* is a silly book that Clemens would later regret having published. To suppress it, he bought the book's printing plates and had them destroyed.

Clemens would not take up serious autobiographical writing for several more decades. Meanwhile, he wrote extensively about himself in other forms—most notably in his travel books. *The Innocents Abroad, or The New Pilgrims' Progress*, is his account of the *Quaker City* cruise on which he visited the Old World for the first time in 1867 (**pages 52–53 and 108–109**). The success of that volume, the best-selling American travel book of the nineteenth century, helped make the name Mark Twain famous and

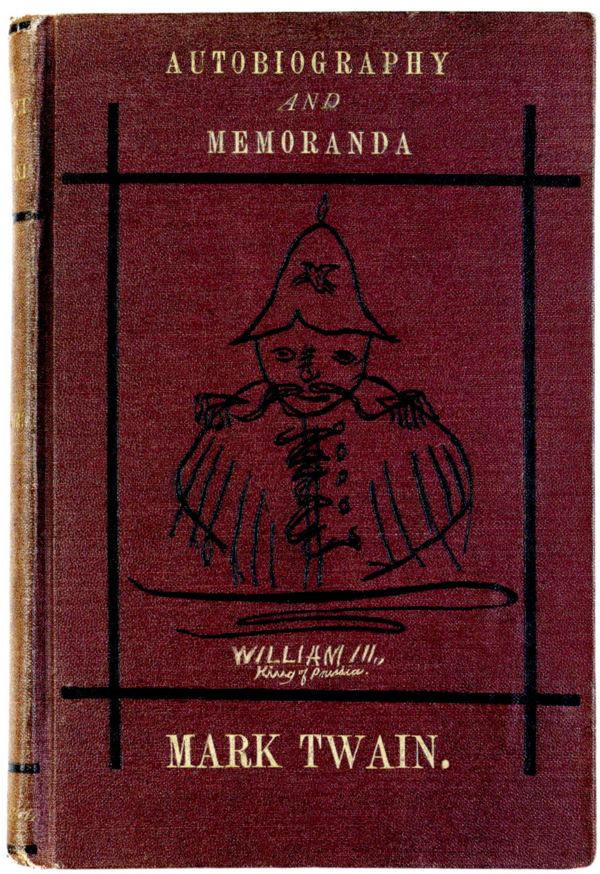

Mark Twain. *Autobiography, Burlesque. First Romance, and Memoranda*. Toronto: James Campbell & Son, [1871?]. (Item no. 40)

This unauthorized collection of Twain sketches features on its cover Twain's caricature of William III of Prussia. Following the publication of this volume, Twain took action to better protect his copyright in England and Canada, leading to a five-year lull in Canadian piracy of his work before the Canadian Copyright Act of 1875, which separated Canada from imperial copyright agreements, enabled a second major phase of unauthorized editions. The eponymous "autobiography" is an entirely fictional account that originally appeared in his "Memoranda" for the *Galaxy*.

set Clemens firmly on a career as an author. The book offers details of his journey and occasional reminiscences about his earlier life, but rich though it is in material about its narrator, it comes with a caveat: Not everything in it is true. Its overall travel account is basically factual, but many incidents it describes are either embellishments or things that never actually happened.

After finding a formula that worked in *Innocents*, Clemens not only repeated but also built on it in *Roughing It* (1872) **(page 231)**. In contrast to *Innocents*, his second travel book looked back further into his past—his six years of prospecting, reporting, and "vagabondizing" in Nevada, California, and Hawaii during the early 1860s. *Roughing It* also differed in focusing even more on its narrator. For these reasons, it resembles true autobiography more closely. Again, however, seeing the book as autobiography comes with a large caveat; it goes further in embellishing and inventing colorful experiences for its narrator, making so much of the book pure fiction that some people consider it a novel.

The very first lines of *Roughing It* signal the mixture of fact and fiction that is to come. Its unnamed narrator begins by announcing that his brother "had just been appointed Secretary of Nevada Territory" at a salary of $1,800 a year and was preparing to travel to the West **(pages 140–141)**. That much was true for Clemens in 1861, but then the narrator adds how much he "envied" his brother, for "his distinction and his financial splendor, but particularly and especially the long, strange journey he was going to make . . . He was going to travel! I never had been away from home, and that word 'travel' had a seductive charm for me."

Charming, but not quite true! By that time, Clemens had already traveled extensively throughout the Midwest and East and had just spent four years piloting Mississippi steamboats between St. Louis and New Orleans. Moreover, as a licensed pilot he had earned substantially more than Orion was ever to earn in Nevada. *Roughing It*'s opening passages thus signal to readers that while much of what follows is a true account of six years of Clemens's life, it cannot all be taken seriously. Clemens deliberately depicted his narrator as a timid and naive greenhorn in order to magnify the dangers and adventures that he himself had actually experienced.

Although Clemens's travel books cover significant periods of his life, their contents are scarcely the stuff of true autobiography. Nevertheless, those books do reveal a great deal about Clemens. In the preface to his Pulitzer Prize–winning biography *Mr. Clemens and Mark Twain* (1966), Justin Kaplan remarked that his biography "begins when its subject is already thirty-one and a journalist in San Francisco." That's the same moment *Roughing It*'s narrative concludes. Kaplan explains that he doesn't cover the earlier years because Clemens "was always his own biographer, and the books he wrote about those years are incomparably the best possible accounts, even if they may not always be the truest . . . " (Kaplan 9). Fair enough, but how can readers distinguish between fact and fiction in those books? In 1880, after having read *The Innocents Abroad*, *Roughing It*, and *A Tramp Abroad*, a correspondent asked Clemens himself that very question: "What I want to know is by what rule a fellow can infallibly judge when you are lying and when you are telling the truth. . . . I would suggest the next volume be published with the truth printed in italics." Clemens responded by jotting on the correspondent's letter: "Ha!--ha! | captured another idiot" (Rasmussen 75).

Clemens's next travel book, *Life on the Mississippi* (1883) **(pages 46–47)**, did not take up the italics suggestion but did add some new autobiographical twists. Eighteen of its sixty chapters comprise a poignant memoir of Clemens's two years as an apprentice steamboat pilot on the Mississippi during the late 1850s. Expanded from articles he had published in the *Atlantic Monthly* under the title "Old Times on the Mississippi" (Item no. 58), these chapters contain some humorous embellishments but otherwise resemble authentic autobiography, offering a coherent linear narrative and reflecting on the cub pilot's professional and personal development. The remaining chapters of *Life on the Mississippi* cover Clemens's return visit to the river in 1882. Along with their travel narrative, they contain some poignant reminiscences about his earlier life, including an apocryphal account of how he adopted his famous pen name, as well as tall tales of little relevance to either the river or Clemens himself.

Through the 1880s and 1890s, Clemens occasionally dabbled at autobiography, but such efforts rarely held his interest for long. Glimpses into his past can nevertheless be found in occasional articles, such as "The Private History of a Campaign That Failed" (1885). In that largely fictionalized account of a poorly understood period in his life, Clemens claimed to have served in an irregular Missouri militia at the start of the Civil War. Significantly, he wrote the piece around the same time the book-publishing firm he owned was preparing to issue Union general Ulysses S. Grant's *Personal Memoirs* **(pages 149–150)**.

A breakthrough in Clemens's motivation to write autobiography finally came in 1904, while he was staying

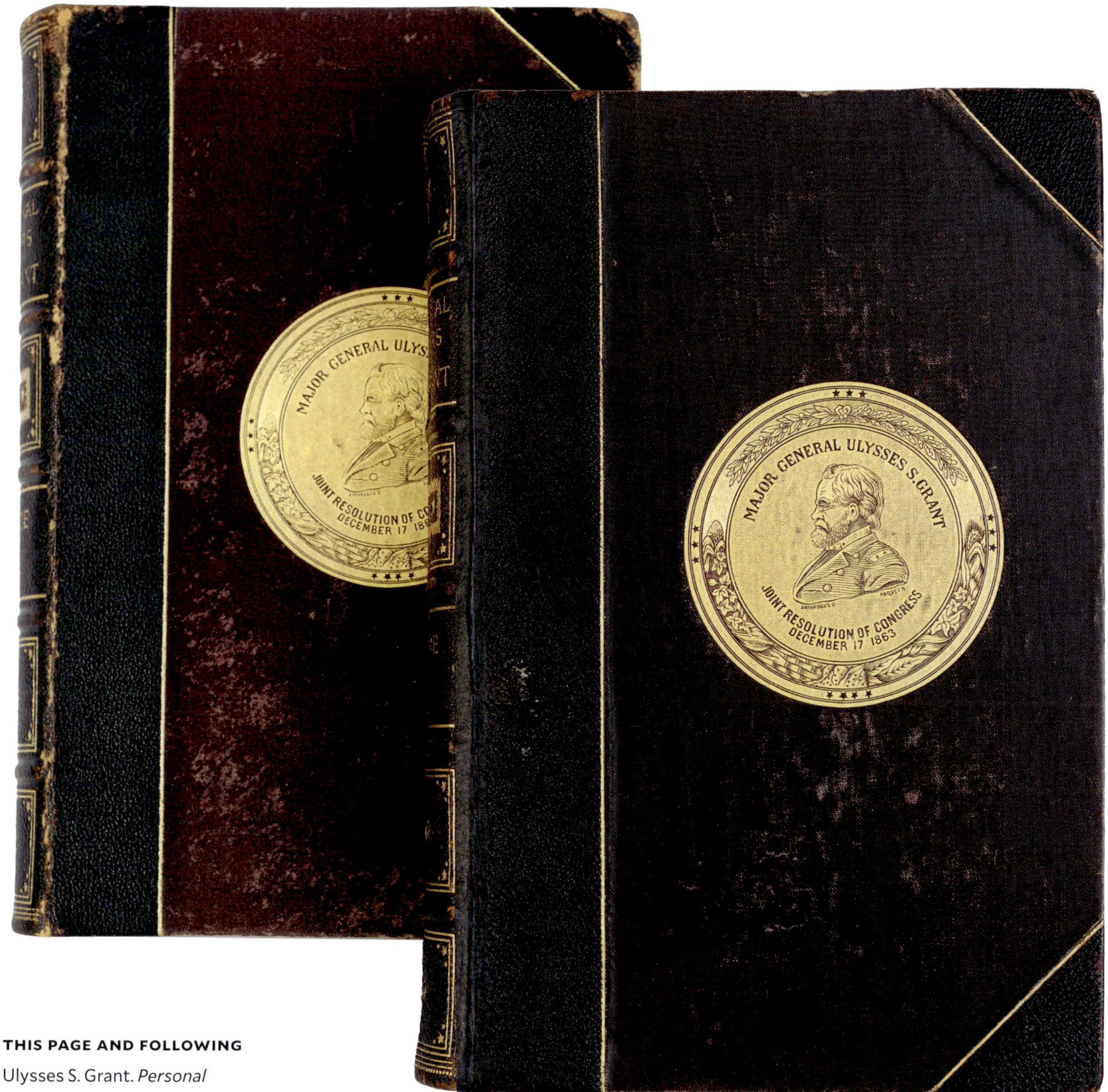

THIS PAGE AND FOLLOWING

Ulysses S. Grant. *Personal Memoirs of U.S. Grant*. New York: Charles L. Webster and Company, 1885–1886. Two volumes. Publisher's deluxe brown half morocco. (Item no. 57)

Twain assisted Grant with his memoirs—which he praised as "the best of any general's since Caesar"—and inscribed this copy to his secretary, Miss Fanny C. Hess.

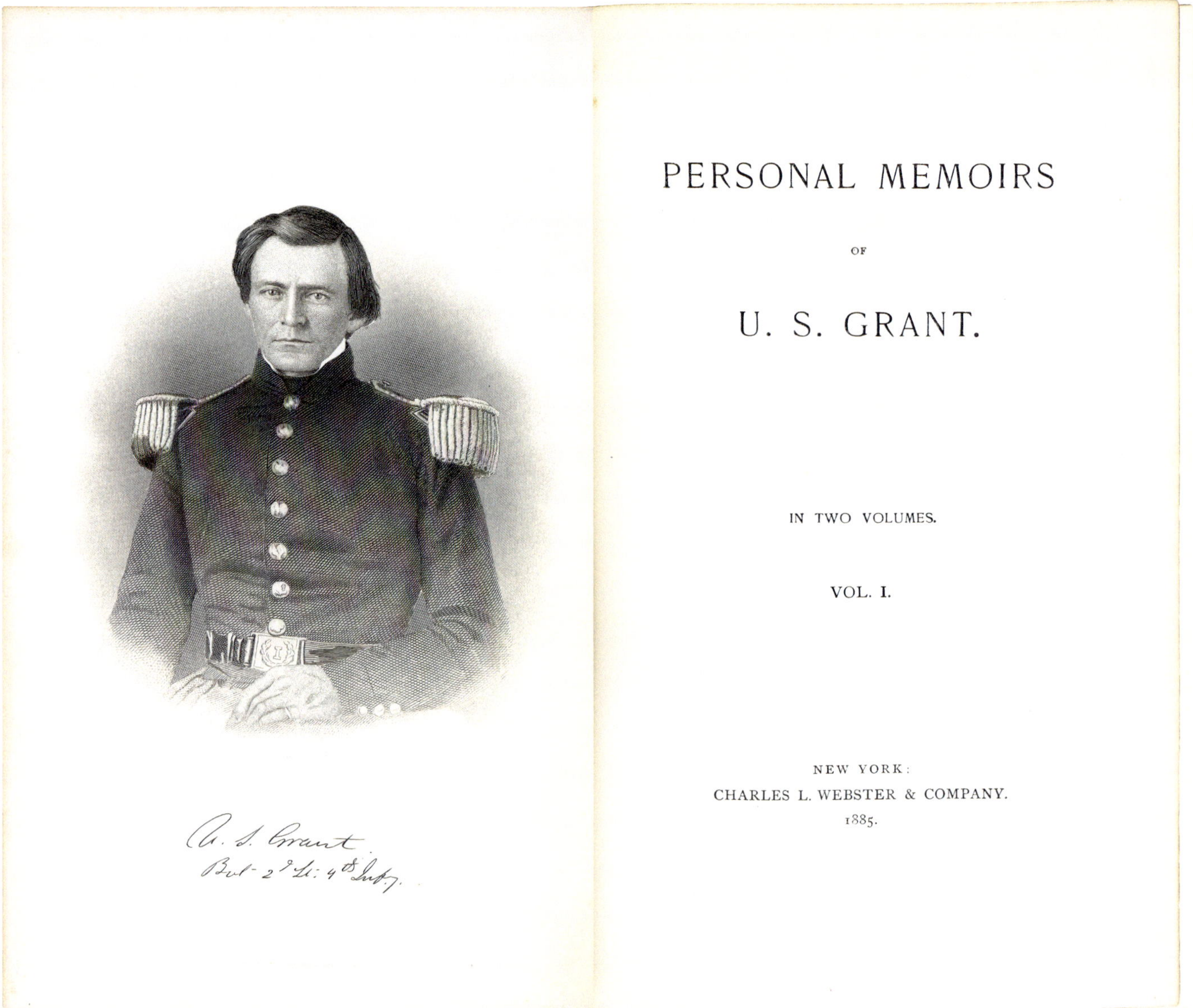

U. S. Grant
Bvt-2d Lt. 4th Inf.

PERSONAL MEMOIRS

OF

U. S. GRANT.

IN TWO VOLUMES.

VOL. I.

NEW YORK:
CHARLES L. WEBSTER & COMPANY.
1885.

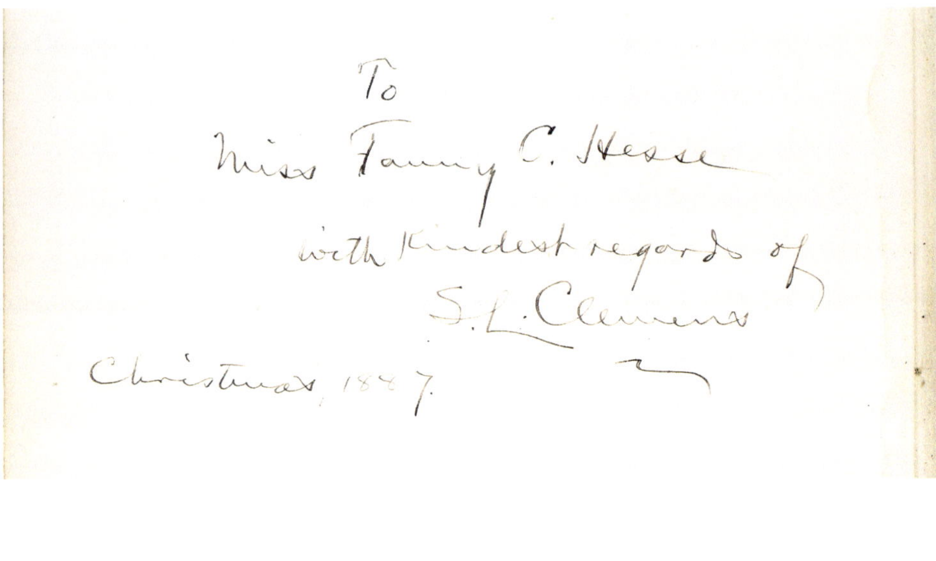

To
Miss Fanny C. Hesse
with kindest regards of
S. L. Clemens
Christmas, 1887.

in Florence, Italy, where his family had gone in the hope of improving his wife Olivia's health. Using his secretary Isabel Lyon as a stenographer, he was exhilarated to discover how easy it was to *dictate* his life story, especially to an appreciative listener. He gushed to his friend William Dean Howells that he felt like he could dictate "to the stenographer two hours a day for a hundred years . . . [and] still never be able to set down a tenth part of the things which have interested me in my lifetime." After Olivia died, however, Clemens returned to the United States and again set aside autobiography writing for more than a year. Finally, in early 1906, his future biographer, Albert Bigelow Paine, came into his life and restored his interest in autobiography. Energized by Paine's enthusiastic encouragement, Clemens dictated to a professional stenographer almost daily over the next two years. A natural speaker and raconteur, he hit upon a system in which he would talk about whatever interested him at the moment and then abruptly drop it and switch to something else the moment his interested flagged. The result was a sprawling, amorphous mass that eventually added up to the nearly half-million words that Clemens regarded as his formal autobiography. Its shapelessness has often perplexed and sometimes infuriated both its editors and its readers. Thanks to the endlessly fascinating complexities of its author's life, however, its contents and the brilliance of Clemens's ability to tell stories more than make up for its awkward structure.

At the time Clemens worked on his autobiography, he proclaimed he didn't want any of it published until one hundred years after he died, but a generous offer from the biweekly *North American Review*—and his need for money—moved him to relent. From September 1906 through December 1907, the *Review* published about 100,000 words in twenty-five installments titled "Chapters from My Autobiography." The same chapters also appeared in many American newspapers, including the *St. Louis Republic*, which printed them in its Sunday magazine (**pages 156–157**). Since 1990, the *Review* articles have been published in at least four different book editions.

The last book Clemens published during his life was the strange little volume titled *Is Shakespeare Dead? From My Autobiography* (1909) (**page 152**). It and his 1871 *Burlesque Autobiography* make curious bookends to his autobiography-writing work. Despite their titles, neither contains much in the way of Clemens autobiography. The Shakespeare book is primarily an unconvincing attempt to argue that Francis Bacon wrote Shakespeare's plays in which Clemens works in occasional comparisons between what is known about his own life and that of Shakespeare to make points about Shakespeare.

After Clemens died in 1910, his biographer, Paine, became his literary executor and then spent the last twenty-five years of his own life writing about Clemens and editing new editions of Clemens's writings, including previously unpublished works. Among the latter was Paine's two-volume edition titled *Mark Twain's Autobiography* (1924) (**pages 153–155**), containing about 195,000 words, including most of the material that had appeared in the *Review*, as well as some that Clemens didn't consider part of his formal autobiography. In 1940, Paine's successor as literary editor, Bernard DeVoto, published *Mark Twain in Eruption: Hitherto Unpublished Pages about Men and Events*, containing about 120,000 words not in Paine's edition. Nineteen years later, Charles Neider published *The Autobiography of Mark Twain* (1959), in which he added more of the unpublished material and reorganized everything into a more traditional chronological narrative, starting with Clemens's birth. Neider's edition was widely praised and remained in print for many years, but it was not the autobiography Clemens intended. Finally, exactly one hundred years after he died—and much longer after he had begun it—his final vision of his autobiography was fully realized. From 2010 to 2015, the University of California Press published *Autobiography of Mark Twain* in three volumes, precisely as he had planned it. Magnificently edited and annotated by the staff of the university's Mark Twain Project, it now constitutes the first and only complete edition of Clemens's *entire* autobiography.

Mark Twain. *Is Shakespeare Dead?: From My Autobiography.* New York and London: Harper & Brothers, 1909. (Item no. 38)

Twain's semi-autobiographical reflection on Shakespeare, with an autograph note by Twain pasted inside the front cover: "Shakespeare gets a lot of applause for Hamlet, but if you had written it you couldn't have got it accepted."

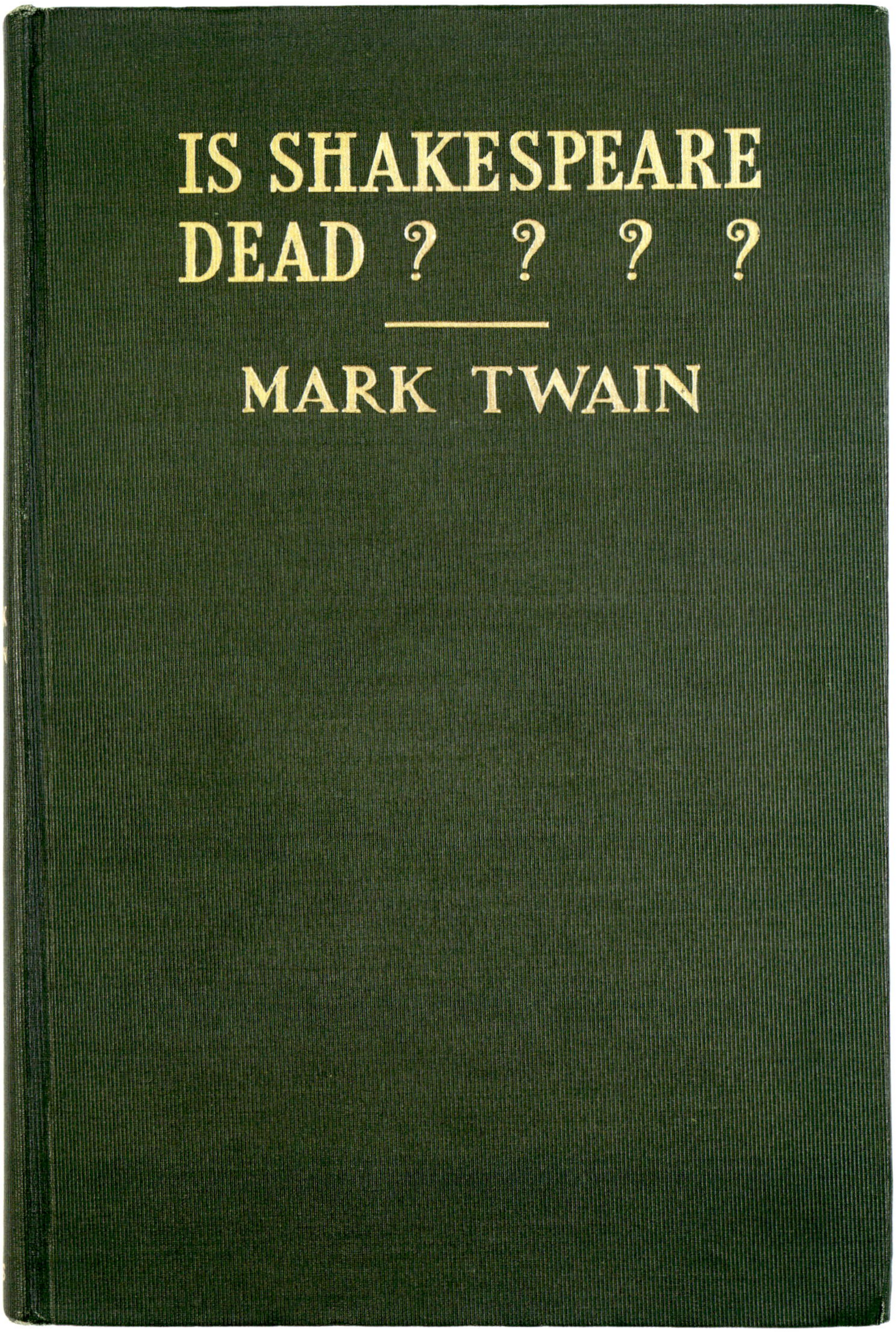

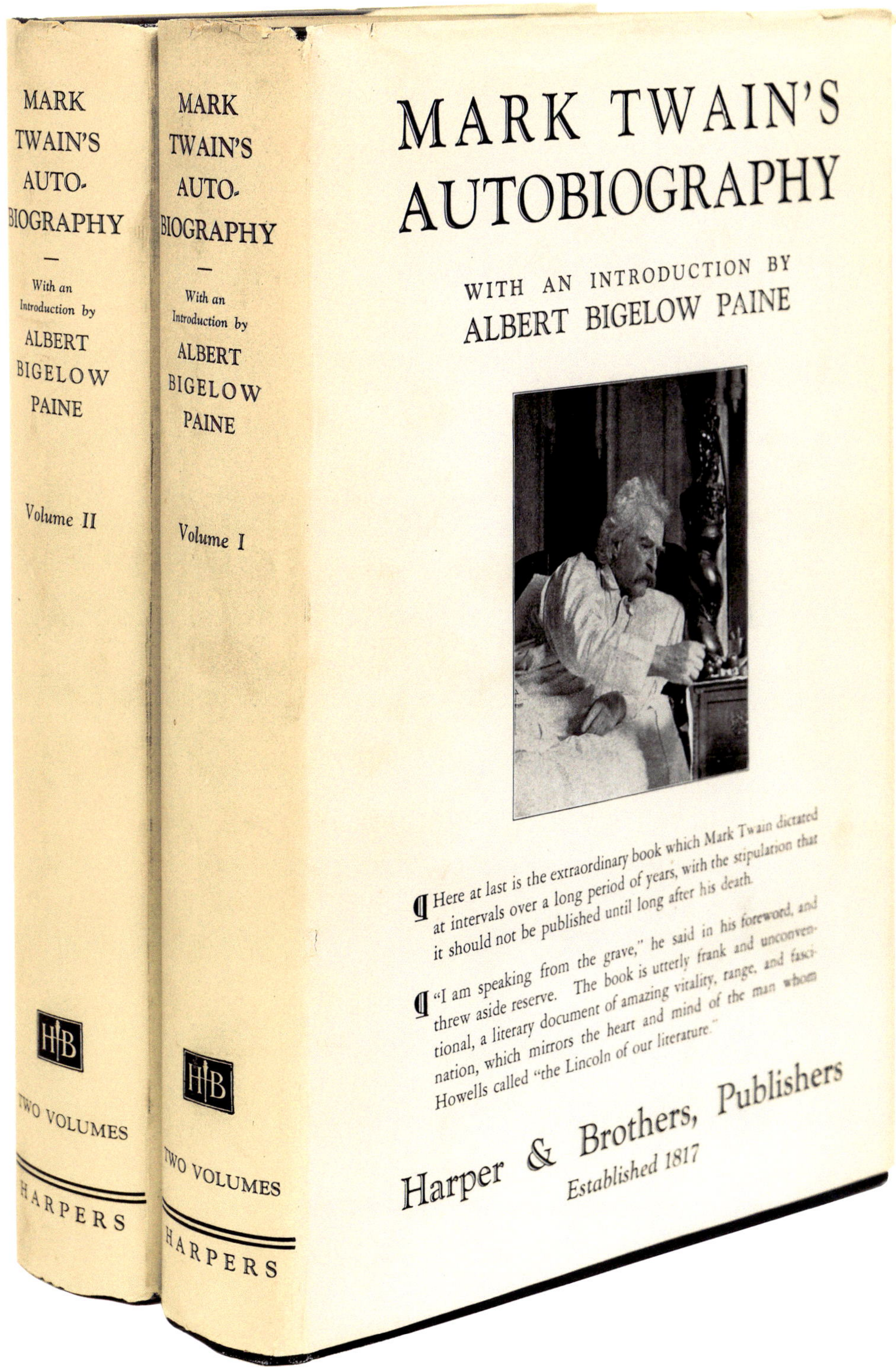

THIS PAGE AND FOLLOWING

Mark Twain's Autobiography. With an introduction by Albert Bigelow Paine. New York & London: Harper & Brothers, 1924. Two volumes. (Item no. 39)

Clemens began work on his autobiography as early as 1870, but intended for major portions of it to remain unpublished until long after his death; his embargo on the full work expired in 2010. The 1924 edition, containing under half of the full work, opens with a facsimile of a handwritten statement: "I am writing from the grave. On these terms only can a man be approximately frank. He cannot be straitly & unqualifiedly frank either in the grave or out of it."

I am writing from the grave. On these terms only can a man be approximately frank. He cannot be straitly & unqualifiedly frank either in the grave or out of it.

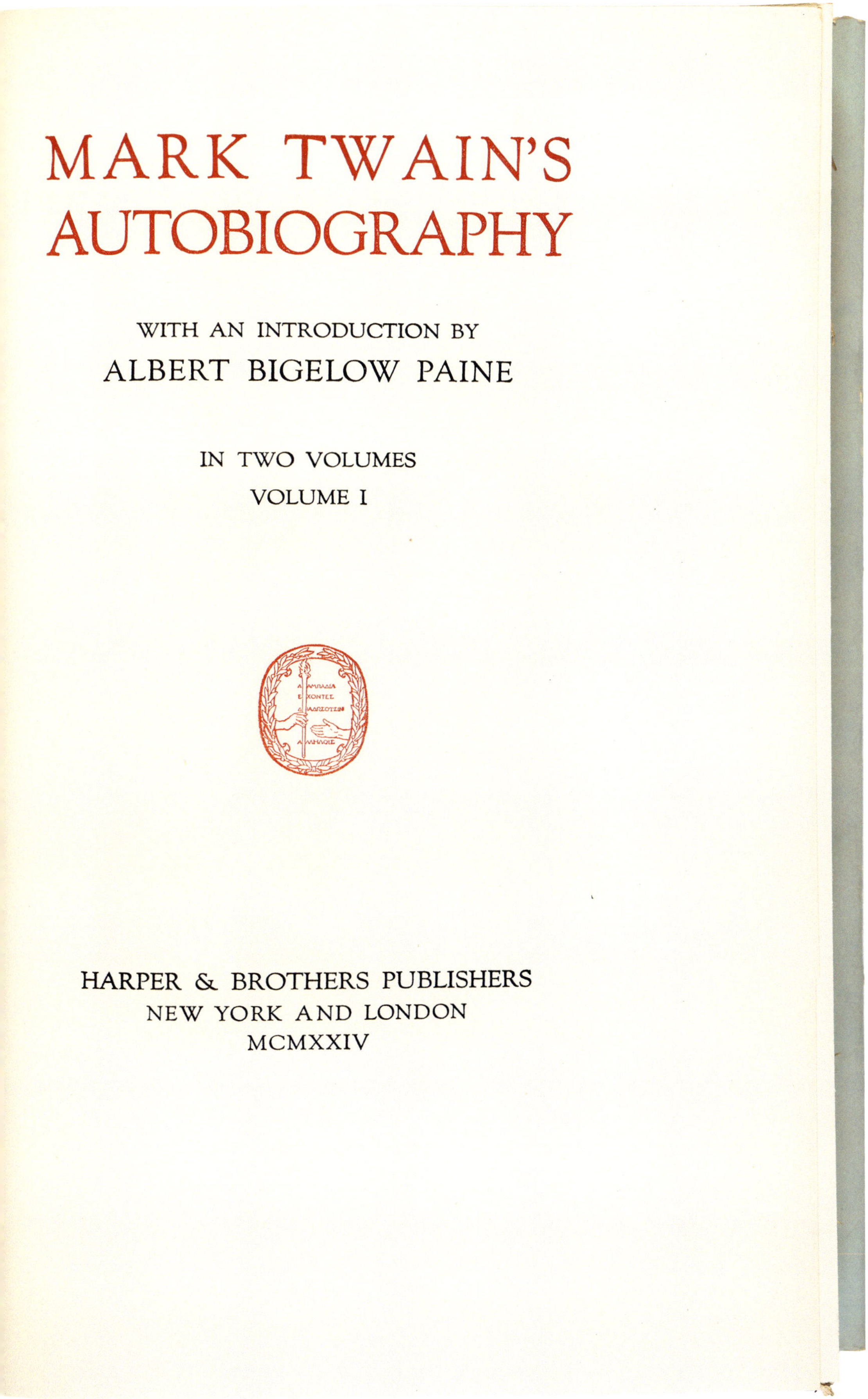
MARK TWAIN'S AUTOBIOGRAPHY

WITH AN INTRODUCTION BY
ALBERT BIGELOW PAINE

IN TWO VOLUMES
VOLUME I

HARPER & BROTHERS PUBLISHERS
NEW YORK AND LONDON
MCMXXIV

THE AUTOBIOGRAPHY OF MARK TWAIN

Drawing by F. Luis Mora

Introduction

I INTEND that this autobiography shall become a model for all future autobiographies when it is published, after my death, and I also intend that it shall be read and admired a good many centuries because of its form and method,—a form and method whereby the past and the present are constantly brought face to face, resulting in contrasts which newly fire up the interest all along, like contact of flint with steel. Moreover, this autobiography of mine does not select from my life its showy episodes, but deals mainly in the common experiences which go to make up the life of the average human being, because these episodes are of a sort which he is familiar with in his own life, and in which he sees his own life reflected and set down in print. The usual, conventional autobiographer seems to particularly hunt out those occasions in his career when he came into contact with celebrated persons, whereas his contacts with the uncelebrated were just as interesting to him, and would be to his reader, and were vastly more numerous than his collisions with the famous.

Howells was here yesterday afternoon, and I told him the whole scheme of this autobiography in my lifetime. I told Howells that this autobiography of mine would live a couple of thousand years, without any effort, and would then take a fresh start and live the rest of the time.

He said he believed it would, and asked me if I meant to make a library of it.

I said that that was my design; but that, if I should live long enough, the set of volumes could not be contained merely in a city, it would require a State, and that there would not be any multi-billionaire alive, perhaps, at any time during its existence who would be able to buy a full set, except on the instalment plan.

Howells applauded, and was full of praises and indorsement, which was wise in him, and judicious. If he had manifested a different spirit, I would have thrown him out the window. I like criticism; but it must be my way.

CHAPTER I.

BACK of the Virginia Clemenses is a dim procession of ancestors stretching back to Noah's time. According to tradition, some of them were pirates and slavers in Elizabeth's time. But this is no discredit to them; for so were Drake and Hawkins and the others. It was a respectable trade then, and monarchs were partners in it. In my time I have had desires to be a pirate myself. The reader, if he will look deep down in his secret heart, will find—but never mind what he will find there; I am not writing his autobiography, but mine. Later, according to tradition, one of the procession was Ambassador to Spain in the time of James I., or of Charles I., and married there and sent down a strain of Spanish blood to warm us up. Also, according to tradition, this one or another—Geoffrey Clement, by name—helped to sentence Charles to death.

I have not examined into these traditions myself, partly because I was indolent, and partly because I was so busy polishing up this end of the line and trying to make it showy; but the other Clemenses claim that they have made the examination and that it stood the test. Therefore, I have always taken for granted that I did help Charles out of his troubles, by ancestral proxy. My instincts have persuaded me too. Whenever we have a strong and is ancestral; it must be in the blood, for I could not have originated it.

And so, by the testimony of instinct, backed by the assertions of Clemenses who said they had examined the records, I have always been obliged to believe that Geoffrey Clement the martyr maker was an ancestor of mine, and to regard him with favor, and in fact pride. This has not had a good effect upon me; for it has made me vain, and that is a fault. It has made me set myself above people who were less fortunate in their ancestry than I, and has moved me to take them down a peg, upon occasion, and say things to them which hurt them before company.

A Question of Ancestry

A CASE of the kind happened in Berlin several years ago. William Walter Phelps was our minister at the Emperor's court then, and one evening he had me to dinner to meet Count S., a Cabinet minister. This nobleman was of long and illustrious descent. Of course I wanted to let out the fact that I had some ancestors too; but I did not want to pull them out of their graves by the ears, and I never could seem to get the chance to work them in in a way that would look sufficiently casual. I

THIS PAGE AND OPPOSITE

Sunday Magazine of the St. Louis Republic, part 6. St. Louis: Associated Sunday Magazines, October 27, 1907. In original wrappers. (Item no. 74)

This Sunday supplement to *The St. Louis Republic* reprinted *The North American Review*'s selections from *The Autobiography of Mark Twain* in 1907, as did the *Sunday Magazine* for many other journals around the nation.

SUNDAY MAGAZINE Of the ST. LOUIS REPUBLIC

PART 6 20 PAGES ST. LOUIS, MISSOURI OCTOBER 27, 1907

FROM PHOTO BY UNDERWOOD & UNDERWOOD, N. Y., COPYRIGHT 1907.

Mark Twain's Autobiography

COLONEL SELLERS FEEDING HIS FAMILY ON EXPECTATIONS.

Plate from: Mark Twain (Samuel L. Clemens) and Charles Dudley Warner. *The Gilded Age: A Tale of To-Day.* Hartford: American Publishing Company, 1873. Publisher's full sheep. (Item no. 12)

When Twain and Warner lamented the quality of the books their wives were reading, the women challenged them to write something better. The resulting collaboration is the book whose name lent itself to the era: *The Gilded Age*, a satire on post–Civil War American corruption. The first edition contained illustrations by Augustus Hoppin.

Photograph of Samuel and Olivia Clemens on a ship, 1895. (Item no. 117)

Even long past his days as a riverboat pilot, Clemens continued to enjoy traveling by water.

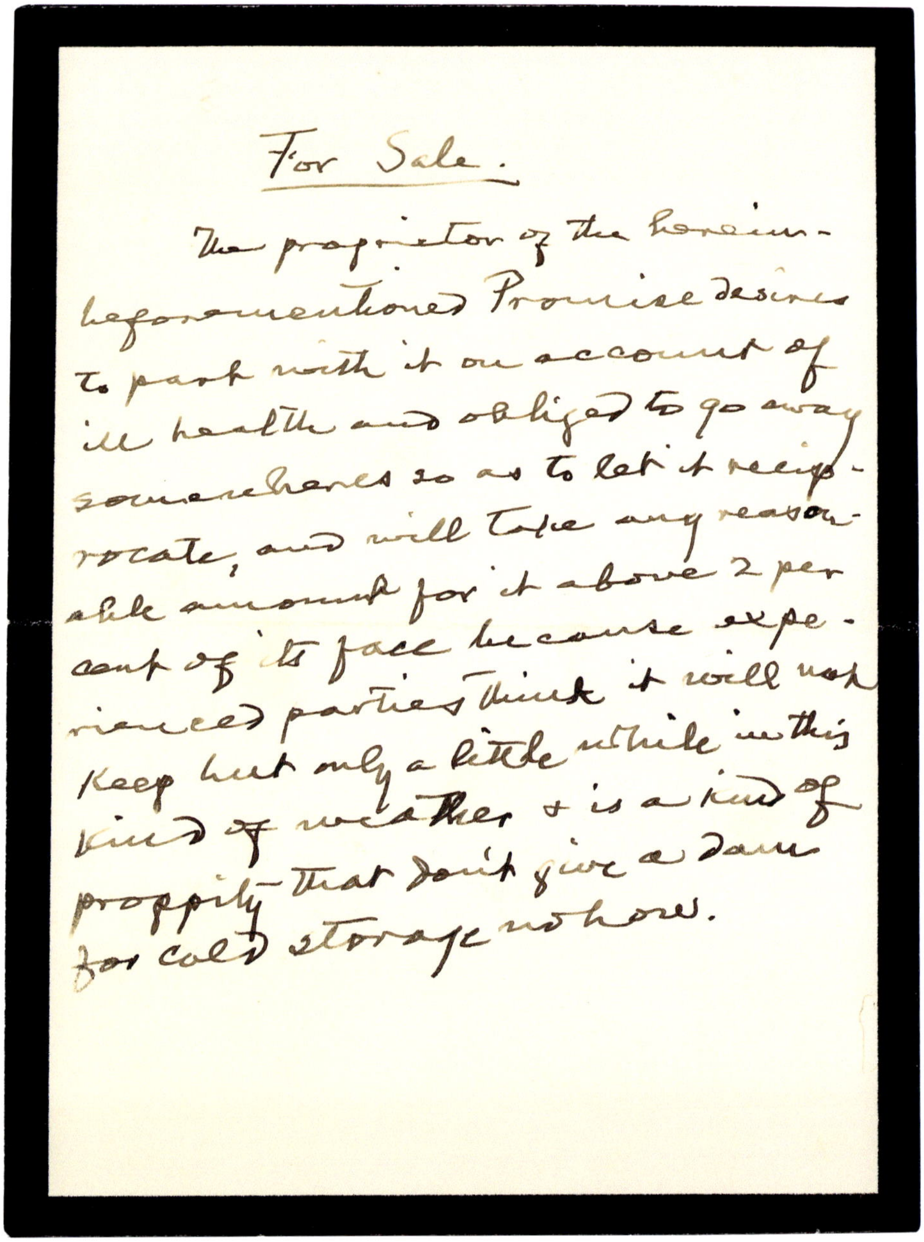

For Sale.

The proprietor of the hereinbeforementioned Promise desires to part with it on account of ill health and obliged to go away somewheres so as to let it reciprocate, and will take any reasonable amount for it above 2 per cent of its face because experienced parties think it will not keep but only a little while in this kind of weather & is a kind of proppity—that don't give a dam for cold storage nohow.

Samuel L. Clemens. Autograph receipt [and] "For Sale." [Bermuda]: March 6 [and ca. March 7–28], 1910. 2 p. (Item no. 89)

These two handwritten documents on a single folded sheet are some of the final writings in Twain's hand. Clemens spent the final months of his life at the home of William H. Allen in Bermuda. In the first document, Clemens writes out a receipt to Allen's daughter Helen, in which she affirms that he had given her two dollars and forty cents in exchange for her "promise to believe everything he says hereafter." Sometime over the course of the next few weeks, he added text to the sheet offering Helen's promise for sale, noting that she "will take any reasonable amount for it above 2 per cent of its face because experienced parties think it will keep but only a little while in this kind of weather & is a kind of proppity—that don't give a dam for cold storage nohow." Even in his final days, Clemens's sense of humor was undiminished.

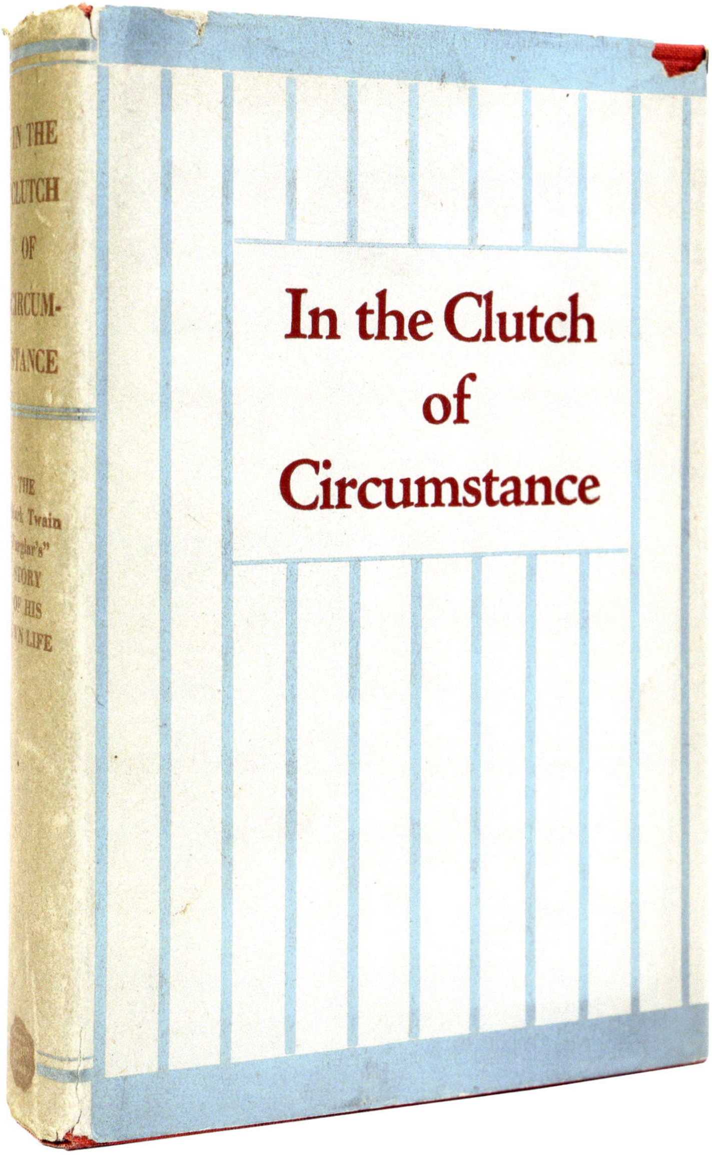

[Henry Williams.] *In the Clutch of Circumstance: My Own Story. By a Burglar.* New York and London: D. Appleton, 1922. (Item no. 83)

Henry Williams's anonymous account of his robbery of Clemens's home at Stormfield in Redding, Connecticut, which he dubs "the Mark Twain burglary."

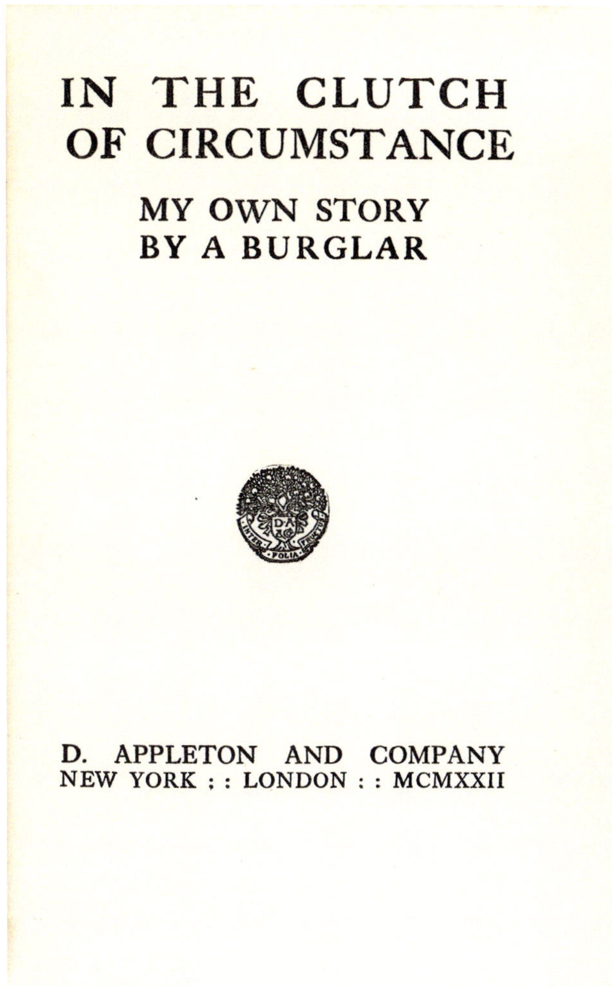

IN THE CLUTCH
OF CIRCUMSTANCE

MY OWN STORY
BY A BURGLAR

D. APPLETON AND COMPANY
NEW YORK : : LONDON : : MCMXXII

Mark Twain Influenced; Mark Twain, Influencer

KEVIN MAC DONNELL

Literary influences flow in two directions; one could even say they are twain. It's easy to imagine that they steadily flow in and out like the tides, but that would be an oversimplification. The influence an author has on readers and the culture does not flow out at a steady rate, but is transmitted through their writings, whose popularity and output can wax and wane. Meanwhile, the influences on an author's writings arrive at unpredictable intervals, and come from many different directions. Literary influences, going in and going out, can be complicated, difficult to pin down, and at times chaotic.

Twain recognized this confusing nature of incoming influences when he witnessed the variety of the influences—he called them "trainers"—that he observed when he and his wife were raising their children, and he knew from his own experience that these influences would continue for their entire lives:

> . . . we were reinforced in our work by the usual and formidable multitude of unconscious and unintentional trainers, such as servants, friends, visitors, books, dogs, cats, horses, cows, accidents, travel, joys, sorrows, lies, slanders, oppositions, persuasions, good and evil beguilements, treacheries, fidelities, the tireless and everlasting impact of character-forming exterior influences which begin their strenuous assault at the cradle and only end it at the grave. Books, home, the school and the pulpit may and must do the directing—it is their limited but lofty and powerful office—but the countless outside unconscious and unintentional trainers do the real work . . . (*A Family Sketch* 29)

Of course, literary scholars look first at an author's writings for evidence of what might have influenced those writings. Ideally, they also examine what an author has read—if there is supporting evidence like letters or books from an author's library. But this commonsense approach cannot ignore those other lifelong influences that Twain himself identified, even if those other influences are inherently speculative and often impossible to prove. It is well established that Twain's parents and siblings, as well as his Hannibal childhood contemporaries, Laura Hawkins Frazer and Tom Blankenship, all provided models for the characters and events in his fiction. Sadly, the identity of the innocent kitty who served as the model for the somersaulting feline who was fed Painkiller in *The Adventures of Tom Sawyer* is probably forever lost to history, as is the model for the hapless dog who disrupted the church service—never mind the model for that beetle who bit him.

The historical record does not always yield the evidence that is desired, but books from an author's library, notebooks, photographs, and even legal papers often bear fruit, as well as correspondence with family, friends, business associates, and even strangers, which often provide additional clues. Books, letters, and other printed and manuscript materials document the influences on Mark Twain's writings, and ample evidence of Twain's cultural influence includes visual materials and examples of products that reflect his status as a cultural icon.

The earliest literary influences on Twain's writings were newspapers and comic magazines, and his earliest writings reflect the tall-tale tradition, American folklore, and southwestern humor. By the 1860s, he was imitating the style of the Phunny Phellows, a distinctively American group of comic writers who pretended to be unlettered. They employed puns, misspellings (cacography), and malapropisms to satirize politics and social norms. Most of those comic writers were witty, but their humor looks strained to modern eyes, and much of it is crude and even racist. The most famous Phunny Phellow of all was Charles Farrar Browne, who wrote under the nom de plume Artemus Ward, and the most popular comic magazine of that era was *Vanity Fair* (1859–63), not to be confused with the later magazine of the same name that is still published today.

Twain was an attentive reader of *Vanity Fair*, as evidenced by his remarks about its rapidly declining quality of humor before, during, and after Artemus Ward's editorship, which he voiced in his oft-repeated 1871 lecture on Ward. In January 1861, shortly before Ward became editor of that magazine, Twain found in its pages a short anonymous comic sketch (probably written by Ward, who was a contributor before becoming editor) that featured some ignorant Confederate characters whose names were all puns on nautical terms, including one fellow named Mark Twain, a pun on the Mississippi River leadsman's call, "mark twain," which meant two fathoms (**page 164**). It was the first time the term appeared in print, used as a proper name. In February 1863, Sam Clemens, after having tried out a long list of pseudonyms, settled on Mark Twain as his nom de plume, and the rest is history.

For the next three decades Twain often found himself lumped together with the Phunny Phellows, and his writings were often compared to theirs, much to his chagrin. He did everything he could to distance himself from their fast-fading slapstick brand of humor as his own satiric and ironic humorous style evolved, but he was still being included in anthologies of Phunny Phellow writings as late as 1885 (**page 166**). Twain even made up a story about how he acquired his nom de plume in an attempt to obscure its Phunny Phellow origin and link it to his Mississippi River heritage, claiming in chapter 50 of *Life on the Mississippi* (**pages 46–47**) that he stole it from an old Mississippi River steamboat captain who had used it when Twain himself worked as a steamboat pilot. That story was debunked in the 1930s, and the name's origins remained uncertain until the 2006 discovery of its appearance in *Vanity Fair* (Mac Donnell, "How Samuel," "Mark Twain at Ten Paces," "Mark Twain Did Read"). By the time *Mark Twain's Library of Humor* appeared in 1888 (**page 49**), there were phar phewer Phunny Phellows left, but they were well represented in that thick anthology that included examples of every kind of humor that had preceded Twain's arrival on the scene.

Although Twain left school at the age of eleven, he was a lifelong voracious reader, a fact he downplayed to preserve his reputation as a popular humorist. He was certainly in tune with the popular tastes of his day from his readings of many comic journals; he also read several newspapers and most of the widely circulated magazines of his day. In reality, however, he was an autodidact who was well read in the Bible; the Greek and Roman classics; English, American, and European literature; and religion, politics, philosophy, and history. His readings were as deep as they were broad, and included poetry, biographies, novels, travelogues, plays, memoirs, anthologies, collected letters, and sometimes even the oddball books that aspiring authors and publishers would send him in hopes of provoking a useful blurb or a few words of encouragement. All of these readings influenced his own writings in ways that continue to be scrutinized by scholars (Gribben, *MTLR*).

Twain had approximately 3,000 books in his library and is known to have read about twice that many books and magazines. Books he owned show both the broad scope of his reading and his frequent annotations, revealing that for Twain reading was a collaborative act between author and audience. For example, in Twain's copy of *The Underground Railroad* (1883), by William Still, Twain has written out an account of two enslaved women who escaped to freedom, ending up in Elmira, New York, near Quarry Farm, where Twain and his family spent nearly every summer with his wife Olivia's family for twenty years (**page 167**). In his copy of *William Allingham: A Diary* (1907), Twain made a number of

THE NORTH STAR.

CONVENTIONS are all the rage. We give a report of one of the latest and greatest.

The Mariners of Charleston, having met to consider the propriety of abolishing the use of the magnetic needle, because of its constancy to the North, the following Resolution was read by the chair:

Resolved, That notwithstanding there is a very praiseworthy variation in the magnetic needle from the due North, still, in view of its uniform tendency to that odious and detested point of the compass, we consider its use, at least during the present juncture, as incompatible with a true affiliation and fealty to the South.

Mr. PINE KNOTT said he did not consider the resolution sufficiently comprehensive. Why not include the North Star? There were plenty of elegant Southern stars, that, as far as he could see, were just as good as the North Star; certainly they were brighter and larger. He had kept the "Ocracoke" full and by, for hours together by means of one or two Southern planets of his own discovery which he would make public if desired.

Mr. LEE SCUPPER didn't see no use in no stars n-o-way, nor no stripes neither. A man that couldn't sail his vessel without them scientific thingemagigs warn't no sailer. People might talk about the star spangled banner, and the bones of their aunt's sisters, in his opinion the star spangled banner was a *rag*. (*Sensation*.)

Mr. MARK TWAIN proposed to insert the words "Northern half," so as to make the resolution apply to the Northern half only of the needle. He did not see why the Southern half should not be retained. (*Applause*.)

Mr. ROBERT STAY didn't know much about the magnetic needle, as he had never used 'em, but he knew it was something like a sail needle with the eye out. He did have a compass once, but when he got outside, and the "Polly Ann" began to jump, the needle wiggled about so that he had to make it fast with a bit of spun-yarn. He generally steered for the fishing banks, and kept the lights abeam. He was in the Tar business himself, and was not ashamed of it. It was a fortunate thing that the South is a tar country, she had her tar and her tars, and the North might find they had caught Tartars. (*Shudders*.) He would advise abolition emissaries to haul their wind out o' this as soon as possible. In his opinion the Ship of State had missed stays and wouldn't go about, they were all "hard up" at the North, instead of being hard down and standing by the sheets and braces; and if Captain BUCHANAN didn't keep his weather eye skinned, they'd be on the banks. The Captain ought to send some one aloft as know'd a flash light from a sailor's pipe, and could tell an outer buoy from a porpoise.

Mr. RATTLIN was glad to hear that Mr. STAY was in the Tar business. He had heard that GERRIT SMITH and WENDELL PHILLIPS were coming South this winter, for the benefit of their health.

After a little further discussion the resolution was carried as amended.

China Ware vs. Domestic.

All are amazed, that John Bull razed
John Chinaman's Pekin,
We are not praised, though we have raised
The hull of John P. King.

Fruits of War.

When an army is about Raisin' a siege, do they always use Grape shot?

BEFORE THE RESTAURANT.

I stand at the corner of Chambers Street
With frozen hands and with frozen feet;
Like ærial diamonds the fine white snow
Wafts on the keen wind to and fro,
And the draught of the cheerless street strikes in
With its cutting fangs through my shivering skin,
Yet I brave the cold and the withering sky;
And stand at the corner—I'll tell you why.

Less than an hour since, down Broadway,
I saw him dash in his splendid sleigh,
With his slender form and his face so fair,
Wrapt in the skin of the Russian bear;
And gay companions were at his side,
Muffled and furred for the joyous ride—
The butterfly friend and the gorgeous swell,
Till they all pulled up at the gay hotel.

I watched the windows and saw the light
Up in the corner room shine bright;
And through dim frost over the glass,
Coming and going I saw him pass;
I couldn't mistake him, and I can swear
That I heard his voice on the frosty air,
Laughing and jesting with careless glee,
But he didn't see me—he didn't see me!

Though I'm almost blind with the thickening snow,
I can tell when the waiters come and go.
I know the thing—'tis the same old strain—
Claret and Burgundy and Champagne,
And delicate dishes to please the sense;
Who cares—not he—for the small expense!
The bill is nothing to him—but I
Am alone and starving—I'll tell you why.

But no—I will not, the tale is old,
And by thousands of quivering lips been told.
'Tis the same old tale, and the same old song
Of man's deception and woman's wrong.
Oh! you curve your lip, and you frown me down,
And you hunt me over the pitiless town,
But look at him—he is blithe and gay,
Which of the two has the best of it, pray?

Thicker and thicker the air becomes,
And the cold my every limb benumbs.
Oh for one deep and vital draught
Of that ruby wine which he just has quaffed!
Is life worth having when this is life?
My heart is crushed with the bitter strife—
So I'll wander down where the ferry-boats lie,
And the morning papers may tell you why!

SEASONABLE THOUGHTS.

How rich a material for costume is fur! how nice Mrs. MENDIP looked to-day in her squirrel cloak, martin boa, mink muff and chinchilla skating cap! But one must be reserved upon the subject of fur; you must not tell the whole truth about it in polite society. Suppose, for instance, that you were to say in some amber-lighted drawing-room—"I saw Mrs. MENDIP to-day, and she was dressed entirely in the skins of wild beasts." Try that once, and you will be socially branded with H for Hottentot and left to perish.

Did anybody ever yet see a man of fashion proceeding through the streets with a pair of boots in his hand? Certainly not, unless the thing was done for a wager; the man who kicked at society with his boots in such a way would find the recoil too much for him. But every day that the "ball is up," swells of the heaviest metal may be seen proceeding in the direction of Central Park, each with a pair of those winter shoes known as skates dangling from his wrist. Fashion then, it seems, forbids its votaries to carry about on any pretext whatever, foot-gear constructed exclusively of leather, while she decidedly encourages the hawking round of that kind into the composition of which steel and wood enter as well. Skate on, Fashion!—since boots are so vulgar, no longer let your children walk!

Our German Again.

I dinks Mishter RAREY soofers pooty bad as some vorse *allaweil*. I sees in de bapers he catches a vresh colt moost avery day.

annotations in the text, calling Teddy Roosevelt "insane," taking issue with Allingham's calling suicide "silly," and even, on a page where Twain's pen dripped some ink, provoking Twain to jot down a note nearby: "Oh, damn!" **(page 168)**. We can continue reading over Twain's shoulder in Moncure Conway's *Autobiography: Memories and Experiences* (1904), with Twain's annotations totaling over 500 words, which no doubt influenced the writing of Twain's own autobiography that he was dictating at the time he was reading this book **(page 169)**. Finally, Richard Irving Dodge's *Our Wild Indians* (1883) is one of several books Twain used when writing one of his sequels to *Adventures of Huckleberry Finn*, heavily marked with more than 350 annotations totaling over 1,200 words (see the essay by Kerry Driscoll in this volume) **(pages 182–183)**.

While the textual influences on Twain can be clearly documented, *his* influence on American literature and culture is more complicated. Unlike most nineteenth-century literary figures, Twain was both an author and a cultural icon, with the result that his influence is felt beyond that of his writings alone. His cultural influence also draws on his celebrity, his carefully crafted public image and persona, and his countless lectures, speeches, aphorisms, and interviews. His influence has flowed out like a high tide in reverse for more than 150 years, at times like a tsunami, extending beyond US borders, and is reflected not only in books, but in the visual arts, the performing arts, the media, politics, education, consumer goods, tourist destinations, and the very character of American humor itself. Very few authors of any era have had this kind of dual influence on their native literature and culture, and even fewer have exerted that influence in so many different venues, for the simple reason that few literary figures have enjoyed a truly iconographic celebrity status during their lifetimes that could be sustained after their death.

Twain's influence has been felt both in literature and on the culture. His influence on American literature has been profound, and the list of authors influenced by Twain is a long one. This influence was expressed in an interesting way when Norman Mailer once wrote that although his first reading of *Huckleberry Finn* (1885) was a disappointment, his second reading was a revelation, and he felt like he was reading a recent novel by a modern author who had been heavily influenced by—and who had borrowed liberally from—older writers like Ernest Hemingway, William Faulkner, John Steinbeck, John Dos Passos, J. D. Salinger, Kurt Vonnegut, Joseph Heller, Saul Bellow, James Dickey, and even the actors John Wayne and Burt Reynolds (Mailer 4–5). Mailer's roster is representative but incomplete, and Twain's influence continues unabated on contemporary authors.

In addition to literature, Twain's influence has permeated American culture, and can appear in some surprising places. His name and image have been attached to more vendable products, places, services—and even living creatures—than might be expected, including hotels, cafés, banks, coal companies, parks, resorts, candies, whiskies, beers, wines, sodas, watches, toys, games, cigars, awards, dolls, motorboats, slingshots, stamps, coins, comics, shirts, pants, suspenders, mink stoles, shoes, soaps, a train, a passenger jet, all kinds of food, several horses, at least one cave, a redwood tree, and one entire national forest.

Mark Twain's name and image have been attached to things associated with his writings (Mark Twain Cave) and his image (Mark Twain Cigars) **(pages 170–173)**, but just as often they have been attached to things that defy logic, like those horses or a jet. But, no matter; given his track record it is safe to assume that Mark Twain's cultural and literary influence will continue unabated for generations to come.

OPPOSITE

Vanity Fair, volume 3. New York: Louis H. Stephens, 1861. (Item no. 81)

The January 26, 1861, issue of *Vanity Fair*—a humor magazine edited by Clemens's friend Charles Farrar Browne aka Artemus Ward that bears no relation to the current serial of the same title—includes a sketch titled "The North Star," which features a character named Mark Twain. This is presumably the original source of Clemens's iconic pen name.

PHUNNY PHELLOWS

Mark Twain,
Josh Billings, Robt. Burdette,
Artemus Ward,
AND OTHERS.

CHICAGO.
RHODES & McCLURE,

Phunny Phellows: Mark Twain, Josh Billings, Robt. Burdette, Artemus Ward, and others. Chicago: Rhodes & McClure, 1885. (Item no. 80)

The group of humorists known as the "Phunny Phellows" produced broad and folksy humor that often depended on comic misspellings. Twain resented being associated with these authors, whose work often lacked his sharper satirical aims.

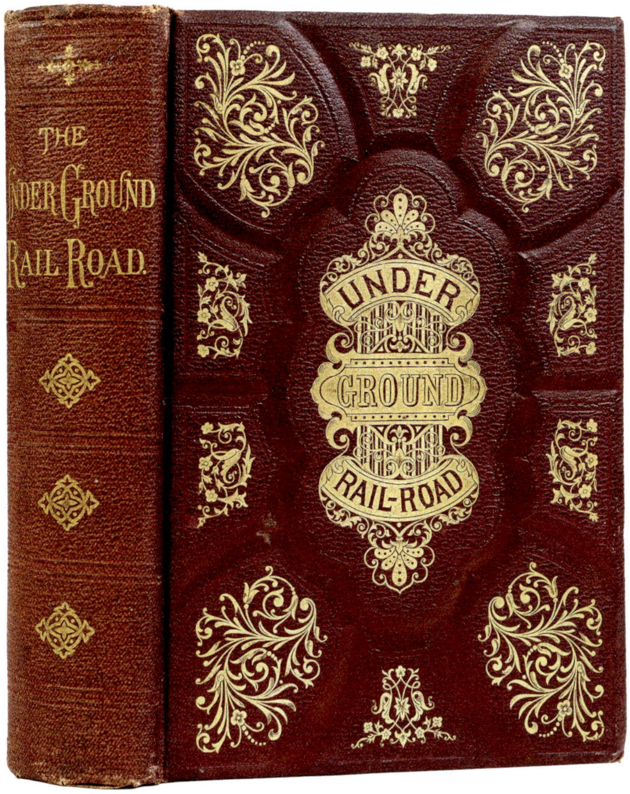

William Still. *The Underground Rail Road. A Record of Facts, Authentic Narratives, Letters, Etc. Narrating the Hardships, Hair-Breadth Escapes and Death Struggles of the Slaves in the Efforts for freedom, as related by themselves and others, or witnessed by the author; together with Sketches of Some of the Largest Stockholders, and Most Liberal Aiders and Advisers, of the Road.* Philadelphia: Wm. Still, 1883. (Item no. 78)

Clemens's copy, with his autograph note recounting the story of two formerly enslaved women who escaped to Quarry Farm, where they reunited with their family member. Still, a leading Black abolitionist hailed as "the father of the Underground Rail Road," collects firsthand accounts of formerly enslaved people's journeys to freedom.

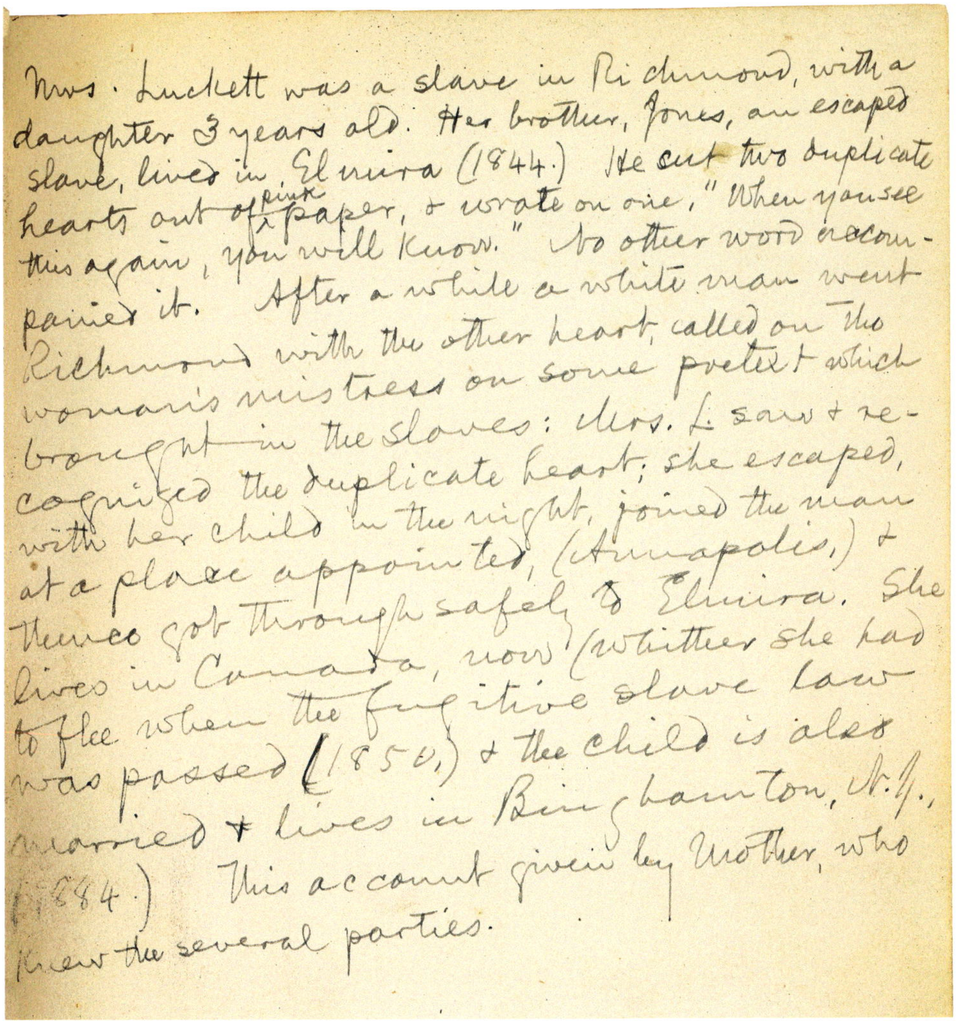

Mrs. Luckett was a slave in Richmond, with a daughter 3 years old. Her brother, Jones, an escaped slave, lived in Elmira (1844.) He cut two duplicate hearts out of pink paper, & wrote on one, "When you see this again, you will know." No other word accompanied it. After a while a white man went to Richmond with the other heart, called on the woman's mistress on some pretext which brought in the slaves: Mrs. L. saw & recognized the duplicate heart; she escaped with her child in the night, joined the man at a place appointed, (Annapolis,) & thence got through safely to Elmira. She lives in Canada, now (whither she had to flee when the fugitive slave law was passed (1850,) & the child is also married & lives in Binghamton, N.Y., (1884.) This account given by Mother, who knew the several parties.

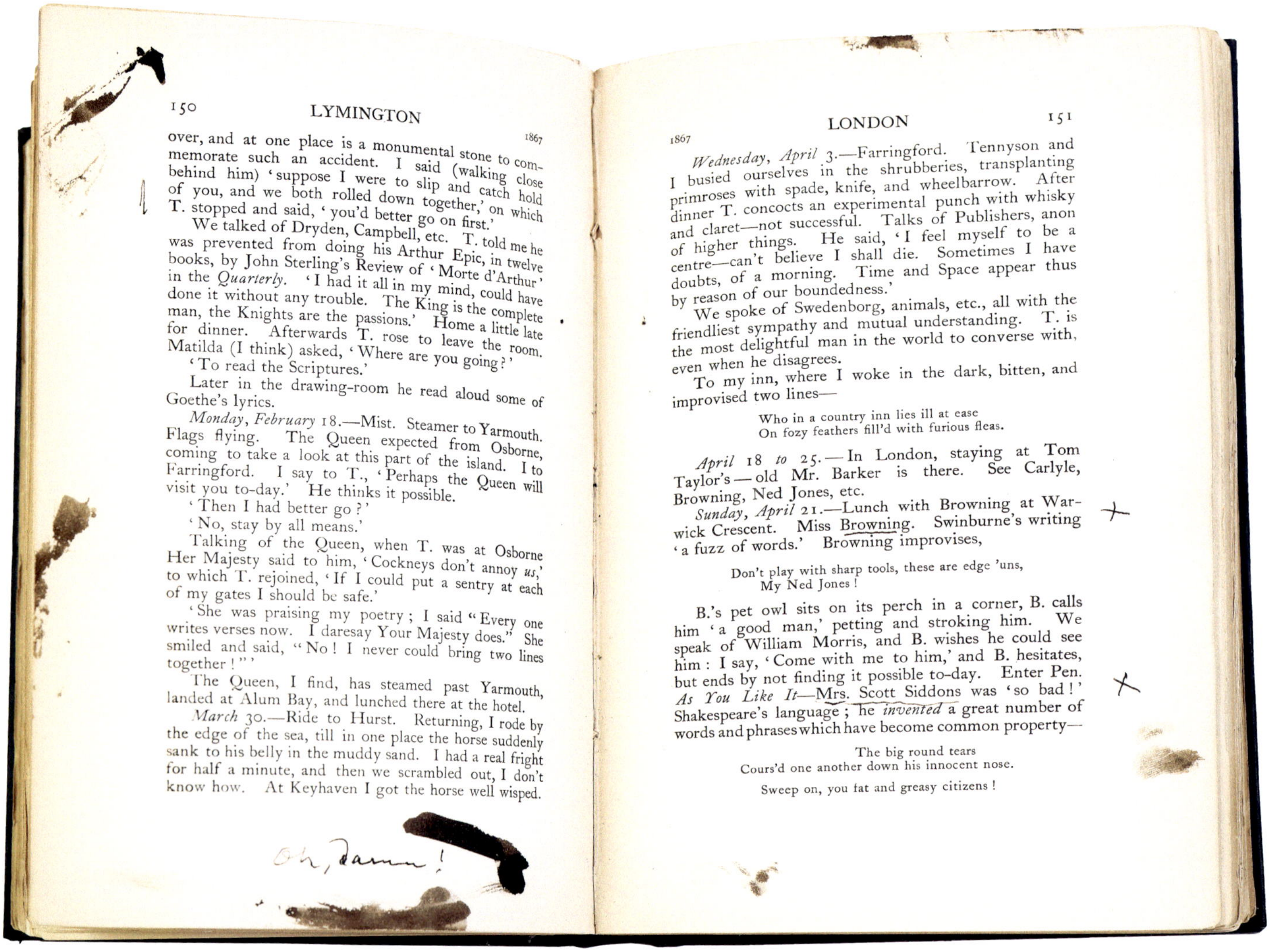

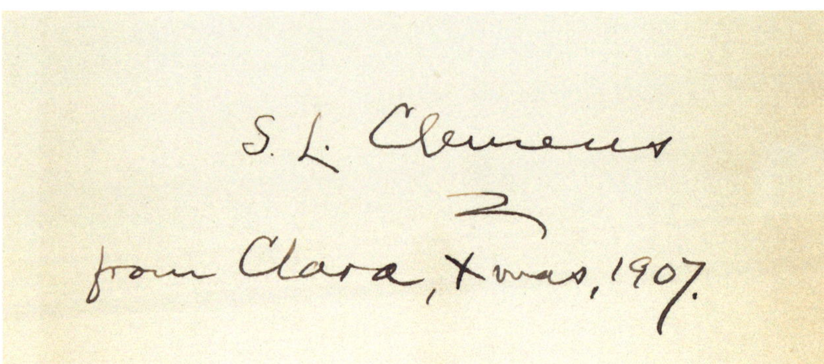

W. H. Allingham and D. Radford, eds. *William Allingham: A Diary*. London: Macmillan and Co., 1907. (Item no. 75)

Clemens's copy, given to him by his daughter Clara for Christmas in 1907. Among his annotations is the amusing note "Oh, damn!" next to an ink blot on page 150.

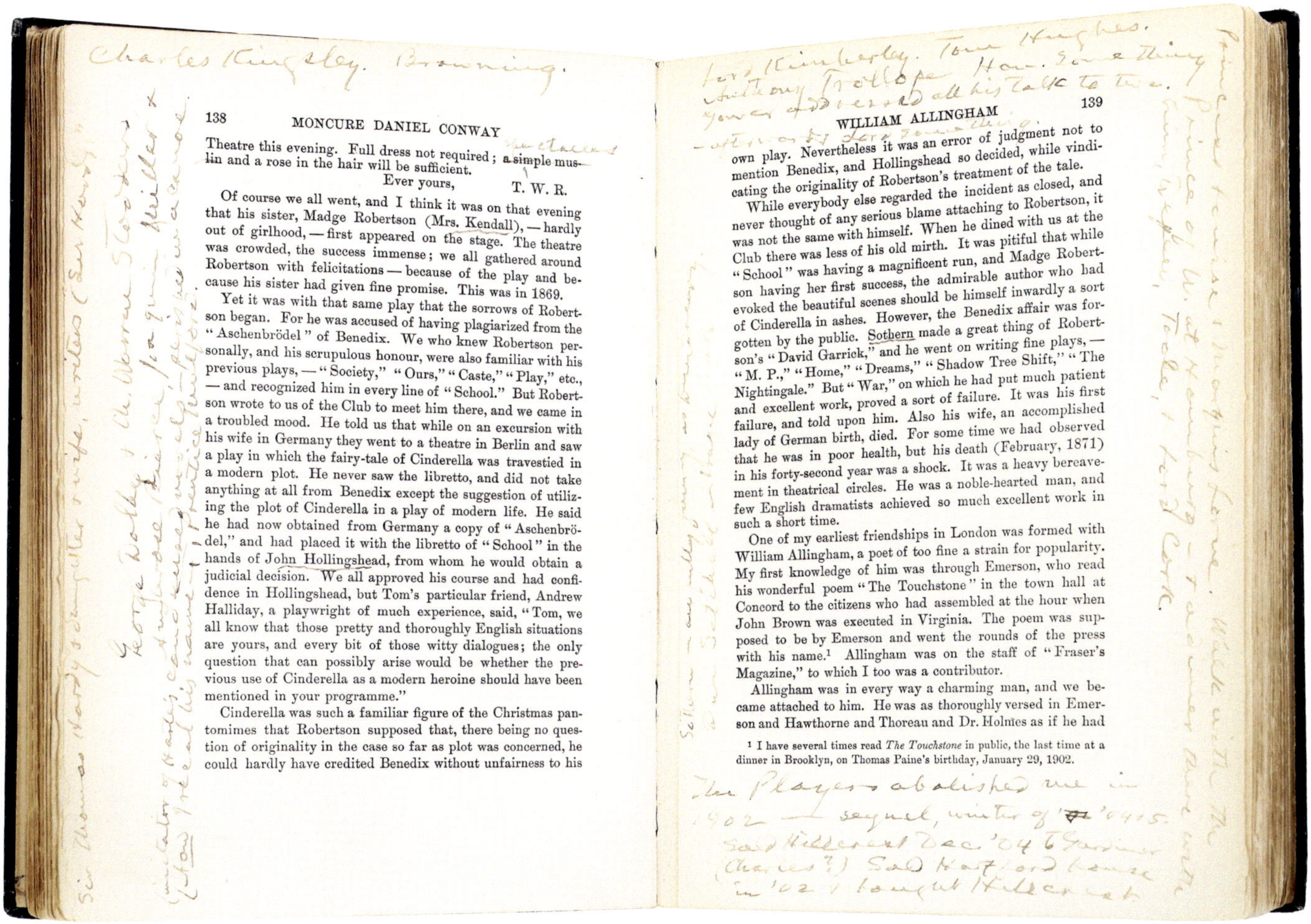

138 MONCURE DANIEL CONWAY

Theatre this evening. Full dress not required; a simple muslin and a rose in the hair will be sufficient.

Ever yours,
T. W. R.

Of course we all went, and I think it was on that evening that his sister, Madge Robertson (Mrs. Kendall), — hardly out of girlhood, — first appeared on the stage. The theatre was crowded, the success immense; we all gathered around Robertson with felicitations — because of the play and because his sister had given fine promise. This was in 1869.

Yet it was with that same play that the sorrows of Robertson began. For he was accused of having plagiarized from the "Aschenbrödel" of Benedix. We who knew Robertson personally, and his scrupulous honour, were also familiar with his previous plays, — "Society," "Ours," "Caste," "Play," etc., — and recognized him in every line of "School." But Robertson wrote to us of the Club to meet him there, and we came in a troubled mood. He told us that while on an excursion with his wife in Germany they went to a theatre in Berlin and saw a play in which the fairy-tale of Cinderella was travestied in a modern plot. He never saw the libretto, and did not take anything at all from Benedix except the suggestion of utilizing the plot of Cinderella in a play of modern life. He said he had now obtained from Germany a copy of "Aschenbrödel," and had placed it with the libretto of "School" in the hands of John Hollingshead, from whom he would obtain a judicial decision. We all approved his course and had confidence in Hollingshead, but Tom's particular friend, Andrew Halliday, a playwright of much experience, said, "Tom, we all know that those pretty and thoroughly English situations are yours, and every bit of those witty dialogues; the only question that can possibly arise would be whether the previous use of Cinderella as a modern heroine should have been mentioned in your programme."

Cinderella was such a familiar figure of the Christmas pantomimes that Robertson supposed that, there being no question of originality in the case so far as plot was concerned, he could hardly have credited Benedix without unfairness to his

WILLIAM ALLINGHAM 139

own play. Nevertheless it was an error of judgment not to mention Benedix, and Hollingshead so decided, while vindicating the originality of Robertson's treatment of the tale.

While everybody else regarded the incident as closed, and never thought of any serious blame attaching to Robertson, it was not the same with himself. When he dined with us at the Club there was less of his old mirth. It was pitiful that while "School" was having a magnificent run, and Madge Robertson having her first success, the admirable author who had evoked the beautiful scenes should be himself inwardly a sort of Cinderella in ashes. However, the Benedix affair was forgotten by the public. Sothern made a great thing of Robertson's "David Garrick," and he went on writing fine plays, — "M. P.," "Home," "Dreams," "Shadow Tree Shift," "The Nightingale." But "War," on which he had put much patient and excellent work, proved a sort of failure. It was his first failure, and told upon him. Also his wife, an accomplished lady of German birth, died. For some time we had observed that he was in poor health, but his death (February, 1871) in his forty-second year was a shock. It was a heavy bereavement in theatrical circles. He was a noble-hearted man, and few English dramatists achieved so much excellent work in such a short time.

One of my earliest friendships in London was formed with William Allingham, a poet of too fine a strain for popularity. My first knowledge of him was through Emerson, who read his wonderful poem "The Touchstone" in the town hall at Concord to the citizens who had assembled at the hour when John Brown was executed in Virginia. The poem was supposed to be by Emerson and went the rounds of the press with his name.[1] Allingham was on the staff of "Fraser's Magazine," to which I too was a contributor.

Allingham was in every way a charming man, and we became attached to him. He was as thoroughly versed in Emerson and Hawthorne and Thoreau and Dr. Holmes as if he had

[1] I have several times read *The Touchstone* in public, the last time at a dinner in Brooklyn, on Thomas Paine's birthday, January 29, 1902.

Moncure Conway. *Autobiography: Memories and Experiences*. Boston & New York: Houghton, Mifflin and Company, 1904. (Item no. 76)

Clemens's copy, with his annotations throughout. His notes, such as "I seem to have met most of the people mentioned in this book" on p. 277 of volume 1 (not pictured here), evidence the early stirrings of Twain's autobiographical recollections; he would publish the *Autobiography of Mark Twain* in 1906.

ABOVE

Aschermann & Co. "Don't Fail to Smoke Mark Twain Cigars." New York: Heppenheimer & Maurer, [ca. 1877–1880]. Lithographed advertising card. (Item no. 140)

RIGHT

Mark Twain cigar box. [Missouri]: Londres, [ca. 1910–1913]. Wooden box with printed labels. (Item no. 142)

OPPOSITE

Mark Twain cigar box. Pennsylvania: Wolf Bros., [ca. 1913–1930]. Wooden box with printed label and one original cellophane-wrapped cigar. (Item no. 143)

FOLLOWING PAGES

"Liked By All: Mark Twain Cigars." Baltimore: Parker Metal Dec. Company, [ca. 1913–1931]. Metal sign. (Item no. 144)

Clemens estimated that he smoked fifteen to twenty cigars a day, and the public image of Mark Twain is closely associated with cigars. Cigar manufacturer Edward Aschermann registered a trademark for Twain-branded cigars in 1877. Clemens does not seem to have received any income from this use of his name, but in 1907 his business manager Ralph Ashcroft registered a new trademark on Twain's name and likeness for whiskey and tobacco, and Twain cigars from other manufacturers continued to be produced until the 1930s.

5¢
SWEET TIP
MARK TWAIN
KNOWN TO EVERYONE - LIKED BY ALL
HOLE IN HEAD
MARK TWAIN
MARK TWAIN
MARK TWAIN

LIKED
MARK
5¢ CIG.

BY ALL
TWAIN
ARS 5¢

B. P. Shillaber. *Life and Sayings of Mrs. Partington, and Others of the Family*. New York: J. C. Derby/Boston: Phillips, Sampson and Company, 1854. (Item no. 169)

As the editor of *The Carpet-Bag*, Shillaber purchased Clemens's first published story, "The Dandy Frightening the Squatter." His fictional creation, Mrs. Partington, was a simple-minded but kind-hearted woman whose speech was laden with malapropisms, and she was a direct influence on *Tom Sawyer*'s Aunt Polly.

RUTH PARTINGTON.

Betsy J. Ward [William Comstock]. *Betsy Jane Ward better-half to Artemus, Hur Book of Goaks, with a full akkownt of the coartship and maridge to a4said Artemus, and Mister Ward's cutting-up with the Mormon fare secks*. London: George Routledge and Sons, 1866. (Item no. 175)

Artemus Ward was a persona adopted by author and speaker Charles Farrar Browne. Ward, an illiterate but ironically wise character, traveled broadly, and his books are filled with humorous observations on the American West and Europe. Browne's humorous lectures influenced Twain as a speaker, and his success led to imitators, including this book credited to his fictional wife. Its authorship is attributed to William Comstock, a prolific dime novelist.

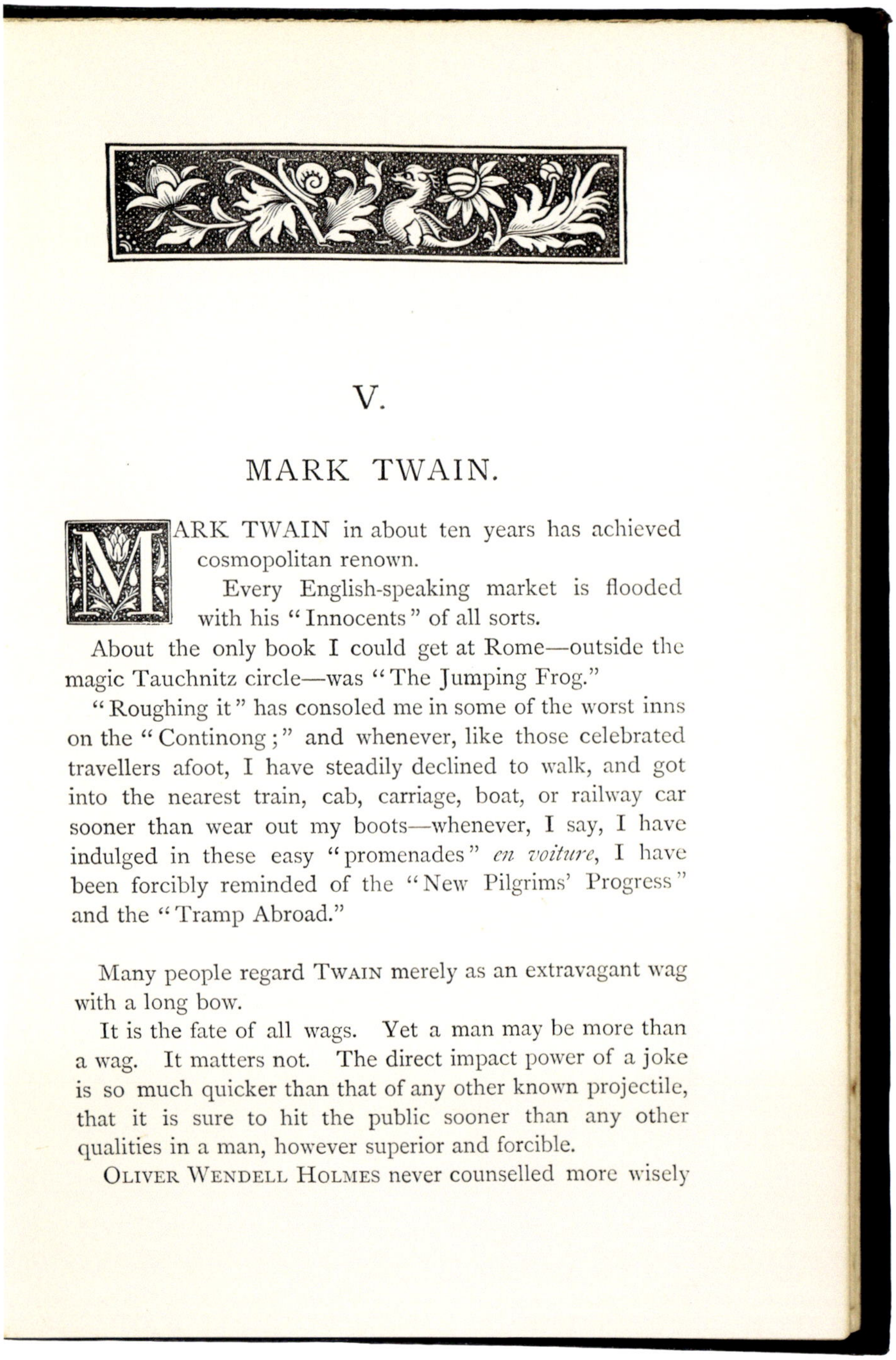

V.

MARK TWAIN.

MARK TWAIN in about ten years has achieved cosmopolitan renown.

Every English-speaking market is flooded with his "Innocents" of all sorts.

About the only book I could get at Rome—outside the magic Tauchnitz circle—was "The Jumping Frog."

"Roughing it" has consoled me in some of the worst inns on the "Continong;" and whenever, like those celebrated travellers afoot, I have steadily declined to walk, and got into the nearest train, cab, carriage, boat, or railway car sooner than wear out my boots—whenever, I say, I have indulged in these easy "promenades" *en voiture*, I have been forcibly reminded of the "New Pilgrims' Progress" and the "Tramp Abroad."

Many people regard TWAIN merely as an extravagant wag with a long bow.

It is the fate of all wags. Yet a man may be more than a wag. It matters not. The direct impact power of a joke is so much quicker than that of any other known projectile, that it is sure to hit the public sooner than any other qualities in a man, however superior and forcible.

OLIVER WENDELL HOLMES never counselled more wisely

Hugh R. Haweis. *American Humorists.* London: Chatto & Windus, 1883. (Item no. 79)

Haweis, an English cleric, profiled Twain alongside Artemus Ward, Washington Irving, and Oliver Wendell Holmes.

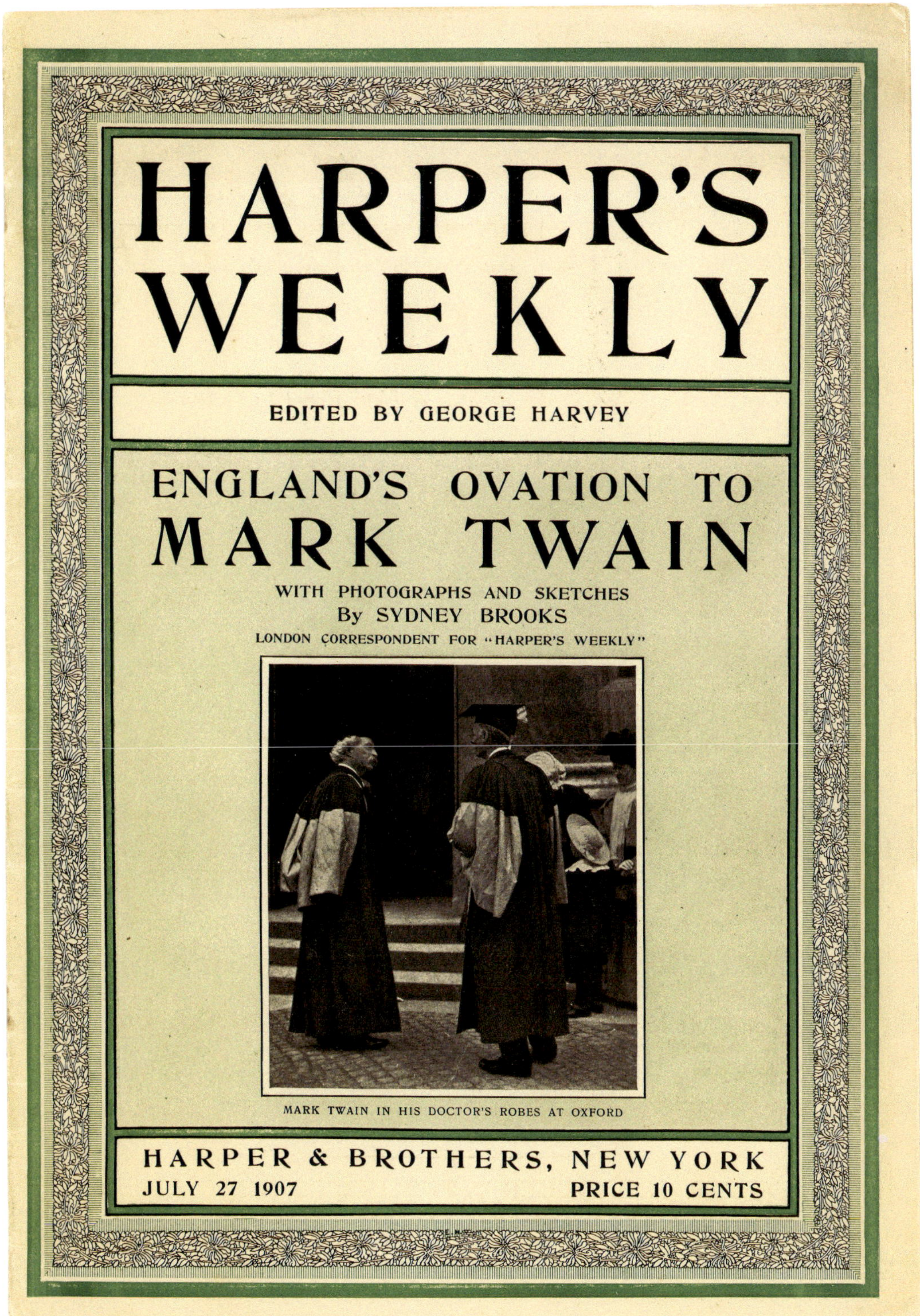
HARPER'S WEEKLY

EDITED BY GEORGE HARVEY

ENGLAND'S OVATION TO MARK TWAIN

WITH PHOTOGRAPHS AND SKETCHES
By SYDNEY BROOKS
LONDON CORRESPONDENT FOR "HARPER'S WEEKLY"

MARK TWAIN IN HIS DOCTOR'S ROBES AT OXFORD

HARPER & BROTHERS, NEW YORK
JULY 27 1907 PRICE 10 CENTS

Harper's Weekly: A Journal of Civilization, volume 51, number 2,640. New York: Harper & Brothers, July 27, 1907. In original wrappers. (Item no. 68)

This issue of the political weekly version of *Harper's*, which has a photograph of Mark Twain receiving his honorary doctorate from Oxford University on the front wrapper, includes the article "England's Ovation to Mark Twain" by Sydney Brooks.

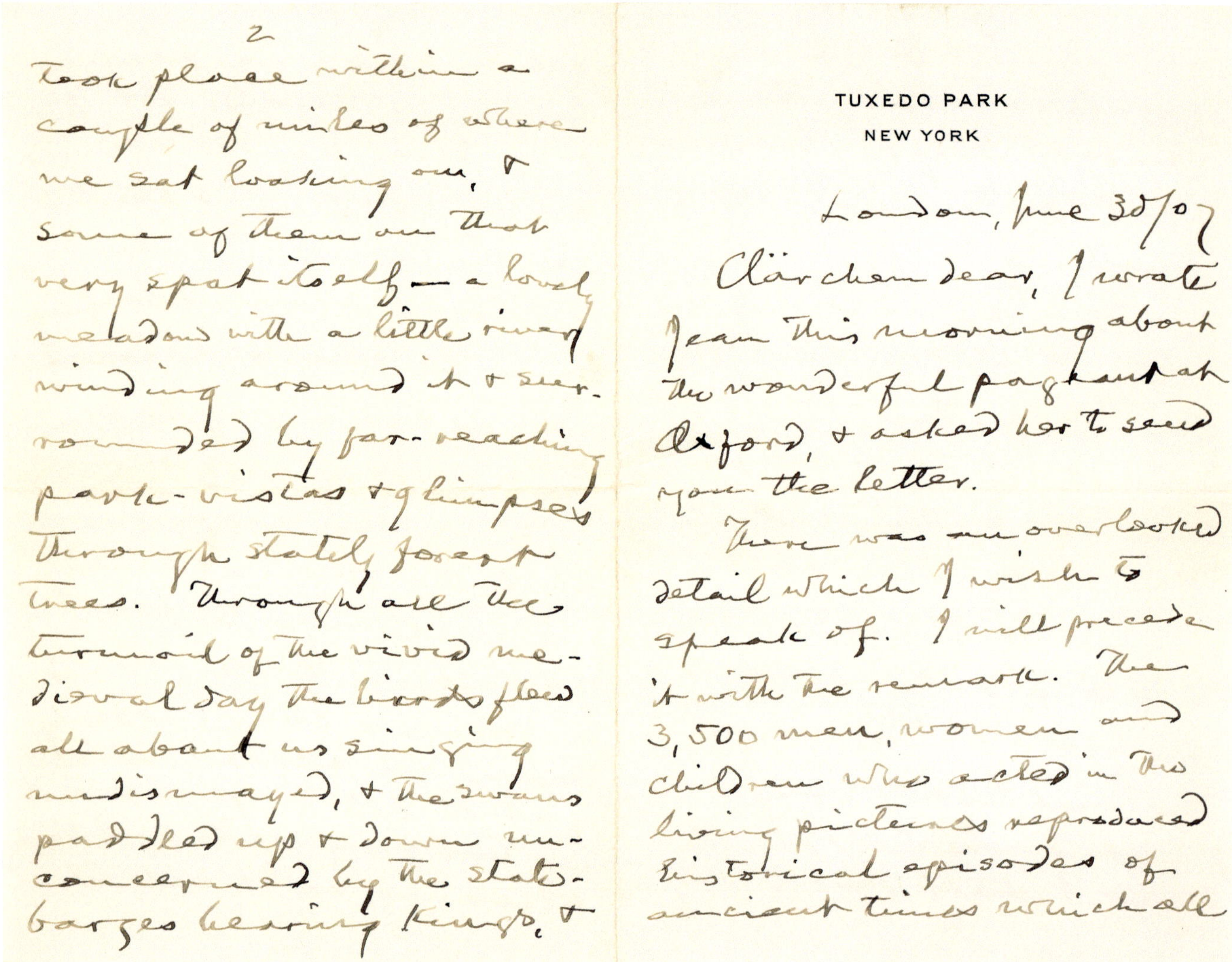

2

took place within a
couple of miles of where
we sat looking on, &
some of them on that
very spot itself — a lovely
meadow with a little river
winding around it & sur-
rounded by far-reaching
park-vistas & glimpses
through stately forest
trees. Through all the
turmoil of the vivid me-
dieval day the birds flew
all about us singing
undismayed, & the swans
paddled up & down un-
concerned by the state-
barges bearing kings, &

TUXEDO PARK
NEW YORK

London, June 30/07

Clärchen dear, I wrote
Jean this morning about
the wonderful pageant at
Oxford, & asked her to send
you the letter.

There was an overlooked
detail which I wish to
speak of. I will precede
it with the remark: The
3,500 men, women and
children who acted in the
living pictures reproduced
historical episodes of
ancient times which all

Samuel L. Clemens. Autograph letter signed "Father" to Clara Clemens. London, June 30, 1907. (Item no. 108)

Clemens writes to his daughter, describing the program of events at the ceremony for the awarding of his honorary doctoral degree from Oxford University.

E. A. *Doctors All, or, More Innocents Abroad*. [June 1907.] Pen and ink on board. (Item no. 127)

This cartoon, drawn for a student publication at Oxford University, depicts the recipients of honorary doctorates in 1907: William Booth, founder of the Salvation Army, leads the procession with a bass drum, followed by Rudyard Kipling, Prince Arthur of Connaught, and Clemens.

Our Wild Indians: A Writer's Sourcebook

KERRY DRISCOLL

In "Chapter the Last" of *Adventures of Huckleberry Finn* **(pages 35–36)**, Tom Sawyer proposes that rather than returning to St. Petersburg from the Phelps Farm, he, Huck, and Jim should "get an outfit, and go for howling adventures amongst the Injuns, over in the Territory, for a couple of weeks or two" (*Huckleberry Finn* 361). While Huck is initially amenable to the idea, upon further reflection, he formulates a different, more open-ended course of action: "I reckon I got to light out for the Territory ahead of the rest, because aunt Sally she's going to adopt me and sivilize me and I can't stand it. I been there before" (*Huckleberry Finn* 362). Within months of penning those famous words, Mark Twain began contemplating a sequel to *Huck*, and by the summer of 1884 was ready to tackle the project. As he settled into his annual writing season at Quarry Farm in Elmira, New York, Clemens fired off an urgent message to his nephew and business manager, Charles L. Webster:

> Dear Charley—
>
> Send to me, right away, a book by *Lieut. Col. Dodge, USA*, called "25 Years on the Frontier"—or some such title—I don't remember just what. Maybe it is "25 Years Among the Indians," or maybe "25 Years in the Rocky Mountains." But the name of the *author* will guide you. I think he has written only the one book; & so any librarian can tell you the title of it.
>
> I want several other *personal narratives* of life & adventure out yonder on the Plains & in the Mountains, if you can run across them—especially life *among the Indians*. Send what you can find. I mean to take Huck Finn out there. (UCCL 08930, Twain to Webster, 6 July 1884)

This letter offers an important hint regarding the origins of Mark Twain's unfinished manuscript, "Huck Finn and Tom Sawyer among the Indians"—nine chapters produced over a three-month period during the summer of 1884, then abruptly abandoned in midsentence. The fragment remained unpublished until fifty-nine years after his death, when the University of California Press included it in a 1969 collection of the writer's other short unfinished works ("Huck Finn and Tom Sawyer").

While Mark Twain generally tapped into the rich store of his Missouri childhood memories to create novels like *The Adventures of Tom Sawyer* and *Huckleberry Finn*, in this instance he needed information concerning the customs, character, and lifeways of Plains Indian tribes—

gleaned from individuals with firsthand experience of these groups—to fashion a realistic backdrop for his story. Webster promptly obliged his uncle's request, posting several books to him in Elmira within a matter of days: George Armstrong Custer's *My Life on the Plains* (1874), Buffalo Bill's *The Life of the Honorable William F. Cody* (1879), and Washington Irving's *The Adventures of Captain Bonneville* (1883), along with copies of two different books by Colonel Dodge, *The Plains of the Great West and Their Inhabitants* (1877) and *Our Wild Indians: Thirty-Three Years' Personal Experience among the Red Men of the Great West* (1882). Clemens acknowledged their receipt, informing Webster, "Don't need any more Injun books" (UCCL 01551, Twain to Webster, 17 July 1884).

The multiplicity of sources Mark Twain consulted in researching "Huck Finn and Tom Sawyer among the Indians" reflects both his abiding commitment to realism and scrupulous professionalism. Of these volumes, *Our Wild Indians* is arguably the most important, mined not only for small ethnographic details but also key features of his emerging plot. Clemens had long admired Dodge's military expertise and no-nonsense views on the so-called Indian Problem, telling William Dean Howells in February 1877:

> I hope he [newly elected president Rutherford B. Hayes] will put Lt. Col. Richard Irwin [*sic*] Dodge (Author of "The Great Plains & their Inhabitants") at the head of the Indian Department. *There's* a man who knows all about Indians & yet has some humanity in him—(knowledge of Indians, & humanity, are seldom found in the same individual). (UCCL 01533, Twain to Howells, 22 Feb. 1877)

The writer's copiously annotated copy of *Our Wild Indians* **(pages 182–184)** is unquestionably one of the most important books in his personal library. Its pages offer a fascinating glimpse into both the sensibility and working habits of one of America's greatest literary geniuses.

THE MARGINALIA: A WINDOW INTO MARK TWAIN'S MIND

Clemens's annotations throughout *Our Wild Indians* are written primarily in pencil—though a handful are in black ink, indicating multiple readings of the text. Moreover, their progression from single words and terse phrases to lengthy passages spilling in all directions across the margins of a given page reflects the writer's deepening immersion in—and attendant fascination with—Dodge's subject matter. While the inherent ethnocentric bias of Dodge's perspective is obvious to modern readers, Mark Twain regarded him as an unimpeachable authority. Though the marginalia cannot be dated with any specificity, circumstantial evidence suggests that Clemens's review of the volume was well underway by mid-July. Next to a passage in chapter 2 describing the Indian's stoic ability to endure "excruciating torture," for example, he made two bold vertical strokes and jotted "Pain." This same idea figures prominently in a letter to Howells recounting the ordeal of having several cavities filled by a local dentist. After spending hours having two teeth "gouged out and stuffed," Clemens states: "I can stand the most exquisite pain, now, without outward manifestation; & indeed without any very real discomfort. The Indian has fallen in my estimation; he is no better than you or me—he is merely the product of education" (UCCL 01529, Twain to Howells, 15 July 1884).

The preliminary nature of the Dodge marginalia is also apparent when examined in the context of the sequel's nine extant chapters. One of Mark Twain's earliest notes in *Our Wild Indians*—"Mills boys teach H. & T" (34), which appears adjacent to Dodge's description about shooting quail—indicates that he had already chosen the surname of the emigrant family that Huck, Tom, and Jim encounter while crossing the Plains. On the other hand, he had not yet determined the name of the sequel's central female protagonist. Several annotations instead refer to "Sal"—evidently an early version of his seventeen-year-old heroine, Peggy Mills. An accomplished horsewoman, Sal handles her animal with "grace and skill" while riding sidesaddle and thereby elicits the tribe's awe (61). Two additional comments are even more intriguing, demonstrating that Mark Twain was actively entertaining several discrete—and at times, contradictory—story arcs. In other words, at the time of his reading, fundamental details of the narrative's plot were still in flux—and would not be finalized until he began writing. Alongside a passage concerning the Indians' brutal mistreatment of white female captives, for example, Mark Twain writes: "T [Tom Sawyer] kills Sal by request to save her from a worse fate," meaning gang rape (529). Then on the very next page, he imagines an entirely different scenario: "Sal is gambled away" (530), callously used as collateral by her captors in a primitive game of chance. These marginalia—and the ominous fates they augur for Sal—highlight the absence of yet another character who plays a pivotal role in the manuscript: Peggy Mills's fiancée, Brace Johnson.

A sequential review of Mark Twain's marginalia is illuminating. In the opening chapters, his comments are succinct and methodical—essentially a checklist of basic demographic facts regarding the history, social organization, and governance of Plains tribes. These entries are clearly intended as "memory jogs," for quick reference and retrieval. Twain notes, for example, that they possess a "Multitude of languages" (44), comprise "60 tribes ½ the In pop of U.S." (53), and live in a "base condition" (55). Similarly, he enumerates the Indians' distinctive character traits, indicating that they are "jolly," "noisy, "easily scared," and consider it "bad to show surprise among strangers" (all on 59).

As Mark Twain delved more deeply into the volume, his marginalia underwent a substantive shift, growing more expansive and interpretive. Sitting in his airy hill-top study amidst the welter of source material supplied by Charlie Webster, he began comparing and actively cross-checking Dodge's text with information in other volumes—jotting "See Parkman's histories also" (106), for example, next to a passage describing the Native concept of "medicine." Similarly, after reading about the Indians' use of hand mirrors as signaling devices in *Our Wild Indians*, he reminds himself: "See that gov't book at home as to signals" (433). He also explicitly references Custer's narrative at the beginning of chapter 10: "Note—In L on P., a chief went into battle unpainted or decorated. Because a relative of his had been scalped (& killed?) by a man of this tribe, & this compliment *had* to be returned before he can appear in war reg[alia] again" (Dodge 148). He would later incorporate this detail into the sequel with chilling effect to explain why "Man Afraid of His Mother-in-law," one of the Sioux warriors whom the Mills family meets on the Plains, refuses to wear "fuss and feathers and war paint" ("Huck Finn and Tom Sawyer" 45). But most significantly, Mark Twain makes repeated allusions to "Bonneville"—Washington Irving's edition of the journals kept by Captain Benjamin Bonneville during his 1832–35 travels in the West. Although he dismissed this work as "a narrative poorly & wordily told" (according to a comment made on the cover of the volume, now housed at the Mark Twain Papers in Berkeley), he nonetheless regarded its content as credible. In several places, he uses Irving's book to corroborate Dodge, e.g., "See Bonneville—confirmation slight" (66) and "Like the N.P$^{s.}$ [Nez Perce] in Bonneville" (442); however, one annotation is especially revealing. Regarding Dodge's description of Native funeral practices, he writes: "Mr. B says cremation would defeat resurrection. What becomes of martyrs [?]" (103).

THIS PAGE, OPPOSITE, AND FOLLOWING

Richard Irving Dodge. *Our Wild Indians: Thirty-three Years' Personal Experience among the Red Men of the Great West.* Hartford: A.D. Worthington and Company, 1883. (Item no. 77)

Clemens studied and extensively annotated this book while preparing to write "Huck and Tom Among the Indians."

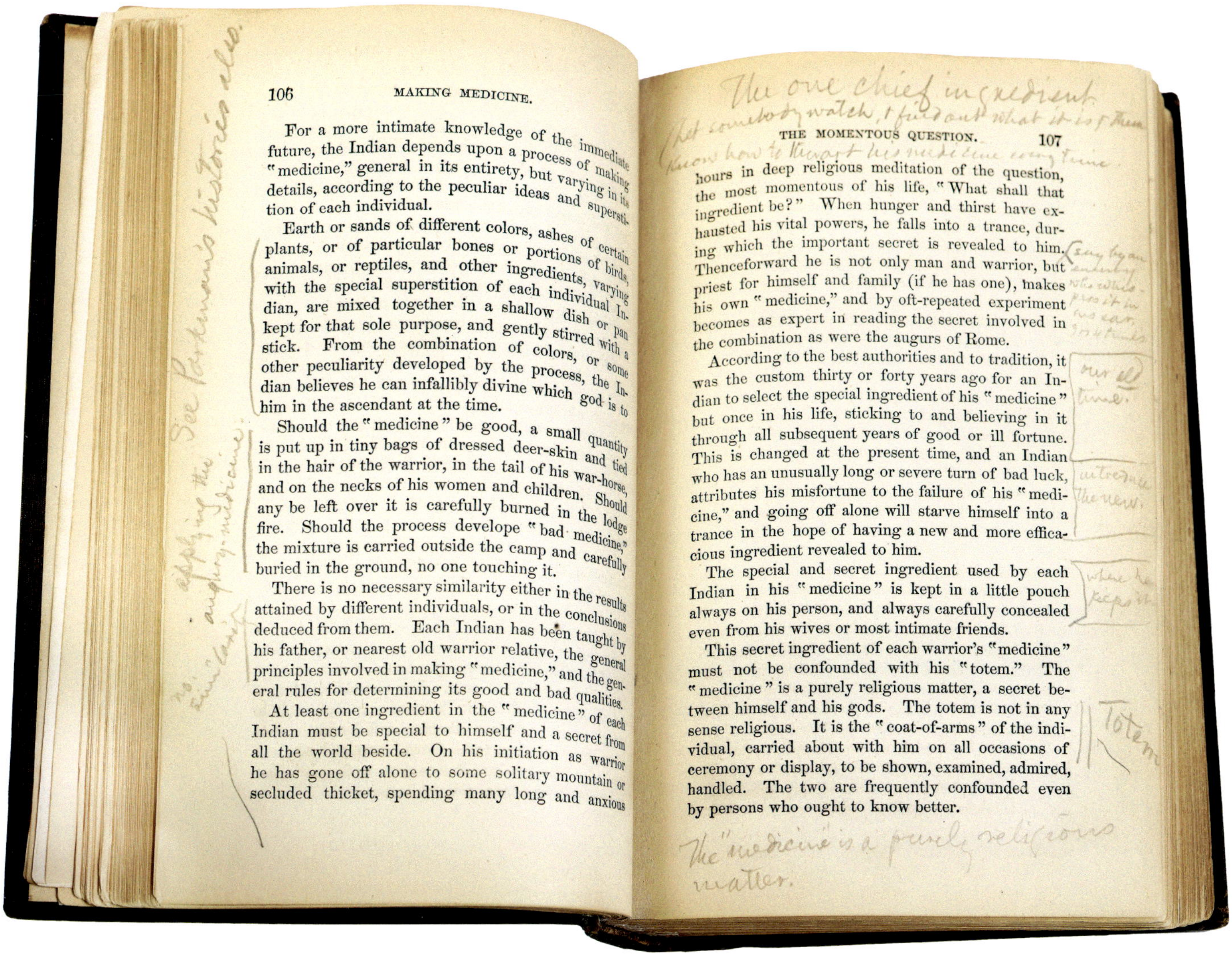

106 MAKING MEDICINE.

For a more intimate knowledge of the immediate future, the Indian depends upon a process of making "medicine," general in its entirety, but varying in its details, according to the peculiar ideas and superstition of each individual.

Earth or sands of different colors, ashes of certain plants, or of particular bones or portions of birds, animals, or reptiles, and other ingredients, varying with the special superstition of each individual Indian, are mixed together in a shallow dish or pan kept for that sole purpose, and gently stirred with a stick. From the combination of colors, or some other peculiarity developed by the process, the Indian believes he can infallibly divine which god is to him in the ascendant at the time.

Should the "medicine" be good, a small quantity is put up in tiny bags of dressed deer-skin and tied in the hair of the warrior, in the tail of his war-horse, and on the necks of his women and children. Should any be left over it is carefully burned in the lodge fire. Should the process develope "bad medicine," the mixture is carried outside the camp and carefully buried in the ground, no one touching it.

There is no necessary similarity either in the results attained by different individuals, or in the conclusions deduced from them. Each Indian has been taught by his father, or nearest old warrior relative, the general principles involved in making "medicine," and the general rules for determining its good and bad qualities.

At least one ingredient in the "medicine" of each Indian must be special to himself and a secret from all the world beside. On his initiation as warrior he has gone off alone to some solitary mountain or secluded thicket, spending many long and anxious

THE MOMENTOUS QUESTION. 107

hours in deep religious meditation of the question, the most momentous of his life, "What shall that ingredient be?" When hunger and thirst have exhausted his vital powers, he falls into a trance, during which the important secret is revealed to him. Thenceforward he is not only man and warrior, but priest for himself and family (if he has one), makes his own "medicine," and by oft-repeated experiment becomes as expert in reading the secret involved in the combination as were the augurs of Rome.

According to the best authorities and to tradition, it was the custom thirty or forty years ago for an Indian to select the special ingredient of his "medicine" but once in his life, sticking to and believing in it through all subsequent years of good or ill fortune. This is changed at the present time, and an Indian who has an unusually long or severe turn of bad luck, attributes his misfortune to the failure of his "medicine," and going off alone will starve himself into a trance in the hope of having a new and more efficacious ingredient revealed to him.

The special and secret ingredient used by each Indian in his "medicine" is kept in a little pouch always on his person, and always carefully concealed even from his wives or most intimate friends.

This secret ingredient of each warrior's "medicine" must not be confounded with his "totem." The "medicine" is a purely religious matter, a secret between himself and his gods. The totem is not in any sense religious. It is the "coat-of-arms" of the individual, carried about with him on all occasions of ceremony or display, to be shown, examined, admired, handled. The two are frequently confounded even by persons who ought to know better.

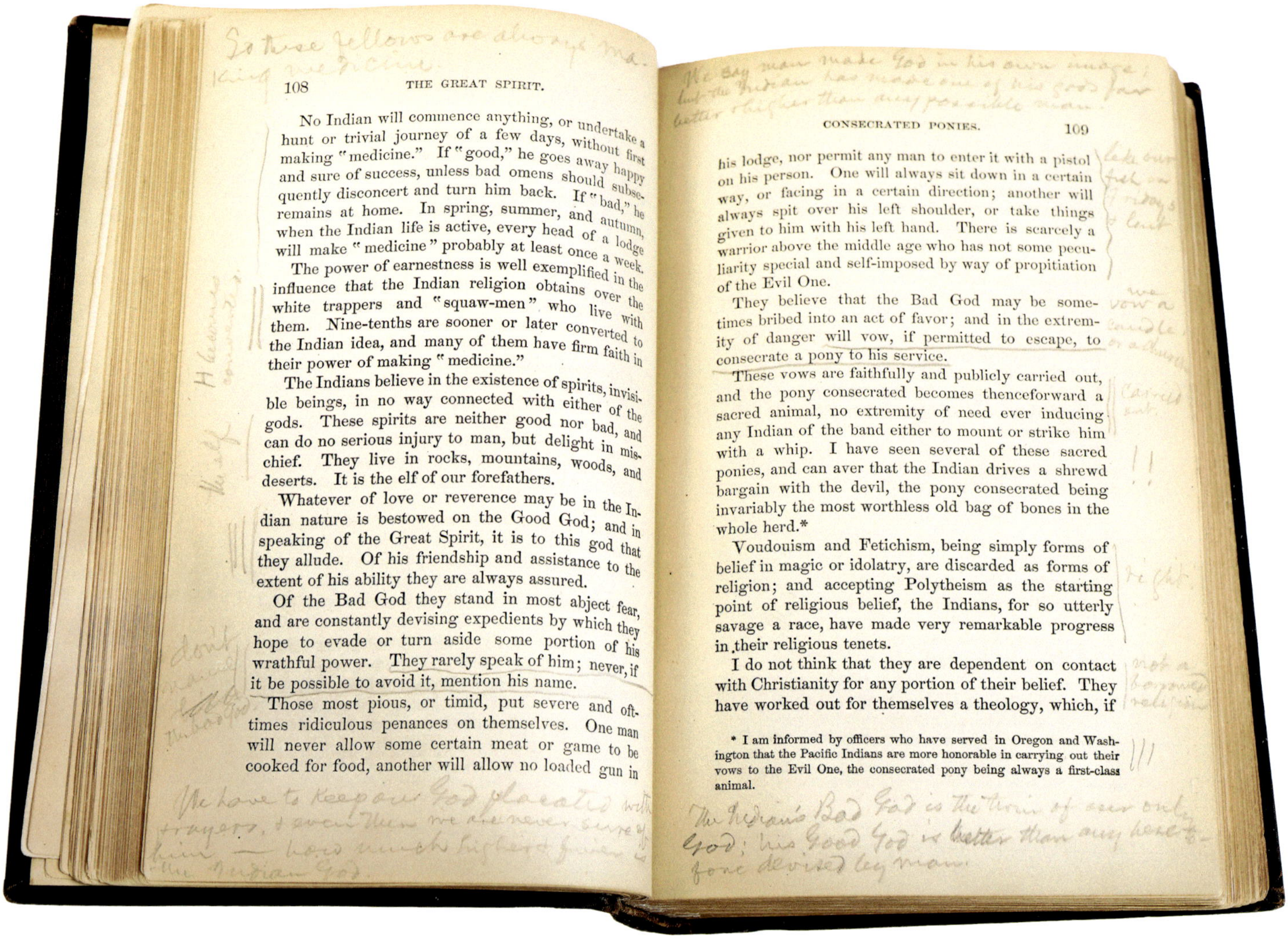
108 THE GREAT SPIRIT.
No Indian will commence anything, or undertake a hunt or trivial journey of a few days, without first making "medicine." If "good," he goes away happy and sure of success, unless bad omens should subsequently disconcert and turn him back. If "bad," he remains at home. In spring, summer, and autumn, when the Indian life is active, every head of a lodge will make "medicine" probably at least once a week.
The power of earnestness is well exemplified in the influence that the Indian religion obtains over the white trappers and "squaw-men" who live with them. Nine-tenths are sooner or later converted to the Indian idea, and many of them have firm faith in their power of making "medicine."
The Indians believe in the existence of spirits, invisible beings, in no way connected with either of the gods. These spirits are neither good nor bad, and can do no serious injury to man, but delight in mischief. They live in rocks, mountains, woods, and deserts. It is the elf of our forefathers.
Whatever of love or reverence may be in the Indian nature is bestowed on the Good God; and in speaking of the Great Spirit, it is to this god that they allude. Of his friendship and assistance to the extent of his ability they are always assured.
Of the Bad God they stand in most abject fear, and are constantly devising expedients by which they hope to evade or turn aside some portion of his wrathful power. They rarely speak of him; never, if it be possible to avoid it, mention his name.
Those most pious, or timid, put severe and ofttimes ridiculous penances on themselves. One man will never allow some certain meat or game to be cooked for food, another will allow no loaded gun in
CONSECRATED PONIES. 109
his lodge, nor permit any man to enter it with a pistol on his person. One will always sit down in a certain way, or facing in a certain direction; another will always spit over his left shoulder, or take things given to him with his left hand. There is scarcely a warrior above the middle age who has not some peculiarity special and self-imposed by way of propitiation of the Evil One.
They believe that the Bad God may be sometimes bribed into an act of favor; and in the extremity of danger will vow, if permitted to escape, to consecrate a pony to his service.
These vows are faithfully and publicly carried out, and the pony consecrated becomes thenceforward a sacred animal, no extremity of need ever inducing any Indian of the band either to mount or strike him with a whip. I have seen several of these sacred ponies, and can aver that the Indian drives a shrewd bargain with the devil, the pony consecrated being invariably the most worthless old bag of bones in the whole herd.*
Voudouism and Fetichism, being simply forms of belief in magic or idolatry, are discarded as forms of religion; and accepting Polytheism as the starting point of religious belief, the Indians, for so utterly savage a race, have made very remarkable progress in their religious tenets.
I do not think that they are dependent on contact with Christianity for any portion of their belief. They have worked out for themselves a theology, which, if
* I am informed by officers who have served in Oregon and Washington that the Pacific Indians are more honorable in carrying out their vows to the Evil One, the consecrated pony being always a first-class animal.

The appearance of such open-ended questions in the marginalia reflects Mark Twain's deepening engagement with Dodge's subject matter. His annotations are most frequent in the pages of chapter 6, concerning the "Religion of the Indian"—demonstrating that he was especially intrigued by the Native concepts of God discussed therein:

> The Indian is as religious as the most devout Christian. . . . He believes in two gods, equal in wisdom and power. One is the Good God. His function is to aid the Indian in all his undertakings, to heap benefits upon him, to deliver his enemy into his hand, to protect him from danger, pain, and privation. . . . Warmth, food, joy, success in love, distinction in war, all come from him.
>
> The other is the Bad God. He is always the enemy of each individual red man, and exerts to the utmost all his powers of harm against him. From him proceed all the disasters, misfortunes, privation, and discomforts of life. (100)

The Good God, Dodge asserts, "demands nothing in return" for his benevolence: "No prayers [or] . . . thanks are necessary, for he does these things because he chooses to do them." Mark Twain reacts to this information with mock incredulity, asking, "not even a candle?" (101).

For Clemens, the Indian's bifurcation of the divine into "Good" and "Bad" gods resolved a vexing paradox at the heart of Christian dogma—namely, the Almighty's capacity for compassion *and* cruelty, comfort *and* terror, love *and* vengeance. As such, the marginalia on pages 108 and 109 of *Our Wild Indians* articulate a remarkable theological epiphany about the superiority of the "savage" religion to those of more allegedly civilized and advanced peoples: "We have to keep our God placated with prayers, and even then we are never sure of him—how much higher and finer is the Indian God" (108). The writer underscores this point in two emphatic comments: "We say man made God in his image; but the Indian has made one of his gods far better and higher than any possible man," and "The Indian's Bad God is the twin of our only God; his Good God is better than any heretofore devised by man" (109). Several pages later, he affirms: "Our illogical God is all-powerful in name, but important in fact; the Great Spirit is not all-powerful, but does the very best for his Injun & does it free of charge," and ultimately declares: "This is very much superior to all other men's religions" (113).

The fervor of Mark Twain's commentary all but assured that the Native concept of a "Good" and "Bad" God would play a key role in his sequel; however, the mechanics of exactly how to incorporate it into the narrative were still unclear. The writer's "solution"—problematic though it would prove—eventually came in the form of Peggy Mills's betrothed, Brace Johnson, an Indian scout who spent many years living among the Sioux:

> He didn't talk very much and when he talked about Injuns, he talked the same as if he was talking about animals; he didn't seem to have much idea that they was men. But he had some of their ways, himself, on account of being so long amongst them; and moreover he had their religion. And one of the things that puzzled him was how such animals ever struck such a sensible religion. He said Injuns hadn't only but two gods, a good one and a bad one, and they never paid no attention to the good one, nor ever prayed to him . . . because the good one loved them and wouldn't ever think of doing them any harm . . . all the trouble come from the bad god, who was setting up nights to think up ways to bring them bad luck and bust up all their plans. ("Huck Finn and Tom Sawyer" 120)

The obvious parallels between this passage and Dodge's discussion of Native religion in *Our Wild Indians* demonstrate the degree of Mark Twain's indebtedness to his source.

A DEEPER IMAGINING OF HUCK

The most intriguing aspect of Mark Twain's annotations in *Our Wild Indians* is the insight they afford into his evolving conception of his most famous character. From his earliest appearance in *Tom Sawyer* (1876), Huckleberry Finn is a marginalized figure, a survivor who exists on the fringes of respectable society. As the son of St. Petersburg's most notorious drunkard, he is regarded as the "juvenile pariah of the village," "hated and dreaded by all the mothers . . . because he was idle and lawless, and vulgar and bad—and because all their children admired him so, and delighted in his forbidden society, and wished they dared be like him" (*Tom Sawyer* 47–48). Huck's outsider status confers autonomy—"he did not have to go to school or church, or call any being master or obey anybody"; in Mark Twain's words, he is a "romantic outcast" who comes and goes "at his own free will," sleeping "on doorsteps in fine weather and in empty hogsheads in wet" (*Tom Sawyer*

48–49). Although Huck briefly experiences the comfort and security of home while drifting down the Mississippi on a raft with Jim, the oppressive strictures and hypocrisy of "sivilization"—incarnated in a series of well-meaning Christian women like Miss Watson, the Widow Douglas, and Aunt Sally Phelps—fuel his irresistible desire to "light out."

Of the fifteen marginal annotations in *Our Wild Indians* specifically related to Mark Twain's plans for "Huck Finn and Tom Sawyer among the Indians," more than half focus exclusively on Huck. In comparison, "T" (for Tom Sawyer) merits only two mentions: "T becomes a chief—maybe a med chief" (120) and "T kills Sal by request" (529). His references to Jim are even more opaque, jotting his name next to Dodge's description of a superstitious African American belief that "an Indian could make himself invisible as air, and was much harder to kill than even a witch" (Dodge 30) and writing "won't scalp J" beside a statement that "An Indian will never take the scalp of a colored soldier . . . [believing] 'Buffalo soldier no good, heap bad medicine' " (Dodge 517). Only one annotation pertains to all three characters: "When H J & T are taken prisoners, it is for the torture. Their devices save them" (Dodge 523), although no further information is included regarding the "devices" in question. Moreover, this comment reinforces the preliminary nature of the marginalia; in the sequel itself, only Jim is taken captive (along with Peggy Mills and her younger sister Flaxy), while Huck, Tom, and Brace Johnson engage in pursuit, hoping to effect a rescue. Mark Twain's emphasis on Huck in the marginalia suggests that the character's extreme social isolation predisposes his attraction toward—and eventual assimilation into—Native society. To this end, the writer underscores several passages concerning "squaw men"—whites married to indigenous women who become integrated into the tribe, fully embracing its beliefs and practices—indicating that this may be Huck's destiny.

Although it is impossible to determine Mark Twain's plans for his sequel with any certainty, his annotations nonetheless offer some tantalizing possibilities. He envisions, for example, Huck entering an Indian camp where he is approached by a medicine man who performs a chant to exorcise the evil spirits traditionally associated with strangers: "H. so received" (Dodge 119). The ritual apparently succeeds because two pages later, next to Dodge's description of the annual visit of an arrow-maker whose charmed projectiles render their possessor immune from injury, Mark Twain writes: "The great arrow maker pays a visit to *H's tribe*" (Dodge 121; emphasis added). This phrase, implying that Huck has not only become an adopted member of the tribe but also one of its respected leaders, is highly significant. He is at home among the Indians, with whom he can be his most free and authentic self.

Several of Mark Twain's other annotations reflect the remarkable degree of cross-cultural integration he imagines for Huck. On page 108, for example, Dodge states: "The power of earnestness is well exemplified in the influence that the Indian religion obtains over the white trappers and 'squaw men' who live with them. Nine-tenths are sooner or later converted to the Indian idea, and many of them have firm faith in their power of 'making medicine.' " The writer made two emphatic vertical strokes next to this paragraph, noting in the margin: "H. becomes converted." At the end of Dodge's subsequent chapter, Mark Twain offers a clue intimating how this conversion occurs: "H. knows [a] young Indian girl whose attitude toward the Good God illustrates the Indian idea. She will indicate the Bad God but refuses to name him" (125).

Other marginalia imply that Huck is initiated into a secret society among the tribe, reflecting the privileged status and trust he has achieved. According to Dodge,

> It is asserted by squaw men, and others in position to know, that almost every tribe of Indians has its secret societies, which have pass-words, grips, and signs as the Masons, Odd-Fellows, etc. I have never been able positively to ascertain the truth or falsity of this statement. Most of the Indians deny it, but . . . I suspect it may be true. (Dodge 131)

Even after thirty years of living among the Cheyenne, Dodge is unable to confirm the existence of these clandestine groups, yet Huck is invited to join one within months of his arrival, as evidenced in the writer's note, "H. gets a grip wh[ich] he recognizes" (Dodge 131).

Two additional annotations flesh out Mark Twain's radical, newfound conception of an Indianized Huck. In a chapter devoted to "The Great Medicine Dance"—more commonly known as the Sun Dance—Dodge describes the elaborate preparations that precede the ceremony and the process whereby young male warriors are selected to participate in it. Once chosen, he explains, each dancer "is stripped to the breech clout (sometimes entirely naked), and holds in his mouth a small whistle of wood or bone, in the lower end of which is fastened a single tail feather of the medicine bird," identified in a footnote as the

Chapparal Cock (Dodge 138). Because these birds are exceedingly rare, only the most skilled hunters succeed in capturing them; as a result, their feathers command "extravagant prices." This small ethnographic detail would not seem particularly important were it not for Mark Twain's comment beside it: "H. sells feathers" (Dodge 145). Huck's role as a supplier of these coveted medicine bird feathers reflects his hunting prowess and revered spiritual stature in the tribe.

The single most provocative comment Mark Twain makes about Huck, however, complicates his character as a result of its ambiguity. While the marginalia do not explicitly confirm Huck's participation in the Sun Dance, Dodge's assertion that "nearly all the unmarried men of the tribe, and numbers of the younger married men, say at least half of the fighting force there present, will go into the dance" (Dodge 144–45) strongly insinuates his involvement. This means that Huck volunteers for "seventy-five hours without sleep, food, drink, or obedience to any demand of nature . . . seventy-five hours of unremitting motion . . . seventy-five hours' expenditure of breath in a constant, monotonous whistle"—the most grueling test of a warrior's stamina and endurance in Plains Indian culture (Dodge 145). Of the one hundred men who enter the dance, Dodge reports that half give up after the first twenty-four hours; "another twenty or twenty-five will collapse before forty-eight hours have expired . . . until the expiration of the dance will find present and at work but ten or fifteen of the original starters . . . those that hold out longest are [deemed] the best men" (Dodge 145–46). The duration of each dancer's participation, moreover, depends on his reason for performing the ceremony: "If that motive is personal to himself, he can cease dancing whenever he thinks he has done enough, either as propitiation or atonement." Mark Twain marked this paragraph with a vertical bracket and wrote next to it: "H. chooses the third night of a dance to help a prisoner escape" (Dodge 146). While it is unclear whether this means that Huck drops out of the dance on the third night or is simply a bystander who seizes the moment as an opportune time to act, his ambition—to free a white captive—belies his position as a "squaw man" and implies an ongoing loyalty to Anglo-American culture. The detail raises the possibility that Huck is a double-agent of sorts, integrating himself into Native culture in order to facilitate a rescue and return to mainstream society.

A CREATIVE CONUNDRUM

Mark Twain's richly detailed marginalia in *Our Wild Indians* offer many suggestive possibilities regarding the sequel to *Huckleberry Finn* that he intended to write during the summer of 1884. Ironically, however, they also prefigure the ultimate cause of its failure. The writer's last entry appears beside a passage describing the sadistic cruelty of Indians "laughing heartily and sometimes positively screaming with delight" not only at the slaughter of Anglo-American settlers but also at violence inflicted on members of their own tribe. "Fun," Mark Twain sardonically comments, "—one's family destroyed" (539). Although Dodge's text continues for a hundred more pages, its margins are empty. The revulsion elicited by this shocking anecdote seems to have thrown the writer's plans into question—challenging and likely overriding the fervent admiration he had previously expressed regarding the "logic," eminent "good sense," and "superiority" of Indian religion.

Unable to reconcile the dissonance of these conflicting responses, Mark Twain found himself at an impasse, and his progress on the sequel stalled. In September, as the family prepared to return to Hartford from Elmira, he gloomily informed his friend Joe Twichell: "The summer has been lost to me. I spent several weeks in the dental chair, coming down from the hill every day for [this] purpose . . . the remnant of the season I wasted in ineffectual efforts to work. I haven't a paragraph to show for my summer" (UCCL 01327, Twain to Twichell, 16 Sept. 1884). Though Mark Twain never finished "Huck Finn and Tom Sawyer among the Indians," his efforts were by no means futile. For in the Dodge marginalia, he left an invaluable record of his keen, insatiably curious mind at work.

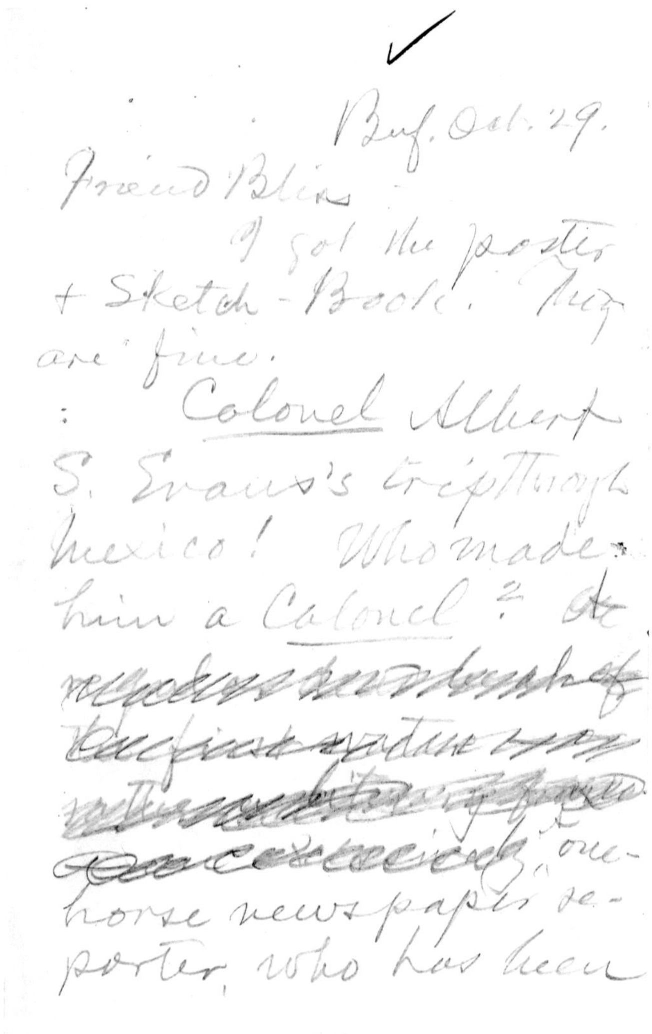

Buf. Oct. 29.

Friend Bliss

I got the poster & Sketch-Book. They are fine.

Colonel Albert S. Evans's trip through Mexico! Who made him a Colonel? A [illegible] one-horse newspaper reporter, who has been

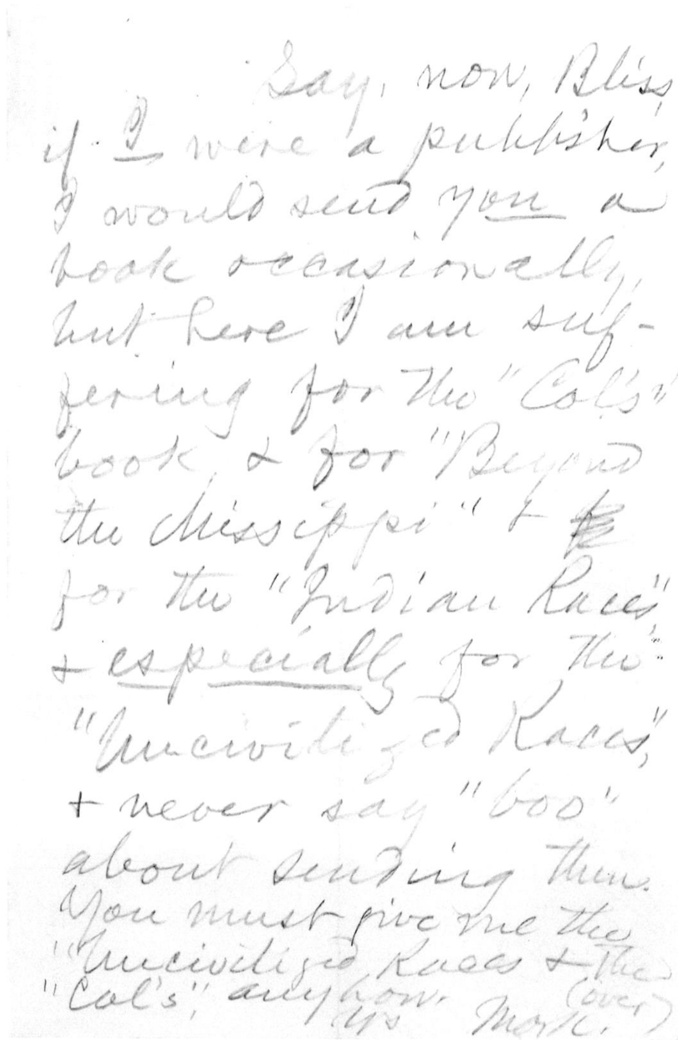

Say, now, Bliss, if I were a publisher, I would send you a book occasionally, but here I am suffering for the "Col's" book, & for "Beyond the Missisippi" & for the "Indian Races" & especially for the "Uncivilized Races," & never say "boo" about sending them. You must give me the "Uncivilized Races & the "Col's," anyhow.

Ys Mark.

(over)

Mark Twain. Autograph letter signed "Mark" to Elisha Bliss, Jr. Buffalo, N.Y., October 29, [1870]. (Item no. 95)

In this letter to his publisher, Twain humorously disparages another author while requesting research materials for *Roughing It*: "*Colonel* Albert S. Evans's trip through Mexico! Who made him a *Colonel*? . . . A one-horse newspaper reporter, who has been trying all his life to make a joke & never has & never *will* succeed. A *Colonel!* He would run from a sheep."

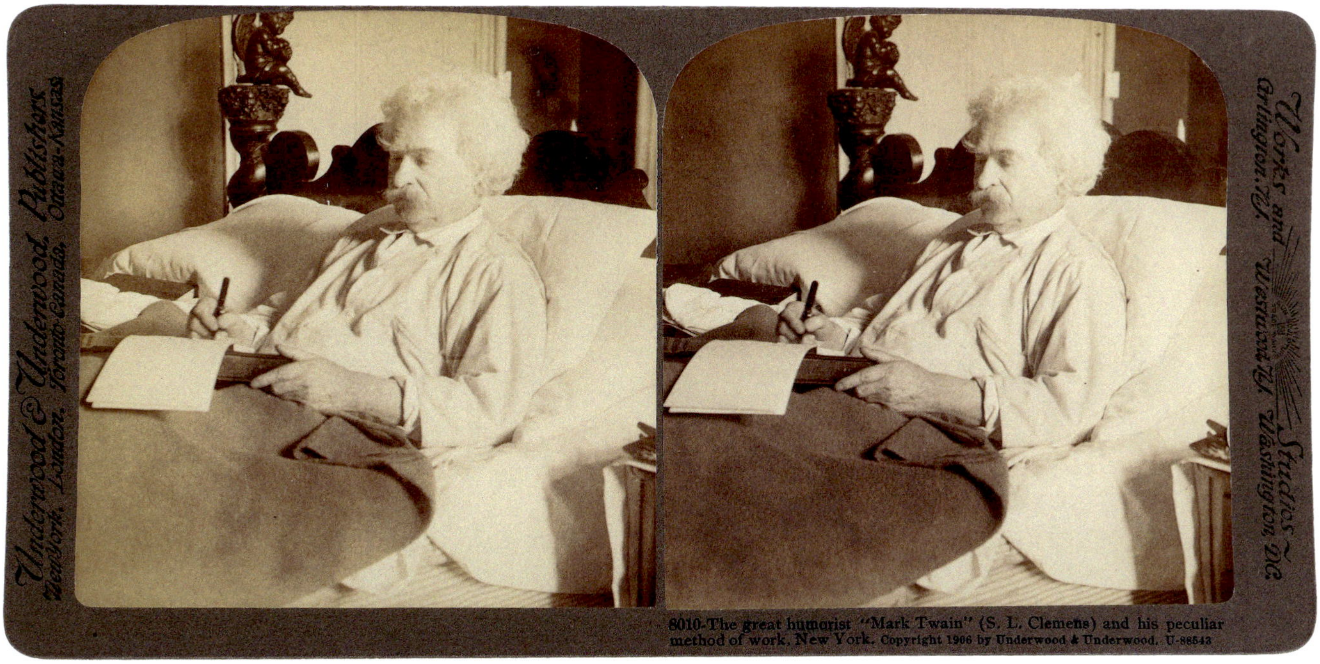

Stereoview of Mark Twain writing in bed. New York: Underwood & Underwood, 1906. (Item no. 119)

This stereoscopic photograph shows "the great humorist 'Mark Twain' (S.L. Clemens) and his peculiar method of work."

THIS PAGE AND OPPOSITE

Life, volume 65, number 25. Chicago: Time, Inc., December 20, 1968. In original wrappers. (Item no. 70)

The unfinished and previously unpublished "Huck Finn and Tom Sawyer Among the Indians" was printed for the first time by Henry Luce's *Life* magazine in 1968, with illustrations by James McMullan.

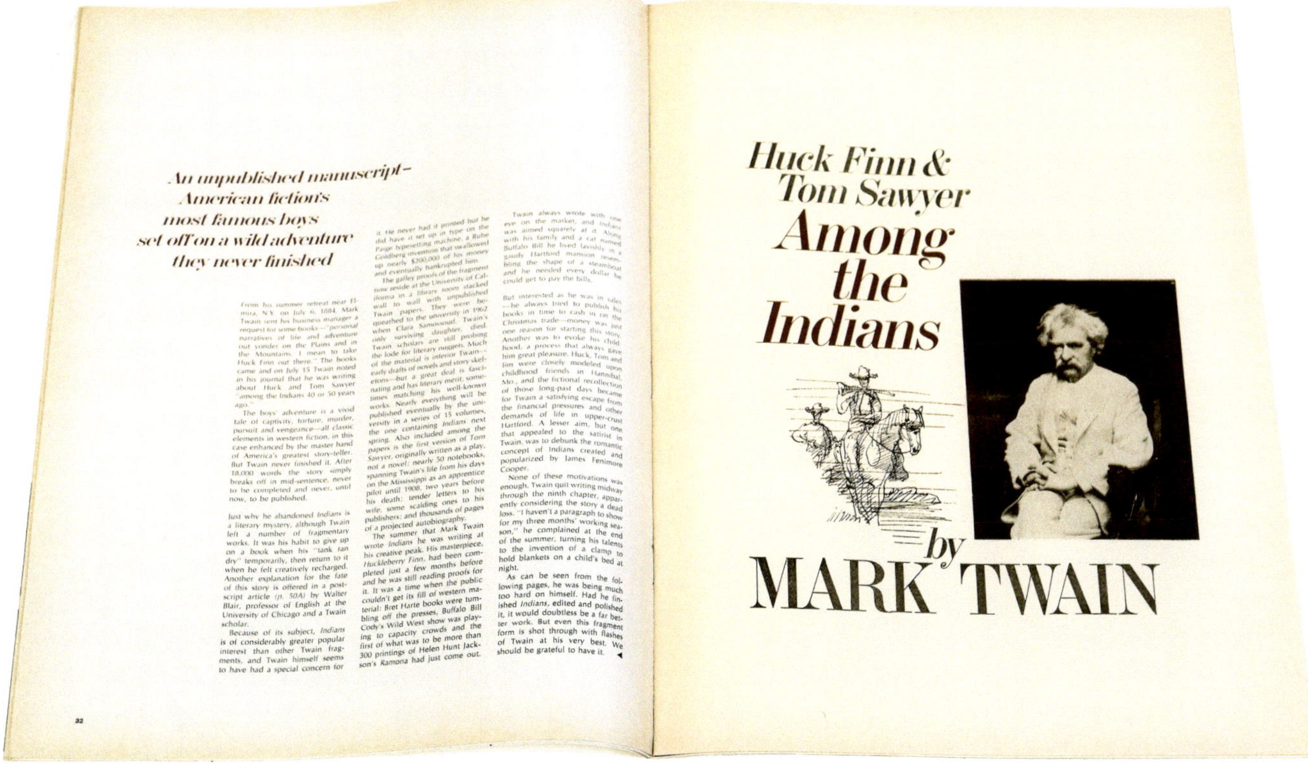

An unpublished manuscript—American fiction's most famous boys set off on a wild adventure they never finished

Huck Finn & Tom Sawyer Among the Indians

by MARK TWAIN

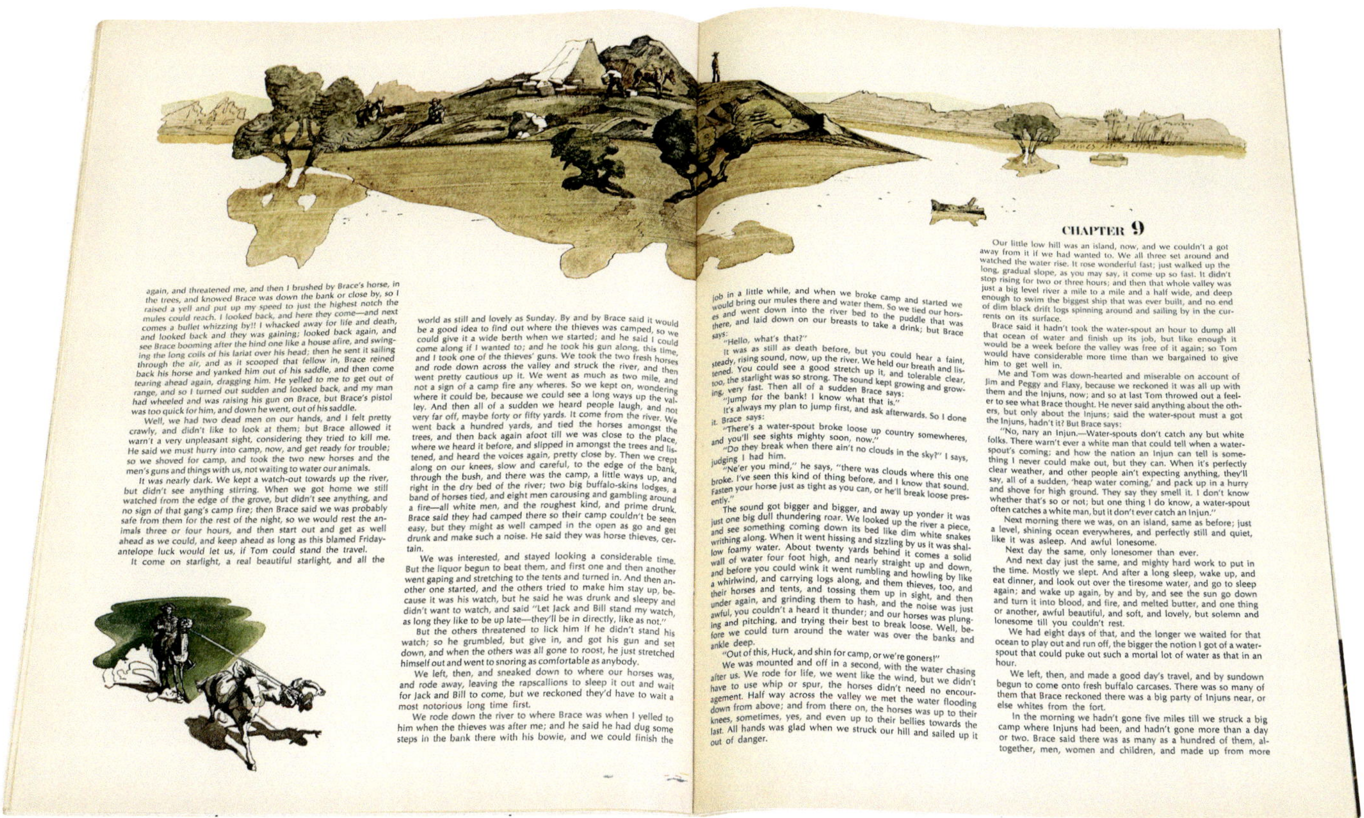

CHAPTER 9

Banning, Editing, and Censoring *Huckleberry Finn*

NICHOLE MISAKO NOMURA

Mark Twain, like most famous authors, has a number of quotes misattributed to him on the internet. His "Censorship is telling a man he can't have a steak just because a baby can't chew it" is more likely a riff on this quote from science fiction author Robert Heinlein's "The Man Who Sold the Moon" than it is Twain's own observation: "The principle [of censorship] is wrong. It's like demanding that grown men live on skim milk because the baby can't have steak."

Wrongly attributed quotes on the internet are more than just the bane of anyone trying to write an article: They're evidence of a cultural schema that understands historical figures as champions of ideas, principled enough that they clearly *could* have said something. We have a clear mental model of what they might have said based on what we know they said. In this case, the Twain/Heinlein mashup points to an important role for Mark Twain in the way we understand book bans. One of the reasons he's fundamental to the way we understand book banning in America is because of the story we tell about banning *Adventures of Huckleberry Finn*—a story Twain, in many ways, taught us to tell.

In book banning, there are always two realities. There are the actual physical books and the various restrictions/disincentives placed on access to them. This is the reality of numbers, policies, and legal actions. Then there is the story we tell about book banning in the press, at school board meetings, and in interviews—no less real for being *made*, sometimes of lies and half-truths—that shapes how we read, purchase, and talk about books. This is the reality of words, public relations, and our own personal experiences with text.

These two realities can be tightly connected, or not. They certainly influence each other—but not always in the directions we think they will. In the case of *Huckleberry Finn*, we can see the ways the stories about banning are simultaneously things made of words and built on numbers—and that they are stories Twain himself was eager to exploit.

In February and March of 1885, newspaper reviews of *Huckleberry Finn* were split—some favorable, and some, including a review from the Boston *Daily Globe* (20 Feb. 1885; quoted in Fischer 10), which pans Twain's command of dialect (arguing that Huck would never have said "commence" and that Twain should have used "begin"), decidedly unfavorable. Despite the mixed critical reception, the book was selling well—39,000 copies by mid-March, which Twain pronounced a "success" (UCCL 03162, Twain to Webster, 10 Feb. 1885).

The *Globe*'s review was positioned against a background of general animosity toward the text that had been brewing in the publishing world: Twain's lawsuit against Estes & Lauriat (for selling the novel below subscription price) was covered negatively by the Boston papers. In mid-March, that animosity took a new form as the Concord Library committee published their decision not to circulate *Huckleberry Finn*, citing some of their reasons included in this infamous quote:

> Said one member of the committee: "While I do not wish to state it as my opinion that the book is absolutely immoral in its tone, still it seems to be that it contains but very little humor, and that little is of a very coarse type. If it were not for the author's reputation the book would undoubtedly meet with severe criticism. I regard it as the veriest trash." Another member says: "I have examined the book and my objections to it are these: It deals with a series of adventures of a very low grade of morality; it is couched in the language of a rough, ignorant dialect, and all through its pages there is a systematic use of bad grammar and an employment of rough, coarse, inelegant expressions. It is also very irreverent. To sum up, the book is flippant and irreverent in its style. It deals with a series of experiences that are certainly not elevating. The whole book is of a class that is more profitable for the slums than it is for respectable people, and it is trash of the veriest sort." (*Globe-Democrat*, 17 March 1885; quoted in Fischer 17)

News of the ban and key snippets of the insults spread quickly—all the way to California within just two days. While the Boston *Daily Advertiser* (23 March 1885; quoted in Fischer 19) announced that papers across the country were reporting on the ban in agreement with Concord, in truth, the landscape was much more varied. Several prominent editorials, including one in the San Francisco *Chronicle*, lampooned the ban as absurd. Reporting on the ban was an opportunity to editorialize on Twain, *Huckleberry Finn*, *Huckleberry Finn*'s expected sales as a result of the ban, and Concord itself, which was the subject of many jokes about Transcendental philosophy and not a little scorn for giving free publicity to the text, rather than silently refraining from adding the book to their library shelves.

Clemens seemed initially pleased by the ban, writing to his publisher that the library committee had "given us a rattling tip-top puff which will go into every paper in the country. They have expelled Huck from their library as 'trash & suitable only for the slums.' That will sell 25,000 copies for us, sure" (UCCL 03192, Twain to Webster, 18 March 1885).

Concord, perhaps trying to make amends, made Clemens a member of the Concord Free Trade Club on the 24th of March. Clemens wrote a satirical letter to the secretary of the club, published in the Boston *Daily Advertiser* on April 2 (quoted in Fischer 25), that thanked Massachusetts for two different harms, which he reframed as benefits—the first, the Estes & Lauriat ruling (decidedly not in his favor), the second, the Concord Library ban. In that letter, Clemens writes:

> In the next place, a committee of the public library of your town have condemned and excommunicated my last book and doubled its sale. This generous action of theirs must necessarily benefit me in one or two additional ways. For instance, it will deter other libraries from buying the book; and you are doubtless aware that one book in a public library prevents the sale of a sure ten and a possible hundred of its mates. And, secondly, it will cause the purchasers of the book to read it, out of curiosity, instead of merely intending to do so, after the usual way of the world and library committees; and then they will discover, to my great advantage and their own indignant disappointment, that there is nothing objectionable in the book after all.

In this letter, we see the stories and numbers merge—first, the surety of "doubl[ing] its sale," then, the speculative impact of absent library copies on readers and sales—the "sure ten and a possible hundred." This is followed by a story about what happens when a book is banned—that curiosity, and a desire to read materials deemed objectionable, increases readers' engagement with the text.

The letter was widely reprinted, and, like the ban, commented upon—although less favorably. It smacked of self-promotion just a little bit too much. Yet Twain's prediction that the ban would result in more sales seemed to be correct, and his use of the ban as continued self-advertisement, however distasteful it may have seemed to a handful of reviewers in the moment, likely helped to cement the story about the book ban as the story of *Huckleberry Finn*—a story that would continue to help sales and direct critical attention for time to come. The ban has been perhaps erroneously taken to represent *Huckleberry Finn*'s American reception (Fischer 17), but a generation of scholars has worked to disentangle the story about the ban from its reality.

Bernadette Lear's study of library holdings of Twain found that *Huckleberry Finn* was rapidly acquired and widely held during Twain's lifetime—in fact, it was adopted by public libraries more quickly than most of Twain's other works. Within two years, Lear found, 41.2 percent of libraries had acquired *Huckleberry Finn*, compared to 31.5 percent holding *The Adventures of Tom Sawyer* or the 26.2 percent that held *Life on the Mississippi* within a similar window (Lear 212). Demand was so high, in fact, that libraries regularly ordered replacements and extra copies (Lear 214).

While the book sold well and was well reviewed after the furor over Concord died down, anxieties about its content and form for audiences of young people remained. By the turn of the century, *Huckleberry Finn* was being cataloged with texts aimed at young readers. Some libraries had specific sections for young readers, and some did not; our understanding of children's and juvenile literature as a thing distinct from literature for adults was burgeoning, but by no means established, at the turn of the century (Lear 218). Some libraries promptly moved it out again—the Brooklyn Public Library moved it into the adult readers' section in 1905. A librarian who was present at the meeting wrote to Clemens in a letter that "the prevailing opinion of Huck was that he was a deceitful boy who said 'sweat' when he should have said 'perspiration' " (UCLC 35703, Asa Don Dickinson to Twain, 19 Nov. 1905). Moving from the library to the school, however, took another thirty years: The first school edition was printed in 1931. The edition was unexpurgated, produced, it was claimed, "scientifically" by two teachers, and included testimony from student readers to assert its value to the classroom—defending it against the bans of the past and hypothetical future ones constructed using the same rationale. While the edition addressed issues of grammar, dialect, and uplift—the concerns of the Concord ban—it did not anticipate the challenges that begin in the 1940s and '50s, such as the challenges centered on the harm of reading a slur repeatedly.

Schools don't have to ban a text to not teach it. As *Huckleberry Finn* enters the public classroom, the kinds of challenge, censorship, and contestation that can be directed at the text change. Outright bans remain a possibility—in 1957, the New York City Board removed *Huckleberry Finn* from the list of approved elementary and junior high textbooks, functionally banning it from those school's classrooms—but it remained permitted in high schools and in libraries. Other kinds of censorship, ranging from expurgation and bowdlerization to the practice of excerpting approved passages for inclusion in anthologies, have been used to minimize or circumvent the challenges of teaching a text that uses the N-word over 200 times.

In 1983, John H. Wallace, a Black educator, produced an edition for classroom use that replaces the N-word with "slave," "dude," and "Black." In 2011, NewSouth Books produced an edition, also aimed at classrooms, that replaces the N-word with "slave"—an edition that was incredibly controversial in both Twain studies and in education. The NewSouth edition spawned several parodies, the most successful of which, Diani & Devine's Robotic Edition, raised over $30,000 on Kickstarter to sponsor its production. Classrooms may censor the use of the N-word by students aloud but permit them to read an unexpurgated text; the Norton Critical Editions, aimed at a college market, remain unexpurgated. Students might have their parents opt them out of particular texts, reading an alternative text independently in the library while their peers discuss *Huckleberry Finn*. There are any number of ways to intervene in the reading experience of *Huckleberry Finn*, some of which look like conventional censorship, and some of which look like standard pedagogical practice.

Bans, however, get the most attention, thanks to the American Library Association's (ALA) banned book list ("100 Most Frequently"; "Top 100 Banned"; "Top 100 Most Banned"). In the 1990s and 2000s, the novel regularly rose to the top of the ALA lists, which include school libraries. Over the past thirty years, its position has fallen, from spot #5 in 1990–1999 to spot #14 in 2000–2009 and, finally, to spot #33 in 2010–2019. The landscape of school and library book bans is changing; while concerns about the N-word and its harms to students persist, they now compete with increasing numbers of challenges to books with LGBTQ+ characters and authors and other identity categories, books that depict sex, pregnancy, or drug use, and books about the Holocaust.

Decisions about what is best for readers, especially young readers in a school context, are easily conflated with decisions about what is legal, given the complicated relationship between public libraries, public schools, the reading public, and the government—but they are worth untangling. At no point has *Huckleberry Finn* ever been illegal to own or read in the United States. Access to the text has been made more expensive, more difficult, and, if Clemens is to be believed about the advertising impact of bans, more appealing by a variety of institutions and agents since the novel's publication. Teachers and schools have been forbidden from assigning the text, libraries have removed it from circulation, editors and censors have swapped words—each its own kind of barrier to entry, with different impacts for different readers.

The story of banning *Huckleberry Finn* reminds us that stories about bans are just that—stories. The story of any book ban is always simultaneously a story with a plot, heroes, and villains, and a story of numbers and real readers. Like all stories, they can be told and retold, reworked, and reimagined. Twain gives us one such template, but so too the activists who redirected our attention from "sweat" to the N-word. What role will the story of *Huckleberry Finn*'s banning play in the broader narrative of contemporary book bans?

W. & A. H. Fry. Carte-de-visite photograph of Mark Twain. Brighton, [U.K.], [September 12, 1872]. (Item no. 114)

Fry's studio took five photographs of Twain during his 1872 visit to England.

Tom Sawyer and Huckleberry Finn bookends. [New York]: Armor Bronze, [ca. 1925]. (Item no. 147)

Twain's characters Tom Sawyer and Huckleberry Finn form a matching pair in these decorative bookends.

THIS PAGE AND FOLLOWING

Edward Ardizzone. 37 original illustrations for *The Adventures of Huckleberry Finn*. [1960–1961.] Pen and ink on paper. (Item no. 128)

Ardizzone, a renowned British illustrator, created this series of pen-and-ink illustrations for a school edition of *Huckleberry Finn* published by Heinemann Educational in 1961.

Huck Finn
Chapt XXXIX

Huck Finn
I read considerable to Jim about Kings & Dukes.

TITLE PAGE
The King
The Duke
Huck Finn
Mary Jane
Jim

THIS PAGE AND OPPOSITE

Samuel L. Clemens. Autograph manuscript, "To the Bride" [and] "S'klk! G'lang!" September 1, 1886. (Item no. 86)

When Olivia Clemens's childhood friend Clara Spaulding was married in 1886, Clemens honored her with a pair of horse-car tickets and a "loving though humble and squalid poem." The poem humorously describes Christopher Columbus, the prophet Elijah, and others who had the courage to "take a ride."

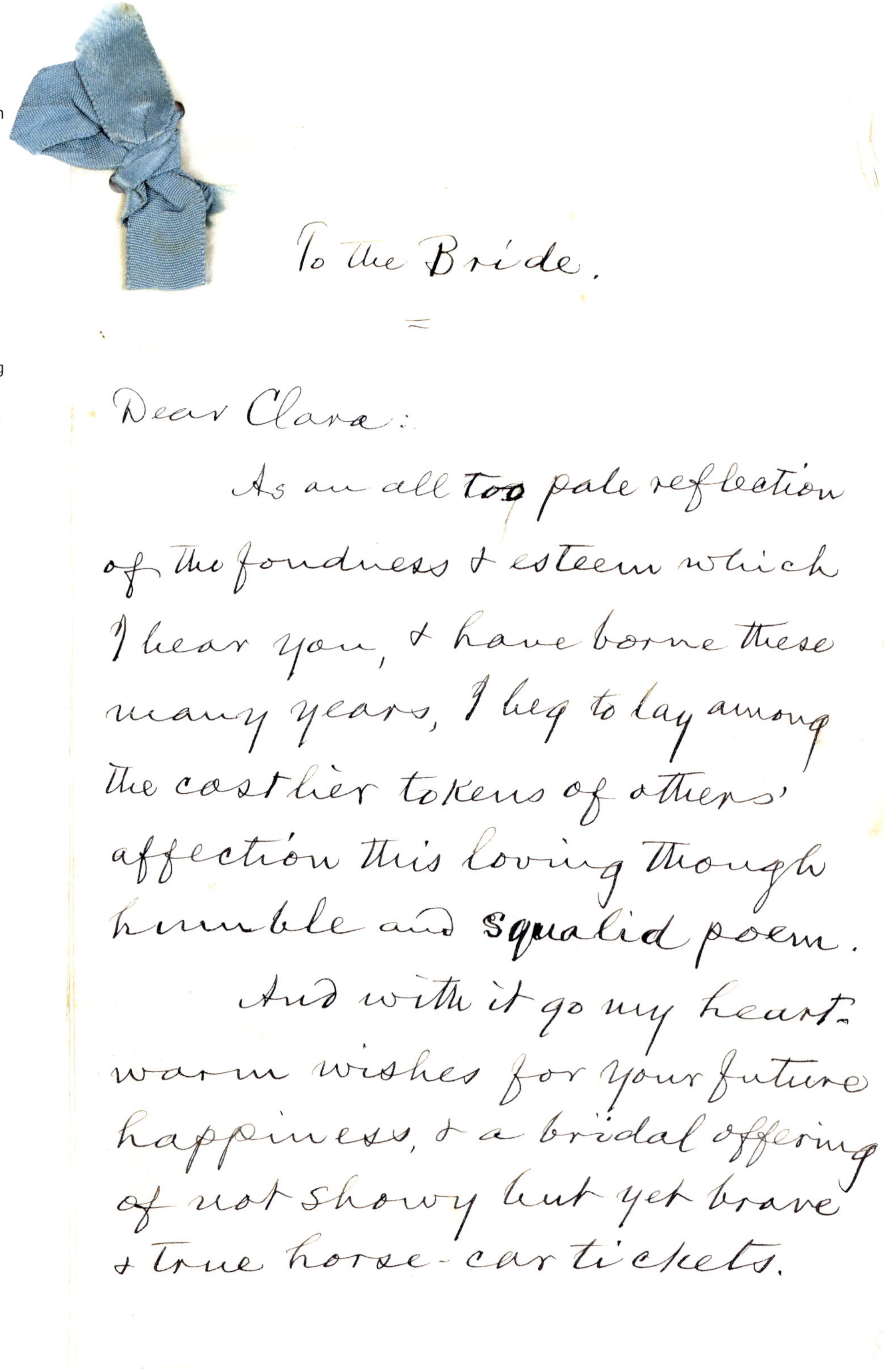

To the Bride.

=

Dear Clara:

As an all too pale reflection of the fondness & esteem which I bear you, & have borne these many years, I beg to lay among the costlier tokens of others' affection this loving though humble and squalid poem.

And with it go my heart-warm wishes for your future happiness, & a bridal offering of not showy but yet brave & true horse-car tickets.

3

S'klk! G'lang!

=

Mongolfier, as people say,
With board-bills gaping wide,
Did not repine, nor bow his spine,
Nor wait to dine, or e'en decline:
But rose + took a ride.

=

In '92, Columbus true
The clamorous world decried:
He never winched, he never flinched!
His contract clinched, his belt he cinched,
Cast off + took a ride.

Mark Twain at Play

GABRIEL MCKEE

Games were an important part of Samuel Clemens's life. His earliest piece for *The Californian* in 1864 discusses a card game of rapid reversals called "Muggins": "In that game, if you make a mistake of any kind, however trivial it may be, you are pronounced a muggins by the whole company. If you play the right card in the wrong place, you are a muggins; no matter how you play, in nine cases out of ten you are a muggins" (Clemens, "A Notable Conundrum"). In 1869, he courted Livy by teaching her cribbage, and when building Stormfield in 1908 he installed a raised platform in the billiard room so that family members and guests could have a better view while watching him play (UCCL 00227, Twain to Langdon, 12 Jan. 1869; UCCL 00235, Twain to Langdon, 19 Jan. 1869; Lyon). Parlor amusements were an important aspect of nineteenth-century family life, and Clemens's family was no exception.

But Clemens turned his imagination to the creation of new methods of play. In 1883, while he was hard at work on the manuscript for *Adventures of Huckleberry Finn*, he devised a game to help his children to learn history, in particular the regnal dates of English monarchs. The first version of this game took on a grand scale:

> I measured off 817 feet of the roadway, a foot representing a year, and at the beginning and end of each rein I drove a three-foot white-pine stake in the turf by the roadside and wrote the name and dates on it. Abreast the middle of the porch-front stood a great granite flower-vase overflowing with a cataract of bright-yellow flowers—I can't think of their name. The vase was William the Conqueror. We put his name on it and his accession date, 1066. We started from that and measured off twenty-one feet of the road, and drove William Rufus's stake; then thirteen feet and drove the first Henry's stake . . . . In our road one could tell at a glance who was who by the size of the vacancy between stakes—with *locality* to help, of course. (Clemens, "How to Make" 5)

The game lent a visual and tactile experience to the abstract dates he wished his children to learn. Within a few hours of devising this game, he imagined a more practical method of envisioning dates, using a scoreboard from the game of cribbage. He developed some simple rules for turning the visualization into a playable experience, in which players would take turns placing a pin on a board representing a century and naming an important event from that year.

Clemens wrote a brief account of the rules to Joseph Hopkins Twichell, and was frustrated to learn that Twichell immediately sent them to a newspaper for publication: He had planned to develop the rules more fully into a marketable product, and Twichell's action potentially undercut his copyright. The game proved difficult to develop, and he cautioned William Dean Howells: "If you haven't ever tried to invent an indoor historical game, *don't*" (UCCL 02572, Twain to Howells, 22 Aug. 1883). In 1885, Clemens patented *Mark Twain's Memory-Builder*, and in 1891 Charles L. Webster & Co. published a game bearing the same name—differing significantly in design, if not general intent, from what had been described in the patent (Rosenberg; Walsh and Zlatic 223).

Mark Twain's Memory-Builder **(page 205)** is more a gamification of learning than a true game, essentially encouraging the process of rote memorization through a simple scoring system. This system is largely arbitrary—accessions of English monarchs are scored at 10 points (compared to 5 for battles and 1 for all other historical events), apparently for no other reason than the fact that this was the historical knowledge he had initially conceived the game to reinforce. The rules explain this preoccupation: "The most conspicuous landmarks in history are the accessions of kings; therefore these events are given the first place in the game and allowed to count the most." The rules are fairly vague—but this also renders them modifiable, and the instruction book provides suggestions for applying the basic rules to different areas of learning.

Clemens had grand plans for the game's success, as Walsh and Zlatic summarize: "National clubs would be organized for the game; newspapers would carry regular columns on it; a book would be written to accompany it; national contests would be held and prizes given; international competition would create millions in royalties!" (Walsh and Zlatic 222–23). The game was a commercial failure, however. Though the rules emphasize the endless versatility of the game for learning history, they give no guidance for restoring the physical board to enable playing the game once the board has deteriorated. The destructive nature of play—which requires punching holes in the paper of the combination scoreboard and rulebook—is an impediment to replayability. But more than play for its own sake, the game's purpose is education—providing a different experience to reading, hearing, or reciting facts, providing a visual and tactile stimulus to associate with historical information. The game's greatest downfall is that it confounds any effort to make it appear fun: Milton Meltzer described it as "a cross between an income tax form and a table of logarithms" (Meltzer 193).

EXPLOITING TWAIN'S IMAGE

Clemens was not the only one seeking to exploit the fame of Mark Twain in a playable format. The card game *Authors*, in which players strive to complete suits matching famous literary figures to their best-known works, was first published in 1861, and saw dozens of editions in the following decades (Strong). It became a bestseller, likely because its original publishers, G.M. Whipple and A.A. Smith, were unable to protect their copyright, leading to imitations and variants from dozens of gamemakers. West & Lee's 1873 edition, published with the name *Portrait Authors*, was the first to include Mark Twain **(page 206)**. He became a mainstay in the game's many editions, and he was highlighted on the boxes of J. H. Singer's *Game of Authors No. 2* **(page 206)**, issued sometime around 1890, and Milton Bradley's *Modern Authors* **(page 207)**, published around 1890–1910.

Another game publisher that sought to benefit from Twain's recognizability was Parker Brothers, founded in 1883. One of its earliest publications was *The Amusing Game of Innocence Abroad*, designed by a Mrs. Shepherd and first published in 1888 or 1889 (Orbanes 16–17) **(page 125)**. The subtle variation on Twain's title suggests a stronger connection to *Innocents Abroad* than the game itself displays. Rather than presenting a steamship voyage overseas, the game appears to focus instead on domestic travel. The players begin in houses at the upper left of the board and travel by train, stagecoach, and boat to the City at the lower right. Each player has two pieces, and can choose which to move after spinning (or, in later printings, rolling dice). The board has several sections—a town in which players shop before beginning their trip, a railroad line, a depot (at which players stop for lunch), a stagecoach path, and a steamboat. Philip Orbanes describes the result as a "smooth-playing, episodic experience" (Orbanes 17).

But despite a colorful board with multiple sections, players have little choice in what route they take, moving wherever the spinner takes them. Thus, the game is almost entirely luck-based, providing little opportunity for players to do anything but spin and move. Where *Authors* and *Mark Twain's Memory-Builder* have an ostensibly educational aim, Parker Bros. were clear that their ambitions for *Innocence Abroad* were simpler, describing it in their trade catalogue as "to a certain degree instructive, but its principal ingredient is PURE FUN" (quoted in Orbanes 17). The game was successful enough to earn a second edition in or after 1901, retitled *The Good Old Game of Innocence Abroad*, and replacing the first edition's spinner with dice—a method of randomizing movement frowned on in the nineteenth century because of their association with gambling (Whitehill 115) **(page 125)**.

Simple race games were popular with young players throughout the nineteenth and twentieth centuries. *The Adventures of Tom Sawyer and Huck Finn*, published in 1925 by Stoll & Edwards, is a roll-and-move game similar to *Innocence Abroad*, but it pays much more attention to the narrative of the book on which it is based, with players collecting a series of sequential picture cards depicting major moments in *Tom Sawyer* **(pages 208–209)**. Milton Bradley's 1937 *Game of Tom Sawyer*, produced as a tie-in with the Selznick motion picture adaptation of the novel, uses the same simple mechanic, but enhances it with a "swapping" system whereby players can play cards that assist or (more often) sabotage one another's progress **(page 213)**.

TOM SAWYER IN PIXELS

As video games took on a central place in the play of the 1980s, publishers again turned to Mark Twain for material to adapt. In 1988, Disney developed *The Chase on Tom Sawyer's Island* for the Apple II and Commodore 64 home computer systems (Item no. 159). The gameplay of this chase game resembles Pac-Man, with a pixelated Tom Sawyer collecting apples while fleeing from Aunt Polly, Injun Joe, and a bear. The following year saw the release of two games based on *The Adventures of Tom Sawyer*. SETA's *Adventures of Tom Sawyer*, for the Nintendo Entertainment System, abandons all but the smallest connections to the novel's setting and plot **(page 210)**. In the simple 8-bit platformer, a daydreaming Tom Sawyer battles giant animals (an octopus, an alligator, and an ape) and an airship before awakening to find his adventures were just a dream. Marketed only in Japan for the Famicom system, *Square's Tom Sawyer* draws far more on the novel's characters and plot, placing them into the general role-playing model that Square had defined with *Final Fantasy* the year before **(page 211)**. The game is marred, however, by a deep racial insensitivity, particularly in the character of Jim, presented as a horrendously racist caricature; this, perhaps even more than the game's overall lackluster gameplay, prevented it from being localized to markets outside of Japan. Neither of these adaptations proved successful, but Twain's work remains a source of inspiration for game designers: Currently in development from game designer Book Games S.E. is a 3-D game entitled *Mark Twain's Tom Sawyer: Survival Game*, aiming to give players an immersive experience of Tom Sawyer's island adventure—simulated with a significantly higher level of realism than that on display in *The Chase on Tom Sawyer's Island*.

Clemens envisioned games as mnemonic strategies for enlivening education. His own effort, *Mark Twain's Memory-Builder*, was a failure, but the success of *Authors* shows that his goal was a reasonable one. The most successful board game based on Clemens's works—*Innocence Abroad*—is the least connected to the details of his works. But more recent developments in digital games suggest that a different approach can provide readers with an immersive experience of his novels. Though past gamemakers have met with limited success turning *Tom Sawyer* into a playable experience, their repeated attempts to do so show that the vividly imagined Mississippi River setting of *Tom Sawyer* remains a world in which readers want to play.

OPPOSITE

Mark Twain's Memory-Builder. A Game for Acquiring and Retaining All Sorts of Facts and Dates. New York: Charles L. Webster, 1891. (Item no. 156)

Clemens patented his rules for a game to assist in the memorization of historical dates in 1885, and finally published this version of his teaching aid in 1891. He anticipated broad interest in the game, but it was a financial failure.

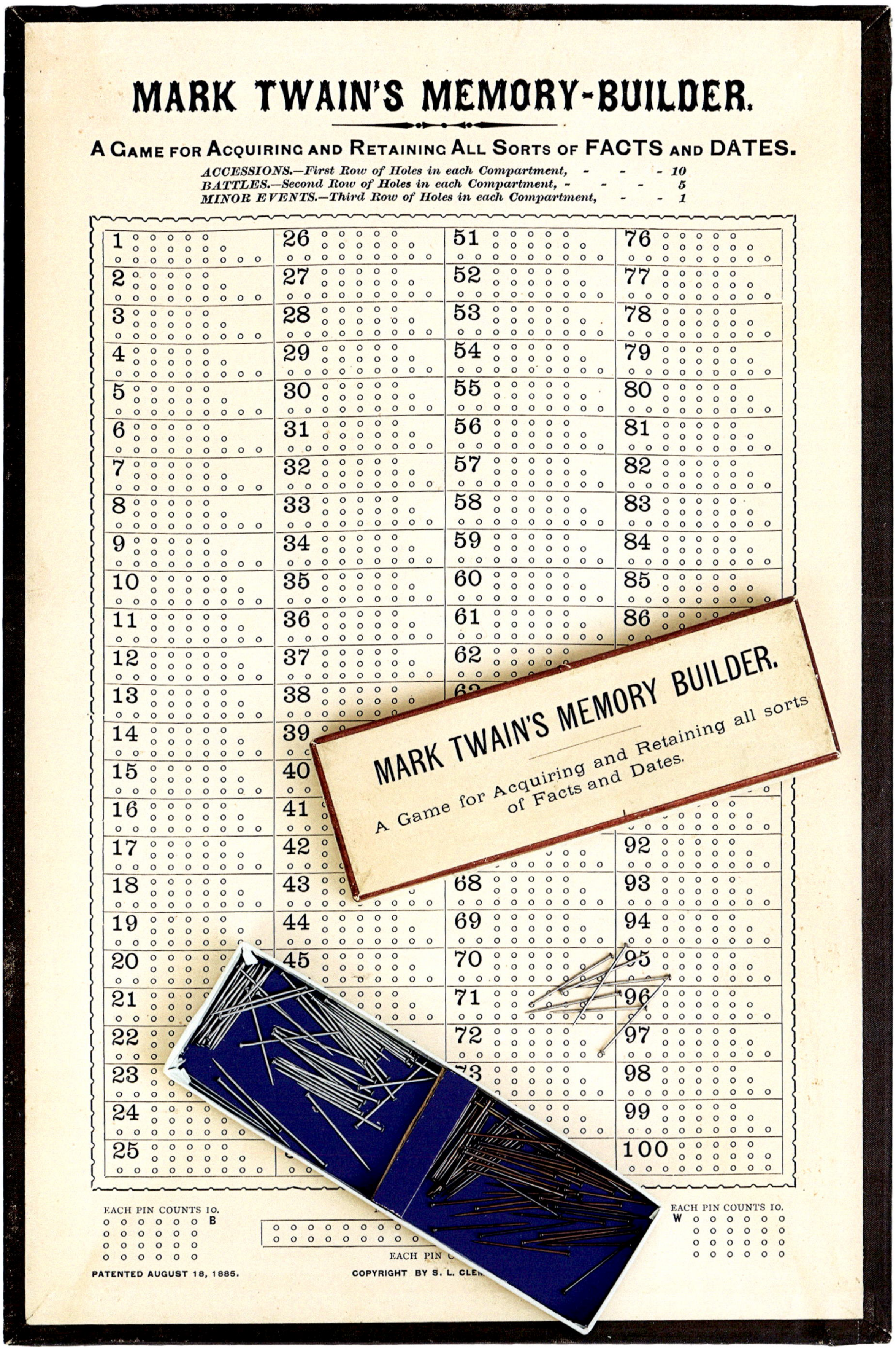
MARK TWAIN'S MEMORY-BUILDER.
A GAME FOR ACQUIRING AND RETAINING ALL SORTS OF FACTS AND DATES.
ACCESSIONS.—First Row of Holes in each Compartment, - - - 10
BATTLES.—Second Row of Holes in each Compartment, - - - 5
MINOR EVENTS.—Third Row of Holes in each Compartment, - - 1
MARK TWAIN'S MEMORY BUILDER.
A Game for Acquiring and Retaining all sorts of Facts and Dates.
EACH PIN COUNTS 10.
PATENTED AUGUST 18, 1885.

BELOW

Portrait Authors. Salem, Mass.: West & Lee Game Co., 1873. (Item no. 149)

TOP AT RIGHT

Authors Improved. Springfield, Mass.: Milton Bradley & Co., [ca. 1890]. (Item no. 152)

BOTTOM AT RIGHT

Game of Authors No. 2. New York: J.H. Singer, [ca. 1890]. (Item no. 151)

OPPOSITE

Modern Authors. Springfield, Mass.: Milton Bradley Co., [ca. 1890–1910]. (Item no. 153)

The suit-building card game *Authors* was patented in 1861, but as a result of a poorly protected copyright it was produced in dozens of different editions from multiple publishers, and remains in print to this day. West & Lee's 1873 illustrated edition *Portrait Authors* was the first to include Twain.

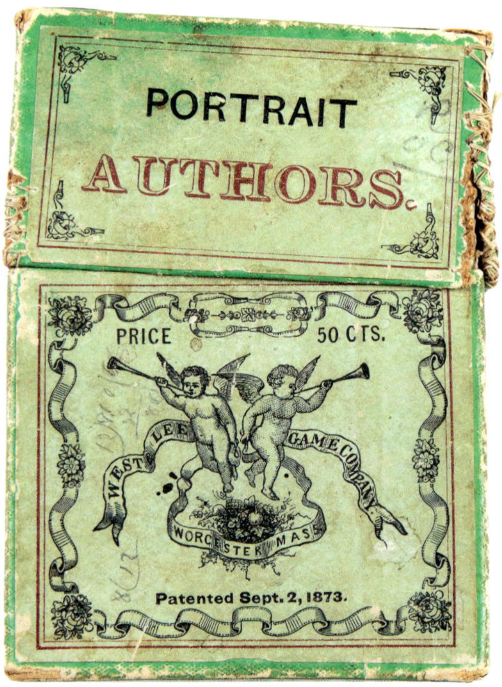

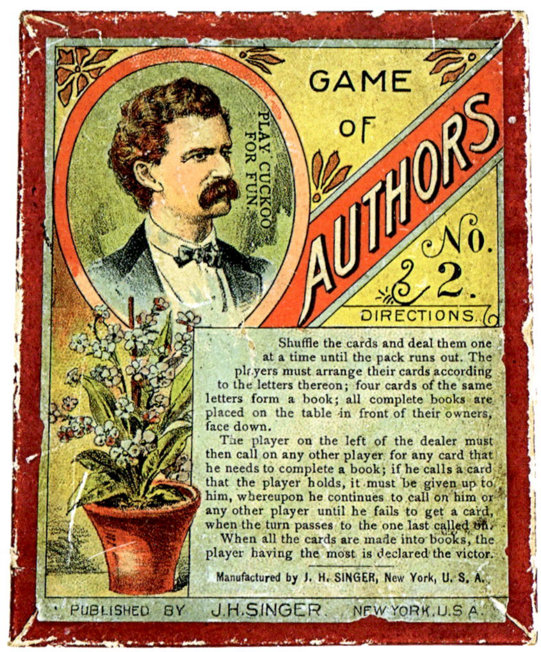

2
The Prince and
2
Innocents Abroad.
2
Huckleberry
2
Samuel L. Clemens.
SAMUEL L. CLEMENS.
INNOCENTS ABROAD.
THE PRINCE AND THE
INNOCENTS ABROAD.
THE PRINCE AND THE PAUPER.
HUCKLEBERRY FINN.

MODERN
AUTHORS
CLEMENS
MILTON BRADLEY COMPANY
SPRINGFIELD, MASS.
4005
Made in U. S. A.

Adventures of Tom Sawyer and Huck Finn: A Game for Boys and Girls. New York: Stoll & Edwards Co., Inc., 1925. (Item no. 157)

This simple race game takes players through the major plot points of *The Adventures of Tom Sawyer*.

GAME OF THE ADVENTURES OF
TOM SAWYER AND HUCK FINN
Village of St Petersburgh Start Here.
Sawyer beguiles the boys into whitewashing the fence. Remain here 2 turns.
The Haunted House. Remain here until one other player passes you.
The boys drag the treasure home in an express wagon.
Tom and Huck dig for hidden treasure. For all your trouble remain here 2 turns.
Tom and Becky lost in the cave. You will be a long time here. Lose 3 turns.
Tom and Huck find the treasure box in the cave. Rich at last. You can run home from here. You win.
Tom Sawyer, the hero of the Sunday School. A fluke, but go ahead 3 spaces.
You may stay here 1 turn for deception.
Commencement exercises, the Schoolmaster loses his wig. For this go back 4 spaces.
Tom, Huck and Joe Harper decide to be pirates. Go ahead to the meeting place.
The meeting place. The pirates capture a raft. Go ahead to Jackson Island.
Tom Sawyer's and Huck Finns midnight adventure in the graveyard. Run ahead 4 spaces.
Tom's great Secret, the return home with his brother pirates and attend their own funerals. Go ahead 6 spaces.
The rendezvous on Jackson Island. Remain here 2 turns and have a good time.
BY PERMISSION OF THE ESTATE OF SAMUEL L. CLEMENS AND THE MARK TWAIN CO.
Tom Sawyer as Robin Hood in grave combat with Joe Harper. Remain here 1 turn.
Tom Sawyer gives Aunt Polly's yellow cat a dose of Pain Killer. Remain here 2 turns and imitate the cat.
Copyright 1925 Stoll & Edwards Co. Inc. New York, N.Y. Made in U.S.A.
1
Tom Sawyer beguiles the boys into whitewashing the fence.
10
Commencement exercises the schoolmaster loses his wig.

The Adventures of Tom Sawyer. Torrance, Calif.: SETA U.S.A., Inc., 1989. Cartridge for Nintendo Entertainment System. (Item no. 161)

In this side-scrolling adventure game with little connection to Twain's novel, a daydreaming Tom Sawyer battles pirates and enormous animals.

Square's Tom Sawyer = *Sukuwea no Tomu Sōya*. Tokyo: Square Co., Ltd., 1989. (Item no. 160)

In this simple role-playing game, players reenact a variation on the plot of *The Adventures of Tom Sawyer*.

RIGHT

Stereoview of Twain's house in Hartford, [ca. 1875]. (Item no. 115)

Twain wrote many of his most famous works while living at this house at 351 Farmington Avenue in Hartford, Connecticut, from 1874 to 1891, although most of his actual writing was done during his summer stays in Elmira.

RIGHT BOTTOM

The Game of Star Authors. New York: McLoughlin Brothers, [1887]. (Item no. 150)

The Game of Tom Sawyer. [Springfield, Mass.]: Milton Bradley Co., 1937. (Item no. 158)

A board game produced as a tie-in with David O. Selznick's 1938 film *The Adventures of Tom Sawyer*.

Illustration from "Tom Sawyer's Gang as Social Ritual: Implications for Modern Social Organization," *Mark Twain Journal*, Spring, 1983.

THIS PAGE AND OPPOSITE

Bill Watterson. Four postcard cartoons of Mark Twain. [Charleston, S.C.]: Mark Twain Journal, 1983. (Item no. 131)

Several years before creating *Calvin & Hobbes*, cartoonist Bill Watterson produced a series of images for the *Mark Twain Journal* that were issued as promotional postcards.

In "A Curious Dream" (1870), Twain satirized the way the citizens of Buffalo had neglected their old North Street graveyard. Tired of having to bail out their graves with their skulls every time it rained, the residents set off with their possessions to find a new home elsewhere.

Twain concluded with a "NOTE:–The reader is assured that if the cemeteries in his town are kept in good order, this dream is not leveled at his town at all, but is leveled particularly and venomously at the *next* town."

WATTERSON Mark Twain Journal ©1983
"I WAS GRATIFIED TO BE ABLE TO ANSWER PROMPTLY, AND I DID. I SAID I DIDN'T KNOW."
–Life on the Mississippi, Ch. 6

"IT COULD PROBABLY BE SHOWN BY FACTS AND FIGURES THAT THERE IS NO DISTINCTLY NATIVE AMERICAN CRIMINAL CLASS EXCEPT CONGRESS."
— Pudd'nhead Wilson's New Calendar
WATTERSON ©1983 Mark Twain Journal

What's in a Name?: Samuel Clemens and Mark Twain

JULIE CARLSEN

Samuel Clemens was working as a journalist in the Nevada Territory when he first introduced the pseudonym Mark Twain in *The Territorial Enterprise* on February 3, 1863. His "Letter from Carson City," a satirical lament of two sleepless nights, begins, "I feel very much as if I had just awakened from a long sleep" and closes with "Yours, dreamily, Mark Twain"—a fitting start for Clemens's illusory alter ego whose identity would become inextricable from his own ("Letter from Carson City"). "A Bloody Massacre Near Carson," a sensational account of a man who murdered his family and took his own life after losing a major investment, is another significant early appearance of Mark Twain, published in the *Enterprise* in October of the same year. Clemens made the whole story up, almost as if warning his audience that as Twain, he could be trusted for good writing—but not the truth.

After achieving national fame as Twain with the success of "Jim Smiley and His Jumping Frog" in 1865, Clemens continued to develop and promote his new image to reach an ever-widening audience. He drew on his personal experiences to inform the character of Twain, but he often adapted, exaggerated, and even fabricated his story along the way, blurring the line between fiction and reality. Louis J. Budd writes in *Our Mark Twain: The Making of His Public Personality*:

> While seeing no logic or profit in splitting off his role as public personality from his writings, he made aggressively sure that Mark Twain the man figured large in the newspapers and common talk . . . he valued the grassroots exposure too; honoring the bonds of sociability with speeches at all kinds of occasions . . . he understood and managed the windings of publicity; and if a little slow to catch on that the fresh genre of the interview played into his strengths, he became its master for quality and quantity. (Budd 25)

Thanks to Clemens's effort, Twain became larger-than-life, prompting some scholars, like Justin Kaplan, to argue that Twain was "an identity in itself," as if existing outside of the man who created it (Kaplan 13). Others, like John C. Gerber, feel that type of analysis goes too far: "The most that can be said for Clemens's famous pseudonym," Gerber argues, "is that it serves as a sign of a comic sensibility at work. To insist on more than this is to indulge in oversimplification that obscures the intricate and successful uses . . . of the comic pose or mask while narrating as 'Mark Twain' " (Gerber 297). And yet both agree: Whether pose or persona, Mark Twain was a figure that Clemens carefully and intentionally cultivated.

Mark Twain's name appears on so wide a variety of consumer products that one could easily assume Clemens was wanton about its use. In fact, he was quite the opposite, even going so far as to create the Mark Twain Company in 1908 in an attempt to control the use of the name. This detail provides a useful tool for understanding the nuances of how and when Clemens chooses to employ his pseudonym in print. The title pages of *Adam's Diary* (1904) and *Eve's Diary* (1906) **(pages 58–59)**, where Mark Twain is credited as the "translator" of Adam and Eve's "original manuscripts," offer a glimpse of the same trickster who peddled a false report of murder decades earlier in Carson City. Determined to extend beyond his reputation as a humorist, Clemens notably considered publishing *The Prince and the Pauper* (1881) anonymously, lest the name Mark Twain work against his intention for the book; that the title page of the first edition bears his pseudonym evidences the unstoppable power of his brand as a selling point—even where it interfered with Clemens's authorial wishes.

SAMUEL CLEMENS: LETTER WRITER

Observing instances of Clemens's choosing *not* to use his pseudonym is also a useful tool for studying his writing, especially his written correspondence. In January 1870, Clemens wrote to his friend Jim Gillis about his upcoming marriage to Olivia Langdon. Clemens begins the heartfelt letter by recounting their time gold-mining together in California and the good fortune he's enjoyed since:

> It makes my heart ache yet to call to mind some of those days. Still, it shouldn't—for right in the depths of their poverty & their pocket-hunting vagabondage lay the germ of my coming good-fortune . . . I mean that day we sat around the tavern stove & heard that chap tell about the frog & how they filled him with shot. . . . I jotted the story down in my note-book that day, & would have been glad to get ten or fifteen dollars for it—I was just that blind. But then we were so hard up. I published that story, & it became widely known in America, India, China, England,—& the reputation it made for me has paid me thousands & thousands of dollars since. Four or five months ago I bought into that *Express* (have ordered it sent to you as long as you live—& if the bookkeeper sends you any bills, you let me hear of it) & went heavily in debt—never could have dared to do that, Jim, if we hadn't heard the Jumping Frog story that day. **(page 13)** (UCCL 00416, Twain to Gillis, 26 Jan. 1870)

He signs the letter: "Truly Your Friend, Saml. L. Clemens." Gillis would not have known Clemens as Twain, but the question still stands: If Clemens wanted to remunerate his friend as thanks, why not send him the autograph of Mark Twain? Perhaps Clemens did not want to appear superior to someone he knew in poorer days (although name-dropping his affluent fiancé later in the letter and the general boasting throughout suggest otherwise). Regardless, Clemens is nonetheless emphasizing the deepness of his affection for the recipient—a clear sign of his awareness that attaching his pseudonym to writing could make it seem less serious.

Similarly, Clemens sometimes signed his legal name to add a note of formality to his correspondence. In a letter from June 1875 **(page 219)** signed "Thankfully yours, S.L. Clemens," he writes to an unidentified group of gentlemen with gratitude for exposing a man who intended to publish his works without authorization, whom he denounces here as a "common thief" (UCCL 13244, Twain to "Gentlemen," 21 June 1875). Clemens, who detested literary piracy and took matters of infringement very seriously, appears to use his legal name to underscore the gravity of his words. Later, in September 1897, Clemens writes to his contemporary Robert Barr **(page 76)**, praising his novel *A Woman Intervenes* (1896), which he says captivated him so that he "read through to the end without stopping (& without skipping a line.) And yet my custom is to skip liberally" (UCCL 10669, Twain to Barr, 18 Sept. 1897). He signs the letter "Sincerely yours, S. L. Clemens," again presumably to emphasize the genuineness of his praise.

But even when he is being serious, Clemens is never completely so. In a letter to Georgia politician Andrew Dawson regarding *A Tramp Abroad* and signed "Truly Yrs, S. L. Clemens" **(page 220)**, Clemens humorously pretends not to be able to spell "hellfire," writing:

> I am in trouble again with my helfiard book. (There— I have probably spelt that word wrong again. Mr. Beecher tried a million times, if he tried once, to teach me how to spell that simple, every-day word, but somehow I never could seem to get the hang of it. I cannot use it with any sort

of confidence especially in print.) (UCCL 09849, Twain to Dawson, 26 Nov. 1879)

Clemens presumably signed this letter with his legal name out of respect for an elected official, but if so, why would he have included this humorous excursus on a purposefully misspelled word? Could he be presenting as Twain to match the fame of his correspondent? Or could he be preemptively diminishing himself, as if to ward off any potential more formal conversation?

MARK TWAIN: LETTER WRITER

Clemens wrote so many letters throughout his lifetime that it is nearly impossible to draw a clear line of demarcation between those he signed as Mark Twain and those he signed as Samuel Clemens—but carefully considering the name he chose to sign can offer additional insight, as explored in a letter to publisher Richard Gilder **(page 221)** (UCCL 05031, Twain to Gilder, 12 March 1896). Clemens wrote this two-part letter to the editor of *The Century* magazine while on his fundraising Around the World Tour in India. The first part of the letter details the author's experiences in India and is signed "Mark Twain." The second part, which is marked "private" and signed "Mark," details a cost-effective publication plan for the public part of the letter.

Clemens's knack for self-promotion is on full display in this letter that is both a proposal and a draft of an article all in one. This tactic is likely why he chose to sign the "public" part of the letter as Mark Twain; he intended it to be published. Clemens's second signature in this letter raises more questions than it answers. On one hand, signing the postscript—which, it should be noted, need not have been signed at all—seems to underscore that the letter is a serious business proposal. But if he wanted to be formal, why didn't he sign his legal name? Could Clemens have been intentionally trying to seem nonchalant lest he come across as desperate for the sale? He was, after all, deeply in debt at the time. Or was this just another one of his jokes—another reminder that Twain should never be fully trusted?

OPPOSITE

Samuel L. Clemens. Autograph letter signed "Samuel L. Clemens" to an unidentified Boston publisher. Hartford, June 21, [1875]. (Item no. 99)

Clemens thanks the unidentified Bostonian for alerting him to the piratical aims of a man named Greer. He advises the publisher that "all of my stuff is amply protected, + none of it is for sale." On the same day as this letter, he made good on his promise to "expose this filthy thief" by writing a brief letter about the matter to the Hartford *Courant*.

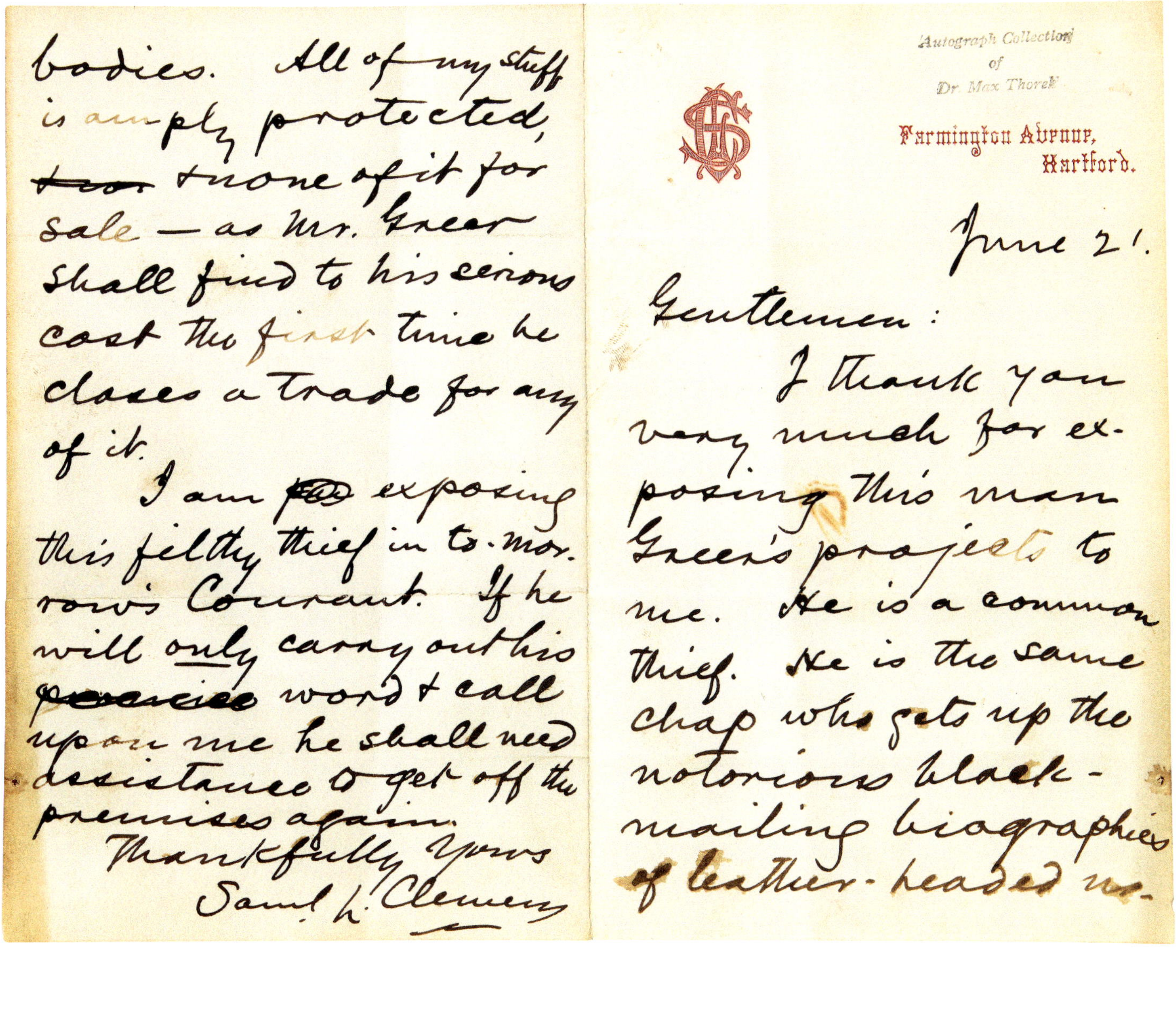

bodies. All of my stuff
is amply protected,
~~too~~ & none of it for
sale — as Mr. Greer
shall find to his serious
cost the first time he
closes a trade for any
of it.

I am ~~[illegible]~~ exposing
this filthy thief in to-mor-
row's Courant. If he
will only carry out his
~~promise~~ word & call
upon me he shall need
assistance to get off the
premises again.

Thankfully Yours
Saml. L. Clemens

Autograph Collection
of
Dr. Max Thorek

Farmington Avenue,
Hartford.

June 21.

Gentlemen:

I thank you
very much for ex-
posing this man
Greer's projects to
me. He is a common
thief. He is the same
chap who gets up the
notorious black-
mailing biographies
of leather-headed us-

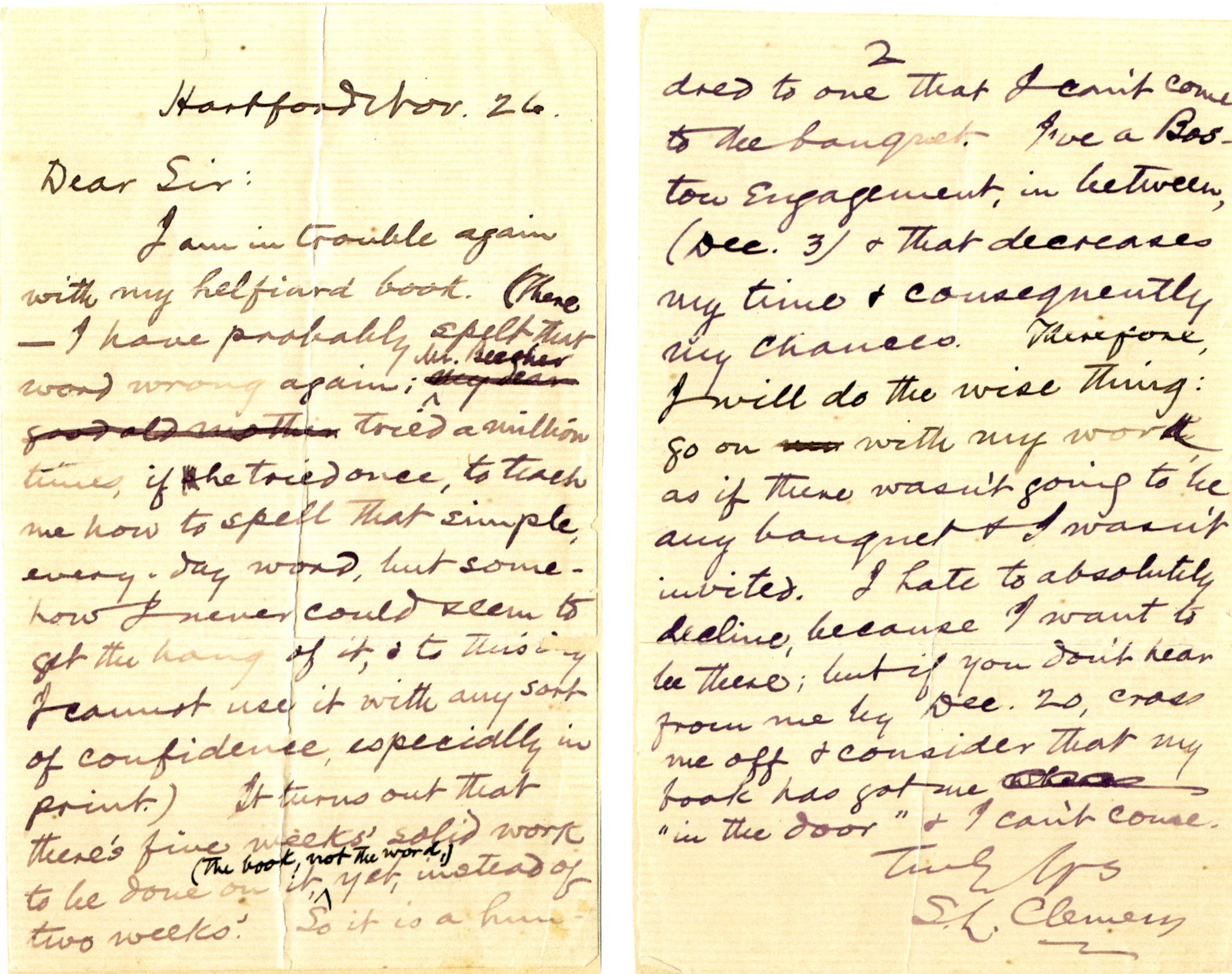

Hartford Nov. 26.

Dear Sir:

I am in trouble again with my helfiard book. (There — I have probably spelt that word wrong again; ~~my dear good old mother~~ Mr. Beecher tried a million times, if ~~s~~he tried once, to teach me how to spell that simple, every-day word, but somehow I never could seem to get the hang of it, & to this day I cannot use it with any sort of confidence, especially in print.) It turns out that there's five weeks' solid work to be done on it, (The book, not the word.) yet, instead of two weeks. So it is a hun-

2

dred to one that I can't come to the banquet. I've a Boston engagement, in between, (Dec. 3) & that decreases my time & consequently my chances. Therefore, I will do the wise thing: go on with my work as if there wasn't going to be any banquet & I wasn't invited. I hate to absolutely decline, because I want to be there; but if you don't hear from me by Dec. 20, cross me off & consider that my book has got me "in the door" & I can't come.

Truly yrs

S. L. Clemens

OPPOSITE

Samuel L. Clemens. Autograph letter signed "S. L. Clemens" to Andrew H. H. Dawson. Hartford, November 26, [1879]. (Item no. 100)

A letter to Georgia politician Andrew Dawson regarding *A Tramp Abroad* in which Clemens humorously pretends not to be able to spell "hellfire," writing: "I am in trouble again with my helfiard book. There—I have probably spelt that word wrong again. Mr. Beecher tried a million times, if he tried once, to teach me how to spell that simple, every-day word, but somehow I never could seem to get the hang of it. I cannot use it with any sort of confidence especially in print."

RIGHT

Mark Twain. Autograph letter signed "Mark Twain" and "Mark" to Richard Gilder. Leypone, India, March 12, 1896. (Item no. 103)

Twain wrote this two-part letter to the editor of *The Century Magazine* while on his fundraising Around the World Tour in India. The first part of the letter, which is signed "Mark Twain," is a travel essay based on the author's experiences in India. The second part, which is marked "private" and signed "Mark," details a cost-effective publication plan for the public part of the letter.

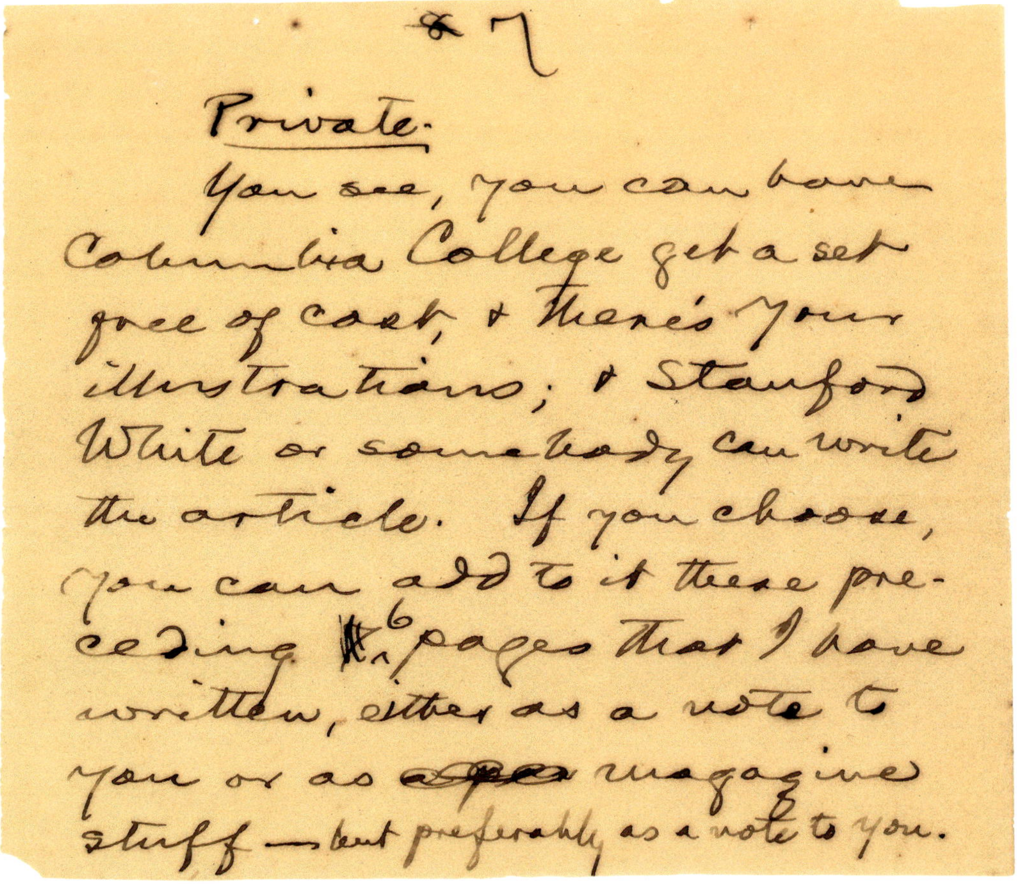

#7

Private.

You see, you can have Columbia College get a set free of cost, & there's your illustrations; & Stanford White or somebody can write the article. If you choose, you can add to it these preceding 6 pages that I have written, either as a note to you or as magazine stuff—but preferably as a note to you.

THIS PAGE AND OPPOSITE

Samuel L. Clemens. Autograph letter signed "Sam. Clemens" to "Aunt Betsy." St. Louis, [October 13?], 1859. (Item no. 90)

Clemens was a twenty-three-year-old riverboat pilot when he wrote this letter to Elizabeth W. Smith, a family friend from Missouri whom he referred to as "Aunt Betsy." This is one of the earliest Mark Twain letters held in a private collection.

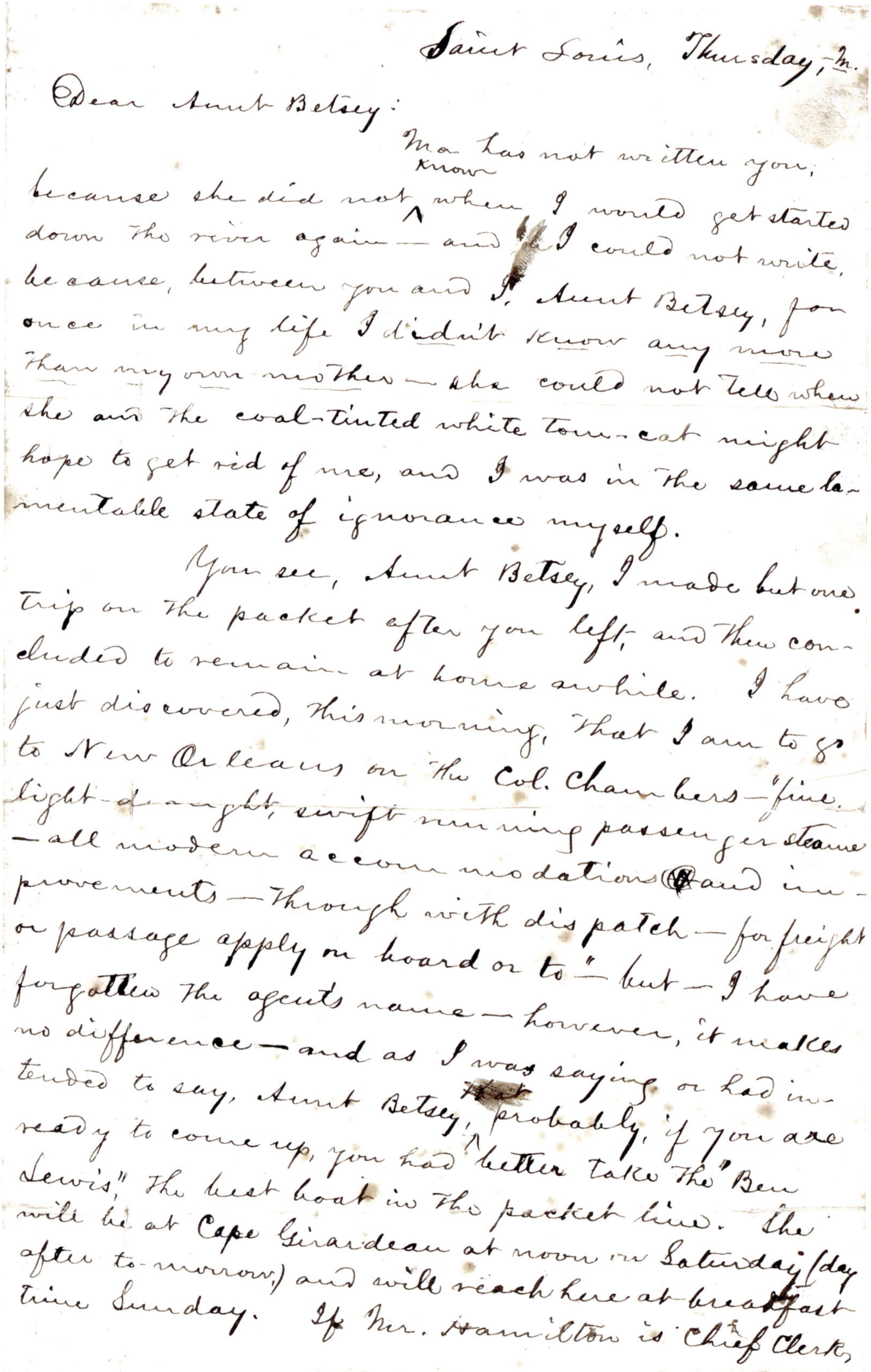

Saint Louis, Thursday, m.

Dear Aunt Betsy:

Ma has not written you, because she did not know when I would get started down the river again—and I could not write, because, between you and I, Aunt Betsy, for once in my life I didn't know any more than my own mother—she could not tell when she and the coal-tinted white tom-cat might hope to get rid of me, and I was in the same lamentable state of ignorance myself.

You see, Aunt Betsy, I made but one trip on the packet after you left, and then concluded to remain at home awhile. I have just discovered, this morning, that I am to go to New Orleans on the Col. Chambers—"fine, light-draught, swift running passenger steamer—all modern accommodations and improvements—through with dispatch—for freight or passage apply on board or to"—but—I have forgotten the agent's name—however, it makes no difference—and as I was saying or had intended to say, Aunt Betsy, probably, if you are ready to come up, you had better take the "Ben Lewis," the best boat in the packet line. She will be at Cape Girardeau at noon on Saturday (day after to-morrow) and will reach here at breakfast time Sunday. If Mr. Hamilton is Chief Clerk,

—very well. I am slightly acquainted with him. And if Messrs. Carter, Gray and Dean Somebody (I have forgotten his other name,) ~~are in the~~ pilot-house—very well again—I am acquainted with them. Just tell Mr. Gray, Aunt Betsey—that I wish him to place himself at your command.

All the family are well except myself—I am in a bad way again—disease, Love, in its most malignant form. Hopes are entertained of my recovery, however. At the dinner-table,—excellent symptom—I am still as "terrible as an army with banners."

Aunt Betsey—the wickedness of this world—but I haven't time to moralize this morning.

Good-bye.

Sam. Clemens

P.S.—All send their love.

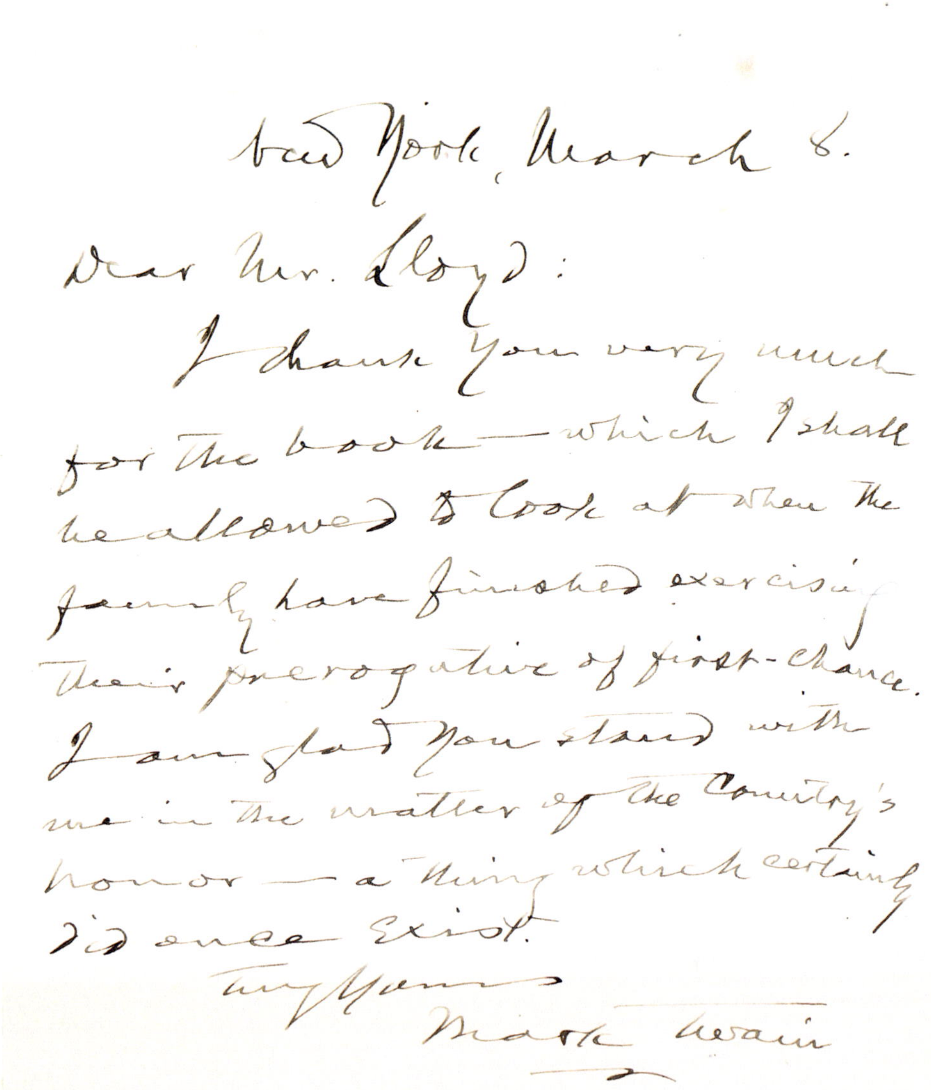

New York, March 8.

Dear Mr. Lloyd:

I thank you very much for the book—which I shall be allowed to look at when the family have finished exercising their prerogative of first-chance. I am glad you stand with me in the matter of the Country's honor—a thing which certainly did once exist.

Truly Yours

Mark Twain

Mark Twain. Autograph letter signed "Mark Twain" to "Mr. Lloyd" (Henry Demarest Lloyd). New York, March 8, no year. (Item no. 109)

Clemens thanks Lloyd, a progressive "muckraking" journalist, for sending a book—likely Lloyd's *Wealth Against Commonwealth*, which condemned the monopolies of the era in general and the Standard Oil Co. in particular.

Napoleon Sarony. Cabinet card photograph of Mark Twain. New York, 1893. (Item no. 118)

Twain signed this photograph taken by celebrity photographer Napoleon Sarony, "This is the very worst!"

Afterword

DECLAN KIELY

"That, of course, is the great secret of the successful fool—that he is no fool at all" (Asimov 1970). This is how Isaac Asimov described the various fools that populate the plays of William Shakespeare. But it is equally applicable to Mark Twain, who shared several characteristics with Shakespeare's fools: an innate ability to outwit others, to sniff out and puncture pomposity, vanity, and hypocrisy in all its forms and, above all, to entertain. In doing so, the fool speaks a vital truth to power.

The range of Twain's humor—from gentle, folksy, Old Southwestern to exuberantly Rabelaisian—is considerable. No person or subject was safe from the razor-sharp, satirical edge of his pen. He was a master of diction and dialogue, whether it be down-home American, or archaic, pseudo-aristocratic English. His ability to parody, to create convincing literary pastiche, is unrivaled. His fiction, often disguised as factual, plain truth, draws upon some of the same literary techniques as his modernist peers: frame narratives, unreliable narrators, non-linear storylines, social criticism, absurdism. But Twain handles these techniques with a lightness of touch that belies his genius.

Inevitably, in presenting himself as "a first-class fool" Twain ran the risk of not being taken as seriously as his literary contemporaries. But as Albert Bigelow Paine, Twain's first biographer (who also served as his editor and literary executor), wrote: "It is very dangerous to take Mark Twain seriously, and still more dangerous not to do so" (Paine to Edward Wagenknecht, 16 Jul. 1935, Morgan Library & Museum MA 4905.24). Susan Jaffe Tane takes Mark Twain very seriously, as her collection—and the exhibition and catalogue that grew out of it—vividly demonstrates. Susan is in august company with some of the great Twain collectors of the past century—J. Pierpont Morgan, Owen D. Young, Walter P. Chrysler Jr., Nick Karanovich, and James S. Copley, to name only a select few. Despite the serious interest (not to say money!) that has been paid to (and for) Twain's work by bibliophiles and admirers of his writing, surprisingly this is the first-ever Grolier Club exhibition devoted to him.

And yet, perhaps my surprise is misplaced. After all, Twain's humor, particularly in his later work when it became darkly comic, was willing to test the boundaries of tolerance and good taste of his own time and the decades following his death. One thinks of his hilarious short story "Cannibalism in the Cars" (first published

[Samuel Clemens, former owner.] Gesteckpfiefe [tobacco pipe]. Germany, undated. (Item no. 124)

Clemens was gifted this two-piece German pipe by his secretary Isabel Lyon, but he purportedly never smoked from it.

in *The Broadway Annual*, November 1868 included in the 1875 collection *Sketches, New and Old*) in which vestigial memories of the recent Civil War and the earlier, ill-fated Donner party hover on the periphery of the reader's consciousness. This exhibition elucidates the full arc of Twain's humor—from "Jim Smiley's Jumping Frog" to *King Leopold's Soliloquy*—revealing a "fool" who speaks to us in our time with undiminished force and relevance. It is well that we pay attention to him and listen.

George Grantham Bain. Portrait photograph of Samuel L. Clemens. [New York?, ca. 1909.]

Works Cited

Asimov, Isaac. *Asimov's Guide to Shakespeare*. New York: Doubleday, 1970.

Blair, Walter, ed. *Selected Shorter Writings of Mark Twain*. Boston: Houghton Mifflin, 1962.

Blanck, Jacob, ed. *Bibliography of American Literature.* 9 vols. New Haven, CT: Yale University Press, 1955–91.

Branch, Edgar M. " 'My Voice Is Still for Setchell': A Background Study of 'Jim Smiley and His Jumping Frog.' " *PMLA* 82 (1967): 591–601.

Budd, Louis J. *Our Mark Twain: The Making of His Public Personality*. Philadelphia: University of Pennsylvania Press, 1983.

Caron, James E. *Mark Twain, Unsanctified Newspaper Reporter*. Columbia: University of Missouri Press, 2008.

Clemens, Samuel L. *Adventures of Huckleberry Finn*. Berkeley: University of California Press, 2003.

——. *The Adventures of Tom Sawyer, Tom Sawyer Abroad, Tom Sawyer, Detective*. Berkeley: University of California Press, 1980.

——. "Almost an Item." San Francisco *Morning Call*, August 5, 1864, 2.

——. *Autobiography of Mark Twain*. 3 vols. Edited by Harriet Elinor Smith et al. Oakland: University of California Press, 2010–15.

——. *The Autobiography of Mark Twain: Including Chapters Now Published for the First Time*. Edited by Charles Neider. New York: Harper & Brothers, 1959.

——. *The Celebrated Jumping Frog of Calaveras County, and Other Sketches*. New York: C. H. Webb, 1867.

——. *Chapters from My Autobiography*. Edited by Shelley Fisher Fishkin, with Introduction by Arthur Miller and Afterword by Michael J. Kiskis. New York: Oxford University Press, 1996.

——. *Early Tales & Sketches.* Volume 1 (1851–1864); Volume 2 (1864–1865). Edited by Edgar Marquess Branch and Robert H. Hirst, and Harriet Elinor Smith. Berkeley: University of California Press, 1979–81.

——. *A Family Sketch and Other Private Writings*. Edited by Benjamin Griffin. Berkeley: University of California Press, 2014.

——. "Forty-Three Days in an Open Boat." *Harper's New Monthly Magazine* 34 (December 1866): 104–13.

——. "How to Make History Dates Stick." *Harper's Monthly Magazine* 130 (December 1914): 3–15.

——. "How to Tell a Story." In *Mark Twain: Collected Tales, Sketches, Speeches, & Essays, 1891–1910*. Edited by Louis J. Budd. New York: Library of America, 1992.

——. "Huck Finn and Tom Sawyer Among the Indians." In *Mark Twain's Hannibal, Huck & Tom.* Edited by Walter Blair. Berkeley: University of California Press, 1969.

——. "Jim Smiley and His Jumping Frog." In *Early Tales & Sketches*. Berkeley: University of California Press, 1981.

——. "Jim Wolf and the Tom-Cats." New York *Sunday Mercury*, 14 July 1867, 3.

——. "The 'Jumping Frog' in English. Then in French. Then Clawed Back into a Civilized Language Once More, by Patient, Unremunerated Toil." In *Mark Twain: Collected Tales, Sketches, Speeches, & Essays, 1852–1890*. Edited by Louis Budd. New York: Library of America, 1992.

——. "Letter from Carson City." *Nevada Territorial Enterprise*, February 3, 1863.

——. "Letter from Honolulu. Burning of the Clipper Ship Hornet at Sea." *Sacramento Union*, 19 July 1866, 1.

——. *Life on the Mississippi.* Boston: James R. Osgood and Co., 1883.

——. "Mark Twain and His English Editor [To the Editor]." *Spectator* [London, England], September 21, 1872, 1201–02.

——. *Mark Twain–Howells Letters: The Correspondence of Samuel L. Clemens and William D. Howells, 1869–1910*. 2 vols. Edited by Henry Nash Smith and William M. Gibson. Cambridge, MA: The Belknap Press of Harvard University Press, 1960.

——. *Mark Twain in Eruption: Hitherto Unpublished Pages about Men and Events*. Edited by Bernard DeVoto. New York: Harper, 1940.

——. *Mark Twain's (Burlesque) Autobiography*. New York: Sheldon, 1871.

——. *Mark Twain's Letters.* Volume 6: 1874–1875. Edited by Michael B. Frank and Harriet Elinor Smith. Berkeley: University of California Press, 2002.

——. *Mark Twain's Notebooks & Journals.* Volume 1 (1855–1873), Volume 2 (1877–1883), Volume 3 (1884–1891). Edited by Frederick Anderson, Michael B. Frank, Kenneth M. Sanderson, Lin Salamo, Bernard L. Stein, and Robert Pack Browning. Berkeley: University of California Press, 1975, 1975, 1979.

——. *Mark Twain's Own Autobiography: The Chapters from the "North American Review."* 2d ed. Edited by Michael J. Kiskis. Madison: University of Wisconsin Press, 2010.

——. *Mark Twain's Speeches.* Edited by Albert Bigelow Paine. New York: Harper and Brothers, 1923.

——. *My Autobiography: "Chapters" from the North American Review*. Introduction by Thomas Wortham. Mineola, NY: Dover, 1999.

——. "My Debut as a Literary Person." *Century Magazine* 59 (November 1899): 76–88.

——. "A Notable Conundrum." *The Californian* (October 1864).

——. *The Prince and the Pauper*. Berkeley: University of California Press, 1979.

——. "Private History of the 'Jumping Frog' Story." In *Mark Twain: Collected Tales, Sketches, Speeches, & Essays, 1891–1910*. Edited by Louis J. Budd. New York: Library of America, 1992.

——. *Roughing It*. Hartford, CT: American Publishing Company, 1872.

——_. Score sheet for a game of Hearts. Jun. 28, 1908, Samuel Langhorne Clemens collection of papers. The Henry W. and Albert A. Berg Collection of English and American Literature, The New York Public Library, Astor, Lenox and Tilden Foundations.

——. *The Unabridged Mark Twain*. 2 vols. Edited by Lawrence Teacher. "Opening Remarks" by Kurt Vonnegut. Philadelphia: Running Press, 1976.

——. "What Have the Police Been Doing?" San Francisco *Golden Era*, 21 January. Reprinted in *Mark Twain: Collected Tales, Sketches, Speeches, & Essays 1852–1890*. Edited by Louis J. Budd. New York: Library of America, 1992.

Dodge, Richard Irving. *Our Wild Indians: Thirty-Three Years' Personal Experience among the Red Men of the Great West.* Hartford, CT: A. D. Worthington and Company, 1882.

Feinstein, Herbert Charles Verschleisser. "Mark Twain's Lawsuits." PhD diss., University of California, Berkeley, 1968.

Fetterley, Judith. "The Sanctioned Rebel." *Studies in the Novel* 3, no. 3 (Fall 1971): 293–304.

Fischer, Victor. "Huck Finn Reviewed: The Reception of 'Huckleberry Finn' in the United States, 1885–1897." *American Literary Realism, 1870–1910* 16, no. 1 (1983).
Fishkin, Shelley Fisher. *Lighting Out for the Territory: Reflections on Mark Twain and American Culture*. Oxford: Oxford University Press, 1997.
Frear, Walter Francis. *Mark Twain and Hawaii*. Chicago: Lakeside Press, 1947.
Gerber, John C. "Mark Twain's Use of the Comic Pose." *PMLA* 77, no. 3 (June 1962): 297–304.
Gribben, Alan. "Autobiography as Property." In *The Mythologizing of Mark Twain*, edited by Sara deSaussure Davis and Philip D. Beidler. Tuscaloosa: University of Alabama Press, 1984.
———. " 'I Did Wish Tom Sawyer Was There' ": Boy-Book Elements in *Tom Sawyer* and *Huckleberry Finn*." In *One Hundred Years of "Huckleberry Finn": The Boy, His Book, and American Culture,* edited by Robert Sattelmeyer and J. Donald Crowley. Columbia: University of Missouri Press, 1985.
———. "Mark Twain, Business Man: The Margins of Profit." *Studies in American Humor* n.s., 1, no.1 (June 1982): 24–43.
———. [*MTLR*] *Mark Twain's Literary Resources: A Reconstruction of His Library and Reading.* 2 vols. Athens: NewSouth Books/ University of Georgia Press, 2019, 2022.
———. "Tom Sawyer, Tom Canty, and Huckleberry Finn: The Boy Book and Mark Twain." In *Mark Twain's Literary Resources: A Reconstruction of His Library and Reading,* Volume 1. Montgomery, AL: NewSouth Books, 2019.
Hooper, Johnson Jones. "The Census Taker." In *The Adventures of Captain Simon Suggs*. Tuscaloosa: University of Alabama Press, 1993.
Jacobson, Marcia. *Being a Boy Again: Autobiography and the American Boy Book*. Tuscaloosa: University of Alabama Press, 1994.
Johnson, Merle. *A Bibliography of the Works of Mark Twain. A List of First Editions in Book Form and of First Printings in Periodicals and Occasional Publications of His Varied Literary Activities.* Revised and enlarged. New York: Harper, 1935.
Kaplan, Justin. *Mr. Clemens and Mark Twain: A Biography.* New York: Simon and Schuster, 1966.
Kipling, Rudyard. *From Sea to Sea: Letters of Travel.* New York: Doubleday & McClure Company, 1899. Project Gutenberg, eBook #32977, updated January 6, 2021.
Lear, Bernadette A. "Were Tom and Huck On-Shelf? Public Libraries, Mark Twain, and the Formation of Accessible Canons, 1869–1910." *Nineteenth-Century Literature* 64, no. 2 (September 2009): 189–224.
Lee, Judith Yaross. "Brand Management: Samuel Clemens, Trademarks, and the Mark Twain Enterprise." *American Literary Realism* 47, no. 1 (Fall 2014): 27–54.
———. "Brand Management: Samuel Clemens, Trademarks, and the Mark Twain Enterprise." In *Mark Twain and Money: Language, Capital, and Culture*, edited by Henry B. Wonham and Lawrence Howe, 39–69. Tuscaloosa: University of Alabama Press, 2017.
———. *Twain's Brand: Humor in Contemporary American Culture*. Jackson: University Press of Mississippi, 2012.
Lorch, Fred W. *The Trouble Begins at Eight: Mark Twain's Lecture Tours.* Ames: Iowa State University Press, 1968.
"Mark Twain in Montreal." *New York Times*, December 10, 1881, 2.
Mac Donnell, Kevin. "How Samuel Clemens Found 'Mark Twain.' " *Mark Twain Journal* 50, no. 1/2 (Spring/Fall 2012): 8–47.
———. "Mark Twain at Ten Paces: Fact Versus Fiction in the Creation of Mark Twain as a Nom de Plume." *Mark Twain Journal* 57, no. 1 (Spring 2019): 77–111.
———. "Mark Twain Did Read *Vanity Fair*—in Nevada." *Mark Twain Journal* 58, no. 1 (Spring 2020): 146–56.
Mailer, Norman. *Huckleberry Finn Alive at 100*. Montclair, NJ: Caliban Press, 1985.
Meine, Franklin J. *Tall Tales of the Southwest*. New York: Alfred Knopf, 1930.
Meltzer, Milton. *Mark Twain Himself: A Pictorial Biography*. New York: Thomas Crowell, 1960.
"100 Most Frequently Challenged Books: 1990–1999." American Library Association, March 26, 2013. http://www.ala.org/advocacy/bbooks/frequentlychallengedbooks/ decade1999.
Orbanes, Philip E. *The Game Makers: The Story of Parker Brothers, from Tiddledy Winks to Trivial Pursuit*. Boston: Harvard Business School Press, 2004.
Paine, Albert Bigelow. *Mark Twain, A Biography: The Personal and Literary Life of Samuel Langhorne Clemens.* 3 vols. New York: Harper, 1912.
Powers, Ron. "Keeping Up with Mark Twain." *Smithsonian Magazine*, September 2003. https://www.smithsonianmag.com/arts-culture/keeping-up-with-mark-twain-89150329/.
Rasmussen, R. Kent, ed. *Dear Mark Twain: Letters from His Readers*. Berkeley: University of California Press, 2013.
Rosenberg, Daniel. "Mark Twain's Memory-Builder." University of Oregon Libraries, 2016. http://timeonline.uoregon.edu/twain/index.php.
"Round About Gotham." Sunday *Herald* (Chicago), September 20, 1891, 22.
Scharnhorst, Gary, ed. *Mark Twain: The Complete Interviews*. Tuscaloosa: University of Alabama Press, 2006.
Schmidt, Barbara. "Illustrating *Tom Sawyer*." In *Critical Insights: The Adventures of Tom Sawyer*, edited by R. Kent Rasmussen. Ipswich, MA: Grey House Publishing, 2022.
———. "Special Feature: Samuel L. Clemens Vs. Belford, Clarke & Company (U.S. Circuit Court, 1883, ILL.)." *Mark Twain Quotations, Newspaper Collections, & Related Resources.* www.twainquotes.com.
Sloane, David E. E., ed. *Mark Twain's Humor: Critical Essays*. New York: Garland, 1993.
The Strong: National Museum of Play. "Portrait Authors." Object ID 107.2718. https://onlinecollection.museumofplay.org/
"Top 100 Banned/Challenged Books: 2000-2009." American Library Association, March 26, 2013. http://www.ala.org/advocacy/bbooks/frequentlychallengedbooks/ decade2009.
"Top 100 Most Banned and Challenged Books: 2010–2019." American Library Association, September 9, 2020. http://www.ala.org/advocacy/bbooks/frequently challengedbooks/decade2019.
UCCL (Union Catalog of Clemens Letters); UCLC (Union Catalog of Letters to Clemens). *Mark Twain's Letters Online*. https://marktwainproject.org/xtf/search?category=letters.
Walsh, Thomas M., and Thomas D. Zlatic. "Mark Twain and the Art of Memory." *American Literature* 53, no. 2 (1981): 214–31.
Whitehill, Bruce. *Games: American Boxed Games and Their Makers, 1822–1992*. Radnor, PA: Wallace-Homestead, 1992.
Wilson, James D. *A Reader's Guide to the Short Stories of Mark Twain*. Boston: G. K. Hall, 1987.

Humorous Highlights from the Mark Twain Collection of Susan Jaffe Tane

JULIE CARLSEN AND
GABRIEL MCKEE

Books by Mark Twain

Ordered by date of first publication, with subsequent editions of each work grouped under the earliest edition.

The Jumping Frog (1867)

1. Mark Twain. *The Celebrated Jumping Frog of Calaveras County, and Other Sketches*. Edited by John Paul. New York: C. H. Webb, 1867. **(pages 16–17)**

A year after the story appeared in *The Saturday Press*, Charles Webb published this first book edition of Mark Twain's jumping frog story in 1867 with his own pseudonym John Paul listed as the editor. It quickly sold out, as did early reprints.

2. Mark Twain. *The Celebrated Jumping Frog of Calaveras County, and Other Sketches*. Edited by John Paul. London: George Routledge & Sons, 1867. **(page 18)**

This pirated edition of *The Jumping Frog*—the first to be published in the United Kingdom—introduces the unknown Mark Twain to British audiences by quoting *The Saturday Review*: "The CELEBRATED JUMPING FROG may be heartily recommended to any one who is capable of appreciating humor, or enjoying a good laugh."

3. Mark Twain. *The Jumping Frog; In English, then in French, then Clawed Back into a Civilized Language Once More by Patient, Unremunerated Toil*. New York and London: Harper and Brothers, 1903. **(pages 20–21)**

Frustrated by the poor quality of unauthorized translations of his works, Twain chose a particularly disagreeable French translation of *The Jumping Frog* and "retranslated" it back into English in order to show how the unskilled adaptation removed the humor from his story.

4. Mark Twain. *The Jumping Frog* [with] *The Private Printing of The "Jumping Frog" Story: An Afterword by Samuel Clemens*. [Easthampton, Mass.]: Cheloniidae Press, 1985. **(pages 24–25)**

This modern fine press edition of *The Jumping Frog* is one of fifteen unnumbered copies bound by Daniel E. Kelm and boxed with a complete suite of wood engravings, a suite of illustrations in proof state, and a copy of the regular edition book.

The Innocents Abroad (1869)

5. Mark Twain. *The Innocents Abroad, or The New Pilgrim's Progress; Being Some Account of the Steamship Quaker City's Pleasure Excursion to Europe and the Holy Land; With Descriptions of Countries, Nations, Incidents and Adventures, as They Appeared to the Author*. Hartford: American Publishing Company, 1869. **(pages 52–53)**

Mark Twain's first major commercial and popular success, *The Innocents Abroad*—a satirical "anti-travel" book based on his 163-day tour of Europe and the Holy Land—would remain his best-selling book throughout his lifetime.

6. Mark Twain. *The Innocents Abroad, or The New Pilgrim's Progress; Being Some Account of the Steamship Quaker City's Pleasure Excursion to Europe and the Holy Land; With Descriptions of Countries, Nations, Incidents and Adventures, as They Appeared to the Author*. Hartford: American Publishing Company, 1869. **(pages 108–109)**

Olivia Clemens's personal copy, bound in a deluxe full morocco binding with her married name stamped on the front cover.

7. Mark Twain. *The Innocents Abroad* [salesman's prospectus]. [Hartford: American Publishing Company, 1869.] **(page 107)**

Many of Twain's books were published as subscription volumes, sold in advance by traveling salespeople who carried incomplete sample copies that highlighted choice selections of text, illustrations, and binding options. This copy is stored in a wooden box engraved with the author's name that was probably handmade by its salesman, William Aldrich of Wisconsin.

8. Mark Twain. *The New Pilgrim's Progress. A Book of Travel in Pursuit of Pleasure: The Journey Home*. London: John Camden Hotten, [1870]. **(page 114)**

London publisher John Camden Hotten exploited the lack of an international copyright treaty to issue pirated editions of many popular American authors. Less than a year after *The Innocents Abroad*'s first publication, Hotten produced his own unauthorized edition, splitting the text into two volumes.

Roughing It (1872)

9. Mark Twain (Samuel L. Clemens). *Roughing It*. Hartford: American Publishing Company, 1872. **(page 232)**

In his follow-up to *Innocents Abroad*, Twain recounts his travels in the American West, from Utah on to California and Hawaii.

10. Mark Twain. *The Innocents at Home*. London: George Routledge and Sons, 1872. **(page 128)**

11. Mark Twain. *Roughing It and The Innocents at Home*. London: George Routledge and Sons, 1882. **(page 239)**

Because of their length, Twain's books were often split into two volumes for their British mass-market "yellowback" editions. Routledge sought to trade on the success of Twain's most successful book by recalling *Innocents Abroad* with its title for the second half—and kept the second title for its single-volume hardcover edition.

The Gilded Age (1873)

12. Mark Twain (Samuel L. Clemens) and Charles Dudley Warner. *The Gilded Age: A Tale of To-Day*. Hartford: American Publishing Company, 1873. Publisher's full sheep. **(page 158)**

When Twain and Warner lamented the quality of the books their wives were reading, the women challenged them to write something better. The resulting collaboration is the book whose name lent itself to the era: *The Gilded Age*, a satire on post–Civil War American corruption.

Tom Sawyer (1876)

13. Mark Twain. *The Adventures of Tom Sawyer*. Hartford: American Publishing Company, 1876. **(pages 31–33)**

The first edition of Twain's classic novel about the mischievous, rough-and-tumble Tom Sawyer's amusing adventures along the Mississippi River.

14. Mark Twain. *The Adventures of Tom Sawyer*. London: Chatto & Windus, [1877]. **(page 39)**

A year after its first publication, *Tom Sawyer* appeared in this mass-market "yellowback" edition in Great Britain, featuring a brightly illustrated cover.

Punch, Brothers, Punch! (1878)

15. Mark Twain. *Punch, Brothers, Punch! and Other Sketches*. New York: Slote, Woodman & Co., 1878. **(page 50)**

The eponymous sketch of this collection also appeared under the title "A Literary Nightmare," and concerns Twain's encounter with what would be called in our day an "earworm"— specifically, a catchy jingle (written by Isaac Bromley and others) about streetcar conductors.

A Tramp Abroad (1880)

16. Mark Twain (Samuel L. Clemens). *A Tramp Abroad*. Hartford: American Publishing Company, 1880. With a tipped-in page from the book's manuscript and a letter (signed "SLC") to "Charley" (Charles Langdon?). **(pages 102–103)**

17. Mark Twain (Samuel L. Clemens). *A Tramp Abroad*. Hartford: American Publishing Company, 1880. With a pencil note (not in Bliss's hand) identifying this as the copy belonging to its publisher, Frank Bliss.

18. Mark Twain (Samuel L. Clemens). *A Tramp Abroad*. London: Chatto & Windus, 1880.

Twain's *A Tramp Abroad* details his humorous observations on his travels in central and southern Europe. The first copy contains a tipped-in letter in which Twain asks "Charley," presumably Olivia Clemens's brother Charley Langdon, to forward the book to supporter E. S. Bowen. He writes: "The correct thing to do on a special occasion is for the notorious author to write his name across a page of MS that helped to make up the book, and send that." This he has done, signing boldly across a page of the book's manuscript: "Yr Truly / S.L. Clemens / Mark Twain."

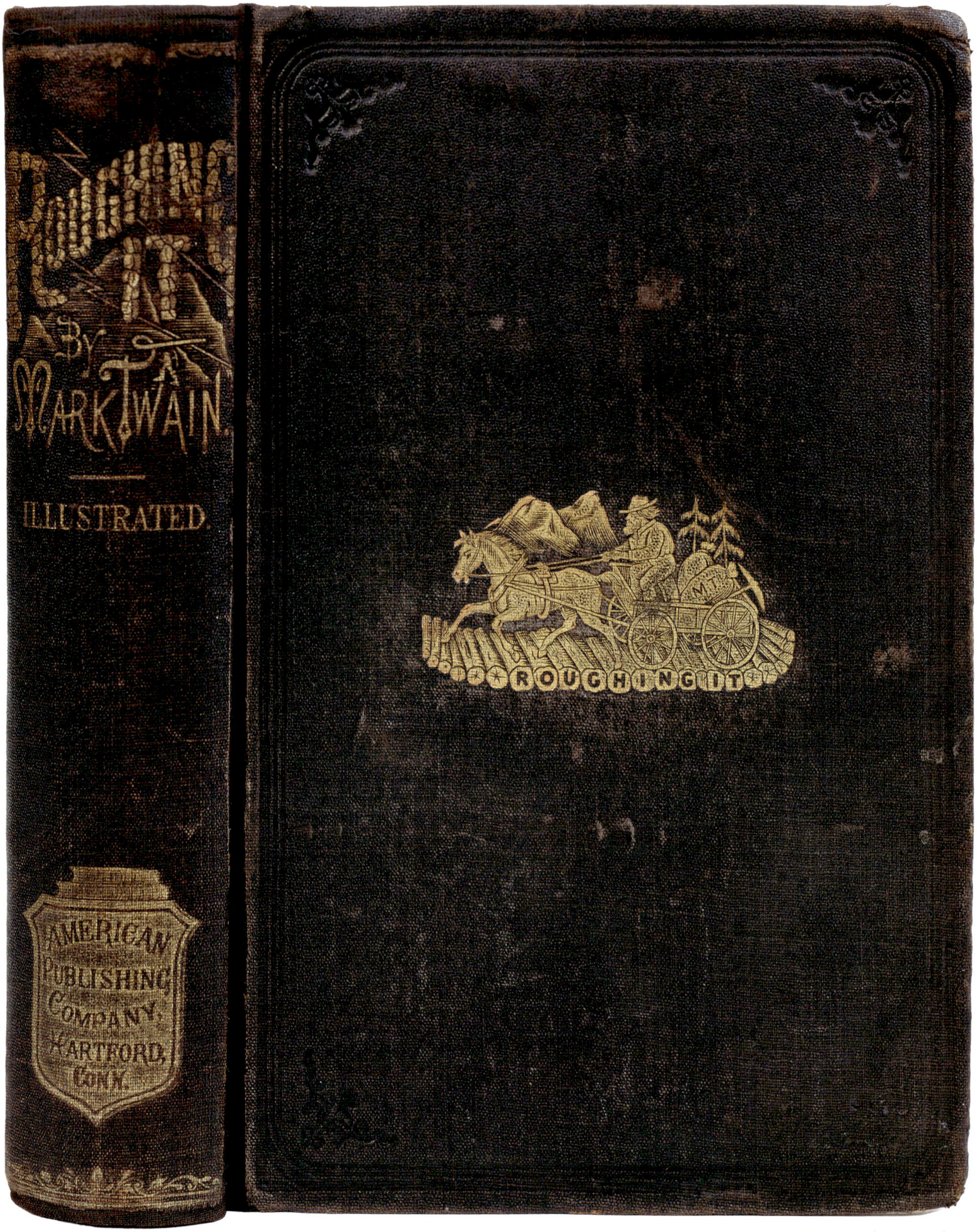
ROUGHING IT
BY MARK TWAIN
ILLUSTRATED
AMERICAN PUBLISHING COMPANY HARTFORD, CONN.
ROUGHING IT

(Item no. 9)

1601 (1880)

19. [Mark Twain.] *Conversation as it was by the Social Fireside in the Time of the Tudors. Date—Sixteen Hundred One*. [New York?]: Privately printed, November 20, 1904. **(page 119)**
20. Mark Twain. *Date, 1601: Conversation as it was by the Social Fireside in the Time of the Tudors*. [New York]: Privately printed [for Merle Johnson and Charles P. Everitt], 1920. **(page 119)**

Twain first published *1601* in 1880 in an anonymous edition of as few as four copies that he shared with a few close friends. The text is a ribald story in which William Shakespeare, Ben Jonson, and other Elizabethan luminaries discuss flatulence, sex, and other taboo topics. Considered obscene under American law until the early 1960s, it was circulated in a variety of privately printed editions in the decades to come. Twain acknowledged his authorship in 1906, telling librarian Charles Orr: "If there is a decent word findable in it, it is because I overlooked it."

The Prince and the Pauper (1881)

21. Mark Twain. *The Prince and the Pauper: A Tale for Young People of All Ages*. Montreal: Dawson Brothers, 1881. **(page 116)**

Clemens long sought to protect his work from unauthorized use, especially outside of the bounds of US law; he published this edition to establish copyright in Canada and to discourage potential piracy.

22. Mark Twain. *The Prince and the Pauper: A Tale for Young People of All Ages*. Boston: James R. Osgood and Company, 1882. **(page 38)**

Twain's first attempt at historical fiction, of which he notes, "It may have happened, it may not have happened: but it could have happened." He presented this copy to Dr. Clarence C. Rice—Clemens's personal physician who introduced the financially troubled author to financial wizard Henry H. Rogers (who ultimately led Clemens to solvency)—and signed it from "the Author."

Life on the Mississippi (1883)

23. Mark Twain. *Life on the Mississippi*. Boston: James R. Osgood and Company, 1883. **(pages 46–47)**

Here Twain turns his traveler's eye to domestic subjects, recounting his brief career as a riverboat pilot along with the history of the river and numerous tall tales from regions on the river's shore.

Huckleberry Finn (1885)

24. Mark Twain. *Adventures of Huckleberry Finn (Tom Sawyer's Comrade)*. New York: Charles L. Webster and Company, 1885. Publisher's green cloth. **(pages 7 and 35–36)**

First edition of Twain's popular sequel to *Tom Sawyer*. He presented this copy to Edith Beecher, the granddaughter of Henry Ward Beecher and grandniece of his Hartford neighbor Harriet Beecher Stowe, and signed it "Mark Twain."

25. Mark Twain. *Adventures of Huckleberry Finn (Tom Sawyer's Comrade)*. New York: Charles L. Webster and Company, 1885. Sheep binding. **(page 40)**

The publication of *Huckleberry Finn* was complicated by the discovery in a salesman's prospectus of a crude addition to Uncle Silas's trousers. Webster and others suspected a disgruntled engraver. But damage to the plate during the printing process is more likely, particularly since the alteration is less pronounced in many copies. Early copies of the book bound in sheep contained the defaced "curved fly" illustrations. Webster required the book's salespeople to destroy the offending sheet in their samples or risk being fired; the illustration was corrected for the copies bound in cloth, and the corrected illustration shows a straighter line on the fly of Silas's trousers.

A Connecticut Yankee in King Arthur's Court (1889)

26. Mark Twain. *A Connecticut Yankee in King Arthur's Court*. New York: Charles L. Webster & Company, 1889. **(pages 56–57)**

In Twain's time-travel story, American engineer Hank Morgan finds himself transported to Camelot, bringing progressive values to the age of chivalry. Twain presented this first edition copy to George L. Bell and signed it "the author."

The American Claimant (1892)

27. Mark Twain. *The American Claimant*. New York: Charles L. Webster & Co., 1892. **(page 65)**
28. Mark Twain (Samuel L. Clemens). *The American Claimant*. London: Chatto & Windus, 1892.

Col. Beriah Sellers, a character featured in Twain and Charles Dudley Warner's novel *The Gilded Age*, became a popular character on the stage in an unauthorized dramatic adaptation of the book. Twain acquired the rights to the play and revised it, and it became a successful touring production. Working with William Dean Howells, Twain authored a sequel in which the character, now renamed Col. Mulberry Sellers, gains a hereditary British title. This play was less successful, but Twain adapted the story into his novel *The American Claimant*.

Tom Sawyer Abroad & Tom Sawyer, Detective (1894–1896)

29. Mark Twain ("editor"). *Tom Sawyer Abroad. By Huck Finn*. New York: Charles L. Webster and Company, 1894. **(page 42)**
30. Mark Twain. *Tom Sawyer Abroad; Tom Sawyer, Detective; and other stories, etc., etc.* New York: Harper & Brothers Publishers, 1896.

Twain completed two short sequels to *The Adventures of Tom Sawyer* and left several others unfinished. In 1896, Harper & Brothers compiled *Tom Sawyer Abroad*, in which Tom and Huck take a hot-air balloon across the Atlantic to Africa, and *Tom Sawyer, Detective*, which places Twain's youthful protagonist into a parody of the detective novel.

Pudd'nhead Wilson (1894)

31. Mark Twain (Samuel L. Clemens). *The Tragedy of Pudd'nhead Wilson, and the Comedy Those Extraordinary Twins*. Hartford: American Publishing Company, 1894. **(pages 54–55)**

This later Twain novel is steeped in irony: Its eponymous character, a lawyer, is dubbed a "Pudd'nhead" not because of his stupidity, but because the unsophisticated inhabitants of his frontier town misunderstand his cleverness. The main plot of the novel updates the basic concept of *The Prince and the Pauper* with biting social criticism, contrasting the lives of a pair of young men—one white, one 1/32 Black (and thus nonwhite under the "one-drop" principle that guided racist legislation of the era)—who are switched in infancy.

32. Mark Twain (Samuel L. Clemens). *The Tragedy of Pudd'nhead Wilson and the Comedy Those Extraordinary Twins* [salesman's prospectus]. Hartford: American Publishing Company, 1894. **(page 29)**

Used to entice potential subscription customers, this presale sample contains sheets from the book, binding samples, and order blanks. Customer information in this copy indicates it was used by a salesman working in Maryland and West Virginia.

Following the Equator (1897)

33. Mark Twain (Samuel L. Clemens). *Following the Equator: A Journey Around the World*. Hartford, Connecticut: The American Publishing Company, 1897. First edition. **(pages 104–105)**
34. Mark Twain. *More Tramps Abroad*. London: Chatto & Windus, 1897.

Mark Twain invested most of his wealth in a typesetting machine called the Paige Compositor in the early 1890s, and the failure of the firm that designed and manufactured the machine left him on the verge of bankruptcy. To recoup some of his losses, he authored another travel book—*Following the Equator*, published in the UK as *More Tramps Abroad*—which detailed a round-the-world tour of the British Empire's colonies.

Adam's Diary & Eve's Diary (1904–1906)

35. Mark Twain. *Extracts from Adam's Diary, Translated from the Original Ms.* London and New York: Harper & Brothers, 1904. **(page 58)**
36. Mark Twain. *Eve's Diary, Translated from the Original Ms.* London and New York: Harper & Brothers, 1906. **(page 59)**

These two novellas purport to tell the biblical story of Adam and Eve from their own perspectives, "translated" here by Mark Twain.

King Leopold's Soliloquy (1905)

37. Mark Twain. *King Leopold's Soliloquy: A Defense of his Congo Rule*. Boston: The P. R. Warren Co., 1905. Second edition, with the publisher's statement on pink paper tipped in. **(page 124)**

King Leopold II of Belgium is notorious for the extent of the atrocities he visited on the Congo Free State between 1885 and 1908. In this bleakly satirical pamphlet, Twain presents the king as offering a self-damning "defense" of his actions. The publisher donated the proceeds from the pamphlet's sale to humanitarian aid in the region.

Autobiography (1909)

38. Mark Twain. *Is Shakespeare Dead?: From My Autobiography*. New York and London: Harper & Brothers, 1909. **(page 152)**

Twain's semi-autobiographical reflection on Shakespeare, with an autograph note by Twain pasted inside the front cover: "Shakespeare gets a lot of applause for Hamlet, but if you had written it you couldn't have got it accepted."

39. *Mark Twain's Autobiography. With an introduction by Albert Bigelow Paine*. New York & London: Harper & Brothers, 1924. Two volumes in slipcase. **(pages 153–154)**

Clemens began work on his autobiography as early as 1870, but intended for major portions of it to remain unpublished until long after his death; his embargo on the full work expired in 2010. The 1924 edition, containing under half of the full work, opens with a facsimile of a handwritten statement: "I am writing from the grave. On these terms only can a man be approximately frank. He cannot be straitly & unqualifiedly frank either in the grave or out of it."

Compilations & Collected Works

40. Mark Twain. *Autobiography, (Burlesque.) First Romance, and Memoranda*. Toronto: James Campbell & Son, [1871?]. **(page 147)**

This unauthorized collection of Twain sketches features on its cover Twain's caricature of William III of Prussia. Following the publication of this volume, Twain took action to better protect his copyright in England and Canada, leading to a five-year lull in Canadian piracy of his work before the Canadian Copyright Act of 1875, which separated Canada from imperial copyright agreements and enabled a second major phase of unauthorized editions. The eponymous "autobiography" is an entirely fictional account that originally appeared in his "Memoranda" for the *Galaxy*.

41. Mark Twain. *A Curious Dream; and Other Sketches*. London: George Routledge & Sons, [1872]. **(page 61)**

In the title story of this collection, a dreamer experiences a macabre vision of a procession of skeletons who protest that the living have allowed their cemetery to fall into neglect.

42. Mark Twain. *Mark Twain's Sketches*. London: George Routledge & Sons, 1872. Copyright edition.

Twain edited the amusing sketches in these collections to soften the language from their original American serial publication so that they would be more suitable for British audiences.

43. Mark Twain. *The Choice Humorous Works of Mark Twain*. London: John Camden Hotten, [1873].

This hardcover collection gathers both volumes of Hotten's pirated *Innocents Abroad* back under a single cover, to which is appended an unauthorized collection of sketches. Hotten's success with his pirated editions infuriated Twain, who referred to him as "Hottentot."

44. Mark Twain. *Mark Twain's Sketches, Number One*. New York: American News Company, 1874. **(page 27)**

This is the first, failed attempt by Twain to publish his sketches as an inexpensive serial series. He used "The Jumping Frog" as an advertising hook, as seen by the cover illustration of a frog smoking a cigar.

45. Mark Twain. *Mark Twain's Sketches, New and Old* [salesman's prospectus]. Hartford: The American Publishing Company, 1875.

The American Publishing Co. issued 1,369 copies of the salesman's sample for Twain's second authorized collection of short fiction; this copy was used by a salesman in Brooklyn and Manhattan.

46. Mark Twain. *Mark Twain's Sketches, New and Old*. Hartford and Chicago: The American Publishing Company, 1875. **(page 62)**

47. Mark Twain (Samuel L. Clemens). *Mark Twain's Complete Works*. Toronto: John Ross Robertson, [1882].

This crudely printed volume collects several of the unauthorized editions of Twain's works issued by Canadian publisher John Ross Robertson. Robertson used various legal means to circumvent international copyright: For this volume, he printed the sheets in the United States, imported them to Canada for binding, and then exported the completed books back over the border for American sale. This elaborate scheme violated the spirit of copyright, but was entirely legal at the time, and the books—boldly marketed as "Robertson's Cheap Series"—were sold at a fraction of the price of the authorized editions. This volume, containing Robertson's editions of *Innocents Abroad*, *A Tramp Abroad*, and a variety of *Sketches*, represents the earliest attempt to gather together a version of Twain's complete works.

48. Mark Twain. *Europe and Elsewhere*. New York: Harper & Brothers, Publishers, 1923.

This posthumous collection of miscellaneous texts includes "The War Prayer," a bleak statement on the meaninglessness of war and nationalistic chauvinism, left unpublished at Twain's death. Though scarcely humorous, the sketch is steeped in irony of a similar flavor present in Twain's lighter material.

Books with Contributions by Mark Twain

Organized by date of publication

49. *Laws of the territory of Nevada passed at the second regular session of the legislative assembly*... Virginia [City, Nev.]: J.T. Goodman & Co., Territorial Enterprise, 1863. **(pages 140–141)**

In November and December of 1862, Clemens worked for Joseph T. Goodman's *Territorial Enterprise*, published in Carson City. During this time, his brother Orion Clemens was Secretary of Nevada Territory, and the two helped draft the language of some of the laws recorded in this volume—though it is impossible to know what texts specifically originated with Clemens's pen. Orion also designed the territory's seal, which appears at the beginning of the volume.

50. Oscar T. Shuck (editor). *The California Scrap-Book: A Repository of Useful Information and Select Reading*. San Francisco: H. H. Bancroft and Company, 1869. **(page 145)**

An early anthology of writing from California, including some of Mark Twain's letters to *The Alta California* that were later incorporated into *Innocents Abroad*.

51. J. Price and C. S. Haley (editors). *The Buyers' Manual and Business Guide; being a description of the Leading Business Houses, Manufactories, Inventions, Etc. of the Pacific Coast, together with copious and readable selections, chiefly from California writers*. San Francisco: Francis & Valentine, Steam Book and Job Printing Establishment, 1872. **(pages 138–139)**

This directory of San Francisco businesses also includes a selection of Californian literature, including Twain's "Jumping Frog," the sketch "The Public to Mark Twain," and the text of a speech he delivered at New York's Aldine Club.

52. Pedro Carolino. *The New Guide of the Conversation in Portuguese and English. With an Introduction by Mark Twain*. Boston: James R. Osgood & Co., 1883. **(page 60)**

Carolino published this phrasebook in Portugal in 1855, which because of his unfamiliarity with English syntax contains innumerable unintentionally amusing mistranslations. Clemens discovered the book several years after its original publication and arranged for its verbatim reprinting, declaring in his introduction: "Whatsoever is perfect in its kind, in literature, is imperishable: nobody can imitate it successfully, nobody can hope to produce its fellow; it is perfect, it must and will stand alone: its immortality is secure." Later reissues did add to the original, however, imposing the title *English As She Is Spoke*—a phrase that appears nowhere in Carolino's original.

53. Mark Twain [edited by Edith Oenone Somerville]. *The Mark Twain Birthday Book*. London: Remington & Co., 1885. **(page 63)**

Containing over 700 quips, maxims, and quotes from Twain's writings, this British publication is the first compilation of Twain quotations.

54. *English as She is Taught, Being Genuine Answers to Examination Questions in Our Public Schools Collected by Caroline B. Le Row. With a Commentary Thereon by Mark Twain*. London: T. Fisher Unwin, 1887. **(page 64)**

Le Row, a Brooklyn schoolteacher, compiled this booklet of her students' most outrageous answers to test questions. Clemens wrote a glowing review of it for *The Century Magazine*, and read from the book in his lectures. Twain's review was reprinted as an introduction to the book's first English edition.

55. [Mark Twain; William Dean Howells, and Charles Hopkins Clark, eds.] *Mark Twain's Library of Humor*. New York: Charles L. Webster & Company, 1888. **(page 49)**

Twain nominally edited this compilation of American humor, but Howells and Clark did the lion's share of the editorial work. The book contains short pieces by dozens of authors, and twenty by Twain himself.

56. Aaron Watson. *The Savage Club: A Medley of History, Anecdote and Reminiscence*. London: T. Fisher Unwin, 1907.

This history of London's Savage Club includes a lengthy account of Twain's visit there for a dinner in his honor in 1899, and summarizes a responsive speech at that event in which Twain called himself "a first-class fool."

57. Ulysses S. Grant. *Personal Memoirs of U.S. Grant*. New York: Charles L. Webster and Company, 1885–1886. Two volumes. Publisher's deluxe brown half morocco. **(pages 149–150)**

Twain assisted Grant with his memoirs—which he praised as "the best of any general's since Caesar"—and inscribed this copy to his secretary, Miss Fanny C. Hess.

Periodicals with Contributions by Mark Twain

Arranged alphabetically

58. *The Atlantic Monthly: A Magazine of Literature, Science, Art, and Politics*, volume 35, numbers 207–212 [and] volume 36, number 214. Boston: James R. Osgood, January–June [and] August 1875. Seven issues in original wrappers.

The New England literary magazine *The Atlantic*, founded by abolitionist James Russell Lowell in 1857, published Twain's memoir "Old Times on the Mississippi," which was later published as *Life on the Mississippi*, over these seven issues in 1875.

59. *Beadle's Dime Book of Fun*, No 3. New York: Beadle and Company, 1866. In original wrappers. **(page 26)**

This volume from publisher Erastus Beadle's series of small, inexpensive books—called dime novels for their 10¢ price tags—includes an early printing of "Jim Smiley's Frog," an abbreviated version of the story that would later become *The Celebrated Jumping Frog of Calaveras County*.

60. *The Californian*, volumes 1–4. San Francisco, May 28, 1864–May 19, 1866. Two bound volumes. **(pages 14–15)**

Founded by Bret Harte and C. H. Webb (who published *The Jumping Frog* in 1867), *The Californian* contains some of Twain's best humor writing. The October 1, 1864, issue contains his earliest article in the journal signed as Mark Twain: "A Notable Conundrum." The December 16, 1865, issue contains an early West Coast printing of "The Celebrated Jumping Frog of Calaveras County."

61. *The Century Illustrated Monthly Magazine*, volume 31, number 2. New York: The Century Co., December 1885. In original wrappers.

The Century, which began as a continuation of *Scribner's Monthly*, was edited by Richard Watson Gilder, a close friend of the Clemens family, and regularly printed pieces by Mark Twain. In "The Private History of a Campaign that Failed," which is accompanied by illustrations by E. W. Kemble and maps by the author himself, Clemens recounts a largely fabricated version of his brief membership in the Ralls County Rangers, a Missouri state guard and pro-Confederate militia from which he deserted after two weeks.

62. *The Day's Doings: An Illustrated Journal of Romantic Events, Reports, Sporting & Theatrical News, at Home & Abroad*, volumes 1–2. London: W. D. Waller, July 30, 1870–July 23, 1871. Bound volume. **(pages 68–69)**

The sensational and richly illustrated English magazine *The Day's Doings* reprinted Mark Twain's "Map of Paris" (first printed in his own magazine *The Buffalo Express*) in the November 5, 1870, issue. Twain teasingly laments that the map was printed backwards, and explains that "this is the first time I attempted to draft and engrave a map, or attempt anything in this line of art at all" and "I have never had so much trouble with anything in my life as I did with this map." Still, he notes that it is perfectly readable to left-handed people and that it can also be viewed easily using a mirror, and he even suggests that the reader frame the map for future reference. Although he did not "fix" the illustration, Twain did tweak the piece for British audiences by substituting Europeans for Americans in the "official" praise that follows his text.

63. *The Galaxy*, volume 9, number 5–volume 11, number 2 [and] volume 11, number 4. New York: Sheldon & Co., May 1870–February 1871 [and] April 1871. 11 issues in original wrappers. **(page 70)**

Clemens was given artistic license to start a humor department for *The Galaxy*; his resulting "Memoranda" was a feature of every issue and advertised on many of the front wrappers: "MARK TWAIN, the Great Humorist, writes for The Galaxy, every month."

64. *The Genesee Valley Post*, volume 2, number 15. Belmont, N.Y., July 19, 1882.

Published in Belmont, New York—a small village located between Buffalo and Elmira—*The Genesee Valley Post* featured "Mark Twain: His First Experience" on its front page in July 1882. Twain amusingly recounts getting started in his present trade: "When I started my first newspaper, I was a Mississippi pilot and didn't start one at all." This appears to be the only appearance of this text, and it may have been a concoction of the newspaper's editors rather than something that Clemens sent to the obscure upstate newspaper.

65. *Harper's New Monthly Magazine*, volume 34, number 199. New York: Harper & Brothers, December 1866. In original wrappers.

This issue contains Twain's first print appearance in a national magazine: "Forty-Three Days in an Open Boat."

66. *Harper's New Monthly Magazine*, volume 90, number 539–volume 92, number 551. New York: Harper & Brothers, April 1895–April 1896. 13 issues in original wrappers. **(page 118)**

Twain's *Personal Recollections of Joan of Arc* was serialized in thirteen issues of the prominent New York magazine *Harper's Monthly*. Because the text was intended as serious, Clemens wanted it to appear anonymously, but *Harper's* advertised the serial as being written by "one of the most successful among American writers of fiction," and the initial installments appeared under the byline of "the Sieur Louis de Conte"—a name that conceals Clemens's initials. Rumors of his authorship spread, and Harper & Bros. published the book as a single volume with the pseudonym on the title page, but the name "Mark Twain" on the book's cover.

67. *Harper's New Monthly Magazine*, volume 93, numbers 555–556. New York: Harper & Brothers, August–September 1896. Two issues in original wrappers.

"Tom Sawyer, Detective" was serialized in two issues of *Harper's* in 1896.

68. *Harper's Weekly: A Journal of Civilization*, volume 51, number 2,640. New York: Harper & Brothers, July 27, 1907. In original wrappers. **(page 177)**

This issue of the political weekly version of *Harper's*, which has a photograph of Mark Twain receiving his honorary doctorate from Oxford University on the front wrapper, includes the article "England's Ovation to Mark Twain" by Sydney Brooks.

69. *Kelley's Weekly, A Journal of the Times*, volume 1, number 1. New York: A. A. Kelley & Co., November 30, 1867. Disbound. **(page 71)**

The New York magazine *Kelley's Weekly*—a rare and presumably short-lived publication styled after *Harper's Weekly*—featured an early reprint of Mark Twain's "A Yankee in the Orient" (first published in the *New-York Daily Tribune* on October 25) in its debut issue.

70. *Life*, volume 65, number 25. Chicago: Time, Inc., December 20, 1968. In original wrappers. **(pages 190–191)**

The unfinished and previously unpublished "Huck Finn and Tom Sawyer Among the Indians" was printed for the first time by Henry Luce's *Life* magazine in 1968, with illustrations by James McMullan.

71. *New-York Daily Tribune*, volume 27, numbers 8,207, 8,240, 8,251, 8,282, 8,289, [and] 8,295. New York, July 30, September 6, September 19, October 25, November 2, [and] November 9, 1867. Six issues.

These contributions to Horace Greely's daily "penny paper" were later collected in *Innocents Abroad*, titled "The Mediterranean Excursion."

72. *The Overland Monthly*, volume 1. San Francisco: A. Roman & Company, 1868. Bound volume. **(page 144)**

The first four issues of this early Californian periodical contained sketches by Twain, all of which were later incorporated into *The Innocents Abroad*.

73. Prospectus for *St. Nicholas for Young Folks*, volume 20, number 12. New York: The Century Company, November 1893. In original wrappers. **(page 41)**

Mary Mapes Dodge, the founding editor of the children's magazine *St. Nicholas*, advertised Mark Twain's *Tom Sawyer Abroad* in this prospectus for the November 1893 issue. She severely revised the story to the point of bowdlerization, removing references she deemed offensive and elevating Huck Finn's dialect, infuriating Twain.

74. *Sunday Magazine of the St. Louis Republic*, part 6. St. Louis: Associated Sunday Magazines, October 27, 1907. In original wrappers. **(pages 156–157)**

This Sunday supplement to *The St. Louis Republic* reprinted *The North American Review*'s selections from *The Autobiography of Mark Twain* in 1907, as did the *Sunday Magazine* for many other journals around the nation.

Books from Samuel Clemens's Library

Arranged alphabetically by author

75. Allingham, W. H. and D. Radford, eds. *William Allingham: A Diary*. London: Macmillan and Co., 1907. **(page 168)**

Clemens's copy, given to him by his daughter Clara for Christmas in 1907. Among his annotations is the amusing note "Oh, damn!" next to an ink blot on page 150.

76. Conway, Moncure. *Autobiography: Memories and Experiences*. Boston & New York: Houghton, Mifflin and Company, 1904. **(page 169)**

Clemens's copy, with his annotations throughout. His notes, such as "I seem to have met most of the people mentioned in this book" on p. 277 of volume 1, evidence the early stirrings of Twain's autobiographical recollections; he would publish the *Autobiography of Mark Twain* in 1906.

77. Dodge, Richard Irving. *Our Wild Indians: Thirty-three Years' Personal Experience among the Red Men of the Great West*. Hartford: A.D. Worthington and Company, 1883. **(pages 182–184)**

Clemens studied and extensively annotated this book while preparing to write "Huck and Tom Among the Indians."

78. Still, William. *The Underground Rail Road. A Record of Facts, Authentic Narratives, Letters, Etc. Narrating the Hardships, Hair-Breadth Escapes and Death Struggles of the Slaves in the Efforts for freedom, as related by themselves and others, or witnessed by the author; together with Sketches of Some of the Largest Stockholders, and Most Liberal Aiders and Advisers, of the Road*. Philadelphia: Wm. Still, 1883. **(page 167)**

Clemens's copy, with his autograph note recounting the story of two formerly enslaved women who escaped to Quarry Farm, where they reunited with their family member. Still, a leading Black abolitionist hailed as "the father of the Underground Rail Road," collects firsthand accounts of formerly enslaved people's journeys to freedom.

Publications Related to Mark Twain

Arranged alphabetically by author or title

79. Haweis, Hugh R. *American Humorists.* London: Chatto & Windus, 1883. **(page 176)**

Haweis, an English cleric, profiled Twain alongside Artemus Ward, Washington Irving, and Oliver Wendell Holmes.

80. *Phunny Phellows: Mark Twain, Josh Billings, Robt. Burdette, Artemus Ward, and others*. Chicago: Rhodes & McClure, 1885. **(page 166)**

The group of humorists known as the "Phunny Phellows" produced broad and folksy humor that often depended on comic misspellings. Twain resented being associated with these authors, whose work often lacked his sharper satirical aims.

81. *Vanity Fair*, volume 3. New York: Louis H. Stephens, 1861. **(page 164)**

The January 26, 1861, issue of *Vanity Fair*—a humor magazine edited by Clemens's friend Charles Farrar Browne (aka Artemus Ward) that bears no relation to the current serial of the same title—includes a sketch titled "The North Star," which features a character named Mark Twain. Presumably the original source of Clemens's iconic pen name.

82. Waddy, Frederick, illustrator. *Cartoon Portraits and Biographical Sketches of Men of the Day*. London: Tinsley Brothers, 1873. **(page 113)**

In this collection of caricatures, Twain is praised as "the best living exponent" of "the peculiar humor invented by our American cousins." A cartoon by Frederick Waddy shows Twain riding a frog as a horse, with the caption "American Humor."

83. [Williams, Henry.] *In the Clutch of Circumstance: My Own Story. By a Burglar.* New York and London: D. Appleton, 1922. **(page 161)**

Henry Williams's anonymous account of his robbery of Clemens's home at Stormfield in Redding, Connecticut, which he dubs "the Mark Twain burglary."

Manuscripts

Arranged chronologically

84. Autograph manuscript table of contents for *Mark Twain's Sketches, New and Old.* [N.p., ca. 1871–1875.] 9 p. **(pages 22–23)**

Clemens organizes a variety of his magazine and newspaper publications for the collection ultimately published in 1875 by the American Publishing Co. as *Mark Twain's Sketches, New and Old.* The selection and order of texts in this list varies slightly from the published edition.

85. Autograph manuscript, *A Tramp Abroad*, chapter 42: "Switzerland." [Paris, ca. May 15–May 25, 1879.] 37 p. **(page 110)**

In the travel book *A Tramp Abroad*, Twain turns his humorist's eye to Central and Southern Europe, lampooning continental and American attitudes with equally mischievous glee. He opens his chapter on Switzerland by describing the country as "simply a large, humpy, solid rock, with a thin skin of grass stretched over it."

86. Autograph manuscript, "To the Bride" [and] "S'klk! G'lang!" September 1, 1886. **(pages 200–201)**

When Olivia Clemens's childhood friend Clara Spaulding was married in 1886, Clemens honored her with a pair of horse-car tickets and a "loving though humble and squalid poem." The poem humorously describes Christopher Columbus, the prophet Elijah, and others who had the courage to "take a ride."

87. Autograph manuscript leaf from "Huck Finn and Tom Sawyer Among the Indians." [Ca. 1884–1889.] 1 p.

At the conclusion of *The Adventures of Huckleberry Finn*, Tom and Huck discuss a plan to "go for howling adventures amongst the Injuns," and shortly after the novel's publication, Clemens began work on a sequel detailing these escapades. He penned over two hundred manuscript pages of the book, but did not complete it, and it remained unpublished until 1968.

88. Autograph manuscript fragment on "Family Hotels" [draft of letter to John Y. MacAlistair]. [Ca. September 1900.] 3 p. **(page 111)**

In this manuscript fragment, Clemens gives a humorous description of "all the modern inconveniences" of lodging in London, with particular opprobrium reserved for Brown's Hotel, where he had recently stayed. He writes: "The lift was a gift of William the Conqueror, some of the beds are pre-historic. They represent geological periods. Mine is the oldest."

89. Autograph receipt [and] "For Sale." [Bermuda]: March 6 [and ca. March 7–28], 1910. 2 p. **(page 160)**

These two handwritten documents on a single folded sheet are some of the final writings in Twain's hand. Clemens spent the final months of his life at the home of William H. Allen in Bermuda. In the first document, Clemens writes out a receipt to Allen's daughter Helen, in which she affirms that he had given her two dollars and forty cents in exchange for her "promise to believe everything he says hereafter." Sometime over the course of the next few weeks, he added text to the sheet offering Helen's promise for sale, noting that she "will take any reasonable amount for it above 2 per cent of its face because experienced parties think it will keep but only a little while in this kind of weather & is a kind of proppity—that don't give a dam for cold storage nohow." Even in his final days, Clemens's sense of humor was undiminished.

ROUGHING IT
AND THE
INNOCENTS
AT HOME
MARK
TWAIN
ILLUSTRATED
ROUTLEDGE
ROUGHING IT
AND THE
INNOCENTS AT HOME

(Item no. 11)

Letters

Arranged chronologically

90. Autograph letter signed ("Sam. Clemens") to "Aunt Betsy." St. Louis, [October 13?], 1859. **(pages 222–223)**

Clemens was a twenty-three-year-old riverboat pilot when he wrote this letter to Elizabeth W. Smith, a family friend from Missouri whom he referred to as "Aunt Betsy." This is one of the earliest Mark Twain letters held in a private collection.

91. Autograph letter signed ("Samuel L. Clemens") to Jim Gillis. Elmira, N.Y., January 26, 1870. **(page 13)**

In this letter, Clemens recalls his days of "picket-hunting vagabondage" in California with the recipient, specifically the day they "heard that chap tell about the frog & how they filled him with shot"—the tall tale that would inspire *The Celebrated Jumping Frog of Calaveras County*.

92. Autograph letter signed ("Mark") to Elisha Bliss, Jr. Elmira, N.Y., July 4, 1870. **(pages 126–127)**

Clemens negotiates a higher royalty fee from Elisha Bliss, Jr., of the American Publishing Company by detailing the generous offer he received from another publisher.

93. Autograph letter signed ("Mark") to William C. Church or Francis P. Church. Buffalo, N.Y., [October] 19, [1870].

Twain writes to the publishers of *The Galaxy* (simply addressed "Friend Church") regarding two articles he had written for the magazine.

94. Autograph letter signed ("Clemens") to Elisha Bliss, Jr. Buffalo, N.Y., October 26, 1870. **(page 73)**

Clemens denies Bliss's request that he stop writing for *The Galaxy* in this letter, contending that "it is good advertising for me—as you show when you desire me to quit."

95. Autograph letter signed ("Mark") to Elisha Bliss, Jr. Buffalo, N.Y., October 29, [1870]. **(page 188)**

In this letter to his publisher, Twain humorously disparages another author while requesting research materials for *Roughing It*: "*Colonel* Albert S. Evans's trip through Mexico! Who made him a *Colonel*? . . . A one-horse newspaper reporter, who has been trying all his life to make a joke & never has & never *will* succeed. A *Colonel!* He would run from a sheep."

96. Autograph letter signed ("S. L. Clemens") to Elisha Bliss, Jr. Buffalo, N.Y., December 2, 1870. **(pages 80–81)**

Clemens proposes and attempts to negotiate terms for a sequel to *Innocents Abroad*. He urges Bliss to formalize the agreement and cautions him to keep their plans secret: "else we'll have somebody standing ready to launch a book right on our big tidal wave and swim it into a success when it would otherwise fall still-born."

97. Final page from an autograph letter signed ("Mark") to publisher Elisha Bliss, Jr. Buffalo, N.Y, December 22, 1870. **(page 28)**

Charles Webb's 1867 publication of *The Jumping Frog* was an instant popular success, but Webb's publishing operation struggled financially, and Clemens accused him of cheating him out of royalties for the book. In this letter on Clemens's personalized stationery, Twain recounts how he bought the *Jumping Frog* back from Webb, and he offers the publisher Elisha Bliss, Jr., an opportunity to print a new "Jumping Frog *pamphlet*."

98. Autograph letter signed ("S. L. Clemens") to Elisha Bliss, Jr. Hartford, February 19, [1874]. **(page 82)**

In this letter, Twain offers a humorous reply to Rufus Hatch, managing director of a steamship company, who had requested copies of Twain's publications to stock his fleet's onboard libraries. Twain responds that Bliss should send the books in exchange for disposing of a troublesome relative: "see that my poor old excellent but imperishable aunt Rachel is shipped westward in the slowest & rottenest craft Mr. Hatch can furnish, even if he has to charter one from some other company; & finally, that you personally superintend the embalming of my aunt— for that, you understand, is the main thing." Later in the year Twain reused the name "Aunt Rachel" in the sketch "A True Story, Repeated Word for Word as I Heard It," which recounts a real-life event from the life of Mary Ann Cord, a cook who had been enslaved in Maryland whom Clemens knew at Quarry Farm. There is no connection between Cord and the vexing, imaginary relative of this letter.

99. Autograph letter signed ("Samuel L. Clemens") to an unidentified Boston publisher. Hartford, June 21, [1875]. **(page 219)**

Clemens thanks the unidentified Bostonian for alerting him to the piratical aims of a man named Greer. He advises the publisher that "all of my stuff is amply protected, + none of it is for sale." On the same day as this letter, he made good on his promise to "expose this filthy thief" by writing a brief letter about the matter to the Hartford *Courant*.

100. Autograph letter signed ("S. L. Clemens") to Andrew H. H. Dawson. Hartford, November 26, [1879]. **(page 220)**

A letter to Georgia politician Andrew Dawson regarding *A Tramp Abroad* in which Clemens humorously pretends not to be able to spell "hellfire," writing: "I am in trouble again with my helfiard book. (There— I have probably spelt that word wrong again. Mr. Beecher tried a million times, if he tried once, to teach me how to spell that simple, every-day word, but somehow I never could seem to get the hang of it. I cannot use it with any sort of confidence especially in print.)"

101. Autograph letter signed ("S. L. Clemens") to Daniel or Charles Frohman. New York, February 2, 1890. **(page 89)**

Clemens denounces a recent stage adaptation of *The Prince and the Pauper* by Abby Sage Richardson as "a mess of idiotic rubbish and vapid twaddle."

102. Autograph letter signed ("Mark") to Frank Bliss. Helena, Mont., August 4, 1895. **(page 91)**

Twain writes to Bliss about the success of his Around the World Tour, boasting, "I always have good houses" despite the Montana heat, and "In a number of instances we have had more people in than were ever in it before, summer or winter."

103. Autograph letter signed ("Mark Twain") and ("Mark") to Richard Gilder. Leypone, India, March 12, 1896. **(page 221)**

Twain wrote this two-part letter to the editor of *The Century Magazine* while on his fundraising Around the World Tour in India. The first part of the letter, which is signed "Mark Twain," is a travel essay based on the author's experiences in India. The second part, which is marked "private" and signed "Mark," details a cost-effective publication plan for the public part of the letter.

104. Autograph letter signed ("S. L. Clemens") to Robert Barr. Weggis, Switzerland, [September 16–30], 1897. **(page 76)**

Clemens writes to his contemporary Robert Barr, praising his novel *A Woman Intervenes* (1896) and reflecting on the qualities of a good novel: "honest, simple, straight-forward, unostentatious, unbruffled; barren of impertinences & familiarities; dignified, refined, self-respectful & respectful toward the reader; bright, snappy, humorous, moving."

105. Autograph letter signed ("S. L. Clemens") to James Tuohy. Vienna, Austria, November 2, 1898. **(page 79)**

Clemens offers two new short stories for sale: "The Man That Corrupted Hadleyburg" and "Wapping Alice."

106. Autograph letter signed ("S.L. Clemens") to Frank or Elisha Bliss, Jr. Vienna, Austria, February 11, 1898. With accompanying postcard. **(pages 78 and 129)**

Both during his lifetime and today, Mark Twain was well known for his maxims: quotations that are simultaneously brief, humorous, and wise. In this letter, Clemens informs his publisher that he has assembled a collection of sixty such quotations—not enough for a daily calendar, but ample to produce a series of postcards that he hopes will sell better than his recent *Following the Equator*.

107. Autograph letter signed ("Mark Twain") to Lilian G. Kimball. Riverdale, N.Y., March 2, 1902. **(page 77)**

Twain reflects on life being "only one long Accident, nothing more," noting that "it begins with the Accidents of birth—place, sex, social degree & the formidable & much-determining Accident of Environment."

108. Autograph letter signed ("Father") to Clara Clemens. London, June 30, 1907. **(page 178)**

Clemens writes to his daughter, describing the program of events at the ceremony for the awarding of his honorary doctoral degree from Oxford University.

109. Autograph letter signed ("Mark Twain") to "Mr. Lloyd" (Henry Demarest Lloyd). New York, March 8, no year. **(page 224)**

Clemens thanks Lloyd, a progressive "muckraking" journalist, for sending a book—likely Lloyd's *Wealth Against Commonwealth*, which condemned the monopolies of the era in general and the Standard Oil Co. in particular.

Photographs

Arranged chronologically

110. Stereoview of the steamship *Quaker City*. Taken on July 4, 1859. **(page 106)**

Popular throughout the latter 19th century, stereoview cards present two photographs of the same subject from slightly different angles, which can be viewed as a single three-dimensional image using a special handheld viewer. The title of this card refers to the steamship *Quaker City*, on which Clemens traveled while gathering material for *Innocents Abroad*. But the ship is not the prominent vessel in the foreground of the image; rather it is a smaller vessel visible in the distance.

111. "The Lecture Platform." New York: American Literary Bureau, ca. 1867–1870. **(page 87)**

Carte-de-visite photograph advertising forty-five available lecturers, including Mark Twain, James T. Fields, Bret Harte, Harriet Beecher Stowe, Ralph Waldo Emerson, Susan B. Anthony, and Elizabeth Cady Stanton.

112. Jeremiah Gurney. Stereoview card of Mark Twain. New York: J. Gurney & Son, [1871]. **(page 143)**

113. Jeremiah Gurney. Carte-de-visite photograph of Mark Twain. New York, [ca. 1871]. **(page 11)**

A young Twain is captured here by preeminent New York photographer Jeremiah Gurney, who founded the first national organization of photographers: the American Daguerre Association.

114. W. & A. H. Fry. Carte-de-visite photograph of Mark Twain. Brighton, [U.K.], [September 12, 1872]. **(page 195)**

Fry's studio took five photographs of Twain during his 1872 visit to England.

115. Stereoview of Twain's house in Hartford. [Ca. 1875]. **(page 212)**

Twain wrote many of his most famous works while living at this house at 351 Farmington Avenue in Hartford, Connecticut, from 1874 to 1891, although most of his actual writing was done during his summer stays in Elmira.

116. Henry William Bradley & William Herman Rulofson, photographers. "Men of Mark." San Francisco: Bradley & Rulofson, 1876. **(page 137)**

A collage made up of 110 separate photographs of famous visitors to Bradley & Rulofson's San Francisco photography studio. Clemens was photographed there in April 1868.

117. Photograph of Samuel and Olivia Clemens on a ship, 1895. **(page 159)**

Even long past his days as a riverboat pilot, Clemens continued to enjoy traveling by water.

118. Napoleon Sarony. Cabinet card photograph of Mark Twain. New York, 1893. **(page 225)**

Twain signed this photograph taken by celebrity photographer Napoleon Sarony, "This is the very worst!"

119. Stereoview of Mark Twain writing in bed. New York: Underwood & Underwood, 1906. **(page 189)**

This stereoscopic photograph shows "the great humorist 'Mark Twain' (S.L. Clemens) and his peculiar method of work."

120. Photograph of Mark Twain aboard the S.S. *Minneapolis*. June 1907.

In June 1907, Twain traveled to England on the S.S. *Minneapolis*, bound for Oxford to receive an honorary degree. Twain is pictured here with two acquaintances he made on the trip. At the right is Carlotta Welles, whom Twain befriended and spent much of his time in transit with, telling her that she reminded him of his daughter Susy, who had died in 1896.

121. Photograph of Mark Twain and Helen Allen in Bermuda. Bermuda, 1908. **(page 255)**

Twain spent his last months in Bermuda with his friend William H. Allen. He is pictured here with Allen's daughter Helen.

Other Items Related to Mark Twain

Arranged by item type, then arranged chronologically

Art & Artifacts

122. *Lloyd's Map of the Lower Mississippi River from St. Louis to the Gulf of Mexico*. New York: J. T. Lloyd, 1863. **(pages 99–101)**

Clemens served on a series of steamships beginning in April 1857. He spent most of October of that year on board the *William L. Morrison*, captained by his neighbor, John N. Bofinger. This hand-colored pilot's map of the Lower Mississippi, mounted into a ledger for ease of use, was used on another ship captained by Bofinger, the *Cora Anderson*, and the manuscript notes detail the sorts of cargo that the ship would have transported during Clemens's time as a cub pilot.

123. [Samuel Clemens, former owner.] Conklin's self-filling pen. Toledo, Ohio: Conklin Pen Co., ca. 1903.

The Conklin Pen Co. of Toledo, Ohio, featured Mark Twain in its advertisement for this self-filling pen, quoting him as saying: "I prefer it to ten other fountain pens because it caries its own filler in its own stomach and I can't mislay it, even by art and intention. I also prefer it because it is a profanity-saver; it cannot roll off the desk." Conklin continues to use Twain for promotional purposes today; each of their fountain pens is engraved with his name along the band.

124. [Samuel Clemens, former owner.] Gesteckpfiefe [tobacco pipe]. Germany, undated. **(page 226)**

Clemens was gifted this two-piece German pipe by his secretary Isabel Lyon, but he purportedly never smoked from it.

125. [Samuel Clemens, former owner.] Black silk cravat. New York: E.A. Newell, undated.

Clemens's careful attention to his image extended to his physical appearance, including his clothing; this is one of the many neckties he owned.

126. [Samuel Clemens, former owner.] Williams No. 6 Typewriter. [New York: 1908.] With accompanying personalized burlap case. **(page 8)**

Clemens famously disliked typewriters, finding them "full of caprices, full of defects—devilish ones." This Williams "grasshopper" typewriter (called such because of the long-legged design that allowed an author to view their work as they wrote it) was one of the last that he purchased during his lifetime. Following her father's death in 1910, Clara Clemens gifted these items to Harry B. Iles, the superintendent and groundskeeper at Stormfield, and they remained in his family through 1982.

127. E. A. *Doctors All, or, More Innocents Abroad*. [June 1907.] Pen and ink on board. **(page 179)**

This cartoon, drawn for a student publication at Oxford University, depicts the recipients of honorary doctorates in 1907: William Booth (founder of the Salvation Army) leads the procession with a bass drum, followed by Rudyard Kipling, Prince Arthur of Connaught, and Clemens.

128. Edward Ardizzone. 37 original illustrations for *The Adventures of Huckleberry Finn*. [1960–1961.] Pen and ink on paper. **(page 197–199)**

Ardizzone, a renowned British illustrator, created this series of pen-and-ink illustrations for a school edition of *Huckleberry Finn* published by Heinemann Educational in 1961.

129. [Unidentified artist.] *A Connecticut Yankee in King Arthur's Court*. 1957. Acrylic on board. **(page 43)**

The comic series *Classics Illustrated* first published its adaptation of Twain's time-travel tale in 1949. For its 1957 reprinting, the story was provided with this new, painted cover depicting a moment of equestrian action.

Cartoons & Promotional Material

130. *Pudd'nhead Wilson's Calendar for 1894*. [New York: The Century Co., 1893.] **(pages 120–121)**

This small pamphlet containing a number of Twain's humorous aphorisms was published as a promotional item for *The Century Magazine*, which serialized *Pudd'nhead Wilson* in 1893–94.

131. Bill Watterson. Six postcard cartoons of Mark Twain. [Charleston, S.C.]: Mark Twain Journal, 1983. **(pages 214–215)**

Several years before creating *Calvin & Hobbes*, cartoonist Bill Watterson produced a series of images for the *Mark Twain Journal* that were issued as promotional postcards.

132. Joseph Keppler. *Mark Twain, America's best humorist*. From *Puck*, new series, number 1. New York: Mayer, Merkel & Ottmann, December 1885. **(page 88)**

This color plate from the humor magazine *Puck* depicts Twain on stage before an amused audience, surrounded by birdlike representatives of his best-known books.

133. Edward Penfield. Poster advertisement for the September 1895 issue of *Harper's*. [New York: Harper & Brothers, 1895.] **(page 72)**

Mark Twain's "Mental Telegraphy Again" is prominently featured in this striking advertisement for *Harper's* magazine.

Menus & Keepsakes

134. [Lotos Club.] Souvenir menu for dinner at the Lotos Club on November 11, 1893. Signed by Mark Twain and ten of the other attendees. **(page 90)**

Clemens was an early member of the Lotos Club in New York, one of the oldest literary clubs in the United States. The Club's first formal dinner in its new clubhouse was held in his honor, and the menu was decorated with illustrations of characters from his books.

135. Mark Twain. Electrotype engraving of self-portrait, with manuscript inscription. [New York, 1902.]

For Twain's sixty-seventh birthday in 1902, Harper Brothers sponsored a dinner in his honor at the Metropolitan Club. Twain gifted each of the fifty-three attendees with a copper plate bearing an engraved self-portrait, with a pasted-on manuscript inscription. The present copy was given to James MacArthur, a frequent contributor to *Harper's*.

136. [Lotos Club.] Souvenir menu for dinner at the Lotos Club, June 17, 1902. **(page 92)**

Clemens spoke at this dinner held in honor of General Horace Porter, a Civil War veteran and US ambassador to France.

137. [Engineers Club.] Commemorative volume for the Engineers Club Inaugural Banquet, December 9, 1907. **(pages 94–95)**

A keepsake for a dinner that featured Andrew Carnegie as guest of honor, this volume, which is bound in Scottish tartan silk and engraved by Tiffany & Co., includes a portrait of Carnegie, illustrations of the Engineers Club clubhouses, the dinner menu and invitation, and other ephemera. It was previously owned by Cleveland engineer Ambrose Swasey, who had the pages signed by Mark Twain, Carnegie, Thomas Edison, and others. Twain entertained the attendees as a speaker, teasing the guest of honor: "just look at Mr. Carnegie's face. It is all scintillating with fictitious innocence. You might think that he had never committed a crime."

138. [Lotos Club.] Souvenir menu for dinner at the Lotos Club, January 11, 1908.

The menu for this 1908 dinner held in honor of "Samuel L. Clemens, Litt. D." featured a photograph of Clemens in his Oxford robes and was presented rolled up like a diploma. The fare was themed after his writings: Innocent Oysters Abroad, Roughing It Soup, Fish Huckleberry Finn, Joan of Arc Filet of Beef, Punch Brothers Punch, Hadleyburg Salad, Pudd'nhead Cheese, and White Elephant Coffee.

139. Mark Twain. "To My Guests" [broadside]. Redding, Connecticut, October 7, 1908. Signed and inscribed by Twain. **(page 93)**

Clemens moved to Stormfield, his home in Redding, Connecticut, in 1908, and helped create the town library with a large donation of books from his personal library. In this humorous broadside given to visitors to Stormfield, he notes that there was only "one detail lacking: a building for the library . . . It seems best to use coercion in this case. Therefore I have levied a tax—a GUESTS' MARK TWAIN LIBRARY BUILDING TAX, of one dollar, not upon the valuable sex, but only upon the other one. Guests of the valuable sex are tax-free, and shall so remain; but guests of the other sex must pay, whether they are willing or not."

Cigars & Smoking Ephemera

140. Aschermann & Co. "Don't Fail to Smoke Mark Twain Cigars." New York: Heppenheimer & Maurer, [ca. 1877–1880]. Lithographed advertising card. **(page 170)**
141. "Smoke the Popular Mark Twain Cigars Sold Everywhere." St. Louis: Compton Label Works, [ca. 1877–1885]. Advertising banner.
142. Mark Twain cigar box. [Missouri]: Londres, [ca. 1910–1913]. Wooden box with printed labels. **(page 170)**
143. Mark Twain cigar box. Pennsylvania: Wolf Bros., [ca. 1913–1930]. Wooden box with printed label and one original cellophane-wrapped cigar. **(page 171)**
144. "Liked By All: Mark Twain Cigars." Baltimore: Parker Metal Dec. Company, [ca. 1913–1931]. Metal sign. **(pages 172–173)**

Clemens estimated that he smoked fifteen to twenty cigars a day, and the public image of Mark Twain is closely associated with cigars. Cigar manufacturer Edward Aschermann registered a trademark for Twain-branded cigars in 1877. Clemens does not seem to have received any income from this use of his name, but in 1907 his business manager Ralph Ashcroft registered a new trademark on Twain's name and likeness for whiskey and tobacco, and Twain cigars from other manufacturers continued to be produced until the 1930s.

145. *Life of "Mark Twain."* [Park Place, N.Y.]: Duke Cigarettes; Knapp and Company, Lithographers & Printers, [1888]. **(page 83)**

Duke Cigarettes' pamphlet series "Histories of Poor Boys Who Have Become Rich, and Other Famous People" offered miniature texts that fit inside a cigarette packet.

Bookends & Busts

146. Joza Krupka. Bronze bust of Mark Twain. [New York]: Armor Bronze, 1912. **(frontispiece)**

Czechoslovakian artist Joza Krupa's bust shows Twain in a large coat—a striking departure from his usual appearance in a jacket and bowtie.

147. Tom Sawyer and Huckleberry Finn bookends. [New York]: Armor Bronze, [ca. 1925]. **(page 196)**

Twain's characters Tom Sawyer and Huckleberry Finn form a matching pair in these decorative bookends.

148. Mark Twain bookends. [Bridgeport, Conn.]: Weidlich Brothers, [1947?]. **(page 134)**

These bookends show a scholarly Twain reading a book that he holds in his lap.

Games

149. *Portrait Authors.* Salem, Mass.: West & Lee Game Co., 1873. **(page 206)**
150. *The Game of Star Authors.* New York: McLoughlin Brothers, [1887]. **(page 212)**
151. *Game of Authors No. 2.* New York: J.H. Singer, [ca. 1890]. **(page 206)**
152. *Authors Improved.* Springfield, Mass.: Milton Bradley & Co., [ca. 1890]. **(page 206)**
153. *Modern Authors.* Springfield, Mass.: Milton Bradley Co., [ca. 1890–1910]. **(page 207)**

The suit-building card game *Authors* was patented in 1861, but as a result of a poorly protected copyright it was produced in dozens of different editions from multiple publishers, and remains in print to this day. West & Lee's 1873 illustrated edition *Portrait Authors* was the first to include Twain.

154. [Mrs. Shepherd.] *The Amusing Game of Innocence Abroad.* Salem, Mass.: Parker Brothers, [ca. 1888–1890]. **(page 125)**
155. [Mrs. Shepherd.] *The Good Old Game of Innocence Abroad.* Salem, Mass.: Parker Brothers, [ca. 1901]. **(page 125)**

George S. Parker copyrighted this map board game in 1888, licensed to his fledgling game publisher by its designer, a Mrs. Shepherd. The subtle change to the title for Twain's *Innocents Abroad* signals the paucity of the game's connection to the book. Still, it proved popular, and was reissued a decade after its original release.

156. *Mark Twain's Memory-Builder. A Game for Acquiring and Retaining All Sorts of Facts and Dates.* New York: Charles L. Webster, 1891. With "Facts for Mark Twain's Memory Builder" pamphlet. **(page 205)**

Clemens patented his rules for a game to assist in the memorization of historical dates in 1885, and finally published this version of his teaching aid in 1891. He anticipated broad interest in the game, but it was a financial failure.

157. *Adventures of Tom Sawyer and Huck Finn: A Game for Boys and Girls.* New York: Stoll & Edwards Co., Inc., 1925. **(pages 208–209)**

This simple race game takes players through the major plot points of *The Adventures of Tom Sawyer.*

158. *The Game of Tom Sawyer.* [Springfield, Mass.]: Milton Bradley Co., 1937. **(page 213)**

A board game produced as a tie-in with David O. Selznick's 1938 film *The Adventures of Tom Sawyer.*

159. *The Chase on Tom Sawyer's Island.* New York: Hi Tech Expressions/The Walt Disney Company, 1988. Disks for Apple IIe/e/GS, IBM, Tandy, and compatible systems.

A maze chase game in the style of *Pac-Man*, licensed in connection with Walt Disney World's Tom Sawyer Island attraction.

160. *Square's Tom Sawyer = Sukuwea no Tomu Sōya.* Tokyo: Square Co., Ltd., 1989. Cartridge for Nintendo Famicom system. **(page 211)**

In this simple role-playing game, players reenact a variation on the plot of *The Adventures of Tom Sawyer.*

161. *The Adventures of Tom Sawyer.* Torrance, Calif.: SETA U.S.A., Inc., 1989. Cartridge for Nintendo Entertainment System. **(page 210)**

In this side-scrolling adventure game with little connection to Twain's novel, a daydreaming Tom Sawyer battles pirates and enormous animals.

Additional Ephemera

162. *Mark Twain Calendar for 1910.* New York: Harper & Brothers, 1909. **(page 122)**

An illustrated calendar issued to promote Harper's National Edition of Twain's *Works.*

163. *Morrell's Mark Twain Calendar* [*1946*]. Ottumwa, Iowa: John Morrell & Co., 1945. **(pages 132–133)**

In this tearaway calendar (missing only January), each month is accompanied by a painted illustration by Norman Rockwell and a quotation from *The Adventures of Tom Sawyer.*

164. "Smiles and Tears. Programme of readings to be given by James Whitcomb Riley the distinguished poet, and Bill Nye, the famous humorist . . . Mr. S.L. Clemens, ('Mark Twain,') will preside" [broadside]. Boston: F. A. Searle, Printer, [1889]. **(page 123)**

James Whitcomb Riley and Edgar Wilson ("Bill") Nye toured together on the lecture circuit for several years in the 1880s, and for this Boston appearance they were introduced by Twain. In his brief speech, Twain offered an extended, joking presentation of the duo as Chang and Eng Bunker, conjoined twins who had appeared at P. T. Barnum's American Museum in 1860 and toured for several years thereafter.

165. United States Postal Service. Tom Sawyer first day of issue cover. Hannibal, Mo., November 30, 1972. **(page 134)**

Illustrated envelope postmarked in Clemens's hometown on the date of issue of an eight-cent stamp commemorating *The Adventures of Tom Sawyer.*

166. Woolson Spice Co. "Shadow Picture [Mark Twain]." Toledo, Ohio: Woolson Spice Co., [1895]. **(pages 130–131)**

Carefully cutting around the lines on the back of this card will turn the floral illustration on the front into a silhouette portrait of Mark Twain.

167. Royal Bobbles. *American Writers: Mark Twain*. Alpharetta, Ga.: Royal Bobbles, 2015. **(page 135)**

A limited edition "bobblehead" figurine featuring Twain in his signature white suit.

168. *Mark Twain's Scrap Book*. New York: Daniel Slote & Company, [1892]. **(page 45)**

Twain patented a self-adhesive scrapbook, which was first issued in 1876. The scrapbook sold well, and was reissued in a variety of sizes and styles for years afterwards.

Influences on Mark Twain

Arranged alphabetically by author

169. B. P. Shillaber. *Life and Sayings of Mrs. Partington, and Others of the Family*. New York: J. C. Derby/Boston: Phillips, Sampson and Company, 1854. **(page 174)**

As the editor of *The Carpet-Bag*, Shillaber purchased Clemens's first published story, "The Dandy Frightening the Squatter." His fictional creation, Mrs. Partington, was a simple-minded but kind-hearted woman whose speech was laden with malapropisms, and she was a direct influence on *Tom Sawyer*'s Aunt Polly.

170. Edgar "Ned" Wakeman. *The Log of an Ancient Mariner. Being the Life and Adventures of Captain Edgar Wakeman*. San Francisco: A. L. Bancroft & Co., 1878.

Storied steamship captain Edgar Wakeman was a folk hero in San Francisco whose exploits included the 1850 hijack of the steam vessel *New World*, which he piloted from New York around Cape Horn and on to San Francisco. His tales influenced Twain's travel letters, and he was the basis for Twain's short story about the comet-racing Captain Stormfield. Wakeman's memoir, published three years after his death, includes material written by Clemens, including the "Tale of Rats," which he based on one of Wakeman's anecdotes.

171. Artemus Ward [Charles Farrar Browne]. *Artemus Ward, His Book*. New York: Carleton, Publisher, 1862.
172. Artemus Ward [Charles Farrar Browne]. *Artemus Ward; His Travels*. New York: Carleton, Publisher, 1865.
173. Artemus Ward [Charles Farrar Browne]. *Artemus Ward in London*. New York: G. W. Carleton & Co., 1867.

Artemus Ward was a persona adopted by author and speaker Charles Farrar Browne. Ward, an illiterate but ironically wise character, traveled broadly, and his books are filled with humorous observations on the American West and Europe. Browne's humorous lectures further influenced Twain as a speaker.

174. Artemus Ward [Charles Farrar Browne], edited by T. W. Robertson & E. P. Hingston. *Artemus Ward's Panorama. (As exhibited at the Egyptian Hall, London)*. New York: G. W. Carleton, 1869.

Browne presented a "panorama"—a lecture delivered in front of a series of unspooling painted backdrops—at London's Egyptian Hall in 1866. He became as successful in England as he had been stateside, but he fell ill while abroad and died at Southampton in March 1867.

175. Betsy J. Ward [William Comstock]. *Betsy Jane Ward (better-half to Artemus), Hur Book of Goaks, with a full akkownt of the coartship and maridge to a4said Artemus, and Mister Ward's cutting-up with the Mormon fare secks*. London: George Routledge and Sons, 1866. **(page 175)**

Ward's success led to imitators, including this book credited to his fictional wife. Its authorship is attributed to William Comstock, a prolific dime novelist.

About the Contributors

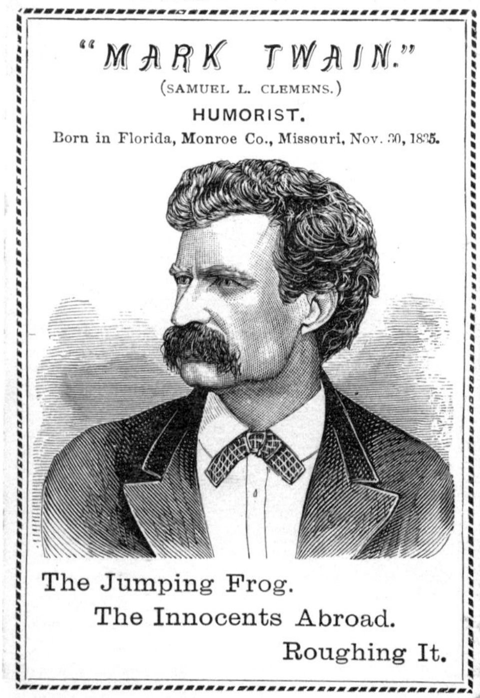

Mark Twain card from *Portrait Authors*. Salem, Mass.: West & Lee Game Co., 1873. (Item no. 149)

JOHN BIRD is Emeritus Professor of English at Winthrop University. He is the author of *Mark Twain and Metaphor* (2007) and the editor of *Mark Twain in Context* (2020), as well as author of numerous articles and book chapters on Mark Twain. He is a past president of the Mark Twain Circle of America and the founding editor of its journal, *The Mark Twain Annual*.

JULIE CARLSEN is the Assistant Curator of the Henry W. and Albert A. Berg Collection of English and American Literature at The New York Public Library. She holds a BA in history from Vassar College and an MLIS from Rutgers University. At the Library, she curated the pop-up exhibition *Lola Szaldits: Devoted Guardian of Literary Delights* (2023) and assisted with *Max Beerbohm: The Price of Celebrity* (2023–24), co-curated by Margaret D. Stetz and Mark Samuels Lasner, and is co-curating *A Century of The New Yorker* (2025) with Julie Golia. At the Grolier Club, where she has been a member since 2019, she co-curated *Magazines and the American Experience* (2020) with Steven Lomazow and assisted with *Poet of the Body: New York's Walt Whitman* (2019), co-curated by Susan Jaffe Tane and Karen Karbiener.

JAMES E. CARON retired as Professor of English at the University of Hawaiʻi, Mānoa, where he taught American literature for thirty-six years. He has published articles on satire, the tall tale, antebellum comic writers, laughter and evolution, Mark Twain, George Washington Harris, Frank Norris, Nathaniel Hawthorne, William Faulkner, Charlie Chaplin, Hunter S. Thompson, and Bill Watterson. In addition, he has published *Mark Twain, Unsanctified Newspaper Reporter* (2008); co-edited a collection of essays on Charlie Chaplin, entitled *Refocusing Chaplin: A Screen Icon in Critical Contexts* (2013); and authored *Satire as the Comic Public Sphere: Postmodern "Truthiness" and Civic Engagement* (2021). His most recent book is *The Modern Feminine in the Medusa Satire of Fanny Fern* (2024). He is the former president of the American Humor Studies Association and former senior associate editor of its journal, *Studies in American Humor*. He is the recipient of the 2023 Charlie Award from the American Humor Studies Association, given for lifetime achievement in service to the AHSA and for research in American humor.

MARK DAWIDZIAK is the author or editor of twenty-five books, including *Mark My Words: Mark Twain on Writing* (1996), *Horton Foote's "The Shape of the River": The Lost Teleplay About Mark Twain* (2003), *Mark Twain in Ohio* (2015), *Mark Twain's Guide to Diet, Exercise, Beauty, Fashion, Investment, Romance, Health and Happiness* (2015), and *Mark Twain for Cat Lovers* (2016). He has four times been the guest scholar at Elmira College's Center for Mark Twain Studies and has had papers accepted for presentation at six consecutive State of Mark Twain Studies international conferences. He also has contributed chapters to such academic anthologies as *A Companion to Mark Twain* (2005) and *Mark Twain and Youth* (2016). His afterword is featured in the most recent Signet Classics edition of *Roughing It*, and he has been portraying Mark Twain on stage for forty-five years. Dawidziak spent most of his journalism career as a television and film critic for such newspapers as the *Akron Beacon Journal* and Cleveland's *The Plain Dealer*. His most recent book is *A Mystery of Mysteries: The Death and Life of Edgar Allan Poe* (2023).

KERRY DRISCOLL, Professor of English Emerita at the University of Saint Joseph (West Hartford, Connecticut) is currently Associate Editor at the Mark Twain Papers and Project at the Bancroft Library, University of California, Berkeley. She is the author of *Mark Twain among the Indians and Other Indigenous Peoples* (2018), the first book-length study of the writer's evolving views regarding the aboriginal inhabitants of North America and Australasia, and his deeply conflicted representations of them in fiction, newspaper sketches, and speeches. She is past president of the Mark Twain Circle of America and a long-time contributing editor to its journal, the *Mark Twain Annual*, as well as a member of the Advisory Council at the Mark Twain House and Museum in Hartford.

JOE B. FULTON is Professor of English at Baylor University in Waco, Texas, where he has been honored as a Baylor University Class of 1945 Centennial Professor. Dr. Fulton has published five books on Mark Twain, including *The Reconstruction of Mark Twain: How a Confederate Bushwhacker Became the Lincoln of Our Literature* (2010) and *Mark Twain Under Fire: Reception and Reputation, Criticism and Controversy, 1851–2015* (2018). He serves as editor of the *Mark Twain Journal*.

ALAN GRIBBEN is the author of the two-volume *Mark Twain's Literary Resources: A Reconstruction of His Library and Reading* (2019, 2022), representing fifty years of travel and research. From 2009 until 2020, Dr. Gribben edited the *Mark Twain Journal: The Author and His Era*. For fifteen years he reviewed books and articles about Mark Twain for *American Literary Scholarship, An Annual*. In 2011, his six variant NewSouth editions of *The Adventures of Tom Sawyer* and *Adventures of Huckleberry Finn* offered instructors and students their choice of the original texts or slightly altered versions omitting racial slurs. He co-edited *Mark Twain on the Move: A Travel Reader* in 2009. Dr. Gribben's *Harry Huntt Ransom: Intellect in Motion* (2008) was the first biography about the eminent library founder at the University of Texas at Austin. He taught American literature and expository writing as an English professor for forty-five years, including seventeen years at the University of Texas at Austin and two decades as head of the Department of English and Philosophy at Auburn University at Montgomery.

BENJAMIN GRIFFIN is an Associate Editor at the Mark Twain Project at the Bancroft Library, University of California, Berkeley. In English literature he holds a BA from UC Berkeley and an MPhil and PhD from Cambridge University; he also studied library science at the Catholic University of America, and electric guitar under Joe Satriani. Before coming to the Project he worked as a lecturer in English at UCLA and Berkeley, a bookseller with Bauman Rare Books, and a rare books cataloger at the Folger Shakespeare Library. Ben's editorial credits with the Mark Twain Project, which since 1967 has been publishing the standard scholarly edition, include the three volumes of Mark Twain's *Autobiography* (2010–15); *A Family Sketch and Other Private Writings* (2014); *Mark Twain's Civil War* (2019); and the three-text edition of *Pudd'nhead Wilson* (2024). During his eighteen years at the Mark Twain Project he has published in many scholarly journals, as well as *Granta* and *Playboy*.

DECLAN KIELY is Executive Director of The Grolier Club. His essay "A Century of Collecting Mark Twain at The Morgan Library & Museum and The New York Public Library" was published in *Mark Twain: A Skeptic's Progress*, the catalogue accompanying the Morgan's 2010 exhibition, co-curated with Isaac Gewirtz. He has curated and co-curated exhibitions on John Milton, Jane Austen, Charles Dickens, William Shakespeare, Edgar Allan Poe, Sir Winston Churchill, Abraham Lincoln, Ernest Hemingway, Henry James, and J. D. Salinger. In 2021, as Director of Exhibitions and Special Collections at The New York Public Library, he inaugurated the first permanent exhibition of its treasures.

JUDITH YAROSS LEE is Distinguished Professor Emerita of Communication Studies at Ohio University (Athens, Ohio), where she taught from 1990 to 2019. Her scholarship on American humor and culture includes six books and five dozen essays, notably *Twain's Brand: Humor in Contemporary American Culture* (2012); *Seeing MAD: Essays on Mad Magazine's Humor and Legacy*, edited with John Bird (2020); and "American Humor and Matters of Empire" (2020). Lee was the 2016 Fulbright Senior Professor of American Culture at Leiden University in the Netherlands and a 2022 Quarry Farm Fellow at Elmira College's Center for Mark Twain Studies, and currently serves as the Vice President of the Mark Twain Circle. She is at work on a study of Mark Twain's long relationship with African explorer Henry Morton Stanley.

KEVIN MAC DONNELL serves on the editorial boards of the *Mark Twain Journal* and *Firsts Magazine*. He holds an MLS from the University of Texas. He co-edited (with Alan Gribben) *Mark Twain's Rubaiyat* (1983), contributed several articles to *The Mark Twain Encyclopedia* (1993), co-edited (with R. Kent Rasmussen) *Mark Twain and Youth* (2016), and has written over sixty book reviews for the Mark Twain Forum. He has published numerous journal essays on Mark Twain and other American authors, librarianship, and antiquarian bookselling. His discovery of the probable source of Mark Twain's nom de plume went viral on the *Huffington Post* and *Salon.com*, and was cited by the *Chronicle of Higher Education* as "research of note." His personal collection of nearly 11,000 Mark Twain first editions, letters, photographs, ex libris, and relics is the largest in private hands and is frequently shared with scholars and museums. He was honored as a Mark Twain Legacy Scholar by the *Mark Twain Journal* in 2016.

ARIL MCKEE is a high school junior with experience in cartooning, animation, and video production. In 2024, they received the Foundation for Beacon Schools' Baldie Award for their short film *Everyone on the Planet and Also Outer Space Has Turned Into a Zombie Except For These Two Specific People: The Movie*. They serve on the Youth Board of the Dutchess County Pride Center. Their current projects include the webcomic *Murderduck* and editing for the web video series *Blue Chair*.

GABRIEL MCKEE is a librarian at New York University's Institute for the Study of the Ancient World. He holds an MTS from Harvard Divinity School and an MLIS from Long Island University. His research concerns popular culture, book history, theology, and parahistoriography. With Susan Jaffe Tane, he curated the Grolier Club exhibitions *Evermore: The Persistence of Poe* (2014) and *"A Literary Fellowship": Relationships and Rivalries in 19th-Century American Literature* (2017). His other works include *The Saucerian: The Unbelievable Life of Gray Barker* (2025), *The Gospel According to Science Fiction* (2007), and *Pink Beams of Light from the God in the Gutter: The Science Fictional Religion of Philip K. Dick* (2003).

NICHOLE MISAKO NOMURA holds a PhD in English and an MA in Education from Stanford University. She is a scholar of English education and pedagogy, digital humanities, and science fiction, and is currently working on a book exploring how and why we might read fictional novels as curricula. She is a member of the Stanford Literary Lab and a postdoctoral researcher at the Center for Spatial and Textual Analysis. Her digital humanities work blends text-mining, critical making, and methods from the social sciences. She collects classroom editions of Twain's *Adventures of Huckleberry Finn* and science fiction–themed educational materials.

R. KENT RASMUSSEN has written and edited fourteen books about Mark Twain over the past three decades, the best known of which is *Mark Twain A to Z* (1995, revised ed., *Critical Companion to Mark Twain*, 2007). He holds a PhD from UCLA. Trained in history, he has published widely in that field. His many other publications include the Penguin Classics edition of Mark Twain's *Autobiographical Writings* (2012). In recent years, he has written extensively about screen adaptations of Mark Twain. He is a member of the editorial board of the *Mark Twain Journal*, which honored him as a legacy scholar in 2015. In 2017, he received the Mark Twain Circle's Thomas A. Tenney Award for Service.

DAVID E. E. SLOANE is Professor Emeritus, University of New Haven. He earned his MA and PhD at Duke University in 1966 and 1970 and his BA at Wesleyan University in 1964. Some of his books are *Mark Twain as a Literary Comedian* (1979); *The Literary Humor of the Urban Northeast, 1830–1890* (1983)—reprints of sketches and stories establishing the importance of northeastern humor; *American Humor Magazines and Comic Periodicals* (1987)—a 650-page descriptive bibliography of known humor magazines from 1765 to 1985; *Adventures of Huckleberry Finn: American Comic Vision* (1988)—an undeservedly neglected classic; *Student Companion to Mark Twain* (2001); as editor, *Mark Twain's Humor: Critical Essays* (1993)—a historical collection with many previously unavailable items from the US and UK; *New Directions in American Humor* (1998); and also *Huckleberry Finn and Race: A Teacher's Toolbox*, in Victor Doyno's CD *Huck Finn: The Complete Buffalo and Erie County Public Library Manuscript* (2003).

BARBARA E. SNEDECOR served as director of the Center for Mark Twain Studies and as assistant professor of American Literature at Elmira College. In addition to editing the second edition of *Mark Twain in Elmira* (2013), she has contributed pieces to the *Mark Twain Annual* and *American Literary Realism*. In 2017, she received the Henry Nash Smith Award. She is the editor of *Gravity: Selected Letters of Olivia Langdon Clemens* (University of Missouri Press, 2023). She holds a PhD from Harpur College of Binghamton University, State University of New York.

SUSAN JAFFE TANE is a longtime bibliophile and philanthropist who holds the foremost private collection of Edgar Allan Poe books, manuscripts, and artifacts in the world. She has been a member of the Grolier Club since 2006. In addition to Poe, Ms. Tane has established notable collections of works by Mark Twain, Herman Melville, Walt Whitman, Ralph Waldo Emerson, Henry David Thoreau, Henry Wadsworth Longfellow, and American presidents. At the Grolier Club, she has curated *Evermore: The Persistence of Poe* (2014) and *"A Literary Fellowship": Relationships and Rivalries in 19th-Century American Literature* (2017) with Gabriel Mckee, and *Poet of the Body: New York's Walt Whitman* (2019) with Karen Karbiener. Most recently, she curated *Presidents and Their Books: What They Read and Wrote* (2023) with her teenage grandchildren Natalie Flaxman and Spencer Flaxman. She sponsors the Susan Jaffe Tane Prize for Student Book Collectors National Collegiate Book Collecting Contest, which gives her enormous pride and pleasure in mentoring young collectors.

Index

[Unidentified artist.] "S.H. Clemmens [*sic*] (Mark Twain)." [N.p.: s.n., ca. 1881.]

Photograph of Mark Twain and Helen Allen in Bermuda. Bermuda, 1908.

Twain spent his last months in Bermuda with his friend William H. Allen. He is pictured here with Allen's daughter Helen. (Item no. 121)

This catalogue is published in conjunction with *A First-Class Fool: Mark Twain and Humor, Featuring the Collection of Susan Jaffe Tane*, on view at The Grolier Club, New York, January 15–April 5, 2025.

Published by The Grolier Club, New York
Produced and designed by Miko McGinty, Miko McGinty Inc.
Copyedited by Janice Fisher
Photography by Nicole Neenan
Decorations by Aril McKee
Typeset in Martina Plantijn, Kalice, and Romie
by Tina Henderson, Miko McGinty Inc.
Production management by Matthew Harvey
Color correction by Thomas Bollier
Printed and bound in China at Artron Art Group

ISBN 978-1-60583-110-7.

Frontispiece: Joza Krupka. Bronze bust of Mark Twain. [New York]: Armor Bronze, 1912. (Item no. 146)

Facing table of contents: *Mark Twain. The Jumping Frog; In English, then in French, then Clawed Back into a Civilized Language Once More by Patient, Unremunerated Toil.* New York and London: Harper and Brothers, 1903. (Item no. 3)